THE GOVERNMENT AND POLITICS
OF NEW YORK STATE

The Government
and Politics
of New York State

JOSEPH F. ZIMMERMAN

New York University Press
New York *and* London
1981

Library of Congress Cataloging in Publication Data
Zimmerman, Joseph Francis, 1928–
The government and politics of New York State.
Bibliography: p.
Includes index.
1. New York (State)—Politics and government—
1951–   . I. Title.
JK3425 1981.Z55   320.9′747   81-9673
ISBN 0-8147-9657-5   AACR2

Manufactured in the United States of America

TO MARGARET AND DEIRDRE

Contents

Preface

GOVERNMENTAL AND POLITICAL developments of great significance have occurred since Lynton K. Caldwell's *The Government and Administration of New York* was published in 1954. While several books and monographs examining aspects of the governance of the Empire State have appeared since 1954, no general book on the subject has been published. This book is designed to fill that gap in the literature of New York State government.

The author's primary goal has been to present a balanced description and analysis of the governance of the Empire State, with particular emphasis upon political processes and institutions and on proposals for change in the governance system. Functional activities of the state government are considered only within the context of the political process.

Studying the government and politics of the Empire State engages one in an analysis of the political system of the second largest state in the Union, a state that has provided national leadership in terms of innovative laws and governmental programs. The importance of gaining a thorough knowledge of the history and political culture of New York cannot be overemphasized if the reader is to gain a proper understanding of current Empire State politics. Nevertheless, space limitations make it impossible to address these topics adequately, and the reader is encouraged to read relevant materials cited in the Bibliography.

Relatively heavy emphasis is placed upon legal foundations, inasmuch as they greatly influence the political behavior of the leading public officials and interest groups. Special attention is paid to constitutional restrictions on the state Legislature and local governments that attempt to shackle these institutions and the ingenious ways by which the restrictions in large measure have been circumvented.

Although this is not a book on New York City politics, sections are devoted to the city because of its political importance. New York City has approximately 40 percent of the state's population and currently supplies all statewide elected officials except the state comptroller. The governor often finds it difficult to deal with the mayor even if both are members of the same political party, a situation traceable in some instances to the presidential ambitions of the two officials.

Three themes are highlighted in this volume. The intergovernmental theme stresses the political importance of national-state, interstate, and state-local relations. Common to this theme is the subtheme of centralization versus decentralization of political authority. Relative to national-state and interstate relations, the key question is the extent to which political power should be concentrated at the national level. Similarly, a question is raised with respect to the concentration of political power at the state level versus affording local governments broad discretionary authority.

The second theme emphasizes the group basis of politics by underlining the importance of the groups that write the rules (e.g., the state constitution) in a state where it is relatively difficult to amend the constitution and the influence these groups bring to bear upon the legislature, the governor, and the bureaucracy.

The third theme is the question of the most desirable degree of executive integration. Two models for the structuring of executive authority have been employed. The first is the traditional weak governor model providing for fragmentation of executive authority; the second provides for the integration of all executive authority in the governor. The first model reflects fear of a strong executive with concentrated powers; a fear attributable to colonial experience under the British Crown and the writings of James Madison. Reenforcing the traditional fear of centralized authority was Jacksonian democracy, which sought to hold public officials accountable to the electorate through population elections and short terms of office.

No book dealing with the politics and governance of the Empire State is the work of one individual. The citations throughout this volume are evidence of the contributions made by numerous individuals and organizations to the promotion of a full understanding of the governance system. While every effort has been made to ensure the accuracy of material included in this book, errors may have crept into this work because of the complexity of the subject matter, and rapidly occurring developments naturally will date some of the factual information. To improve subsequent editions of this book, the author welcomes the receipt of corrections and suggestions.

In closing this preface, a sincere debt of appreciation must be expressed to the following individuals for kindly reading and commenting upon various chapters: Dr. T. Norman Hurd, former secretary to Governor Nelson A. Rockefeller and former Director of the Budget; Albert J. Abrams, former Secretary of the State Senate and currently a Special Consultant to the Senate; Dr. Troy R. Westmeyer, former Director of the Legislative Commission on Expenditure Review; Dr. George H. Hallett, Jr., former Executive Secretary of the Citizens Union of the City of New York; Dr. Frank W. Prescott of the University of Tennessee at Chattanooga; and colleague Dr. Ronald M. Stout. Their comments and suggestions greatly improved the quality of the manuscript. A debt of gratitude is owed to Mrs. Edith Connelly for typing the manuscript and to Mr. Frank Kirk for his copyediting.

Delmar, New York   J.F.Z.
January 1981

CHAPTER I
The Empire State

THE STUDY OF the government and politics of New York State involves a study of an important segment of the political history of the United States, since the Empire State has played a major role in the political development of the United States by contributing "big" men to the service of the nation and innovative laws, governmental programs, and projects. As the center of national finance and the national communications system and as the most populous state until 1960, the Empire State was the natural center of political attention. The loss of its status as the largest state in terms of population has not diminished the political and economic importance of the Empire State, which has the second largest executive budget, after the federal budget, in the nation.

The Empire State has been the home of big men—Alexander Hamilton, the two George Clintons, John Jay, De Witt Clinton, Grover Cleveland, Theodore Roosevelt, Charles Evans Hughes, Alfred E. Smith, Franklin D. Roosevelt, Herbert H. Lehman, Thomas E. Dewey, and Nelson A. Rockefeller, among others—and big projects—the Erie Canal, the Thruway, the university system—as well as an innovator of policies and programs subsequently adopted by the federal government and other states. Relative to the latter, Professor Jack L. Walker of the University of Michigan developed "composite innovation scores" for the states, and New York State ranked the highest.[1]

Although many of the dramatic and highly publicized activities of the federal government, by preempting public attention, tend to overshadow the activities of state governments, one should not lose sight of the fact that state governments and their political subdivisions provide the bulk of governmental services to citizens and affect their lives most directly. While conducted on a smaller scale, the politics of state decision making can be as fascinating and intriguing as the politics of federal decision making.

Possessing the police power, which the federal government lacks, the Empire State can regulate persons and properties in order to promote and protect public health, safety, welfare, morals, and convenience. The scope of the police power, exercisable summarily or through the enactment and implementation of statutes, is undefinable except in the broadest of terms. In contrast, the direct activities of the national government are remote from the daily lives of average citizens.

POLITICAL DEVELOPMENT OF NEW YORK

The Dutch in 1613 commenced to establish trading posts on the Hudson River and claimed jurisdiction over the territory between the Connecticut River and the Delaware River. The Empire State was originally known as New Netherlands following its permanent settlement by the Dutch in May 1624 and acquired the name New York four decades later when the Dutch colony under Governor Peter Stuyvesant surrendered to an English expedition led by Richard Nicolls, the newly appointed provincial governor, and English possession was confirmed by the Treaty of Breda in July 1667.[2] Although the Dutch recaptured New York in August 1673, the Treaty of Westminster restored British rule effective in November 1674.

Col. Richard Nicolls was governor between 1664 and 1668 and published the "Duke's Laws" in 1665, the first English code of law. The duke of York in 1683 authorized the calling of a general assembly to draft the Charter of Liberties and Privileges, which was signed by the duke who, as King James two years later, revoked the charter. In 1691 a new assembly reaffirmed the charter, which met with neither the approval nor the disapproval of the new king, William III. Citizens in general viewed the charter as the fundamental law of the colony. Historians are in general agreement that the quality of the royal governors was mixed—ranging from excellent to fair to poor—although Leonard W. Labaree maintains that "the Governors appointed by the Crown compare not unfavorably in honesty and ability with the men now elected by the people of the several States of the Union."[3]

The next governing document was the constitution of 1777 providing for a strong Legislature and a weak governor, a document described in more detail in Chapter IV. Dissatisfaction with the Council of Appointment and the Council of Revision led to the adoption of a new constitution in 1821 abolishing the two councils and transferring the appointment power, subject to Senate confirmation, and the veto power to the governor.

The laissez-faire theory of Adam Smith, developed in 1776, rejected government control and regulation of the economy and restricted the functions of government to national defense and to the maintenance of public order, public institutions, and public works.[4] Jeffersonians, who were fearful of centralized political power, agreed with the laissez-faire economists and exerted a powerful influence upon the governance system. New York State, however, underwent a dramatic transformation in the nineteenth century as the state was converted from one composed chiefly of small farming communities into a state with a population of 959,049 in 1810, 3,880,735 in 1860, and 5,082,871 in 1880, and that became the leading manufacturing and commercial state in the nation. The dramatic economic changes necessitated the growth of the state government to cope with the problems that arose concomitantly with urbanization and industrialization and to provide services needed by a more urban population.

In particular, the development of monopolies and restrictive trade practices in the post–Civil War period led to governmental intervention in the economy in the form of regulation, a type of intervention that accelerated in the twentieth century. Relative to the control of local governments, John A. Fairlie in 1898 pointed out that "the revolution in the means and conditions of transportation has opened the way to centralizing influences. Central control of local officials under the conditions of communication existing before the middle of the century would necessarily have been exercised without any adequate knowledge of the local situation."[5]

The period from 1821 to 1929 was characterized by the placing of constitutional restrictions upon the power of the legislature and a gradual strengthening of the powers of the governor; the latter development is discussed in more detail in Chapter VII. Scandals in the financing of canal construction and resentment of legislative interference in local governments produced a reaction in the form of a new constitution in 1846 imposing the first restrictions, other than guarantees of civil liberties, upon the power of the legislature, restrictions found in the present constitution. Additional restrictions were placed upon the legislature by constitutional amendments in 1874 and a new constitution in 1894. These restrictions are discussed in detail in Chapter VI.

The first three decades of the twentieth century witnessed efforts by governors to promote the administrative reorganization of the state government and the adoption of the executive budget system. Success in achieving these two objectives produced a transformation in gubernatorial-legislative relations as the balance of formal political power was tipped in favor of the governor and charges began to be made relative to executive dominance of the state government, a subject examined in more detail in Chapters VI–VII.

IMPORTANCE OF THE EMPIRE STATE

The Empire State has been a giant in terms of its contribution to the nation's economy in the period subsequent to independence. In part, the state's economic prominence was a product of its location between the Atlantic Ocean and the Great Lakes and between New England and the states to the south and west. With a superb natural harbor in New York City and development of an extensive canal system, the Empire State was blessed with an outstanding transportation system that facilitated economic development. Neal R. Peirce includes the Empire State among his ten "Megastates."[6] Not surprisingly, interest groups engage in continual battle because of the great importance of many of the decisions made by the legislature and the governor.

With 38,341 manufacturing establishments employing approximately 1,679,000 persons, the Empire State leads all others as a manufacturing giant. The approximately 57,000 farms make New York one of the leading agricultural states, and agriculture's contribution of more than $1.7 billion annually to the economy makes farming the state's largest industry. New York is the largest producer of cabbage; the second largest producer of apples, grapes, ice cream, maple syrup, and wine; and the third largest producer of milk and cheese. Yet the state ranks only twenty-first in agricultural income.

The Empire State's population increased from 16,838,000 in 1960 to 18,384,000 in 1970, a total exceeding the population of many nation-states including Australia, Austria, Chile, Sweden, and Switzerland. Although projected to reach a population of 20,660,000 in 1985, New York suffered a 1.7 percent population decline (318,000 persons) between 1970 and 1977. Births in the state exceeded deaths by 555,000 in this period, but the state suffered a net out-migration of 873,000 persons, or 4.8 percent of the state's population.

The relative economic prosperity and population density of a state influences the nature of its problems. New York State generally is an economically prosperous state and ranks seventh among the fifty states as measured by per capita income, but it has pockets of poverty.

The population center of the state is the town of Forestburgh in Sullivan County in the southern Catskill Mountains. The Empire State, with a land area of 47,831 square miles, ranks thirtieth among the states but fifth in population density, which increased from 217.9 persons per square mile in 1920 to 381.3 in 1970, reflecting urbanization and the impact of New York City on the average figure. In 1973, 89.3 percent of the citizens resided in eight metropolitan areas, including the New York City area, which is the largest metropolitan area in the nation. The second largest such area in the state is the Buffalo Metropolitan Statistical Area (MSA), which ranks twenty-sixth in population nationally. Relative to race and country of origin, approximately 12 percent of the population are black and approximately 32 percent were born in foreign countries. New York in 1976 had the largest number of blacks—approximately 2.2 million—and was followed by California and Illinois, which each had approximately 1.6 million blacks. During the 1970s, New York State gained more blacks than it lost, primarily because of immigration of blacks from overseas. In terms of persons of Spanish origin, New York State ranks third (1.4 million) after California (3.3 million) and Texas (2.6 million).

State politics bears a close relation to national politics because

of the political importance of the Empire State, which had 45 votes
in the electoral college until 1962, when the number was reduced
to 41—the second largest number of electoral votes possessed by a
state in the election of a president of the United States. The number
of electoral college votes probably will decline by 5 following certification of the 1980 federal decennial census.

The size of its voting bloc in the electoral college and the strong
executive system on the state level have encouraged potential national leaders to seek the office of governor as a stepping-stone to
the presidency and make the state a political "heavyweight" among
the states. Not surprisingly, the state has been a major supplier of
presidential nominees.

PROBLEMS OF A MATURE STATE

During the past decade, significant developments of a fundamental nature have combined to produce major problems for the
Empire State. Whereas the state as recently as the halcyon days of
the economic boom of the 1960s, under Governor Nelson A. Rockefeller, was clearly the leader in inaugurating new and innovative
state programs, the failure of the entire northeastern section of the
United States to recover fully from the recession that commenced
in the early 1970s and the movement of industry and population to
the Sunbelt states—induced in part by high taxes, high labor costs,
and high energy costs—have combined to limit the ability of a mature state, which has lost many of its comparative advantages, to
remain innovative in terms of launching expensive new programs.
The Empire State, for example, lost 5.5 percent of its jobs in the
period 1970–77, whereas the remainder of the nation increased jobs
by 8.7 percent. In 1956 the state's share of national manufacturing
employment was nearly 12.0 percent, but the share dropped to 7.5
percent by 1976.

New York State, according to a survey of corporate executives,
is viewed as a high-wage, high-tax, and high-cost state and is placed
last among the forty-eight continental states in terms of a desirable
location for a new factory.[7] Public school costs, the per capita income
tax, and the per capita state-local debt in the state are the highest

among the fifty states, and the state-local tax burden in the Empire State is second only to the burden in Alaska. The strength of labor unions in the Empire State—more than 36 percent of the work force is unionized—is viewed by some industrial firms as a negative location factor when compared with a state such as North Carolina with a work force that is only 7 percent unionized. Available evidence suggests that the state will continue to experience a slower rate of economic growth than states in the South and the West. Contributing to the slow rate of economic growth will be high energy costs.

Certain federal policies have aggravated the problems of New York State. Increased federal farm subsidies promoted the mechanization of agriculture subsequent to World War II, forcing poor blacks and whites off many southern farms and resulting in their migration to northern cities, where they often became "high-cost" citizens in great need of governmental services. The Empire State has the highest per capita expenditures for welfare in the nation and has 1.2 million citizens on welfare. Two, the interstate highway program, launched in 1956, encouraged industry to leave the older central cities for suburban areas, thereby increasing the problems of the cities.

New York State has recovered slowly from the recession of the early 1970s and in January 1981 had an unemployment rate of 7.6 percent. Unemployment was a more serious problem in New York City, where 8.8 percent were officially unemployed, compared with the national unemployment rate of 7.5 percent. Unemployment is concentrated among young black males in the city. Between 1969 and 1978 employment in the city declined by 625,000 jobs, or 16.5 percent.[8]

The near financial collapse of New York City in 1975 severely strained the resources of the state as it attempted to assist the city. Available evidence suggests that New York City and the city of Yonkers will continue to experience serious financial problems and that several other large cities—Buffalo and Rochester in particular—will come under increasing financial pressures. In 1980 the Citizens Budget Commission, Inc., projected that potential New York City's budget shortfalls, defined as the excess of expenditures over revenues, could total $1,142 million in fiscal 1981, $2,143 million in fiscal 1982, and $2,744 million in fiscal 1983.[9] Deficits of this magnitude obviously will continue to strain the financial resources of the Empire State. Complicating the financial problems of hard-pressed local governments is a 1978 Court of Appeals decision invalidating a law allowing local governments to exclude from the constitutional tax limits taxes levied for pensions and other fringe benefits, a subject discussed in detail in Chapter X.

International developments also have affected the Empire State adversely. The sharp increase in the price of oil by the Organization of Petroleum Exporting Countries (OPEC) since 1973 has hit the state hard, since it relies upon oil for 65 percent of its energy needs and upon natural gas for an additional 15 percent. Relative to the latter, a 1978 change in federal regulation of natural gas has led to a steep rise in its cost. The state may be viewed, as one views a nation-state, in terms of balance of payments, and it is apparent that energy costs will exert a drain on the state's balance of payments within the foreseeable future.

AN OVERVIEW

To facilitate an understanding of the powers of the New York State government, Chapter II focuses upon the division of governmental power between the national government and the Empire State. Particular emphasis is placed upon the changing division of powers and the growth in the sharing of governmental powers. The debate launched at the Philadelphia Constitutional Convention in 1787 over the proper role of the national government continues today, and charges have been made that the national government—through the use of conditional grants-in-aid and its preemptory powers—has encroached seriously upon the traditional sphere of state responsibility. Fear is expressed by some observers that states are becoming more and more the ministerial arms of the national government, in that states must abide by federal conditions to be eligible for the receipt of grants-in-aid and must adopt standards meeting federal criteria in functional areas partially preempted by Congress to avoid total preemption.

While federal-state conflicts occur, cooperation is more typical, as the sharing of governmental responsibilities—a partnership approach to solving problems—has become common, and in recent years the state has accelerated its efforts to influence federal policymaking.

Chapter II also examines interstate relations, another area involving conflict and cooperation. The use of interstate and federal-state compacts to solve problems overspilling the boundaries of the Empire State are examined, as are the efforts made to promote the adoption of uniform laws by all fifty states. The relative economic decline of the northeastern states has promoted several cooperative interstate efforts to improve the economy of the region.

Continuing the subject of intergovernmental relations, Chapter III examines state-local relations over the years with emphasis placed upon the development of constitutional home rule and the problem of state mandating of local expenditures. While state mandates increase the fiscal burden of local governments, the Empire State has been a generous provider of financial assistance to local governments, with approximately 61 percent of executive budget appropriations assisting localities. The helpfulness of the state is highlighted by its rescue operation to save New York City from bankruptcy.

A search for an understanding of political behavior in the Empire State leads in part to the state constitution, the subject of Chapter IV, which not only establishes the framework of government and allocates power but also places important restrictions upon the powers of the state legislature and local governments, thereby leading to the employment of ingenuity to discover ways of avoiding the restrictions. The state constitution is the fundamental law of the Empire State and is largely the product of interest groups. Since the relatively detailed document contains numerous provisions inserted through the influence of interest groups, it is not surprising that interest groups benefiting from the various provisions closely monitor attempts to amend the constitution and employ their full political resources to resist assaults upon their entrenched interests. The political nature of constitution making is revealed clearly to the public when a constitutional convention, such as the one in 1967, is held as lobbyists flock to the convention because of the high stakes involved.

Politics in the Empire State is colored and flavored by an upstate-downstate division, with downstate often referring only to New York City, which traditionally has been dominated by the Democratic party, whereas the upstate area in general has been dominated by the Republican party, a subject discussed more fully in Chapter V. Today, five political parties officially are recognized—Democratic, Republican, Conservative, Liberal, and Right-to-Life. The two largest parties may be viewed as pragmatic ones that attempt to appeal to all voters and often have platforms that are generally similar. The Liberal party, while oriented somewhat along philosophical lines, has been a "swing" party often able to influence the outcome of an election by its endorsement of Democratic or Republican candidates. The Conservative party is a "philosophical" party that espouses a discrete ideology and has been gaining strength at the polls. The Right-to-Life is distinctive as a one-issue political party.

As we will see in Chapter V, interest-group activity is not confined to the process of state constitution making and extends to the legislative function and the rulemaking function. Many of the issues—abortion and capital punishment in particular—are highly emotional issues, supported or opposed by single-issue groups. While public utility and railroad lobbies were the most powerful lobbies for a long period of time, their influence in the political process today is small, and they have been replaced in strength by the public employee unions and public interest groups. Lobbying by public officials, especially officials of local governments and public authorities, also has increased substantially.

Chapter VI focuses upon the legislature, the annual forum attended by all political interest groups and the principal resource distributor in the Empire State. Abuse of the public trust by the legislature in the nineteenth century prompted public reaction in the form of constitutional restrictions that today impede legislative action and discretion. Many of the shackling provisions adopted in the nineteenth century have proved to be less restrictive than their sponsors hoped, as the legislature has discovered how to work around many of the inhibiting provisions.

The most significant development of the second half of the twentieth century has been the gradually growing strength of the legislature as it expanded its oversight of administration, participated more fully in the budget-making process, and increased its professional staff substantially. To a large extent, a troika—the governor, speaker of the Assembly, and the president pro tempore of the Senate—dominate the policymaking process of the Empire State.

Gubernatorial-legislative relations underwent a substantial change in the twentieth century as the reorganization of the executive branch and adoption of the executive budget system produced the emergence of the strong governor in terms of formal powers, a subject analyzed in Chapter VII. Forces favoring a weak governor were successful in ensuring through the constitution of 1777, that the governor would possess relatively few powers. The history of the Empire State until 1929 witnessed the gradual strengthening of the Office of the Governor as forces committed to the integration of executive powers grew in strength. In the 1930s charges of executive dominance began to make their appearance and reached a peak during the governorship of Nelson A. Rockefeller (1959–73). Chapter VII examines these charges and draws conclusions as to their accuracy.

Chapter VIII focuses upon the administrative departments, boards, commissions, agencies, and public authorities of the state. Whereas the government established by the constitution of 1777 was relatively unimportant in terms of its administrative activities, the agencies of the Empire State today touch all phases of the daily lives of citizens. Chapter VIII also examines several highly political topics, including the use of public authorities and the "moral obligation" bond; the civil service system, the Taylor law; the retirement system; and various proposals for reforming the civil service system, including creation of a Department of Personnel Management, elimination of the "Rule of Three," and establishment of a Senior Management Service.

The importance of the subject of Chapter IX—the state judiciary—cannot be overestimated, inasmuch as the role of the judiciary has expanded as society has become more complex. In examining the various courts, ranging from minor courts to general trial courts to appellate courts, particular attention is paid to proposals for change, including the greater use of administrative adjudication and arbitration. One of the most important political questions in the Empire State involves the popular election or the appointment of judges. Part of this controversy was resolved in 1977 when voters ratified a constitutional amendment providing for gubernatorial appointment of members of the highest court—the Court of Appeals. The last section of Chapter IX examines the policymaking role of the judiciary and notes that, while this role has been a relatively minor one, judicial decisions have had major financial implications for the Empire State.

The concluding chapter deals with financing the state and includes sections on federal funds, state budgets, constitutional restrictions, the fund structure, the accounting and the auditing systems, the revenue and the debt system, and state-local fiscal relations. While any effort to change the system of financing the state activates political forces, attempts to change the formulas for distributing state financial assistance to local governments immediately result in the marshaling of political resources by interest groups attempting to maximize their advantage.

NOTES

1. Jack L. Walker, "The Diffusion of Innovations Among the American States," *The American Political Science Review*, September 1969, p. 883. Professor Walker defined an innovation "as a program or policy which is new to the state adopting it, no matter how old the program may be or how many other states may have adopted it."

2. For the Dutch period, see John Fiske, *The Dutch and Quaker Colonies in America* (Boston: Houghton Mifflin and Company, 1899); Ellis L. Raesly, *Portrait of New Netherland* (New York: Columbia University Press, 1945); Samuel G. Nissenson, *The Patroon's Domain* (New York: Columbia University Press, 1937); and David M. Ellis, James A. Frost, Harold C. Syrett, and Harry J. Carman, *A History of New York State* (Ithaca: Cornell University Press, 1957), pp. 18–28.

3. DeAlva S. Alexander, *Political History of the State of New York* (New York: Henry Holt & Company, 1906), Vol. I, p. 10; Allan Nevins, *The American States During and After the Revolution: 1775–1789* (New York: The Macmillan Company, 1924), pp. 9–10; and Leonard W. Labaree, *Royal Government in America: A Study of the English Colonial System Before 1783* (New Haven: Yale University Press, 1930), p. 287.

4. Adam Smith, *An Inquiry into the Nature and Causes of the Wealth of Nations* (Oxford: Clarendon Press, 1976).

5. John A. Fairlie, *The Centralization of Administration in New York State* (New York: Columbia University Studies in History, Economics, and Public Law, 1898), Vol. IX, No. 3, p. 194.

6. Neal R. Peirce, *The Megastates of America* (New York: W. W. Norton Company, 1972).

7. *Annual Report: 1975–1976* (Albany: New York Job Development Authority, 1976), p. 4.

8. Jacob K. Javits, "The Hemorrage of Jobs," *Congressional Record,* March 1, 1979, p. S1853.

9. *Statement on New York City's Fiscal Situation* (New York: Citizens Budget Commission, Inc., January 1980), p. 4.

CHAPTER II
Federal-State
and Interstate Relations

TO UNDERSTAND PROPERLY *the* operation of a federal system of government, one must gain a full appreciation of the complexities and dynamics associated with the changing division and sharing of governmental power. Individual states must establish relationships with the national government and with other states under rules and guidelines set down in the United States Constitution as interpreted by the United States Supreme Court, and they also must establish relationships with local governments.

FEDERAL-STATE RELATIONS

Although the United States Constitution might have been designed to allocate specified functions to each of the two levels of government, a decision was made to have the Constitution delegate enumerated powers only to the national government. To make crystal clear that the national government possessed only enumerated powers, the Tenth Amendment to the United States Constitution was adopted stipulating that powers not delegated to the Congress nor prohibited to the states were reserved to the states and the people. This division-of-powers approach to government often is labeled "dual" or "layer-cake" federalism. In practice, however, there is a sharing of most powers by the levels of government rather than the complete division of powers suggested by the term "dual federalism." The term "cooperative federalism" is often used to describe the cooperative activities of the national, state, and local governments involving a sharing of powers.

Powers delegated to the Congress and not forbidden to the states—concurrent powers—may be exercised by either or both levels of government. The power to tax and the power to construct roads are examples.

Powers of the Federal Government

Most of the delegated or enumerated powers of the federal government are found in Section 8 of the United States Constitution authorizing Congress to tax, borrow money, regulate interstate commerce and bankruptcies, establish a uniform rule of naturalization, coin money, fix the standard of weights and measures, punish counterfeiters of money, establish post offices and roads, provide for patents and copyrights, constitute inferior courts, punish piracies and felonies committed on the high seas, declare war, raise and support armies and a navy, call forth the National Guard to execute laws, and govern the District of Columbia.

Article II of the Constitution assigns the duty of conducting foreign relations and military operations to the president, and Article III establishes the Supreme Court and its trial jurisdiction. In addition to enumerated powers, the "elastic clause" stipulates that Congress has the power "to make all laws which shall be necessary and proper for the carrying into execution the foregoing powers, and all other powers vested by this Constitution in the government of the United States or officer thereof."

The Constitution contains a number of restrictions on the powers of the national government. Section 9 of Article I forbids the suspension of the writ of habeas corpus (court order directing the jailer to bring a prisoner before the judge) except in the event of invasion or rebellion, enactment of a bill of attainder (legislative declaration of guilt and imposition of punishment), or ex post facto law (a retroactive criminal law); levying of an export tax; and preference being given to ports of one state over ports of other states. Section 8 of Article I requires all duties, imposts, and excises to be uniform throughout the nation. And the Bill of Rights, the first ten amendments, contains many restrictions upon federal powers by guaranteeing freedom of assembly, petition, press, religion, and speech, and protection of the rights of persons accused of crime, among other guarantees.

With the passage of time, the powers of the national government have been expanded by constitutional amendments, judicial decisions, and statutory elaboration of delegated powers. We also find the federal government engaged in activities that once were considered to be the exclusive responsibilities of state and local governments. This expansion of federal powers has produced a continuing ideological debate over the proper roles of the national government and that of the states.

Constitutional Amendments. No constitutional amendment directly restricted the powers of the states until the Fourteenth Amendment, with its "due process of law" and "equal protection of the laws" clauses, was adopted. These two clauses have served as the basis for numerous federal court decisions striking down as unconstitutional actions taken by states. To cite only one example, the United States Supreme Court in 1964 ruled that both houses of a state legislature must be apportioned on the basis of population—one person, one vote—because apportionment on the basis of geographical areas violated the equal protection of laws clause of the Fourteenth Amendment.[1] This decision necessitated the reapportionment of both houses of the New York State legislature (discussed in more detail in Chapter VI).

The Fifteenth Amendment guarantees the voting rights of blacks, and Congress enacted the Voting Rights Act in 1965 to implement the constitutional guarantees, a subject discussed in Chapter VI relative to the 1974 redistricting of Assembly seats in Brooklyn.

Whereas the Fourteenth Amendment provides the basis for federal judicial intervention in what previously had been the affairs of the states, the Sixteenth Amendment's authorization for Congress to levy a graduated income tax gave the Congress power to raise sufficient funds to finance more than 1,100 domestic categorical grant-in-aid programs with conditions attached. As a result, Congress has considerable influence over reserved powers matters. While it is true that a state may avoid federal controls inherent in grant-in-aid programs by refusing to apply for and accept grants, the fiscal pressures bearing upon most states make such a refusal politically impossible.

The sharp rise in conditional federal grants-in-aid to states during the 1950s and the 1960s led some observers to express the view that states would become little more than ministerial arms of the federal government. This view has proven to be unfounded; states continue to be important units of governments possessing broad discretionary powers. Furthermore, states retain a considerable amount of discretionary authority in administering federally aided programs and also are able to influence federal policies embodied in statutes enacted by Congress, as well as rules and regulations adopted by federal agencies administering the grant programs.

Federal grants-in-aid have strengthened the position of the governor vis-à-vis a legislature of the Empire State, since most federal grants are applied for, and received by, executive agencies under the control of the governor. In consequence, the governor is less dependent upon appropriations by the legislature than he would be in the absence of federal grants, and this is the reason that controversy has raged over the question of whether all federal funds received by the state should be placed in the general fund of the State Treasury and be subject to appropriation by the legislature before the funds can be spent (discussed in Chapter VI).

Judicial Decisions. The doctrine of implied powers, originating in a United States Supreme Court decision in 1819, has led to a significant expansion of federal powers. In *McCulloch* v. *Maryland* the Court held: "Let the end be legitimate, let it be within the scope of the Constitution, and all means which are appropriate, which are plainly adopted to the end, which are not prohibited, but consistent with the letter and spirit of the Constitution, are constitutional."[2]

In general, the Court has interpreted broadly the powers granted to the national government by the Constitution. To cite only one relatively recent example, the Court upheld the constitutionality of the Federal Voting Rights Act of 1965, which had been challenged by South Carolina on the grounds that the act encroached on the powers reserved to the states by the Tenth Amendment and that the act was aimed at one region of the nation.[3]

Statutory Elaboration. Although Congress was delegated specific grants of power in many areas of government concern, a few of the delegated powers were not exercised for many decades. To cite two examples, Congress did not utilize its grant of power to regulate interstate commerce in a comprehensive manner until passage of the Interstate Commerce Act of 1887, and Congress did not use its supersessive power to regulate bankruptcies until 1933.

During the past three and one-half decades Congress has increasingly used its powers of partial and total preemption to supersede state laws. The Atomic Energy Act of 1946, for example, totally preempted responsibility for the regulation of ionizing radiation, and states were forbidden to regulate such radiation until a 1954 amendment authorized the former Atomic Energy Commission, now the Nuclear Regulatory Commission, to enter into agreements with states under which a state would be allowed to assume certain regulatory responsibilities.[4] And the Uniform Time Act of 1966 totally preempted responsibility for determining the dates on which standard time is changed to daylight saving time and vice versa.[5]

The most important preemptory actions by Congress have involved environmental protection. By the mid-1960s, Congress decided that a number of areawide problems—particularly environmental ones—could not be eliminated by reliance upon state and local governmental action encouraged by the "carrots" of federal grants-in-aid. Enactment of the Water Quality Act of 1965[6] and a similar air quality preemptory act have had great significance for the system of intergovernmental governance. The Water Quality Act required each state to adopt "water quality standards applicable to interstate waters or portions thereof within such State" as well as an implementation and enforcement plan. The administrator of the Environmental Protection Agency is authorized to promulgate water quality standards that become effective at the end of six months in the event a state fails to establish and enforce adequate standards. The federal role has been strengthened by other statutory enactments, particularly the Federal Water Pollution Control Act Amendments of 1972 that established July 1, 1977, as the deadline for the secondary treatment of sewage, and July 1, 1983, as the date for achieving "water quality which provides for protection and propagation of fish, shellfish, and wildlife," and required the elimination of the "discharge of pollutants into navigable waters by 1985."[7]

Mention must be made of the fact that the political power of the governor has been increased by partial federal preemption of functional responsibility, since the governor is authorized by federal law and regulations to designate metropolitan planning organizations, which have major transportation responsibilities, and Section 208 water quality planning agencies, and to balance the need for economic development with preservation of air quality, provided pollutants emanating from new developments do not exceed national standards. Prior to the enactment of the Clean Air Act Amendments of 1977, Environmental Protection Agency regulations forbade significant deterioration of existing air quality.[8]

Powers of State Governments

In contrast to the expressed powers of the national government, the powers of the states are reserved or residual. The major reserved powers are the police power and the power to provide services and control local governments.

The police power, although undefinable in precise terms, is a power of utmost importance to the states and may be delegated to local governments. In its broadest terms, the police power may be defined as the authority of the state to regulate personal and property rights in order to promote public health, safety, morals, welfare, and convenience. States may exercise the police power by the enactment and enforcement of a statute, or the power may be exercised summarily to deal with health and safety emergencies such as epidemics and fires.

Although the powers of the states have not been expanded by amendments to the United States Constitution or judicial decisions, states have made increased use of their residual powers to cope with the challenges presented by industrialization, urbanization, increasing number of motor vehicles, and other developments.

Restrictions on State Powers. Section 10 of Article I of the United States Constitution enumerates restrictions upon the powers of states. Specifically, states may not engage in relations with other nations, coin money or emit bills of credit, pass a bill of attainder or ex post facto law, impair the obligation of contract, levy import or export duties, "keep troops or ships of war in time of peace," grant a title of nobility, or engage in war. Section 10 is reinforced by Article VI, the "supremacy" clause.

Five constitutional amendments specifically limit the powers of states. The most important—the Fourteenth Amendment—contains the famous due process of law and equal protection of the laws clauses that have been interpreted by the United States Supreme Court to encompass most of the guarantees of the Bill of Rights. The Fifteenth Amendment forbids states to restrict the right to vote because of race, color, or previous condition of servitude, and the Nineteenth Amendment forbids states to deny women the suffrage right. The Twenty-fourth Amendment outlawed the poll tax as a condition for voting, and the Twenty-sixth Amendment lowered the voting age to eighteen in all elections.

Action initiated by the Empire State on a number of occasions has been restricted by an act of Congress or by federal court decisions, as illustrated by the following two examples. The Federal Voting Rights Act of 1965 as amended necessitated a special session of the state legislature in 1974 to reapportion congressional and state Senate and Assembly districts in portions of New York City, including the drawing of an Assembly district's lines in such a manner that the district contained a black population of 65 percent.[9] In 1977 the United States Supreme Court invalidated a 1972 New York State law providing approximately $11 million in financial assistance to private and parochial schools on the ground the aid could result in "excessive State involvement in religious affairs."[10] The financial assistance was designed to compensate the schools for state-mandated recordkeeping and testing expenditures. In 1980 the United States Supreme Court, in *Committee for Public Education* v. *Regan,* by a 5 to 4 vote, upheld a similar law by ruling that it "has a secular legislative purpose," does not advance or hinder religion, and "does not foster an excessive government entanglement with religion."[11]

Federal Guarantees to the States

Four provisions of the United States Constitution contain guarantees to the states. Article IV contains a pledge to protect the states against foreign invasion and domestic violence, and it stipulates that Congress may neither take territory from one state to form a new state without the consent of the concerned state nor combine two or more states without their consent. A republican form of government also is guaranteed to each state by Article IV.

Article V guarantees each state equality of representation in the United States Senate, and the Eleventh Amendment forbids federal courts to accept jurisdiction in cases involving suits against a state by citizens of another state. The latter guarantee means that a state can be sued only with its permission in its courts.

Federal-State Cooperation

The United States Constitution provides that states are responsible for determining suffrage requirements, subject to four amendments, and conducting the elections for members of Congress and the electoral college. In addition, the Constitution cannot be amended unless the legislature or specially chosen conventions in three fourths of the states approve the amendments proposed by Congress or a constitutional convention.

The history of federal-state relations has been one of cooperation and conflict, the former being more common than the latter. The cooperation can be "one-way," with either the state or the national government lending the other unit equipment, or "two ways," as illustrated by the New York State Department of Taxation and Finance exchanging with the United States Internal Revenue Service state income tax returns for federal income tax returns of the state's citizens in order to enable each government to detect individuals who filed a return with only one government or failed to report the same income on the two returns.

To assist states in apprehending criminals, Congress enacted numerous laws, and federal agencies have issued regulations making it a federal crime for a person violating a state law to cross a state boundary into another state. Examples include the prohibition of the transportation across state lines of kidnapped persons, other persons for immoral purposes, stolen automobiles, and wild animals killed in violation of state laws or regulations.

Relative to financial assistance to state and local governments, Congress enacted a $30.2 billion general revenue-sharing program in 1972 and extended the program in 1976 by authorizing $6.65 billion to $6.85 billion annually through fiscal year 1980.[12] In 1974 Congress authorized a $8.4 billion special revenue-sharing program for community development, and in 1977 the program was extended with an authorization of $3.5 billion for fiscal year 1978, $3.65 billion for fiscal year 1979, and $3.8 billion for fiscal year 1980.[13]

Rapidly changing conditions have outdated a 1954 statement by Lynton K. Caldwell: "Because of the financial resources and the strength of its administrative system, the State of New York is relatively less dependent upon federal assistance than are most States."[14] The importance of direct federal financial assistance is highlighted by the approximately $8 billion annually provided to New York State and its local governments. Without such funds, the state and its political subdivisions would be unable to provide the current level of services.

The growing importance of the federal government led the governor to establish in Washington, D.C., an Office of Federal Affairs that seeks increased financial aid for the state, medicaid and welfare changes lightening the state's financial burden relative to these two programs, development of a national energy policy favorable to the state, changes in federal military policies regarding bases and supplies, and other functions.[15] In 1977 the Assembly and the Senate each established a Washington office and also are represented by the National Conference of State Legislatures (NCSL). In addition, the mayor of New York City, the State Board of Education, the New York City Board of Education, the State University of New York, and Nassau County each maintain a Washington office.

The New York City Fiscal Crisis. A dramatic example of federal-state cooperation is the emergency loan program authorized by Congress in 1975 to help solve the fiscal crisis experienced by New York City.[16] Under the act, the secretary of the treasury is authorized to loan up to $2.3 billion annually to New York City to cover seasonal shortfalls in revenue, and the city is required to repay the loan at the end of the city's fiscal year with interest equal to the Treasury's borrowing cost plus 1 percent.

In part, the federal action is a response to intense lobbying by the governor; the mayor; the state's congressional delegation; and the Coalition for New York, composed of representatives of major corporations and labor unions in New York City, that requested their counterparts in other states, via the telephone and meetings, to put pressure on their senators and representatives to prevent the bankruptcy of the city, which would have national repercussions on the financial markets and the economy.

Regional Lobbying

More recently, the governors of the northeastern states discovered that it is good internal politics to attribute part of their states' economic difficulties to an alleged "shortchanging" of the states by the federal government and began to lobby more strenuously to obtain increased federal financial assistance for their states by altering the states' balance of exchange with the federal government.

The governors have been joined in their efforts by a number of senators and representatives, including Senator Daniel P. Moynihan of New York, who issued a report in 1977 that the federal government takes $17.1 billion more out of New York State than is returned in federal outlays in the state.[17] Determining precisely the relationship between federal outlays in a given state and the amount of federal tax revenue raised in the same state is an impossible accounting task. Included in Senator Moynihan's calculations, for example, are the federal corporate income tax payments made by national and multinational corporations with headquarters in New York State, even though a large proportion of their revenues were generated outside the state. The accounting problem is complicated further by the fact that federal funds reported as distributed in a state, such as New York, immediately may be transferred to another state, as frequently happens with social security checks forwarded to New York recipients spending the Winter in Florida or Arizona.

INTERSTATE RELATIONS

Inherent in a federal system of government is the need for formalizing relations between the individual states and providing a mechanism for settling interstate disputes. Section 2 of Article III of the United States Constitution grants the United States Supreme Court original jurisdiction in cases involving disputes between states. The first such case adjudicated by the Court involved a boundary dispute between New York and Connecticut.[18]

The drafters of the United States Constitution recognized the need for formalizing interstate relations by authorizing states to enter into political compacts or agreements with each other, provided Congress gave its consent to the compacts or agreements.[19] Congressional consent is not required if a compact is nonpolitical, such as one providing for reciprocity in licensing medical doctors, and Congress since the Weeks Forest Fire Protection Act of 1911 has given its consent in advance for states to enter into a number of specified compacts.[20]

Compact Membership

New York State is a member of a relatively large number of interstate compacts, as revealed by Table I, whose importance varies considerably from compact to compact as measured by the nature of the problem designed to be solved by the compact. Certain compacts—the Civil Defense Compact and the Northeastern Forest Fire Protection Compact—are mutual assistance or "standby" compacts that generally are activated only if an emergency develops. Many compacts, such as the one on moving traffic violations, are administered by regular state agencies. Other compacts establish agencies, such as the Port Authority of New York and New Jersey, to administer the compacts.

In addition to the interstate compacts listed in Table I, the Empire State in 1933 entered into a compact with the government of Canada to create the Buffalo and Fort Erie Public Bridge Authority composed of five New York State members and five Canadian members.[21]

The federal-state compact is an organizational innovation of the second half of the twentieth century and involves the federal government becoming a direct partner with several states to solve multistate problems. New York is a member of three federal-state compacts—the Appalachian Regional Compact (1965),[22] the Delaware River Basin Compact (1961), and the Susquehanna River Basin Compact (1971). The Delaware River Basin Compact was the first such compact enacted into law by Congress, thereby providing for the federal government to join in a partnership with New Jersey, New York, and Pennsylvania. Previously, Congress had only given its consent to compacts but never had joined a compact.

Uniform State Laws

The National Conference of Commissioners on Uniform State Laws, established in 1892 and composed of three commissioners

TABLE II.I NEW YORK'S MEMBERSHIP IN INTERSTATE COMPACTS 1981

Compact	Year Entered	Compact	Year Entered
Appalachian Regional Compact	1965	Motor Vehicle Registration	1968
Atlantic States Marine	1941	Compact	
Fisheries Compact		Moving Traffic Violations	1977
Bus Taxation Proration	1964	New England Interstate Water	1949
Champlain Basin Compact	1966	Pollution Control Compact	
Civil Defense Compact	1951	New York, New Haven, and	1968
Commerce Department,	1945	Hartford Railroad Compact	
Cooperating in Promoting		New York–Rhode Island	1943
Delaware River Basin Compact	1961	Boundary Compact	
Detainers, Criminal	1936	Northeastern Interstate Forest	1949
Proceedings		Fire Protection Compact	
Driver License Compact	1965	Ohio River Valley Water	1939
Educational Personnel,	1968	Sanitation Compact	
Qualifications of		Oil and Gas, Conservation of	1941
Failure to Appear, Suspension	1959	Palisades Interstate Park	1937
of Licenses		Compact	
Great Lakes Compact	1960	Parole and Probation Compact	1977
Holland Tunnel Compact	1931	Placement of Children Compact	1960
Hudson River Valley	1972	Port Authority of New York	1921
Commission		and New Jersey Compact	
Income Tax, interest on	1919	Sanitation Compact	1936
obligations of instrumentality		Supervision of Parolees and	1936
created by compact		Probationers	
Interpleader Compact	1963	Susquehanna River Basin	1971
Interstate Library District	1963	Compact	
Juvenile Delinquents	1955	Traffic Violations Compact	1965
Lake Champlain Bridge	1927	Guaranteeing Appearances	
Compact		Tri-State Regional Planning	1965
Limited-Profit Housing	1961	Compact	
Companies Compact		Vehicle Equipment Safety	1962
Mental Health Compact	1956	Compact	
Military Aid Compact	1951	Waterfront and Airport	1953
Milk Control Compact	1937	Commission Compact	

appointed by the governor of each state, meets annually to draft "model laws" for submission to the members' legislatures. Most model laws deal with regulation of commerce, taxation, and family matters. Uniformity is achieved throughout the fifty states whenever all legislatures enact a model law. To date, only the model laws providing for reciprocal enforcement of support and a commercial code have been enacted by all the legislatures. Of the eighty-three model laws, New York State has enacted twenty-four.

The federal government promotes uniform state laws by attaching conditions to grants-in-aid and tax credits. What is commonly referred to as the fifty-five-mile-per-hour "national" speed limit actually is the result of the enactment of a uniform maximum speed law by each of the fifty state legislatures in response to a stipulation of the Emergency Highway Energy Conservation Act of 1974 that the secretary of transportation withhold approval of any federally aided highway construction project in any state with a maximum speed limit in excess of fifty-five miles per hour.[23]

Tax credits are utilized by the federal government to effectuate uniform state tax laws in two areas. Under provisions of the Revenue Act of 1926, estates are granted an 80 percent tax credit against the federal estate tax due for state inheritance tax payments.[24] Similarly, the Social Security Act of 1935 allows an employer to credit state unemployment compensation taxes up to 90 percent of the federal unemployment compensation tax due.[25] These two federal laws encouraged states without such taxes to adopt them with the same rates as the federal rates in order to maximize state revenue. Failure to enact a state estate tax or state unemployment compensation tax would lead to the entire amount of the tax revenue going to the federal Treasury, instead of 20 percent under the first tax and 10 percent under the second act.

Administrative Agreements

In addition to interstate compacts enacted by the New York State legislature and other legislatures, a large number of reciprocal agreements have been signed by New York State administrators and their counterparts in other states. Reciprocal agreements permitting police in hot pursuit to cross into another state are common, as are similar agreements relative to motor vehicle registrations and drivers' licenses. The Department of State has reciprocity agreements for real estate brokers with other states, and the Education Department has similar agreements with many States relative to professions the department regulates. There is no central file of administrative agreements with other states, and the total number of such agreements is unknown.

Major Interstate Problems

Interstate disputes over water have been common and have occasionally led to New York State suing another state or being sued, as in 1931 when New Jersey sued the Empire State to prevent the state and New York City from diverting water from the Delaware River.[26]

A major water dispute involves the control of the flow of water from three huge upstate reservoirs supplying water to New York City. Since these reservoirs also feed into the headwaters of the Delaware River, which supplies water to communities in Delaware, New Jersey, and Pennsylvania, these states announced their strenuous opposition to two 1976 New York State laws allowing the State Department of Environmental Conservation to control the flow.[27]

In 1978 five Pennsylvania property owners won a suit in a United States district court for nearly $250,000 as damages for losses caused by trespass by New York City on their property by diminishing the volume of Delaware River water to the extent of turning parts of the riverbed into a swamp at times.

Another water dispute involved Vermont, which has been attempting since 1968 to force the Empire State to remove the sludge deposited in Lake Champlain by the former International Paper Company plant in Fort Ticonderoga on the ground that the decaying organic material and wood chips were killing the lake. New York contends that the attempt to remove the sludge will cause serious pollution in the lake and that less environmental damage will result if the sludge is allowed to remain on the lake bottom.

"Buttlegging." The most serious interstate problem faced by the Empire State today is "buttlegging," that is, the illegal importation of cigarettes from North Carolina where the state excise tax is only 2 cents and their sale in New York State without the payment of the New York State and City cigarette excise taxes, causing a loss of an estimated $100 million annually in state and city revenue. An estimated 50 percent of the cigarettes purchased in New York City are sold by the underworld, which has driven nearly half of the legitimate wholesalers out of business, resulting in the loss of employment for in excess of 2,500 drivers, packers, and salesmen in the state.

In 1978 Congress attempted to solve the problem by passing a law making it a federal offense, subject to a maximum fine of

$100,000 and five years in federal prison or both, "for any person knowingly to ship, transport, receive, possess, sell, distribute, or purchase contraband cigarettes."[28]

SUMMARY AND CONCLUSIONS

A review of intergovernmental relations since 1787 reveals that amendments to the United States Constitution, statutory elaboration, and broad judicial interpretation of constitutional grants of power, and conditional grants-in-aid to states and their political subdivisions, have produced a substantial increase in the involvement of the national government in functional activities that once were considered to be the exclusive responsibility of state and local governments. The response of the federal government to emerging problems has been practical in nature, and the term "pragmatic federalism" aptly describes the federal system today.

Partial federal preemption of regulatory activities, particularly in the environmental field, has led to a new relationship between the federal government and the Empire State, as the latter has had to develop and implement programs meeting the former's standards. Relations between the two units of government, despite occasional friction, have become closer during the past three decades.

Evidence suggests that the Empire State will become more dependent upon federal financial assistance in the future. The state is in no danger of becoming a mere administrative appendage of the national government, however, since a significant expansion of the use of reserved powers has occurred in recent decades. The greatest assistance the federal government could provide the state in general and New York City in particular would be assumption of financial responsibility for public welfare.

The relative economic decline of the northeastern states will promote cooperative efforts to improve the economy of these states and gain additional assistance from the federal government. Although interstate disputes involving the Empire State will occur in the future, conflict will be relatively minor and overshadowed by cooperative activities.

As we have seen, the relationships between New York and the

federal government have undergone significant changes since World War II. Chapter III traces a somewhat similar changing relationship between the Empire State and its political subdivisions.

NOTES

1. *Reynolds v. Sims,* 377 U.S. 533 (1964).
2. *McCulloch v. Maryland,* 4 Wheaton 316 (1819).
3. *South Carolina v. Katzenbach,* 383 U.S. 309 (1966).
4. *Atomic Energy Act of 1946,* 60 Stat. 755, 42 U.S.C. §§ 2011 *et seq.* (1947 Supp.). *Atomic Energy Act of 1954,* 68 Stat. 919, 42 U.S.C. §§ 2011 *et seq.* (1954 Supp.).
5. *Uniform Time Act of 1966,* 80 Stat. 107, 15 U.S.C. §§ 260 *et seq.* (1966 Supp.).
6. *Water Quality Act of 1965,* 79 Stat. 903, 33 U.S.C. §§ 1151 *et seq.* (1965 Supp.).
7. *Federal Water Pollution Control Amendments of 1972,* 70 Stat. 498, 33 U.S.C. §§ 1151 *et seq.* (1972 Supp.).
8. See *Clean Air Act Amendments of 1977,* 91 Stat. 734, 42 U.S.C. § 7474 (1977 Supp.).
9. The controversy surrounding this reapportionment is analyzed in Chapter VI.
10. *New York v. Cathedral Academy,* 434 U.S. 1205 (1977). See also *New York Laws of 1972,* chap. 996.
11. *Committee for Public Education and Religious Liberty et al. v. Regan,* 100 S. Ct. 840 (1980).
12. *State and Local Fiscal Assistance Act of 1972,* 86 Stat. 919, 31 U.S.C. §§ 1221 *et seq.* (1972 Supp.). *State and Local Fiscal Assistance Amendments of 1976,* 90 Stat. 2341, 31 U.S.C. §§ 1221 *et seq.* (1976 Supp.). In 1980, Congress extended the program for three years, but excluded States in fiscal 1981. If Congress desires, States may be included in fiscal 1982 and fiscal 1983.
13. *Housing and Community Development Act of 1974,* 88 Stat. 633, 42 U.S.C. §§ 5301 *et seq.* (1974 Supp.). *Housing and Community Development Act of 1977,* 91 Stat. 1111, 42 U.S.C. §§ 5301 *et seq.* (1977 Supp.).
14. Lynton K. Caldwell, *The Government and Administration of New York* (New York: Thomas Y. Crowell Company, 1954), p. 180.
15. Edward C. Burks, "8 Units Lobby for New York in Washington," *The New York Times,* April 26, 1978, pp. B-1 and B-5.
16. *New York City Seasonal Financing Act of 1975,* 89 Stat. 797, 31 U.S.C.

§§ 1501 *et seq.* (1975 Supp.). The act was entended by Congress in 1978. See 92 Stat. 460, 31 U.S.C. §§ 521–31.

17. Daniel P. Moynihan, *The Federal Government and the Economy of New York State* (Washington, D.C.: July 15, 1977), p. 1 (Multilithed).

18. *New York v. Connecticut,* 4 Dallas 1 (1799).

19. *Constitution of the United States,* art. 1, § 10.

20. 35 Stat. 961, 16 U.S.C. § 552 (1911).

21. *New York Laws of 1933,* chap. 824, and Bill 13 of the House of Commons of Canada, Fifth Session, Seventeenth Parliament, 24 George V 1934. See also the congressional joint resolution giving the consent of Congress to the compact. Chapter 196 of 1934. 48 Stat. 662 (1934).

22. *Public Works and Economic Development Act of 1965,* 79 Stat. 552, 42 U.S.C. § 3121. (1965 Supp.).

23. *Emergency Highway Energy Conservation Act,* 87 Stat. 1046, 23 U.S.C. § 141 (1974).

24. *Revenue Act of 1926,* 44 Stat. 9, 48 U.S.C. § 845 (1926 Supp.).

25. *Social Security Act of 1935,* 49 Stat. 620, 42 U.S.C. *passim* (1935 Supp.).

26. *New Jersey v. New York,* 283 U.S. 336 (1931). The degree later was modified. See *New Jersey v. New York,* 347 U.S. 995 (1954).

27. *New York Laws of 1976,* chap. 888–89, and *New York Environmental Conservation Law,* § 15–0803 (McKinney 1977 Supp.).

28. 92 Stat. 2463, 18 U.S.C. § 2341 (1978 Supp.).

CHAPTER III
State-Local Relations

WE CONTINUE the intergovernmental theme by examining the legal relationship existing between the Empire State and its 1,605 general-purpose local governments—57 counties, 62 cities, 931 towns, and 554 villages—that play important governance roles, as do the 743 school districts.[1]

Because of its overshadowing economic and political importance, New York City is accorded a special legal status by the legislature, which enacts a number of "general" laws affecting all cities with a population exceeding 1 million. Since 1975 the legislature has also subjected New York City to special financial controls and provided additional fiscal assistance to help avert the bankruptcy of the city.

In common with national-state relations, cooperation and conflict have marked state-local relations. The legal doctrine of state supremacy over local governments is the root cause of state-local conflicts centering on the issue of the amount of freedom citizens should possess to run local governments without state interference in the form of mandates and restraints. This issue often involves a struggle in the legislature between two important types of pressure groups—associations of local government officials and municipal unions.

A fuller appreciation of state-local relations can be gained by an examination of the development of constitutional home rule modifying Dillon's rule, which holds that local governments are creatures of the state and may be abolished or modified at the will of the state.[2]

CONSTITUTIONAL HOME RULE

"Home rule" has been a rallying cry of local officials and citizens seeking to block state interference in their political subdivisions and/or seeking a grant of additional discretionary authority from the state. The term unfortunately often is employed without a definition or with a loose definition. For our purposes, home rule is the legal right of the electorate in a political subdivision of the state to draft, adopt, and amend a charter, and to supersede certain special laws—each affecting only one local government—and certain general laws of the state.

Abuse of the legislature's plenary power to control local governments in the nineteenth century generated a movement to amend the state constitution to grant local governments substantial powers and to limit legislative interference in the affairs of local governments. Commencing with the 1820 constitutional convention, home rule was urged for cities.[3] However, the first limitation upon the legislature's plenary power over political subdivisions was not effectuated until 1874 when the power of the legislature to enact a special law was limited by adoption of an amendment to the 1846 state constitution forbidding the legislature to enact a private or local bill in seven areas, including the incorporation of villages.[4] Twenty years later the electorate ratified a new constitution containing a stipulation that all "special city" acts were subject to a suspensory veto by concerned cities; that is, the veto of a bill by a city kills the bill unless the legislature repasses the bill.[5]

The first constitutional home rule amendment, adopted in 1923, limited state intervention in city affairs by forbidding the enactment of a law concerning the "property, affairs, or government" of a city if the law was "special or local either in its terms or effects," and granted cities general power to enact local laws in nine specified areas, provided the local laws were not inconsistent with the constitution or the general laws.[6] The following year, the legislature enacted the City Home Rule Law implementing the constitutional grant of power by authorizing cities to draft, adopt, and amend charters and by local law to supersede existing special acts, with nine exceptions.[7]

The 1923 constitutional amendment embodied the *Imperium in Imperio* model of home rule by attempting to divide power between the state and local governments, and in theory the legislature could interfere with the "property, affairs, or government" of cities only by general law or pursuant to an emergency message from the governor, provided two thirds of the members of each house approved the special act.[8] The amendment, however, was emasculated by the Court of Appeals, which applied Dillon's rule and decreed that the legislature might intervene in the "property, affairs, or government" of a city.[9] The court held that the people had placed these words in the constitution "with a Court of Appeals' definition and not that of Webster's Dictionary."[10]

Constitutional amendments ratified in 1935 and 1938, respectively, restricted the ability of the legislature to enact special laws affecting counties and villages with a population exceeding 5,000, and in 1958 voters ratified a proposed constitutional amendment granting home rule powers to counties and villages.[11]

The 1963 Constitutional Amendment

In 1959, the Temporary Commission on the Revision and Simplification of the Constitution issued a report calling for a constitutional amendment embodying the devolution-of-powers approach to home rule, with the legislature, not the courts, determining the scope of local government powers.[12] Supporters of the *Imperium in Imperio* approach initiated efforts to draft a new constitutional home rule article that subsequently was proposed by the legislature, ratified by the electorate in November 1963, and became effective on January 1, 1964.

The amendment continues the *Imperium in Imperio* doctrine by retaining the phrase "property, affairs, or government" and the prohibition of special legislation but grants local governments a "bill of rights"; directs the legislature to enact a "Statute of Local Governments" expanding the powers of local governments; grants local governments authority to act relative to ten specific matters beyond the scope of "property, affairs, or government"; and declares that the grants of power are to be interpreted liberally.[13]

The amendment has made no substantial change in the legal position of local governments. The Suburban Town Law, enacted in 1962, increases significantly the powers of suburban towns and has proved to be of greater importance to these towns than the 1963 amendment.[14] And the 1976 revision of the Municipal Home Rule

Law augmented greatly the power of nonsuburban towns, as they were authorized to supersede "any provision of the Town Law relating to the property, affairs, or government of the town . . . unless the Legislature expressly shall have prohibited the adoption of such law." [15]

To sum up, the state constitution clearly reserves complete power over certain subjects to the legislature and grants it plenary power to impose "mandates" on local governments by general law. Furthermore, the legislature's use of special laws to impose "mandates" in the areas of "property, affairs, or government" of local governments is apt to be upheld by the Court of Appeals under its "state concern" doctrine.

THE MANDATE PROBLEM

A state mandate is a legal requirement that a local government must undertake a specific activity or provide a service meeting minimum state standards. A 1977 national survey revealed that New York State with mandates in sixty of seventy-seven listed functional areas apparently has the largest problem with mandates.[16] The constitutional home rule movement may be viewed in part as a reaction against state mandates, since inherent in proposed home rule provisions were prohibitions against special legislation and formal assignment of complete power in specified areas to local governments. By 1938 the state mandate problem in New York State had reached a crisis stage in the view of many local officials and resulted in the constitutional convention devoting an entire chapter of its report to "The Problem of Mandatory Expenditures and State Financial Supervision."[17] Similar concerns were expressed at the 1967 constitutional convention.[18]

The governor has acted on occasion as a check on the legislature's proclivity for imposing mandates on local governments. Governor Nelson A. Rockefeller vetoed a number bills imposing mandates on local governments during his nearly fifteen years in office. To cite only one example, he disallowed Assembly bill 4680 of 1967 requiring New York City to pay election inspectors a minimum of $15 a day and wrote that "the Mayor of the City of New York has stated that the effect of the bill would be to mandate upon the City of New York an estimated increased cost of $366,000. Since there has been no demonstrated justification for the bill, the bill should be disapproved."[19]

More recently Governor Hugh L. Cary disallowed several bills imposing mandates on local governments. A controversy over an educational mandate in 1976 led to the first gubernatorial veto in 104 years being overridden by the legislature. The Stavisky-Goodman law, strongly supported by the education lobby, requires New York City to appropriate a fixed proportion of its expense budget for education.[20] The bill was vetoed by Governor Carey, but the veto was overridden by the Assembly and by a second controversial veto in the Senate. A roll call veto in the Senate resulted in a failure to override, but a motion to reconsider was approved and the veto was overridden by the necessary two-thirds majority five days later.[21]

Opponents of the bill maintained that the constitution requires a single reconsideration by a house of a vetoed bill[22] and that the bill violates the constitutional home rule provision. Justice Abraham J. Gellinoff of the Supreme Court invalidated the law because it "dictates the expenditure priorities and programs for the City, and thereby directly interfere with its property, affairs, and government."[23] The Court of Appeals, however, in 1977 reversed the lower court decision by upholding the constitutionality of the law and the legislative override of the veto.[24]

The most dramatic citizen protest of mandates involved the ordination of in excess of 50 percent of the 236 Hardenburgh residents as ministers of the Universal Life Church, an organization that mails divinity degrees to applicants who pay the requisite fee.[25] The newly ordained residents were protesting the current state law[26] granting real property tax exemptions to "religious" institutions, including Transcendental Meditationists and Zen Buddhists, and other tax exempt groups, such as the Boy Scouts, which have purchased large parcels of land in the area.

The Conference of Mayors and Municipal Officials annually sponsors a bill requiring a fiscal note on bills mandating local governments to initiate or expand a program or service, or reducing the revenue of local governments.[27] The conference believes that legislators will be reluctant to approve bills imposing mandates on local governments if the legislators were aware of the additional fiscal burden that would be imposed or local governments by the mandates. The bill, however, is opposed by a number of city and village mayors who fear that the bill will increase local expenditures because of the need to prepare fiscal notes for bills their cities and villages sponsor in the legislature.

Mandates are viewed in a different light by state officials, who maintain that there is a tendency by local officials to perceive the fiscal implications of state mandates only in terms of the mandates, completely overlooking the fact that the state is meeting its obligations to local government through assistance totaling $8,287 million in fiscal year 1981.

The Politics of Change

What are the prospects for legislative and gubernatorial approval of bills designed to reduce the enactment of mandates, reimburse local governments for additional costs imposed by mandates, and remove mandates?

A bill has been introduced requiring the state to reimburse municipalities for one fourth of the revenue loss caused by real property tax exemptions granted by local governments to homeowners over sixty-five years of age.[28] Since the state law authorizing the partial tax exemption is an "acceptance" statute,[29] the law is not a formal mandate even though local officials maintain that the law is a "back-door" mandate producing irresistible pressure upon local government officials to grant the exemptions. It appears improbable that the legislature will enact the reimbursement bill for two principal reasons: the property tax exemption law is an "acceptance" statute, and the state is experiencing financial problems resulting in part from the fiscal crisis in New York City.

In his 1977 budget message to the legislature, Governor Hugh L. Carey devoted a section to the "Relaxation of State-Imposed Local Government Mandates," the first time a governor devoted a section of a message to the legislature to the problem of state mandates, and reported that "the State has started to analyze all the mandates it imposes on local governments with the aim of reducing unnecessary administrative and financial burdens."[30] A survey of state agencies relative to the existence of state mandates, conducted by the State Division of the Budget in 1976, proved to be totally unsatisfactory because several agencies reported that they imposed no mandates on local governments and the division was aware of mandates imposed by these agencies. The division decided to call upon associations of local government officials to provide information on the mandate problem, but the response of the associations was limited.

As an initial step, the governor proposed the removal of seven relatively minor mandates as measured by their fiscal impact upon local governments. The governor made no reference in his message to mandates imposing a heavy fiscal burden upon local governments. The personnel mandates are the most troublesome and expensive ones, and any attempt to repeal the mandates will lead to a confrontation in the legislature between organized labor and local governments. Organized labor has demonstrated its strength in the legislature in the past and no doubt will be able to muster sufficient support to defeat attempts to repeal major personnel mandates.

Indicative of the strength of unions representing local government employees is the fact that a 1977 bill, sponsored by the Conference of Mayors and Municipal Officials and the chairman of the Assembly Local Government Committee, authorizing the assignment of tours of duty for police officers in upstate cities in accordance with the incidence of crime, was defeated by a vote of 21 to 3 in the committee.[31] The conference was unable to persuade any senator to sponsor the bill.

Stanley Raub, executive director of the New York State School Boards Association, reports that "every time we initiate a bill for savings that will actually reduce some costs, we can't get it through the Legislature."[32] As one might anticipate, the School Boards Association encounters opposition from teachers' unions, including the New York State United Teachers, AFL-CIO, with an annual budget approximately fifteen times larger than the budget of the association.

STATE RESTRAINTS

Related to, and often confused with, state mandates are state restraints limiting the ability of local governments to undertake activities, incur debt, or levy taxes and fees. Local government officials often label as a "state mandate" what more properly should be labeled a "state restraint." For example, the lack of constitutional or statutory authority for cities (other than New York), towns, and villages to levy a major tax other than the general property tax is cited by some local officials as a "state mandate" on the ground that their governments are mandated to rely upon the general property tax as their principal source of locally raised revenue.

Many restraints were incorporated in the state constitution and statutes in the nineteenth century because of corruption and/or financial irregularities and irresponsibility. Constitutional tax limits, defined in terms of percentages of average full valuation of taxable real estate and usually excluding taxes to pay debt service, apply to all local governments except towns and school districts located outside the cities. The limit is 2.5 percent for New York City, 2 percent for other cities and villages, 1.5 to 2 percent for upstate counties, and 1.25 to 2 percent for school districts in cities with a population under 125,000.[33]

Debt limits also are established by the constitution on all local governments except school districts not located in cities.[34] The budgets of these school districts are subject to voter referenda. Limits range from 5 percent for school districts in cities to 10 percent for New York City and Nassau County.

Article IX of the state constitution contains restraints on the adoption of a county charter and transfer of functional responsibilities from cities, towns, and villages to a county. To become effective, a county charter or transfer of a city or town function to a county must be approved by a concurrent majority; that is, voters in cities, if any, in the county and voters in towns. If a charter contains a provision for the transfer of a village function to a county, a triple concurrent majority is required—separate approval by city voters, town voters, and village voters. The latter, of course, also vote as town voters, since villages are located within towns.

Although a three-judge United States District Court for the Western District of New York in 1974 declared the New York State constitutional requirement of a concurrent majority for adoption of a county charter to be violative of the United States Supreme Court's "one-person, one-vote" dictum,[35] the Supreme Court in 1977 ruled that the concurrent majority requirement did not violate the one-person, one-vote dictum, inasmuch as cities and towns had distinctive interests.[36]

Other examples of state restraints include requirements for formal competitive bidding on local government contracts, preference for local and "in-state" bidders, and dedication of revenue from a locally levied tax for certain functions. Illustrative of state restraints impeding the economic operation of local governments is the lack of authority for a county sheriff to enter into a contract for police protection with a town or village desiring to abolish its police department. The Village Law authorizes a village to create or abolish a police force,[37] yet the state comptroller in 1962 ruled that a "sheriff may not enter into a contract with a village or town in order to receive compensation for the added expense of furnishing additional police protection."[38]

A local government is forced to seek a special law if the local government desires to be granted an exception to a state restraint. As a result, legislators from the entire state determine whether the exception will be made. To cite one example, Mayor Edward I. Koch of New York City pledged during his 1977 election campaign to seek a state law authorizing New York City to enact a local law requiring all city employees to live within the city; 40 percent of the city's policemen are nonresidents. On February 4, 1978, the mayor announced he was abandoning his efforts, since legislative leaders informed him that his bill would die because suburban legislators would follow the desires of their constituents.

Governor Carey in his 1977 budget message to the legislature proposed the removal of the following "state restraints," which he labeled "state mandates": allowing counties to charge an annual fee for inspecting or testing weight and measuring devices, fixed dog licensing fees, and adjustment of the fee schedule for birth and death record information.[39]

STATE FINANCIAL ASSISTANCE

A partnership approach has been developed by the Empire State and its political subdivisions that is similar in many respects to the partnership approach developed by the federal government and the states. Local governments in attempting to solve problems often feel constrained by the state, yet the latter provides a considerable amount of technical and financial assistance to the former.

The magnitude of state financial assistance for local governments is indicated by the fact the state legislature appropriates more than twice as much for local assistance and grants than for state operations. Approximately 60 percent of the funds in the executive budget are targeted for local assistance, compared with only 27 percent targeted for state operations.[40]

Development of state aid formulas is an adventure in the politics of resource distribution. Since resources are relatively scarce, an annual battle among interest groups, including local governments, occurs as the groups attempt to increase their relative shares of state financial assistance. The governor and the legislature have assigned highest priority in local assistance to education and social services, with public school systems receiving approximately 90 percent of the education aid distributed under an equalization grant program designed to provide the most assistance to school districts that have a low real-property value/pupil ratio. In general, the large cities receive less aid per pupil under this program than suburban municipalities.

Governor Carey triggered a major resource allocation fight by proposing a change in the education assistance formula in his fiscal 1978–79 budget.[41] Although state aid for schools would be increased by $152 million to a total of $3.32 billion in the 1978–79 school year, many suburban school districts would receive less aid than in the previous year, while financially hard-pressed cities would receive additional aid. Reductions would be limited to the ninety-six wealthy school districts in the upper tenth in terms of school spending; that is, expenditures exceeding $2,250 annually or a real property value per student in excess of $110,000. Sixty school districts would suffer reductions because of the wealth per student factor. The governor's proposal was tilted in the direction of large city school districts by basing aid on enrollment rather than on attendance and a save–harmless aid provision stipulating that no district would receive less aid, even if enrollment declined, if the district was below the ninetieth percentile in property per pupil or operating expenses per pupil. Since truancy is a major problem in large cities and enrollment is projected to decline, these two provisions favor the large city school districts.[42] In the inevitable compromise, suburban legislators were able to protect their school districts.

The New York City Fiscal Crisis

New York City verged on bankruptcy twice since 1930. The fiscal crisis of 1933 stemmed from the huge relief burden engendered by the Great Depression, the debt-service burden, and the corruption associated with the administration of Mayor James Walker. A special session of the state legislature in December 1933 enacted laws ratifying an agreement between large banks and New York City, rescuing it from bankruptcy.

The near financial collapse of the city and the technical bankruptcy of the New York State Urban Development Corporation, a state-controlled public authority (described in Chapter VIII), in early 1975 had serious repercussions for the state, including the inability of the state to enter the financial markets to borrow money and the need to curtail growth in state spending and to levy new taxes. The crisis preempted much of the attention of the governor and legislative leaders, and it resulted in the relative neglect of state administration by the governor.

The problems facing New York City in the early 1970s had been accumulating over a period of many years, commencing with the exodus of many middle-class citizens and business firms to suburbia subsequent to World War II and with an influx of poor persons. Over a period of two decades, the population movements resulted in the city retaining its population of approximately 8 million persons but undergoing a major change in the composition of the population. The sharp increase in the number of poor and elderly citizens placed a heavy burden upon municipal services during a period when the tax base did not grow at the same rate. The city's expense budget currently provides approximately $1 billion annually for welfare.

Part of the blame for New York City's financial problems must be placed upon the mayors and a majority of the members of city councils who borrowed funds for current expenses, leading to a sharp increase in the size of the city's debt and the annual cost of servicing the debt. The city, for example, borrowed $255 million to cover a projected deficit in its fiscal 1965–66 operating budget despite warnings from the Temporary Commission on City Finances against the practice. The city's debt on June 30, 1975, was $12.3 billion, and 40 percent of the total was in notes maturing within one year. The city's expense budget includes approximately $2.3 billion annually in interest and debt repayment, or 30 percent of the locally raised tax revenue.

State Assistance. To assist New York City in overcoming its financial crisis, the state legislature declared the existence of a financial emergency in the city and created the Emergency Financial Control Board and the Municipal Assistance Corporation.[43] The former is composed of the governor as chairman, the state comptroller, the mayor and the comptroller of New York City, and three others appointed by the governor with the consent of the Senate.

The Emergency Financial Control Board, in conjunction with the city, was directed by law to develop a financial plan for the city and authorized to review and disapprove city contracts as well as proposed long-term and short-term borrowing by the city. The act also froze municipal wages, established an Emergency Financial Control Board fund for the receipt of all revenues, and provided that disbursements from the fund are under control of the board.

The Municipal Assistance Corporation (MAC) is governed by a nine-member board of directors appointed by the governor with the advice and consent of the Senate. Four directors are appointed by the governor upon the written recommendation of the mayor. The MAC was initially authorized to issue bonds and notes in an aggregate principal amount up to $3.0 billion, but the amount was increased to $5.8 billion in 1977.[44] Proceeds of MAC bonds and notes, secured by the city's sales tax receipts, are used to pay off the city's notes as they mature.

To assist the MAC, the legislature authorized pension and retirement funds and systems for city and state employees to purchase MAC bonds worth $725 million. The use or attempted use of employee pension funds to assist New York City aroused the concern of powerful interest groups. The New York State Teachers Retirement System, for example, strongly supported the position of then State Comptroller Arthur Levitt, the sole trustee of the system, that pension funds should not be used to assist the city unless there were suitable guarantees.

The legislature took a series of other actions to aid the city, including an appropriation of $250 million to the city from the local assistance fund as an advance and an additional $500 million from the fund as an advance to the MAC. The legislature also decided to aid the city by placing a moratorium on the city's note obligation. This action was challenged as an unconstitutional impairment of the obligation of contract. While the Court of Appeals declared the moratorium unconstitutional, the court did not order the immediate repayment of principal and interest, thereby providing temporary relief for the city.[45]

In the first three years following the fiscal crisis the state provided approximately $3.3 billion in advanced financing to the city, and state aid to the city in fiscal 1978 totaled $3.16 billion, a 34 percent increase since fiscal 1974.

An election year often influences a governor's decision relative to state financial aid for local governments. To cite only one example, on February 5, 1978, Mayor Koch expressed confidence that the state would provide in its fiscal 1978–79 budget the funds New York City needed because "the Governor wants to help and he also wants to get re-elected."[46]

Although federal and state assistance averted a financial collapse of New York City, sound finances have not been restored, as there was a $439 million deficit in the city's financial plan for fiscal 1980.[47] The outgoing chairman of the Municipal Assistance Corporation in 1979 warned the city to cut back spending more sharply to avoid what he labeled "really terrifying surgery" in 1981.[48] And an internal White House memorandum indicated that New York City had been relatively slow in implementing budget cuts and that pressure needed to be applied to the mayor to cut back spending further.[49]

The city of Yonkers also experienced a financial emergency commencing in 1975, and the legislature created a New York State Emergency Financial Control Board for Yonkers consisting of the state comptroller, the mayor, the city manager, the secretary of state, and three members appointed by the governor with Senate approval.[50] The powers of the Yonkers Emergency Finance Control Board were similar to the powers of the New York City Emergency Financial Control Board. With the restoration of Yonkers's fiscal health, the board was dissolved on December 31, 1978.

SUMMARY AND CONCLUSIONS

A review of state-local relations in the Empire State reveals that local governments commenced to acquire a degree of protection from state interference a century ago when restrictions upon the power of the legislature to enact special laws were added to the constitution. However, it was not until the adoption of a 1923 constitutional amendment that cities acquired home rule, a power that counties did not receive until 1958. Although all general-purpose local governments have been granted increased discretionary authority in the twentieth century, the state legislature retains the power to enact general laws imposing mandates upon local governments and to restrain local governments by withholding authority to initiate certain types of action.

Currently, there is no strong movement to amend the state constitution to curtail or expand greatly the powers of local governments. Unless a constitutional convention is held, evidence suggests that no significant constitutional changes in state-local relations will occur in the foreseeable future. This conclusion, however, does not suggest that state-local relations will remain static. Partial federal preemption, discussed in Chapter II, will force the Empire State to assume additional responsibility for environmental protection and enhancement, and such action may be viewed by local officials as state encroachment upon local prerogatives. Furthermore, the fiscal problems of a number of local governments probably will necessitate state intervention, as occurred in 1975 when New York City and Yonkers experienced financial crises.

NOTES

1. There are 5 unorganized counties in New York City and more than 800 fire districts. Green Island, Harrison, Scarsdale, and Mount Kisco are each a town and a village. There also are 44 boards of cooperative educational services (BOCES).

2. *City of Clinton v. Cedar Rapids and Missouri Railroad Company*, 24 Iowa 455 (1868).

3. Joseph D. McGoldrick, *Law and Practice of Municipal Home Rule: 1916–1930* (New York: Columbia University Press, 1933), p. 265.

4. *New York Constitution*, art. III, § 18 (1874).

5. *New York Constitution*, art. XII, § 2 (1894).

6. *New York Constitution,* art. XII, §§ 2–3 (1923).

7. *New York Laws of 1924,* chap. 363, and *New York Consolidated Laws,* chap. 76 (1924).

8. *New York Constitution,* art. XII, § 2 (1923).

9. *Adler v. Deegan,* 251 N.Y. 467, 167 N.E. 705 (1929).

10. *Ibid.,* 251 N.Y. at 473, 167 N.E. at 707.

11. *New York Constitution,* art. IX, § 11 (1938), and *New York Constitution,* art. IX, §§ 1–2 and 16 (1958).

12. *First Steps Toward a Modern Constitution* (Albany: New York State Temporary Commission on the Revision and Simplification of the Constitution, 1959). The report was published as Legislative Document Number 58 of 1959.

13. *New York Constitution,* art. IX (1963). There has been no New York Court of Appeals ruling on the subject of classified legislation since the current constitutional home rule provision became effective.

14. *New York Laws of 1962,* chap. 1009, and *New York Town Law,* §§ 50–58-a (McKinney 1980 Supp.).

15. *New York Laws of 1976,* chap. 805, § 1, and *New York Municipal Home Rule Law,* § 10 (d) (3) (McKinney 1980 Supp.).

16. *State Mandating of Local Expenditures* (Washington, D.C.: United States Advisory Commission on Intergovernmental Relations, 1978).

17. *1938 Reports. Vol. X: Problems Relating to Taxation and Finance* (Albany: New York State Constitutional Convention, 1938), pp. 267–83.

18. "Lindsay Seeking More Home Rule," *The New York Times,* October 4, 1966, p. 1.

19. *Public Papers of Nelson A. Rockefeller: Fifty-Third Governor of the State of New York, 1967* (Albany: State of New York, n.d.), p. 325.

20. *New York Laws of 1976,* chap. 132, and *New York Education Law,* § 2576 (McKinney 1976 Supp.).

21. Russ Pulliam, "State Senate Hands Carey Twin Slaps," *The Knickerbocker News* (Albany, New York), April 14, 1976, pp. 1 and 4; and Linda Greenhouse, "Carey: 'Double Knockout' or a Victory of Sorts?" *The New York Times,* April 15, 1976, p. 22.

22. *New York Constitution,* art. IV, § 7.

23. *Board of Education v. City of New York,* 387 N.Y.S. 2d 195 (1976). See also Steven R. Weisman, "Rise in Spending for Schools Void; 3,500 Face Ouster," *The New York Times,* August 24, 1976, p. 1, and an editorial entitled "Sound Rule on Stavisky," *The New York Times,* August 25, 1976, p. 32.

24. *Board of Education v. City of New York,* 41 N.Y. 2d 535 (1977).

25. "Upstaters' Tax-Protest Ordinations May Spur New Laws on Exemptions," *The New York Times,* September 24, 1976, p. B-16.

26. *New York Real Property Tax Laws,* § 421 (1) (McKinney 1975).

27. For an example, see *New York State Legislature,* S. 852 and A. 1074 of 1977.

28. *New York State Legislature,* S. 5289 and A. 7700 of 1977.

29. *New York Real Property Tax Law,* § 467 (McKinney 1975).

30. Hugh L. Carey, *Annual Budget Message: 1977–1978* (Albany: Executive Chamber, January 18, 1977), pp. s10–s12.

31. *New York State Legislature,* A. 2395 of 1977.

32. John F. Moore, "State School Boards Chief Blames Legislature for High

Education Cost," *The Knickerbocker News* (Albany, New York), April 27, 1977, p. 3A.

33. *New York Constitution*, art. VIII, § 10.

34. *Ibid.*, §§ 4–7.

35. *Citizens for Community Action at the Local Level, Incorporated v. Ghezzi*, 386 F. Supp. 1 (1974).

36. *Town of Lockport v. Citizens for Community Action at the Local Level, Incorporated*, 423 U.S. 808 (1977).

37. *New York Village Law*, § 8–800 (McKinney 1978 Supp.).

38. 18 *Op. N.Y. State Comptroller* 454 (1962).

39. Carey, *Annual Budget Message: 1977–1978*, p. s11.

40. For details on general state financial assistance, see *State Revenue Sharing* (Albany: Temporary State Commission on State and Local Finances, 1975). For details on state financial assistance for public schools, see *Financial Data for School Districts: Fiscal Year Ended June 30, 1976* (Albany: New York State Department of Audit and Control, n.d.).

41. Hugh L. Carey, *State of New York Executive Budget for the Fiscal Year April 1, 1978 to March 31, 1979* (Albany: Executive Chamber, January 17, 1978), pp. M24–M25. For details on educational finance, see *The Fleischmann Report on the Quality, Cost and Financing of Elementary and Secondary Education in New York State* (New York: The Viking Press, 1973).

42. For further details on school finance, see *The Fleischmann Report, Apportionment of Operating Aid for the 1977–1978 School Year: A Complex Status Quo* (Albany: New York State Division of the Budget, September 1977), and *Current Components of New York State's Educational Finance System: A Review* (Albany: New York State Division of the Budget, October 1977).

43. *New York Laws of 1975*, chap. 868–70. *New York Laws of 1975*, chap. 168–69, and *New York Public Authorities Law*, § 3033 (McKinney 1979 Supp.). For a discussion of federal financial assistance to alleviate the New York City fiscal crisis, see Chapter II.

44. *New York Laws of 1977*, chap. 456, and *New York Public Authorities Law*, § 3033 (McKinney 1979 Supp.).

45. *Flushing National Bank v. Municipal Assistance Corporation for the City of New York*, 40 N.Y. 2d 1094 (1977). The court also upheld provisions of the New York State Financial Emergency Act for the City of New York freezing wages of city employees. See *Subway Surface Supervisors Association v. New York City Transit Authority*, 44 N.Y. 2d 101 (1978).

46. Maurice Carroll, "Koch Looks to State to Rescue His Budget," *The New York Times*, February 6, 1978, p. B-11.

47. "Cutting Spending in New York City," *The New York Times*, January 8, 1979, p. A-20.

48. Lee Dembart, "Rohatyn Urges More City Cuts Now to Avert 'Surgery,'" *The New York Times*, January 6, 1979, p. 1.

49. Steven R. Weisman, "Carter Aide Says Koch Agreed to More City Budget Cuts Soon," *The New York Times*, January 8, 1979, p. 1.

50. *New York Laws of 1975*, chap. 871. See also *New York Laws of 1976*, chap. 488–89, and *New York Laws of 1977*, chap. 445.

CHAPTER IV
The Fundamental Document

THE FUNDAMENTAL DOCUMENT establishing the state government, assigning powers to the three branches and various officials, and limiting the powers of the state government and local governments is the state constitution, which is subordinate to the United St.tes Constitution only with respect to "forbidden" powers and functions assigned to the federal government. The themes of group politics, intergovernmental relations, and executive integration are illustrated by constitutional developments in the Empire State.

The constitution is a product of the interaction of political interest groups and efforts to revise the constitution mobilize and impel certain groups to protect their vested interest against groups seeking advantages through constitutional changes. As documented in Chapter III, local government officials began to seek freedom from state legislative interference at the 1820 constitutional convention and later were successful in having the constitution amended to prohibit special legislation and to grant home rule to general-purpose local governments. Commencing in 1821, constitutional amendments were adopted strengthening the formal powers of the governor that culminated in executive integration with the reorganization of the executive branch and the adoption of the executive budget in the 1920s (considered in detail in Chapter VII).

A state constitution is an evolving document as amendments are adopted; a proposed new constitution, incorporating sections of the existing document, occasionally is ratified by the voters; judicial decisions are rendered providing new interpretation of constitutional provisions; and custom and traditions become established. Constitutional development in the Empire State has been characterized by the placing of limitations upon the powers of the state legislature and the strengthening of the powers of the governor.[1] As we will see in Chapter VI, the legislation has employed ingenuity to get around many of the restrictions.

THE CONSTITUTION OF 1777

Meeting in White Plains on July 9, 1776, the fourth provincial congress transformed itself from an extralegal body of 106 members into the "Convention of the Representatives of the State of New York," a de facto government charged with the task of writing a constitution.[2] Without providing for a popular referendum, the convention, with 1 dissenting vote on April 20, 1777, adopted a relatively short constitution establishing a state government with a two-house legislature, subject to few restrictions, as the dominant branch.[3]

To ensure that the chief executive would be a weak official in terms of formal powers, the constitution did not invest the governor with the power of appointment or the power to disallow bills enacted by the legislature, as these powers were vested in the Council of Appointment and the Council of Revision, respectively.[4] The former was composed of the governor and one senator from each "great district" appointed by the Assembly.[5] The Council of Revision was composed of the governor, the chancellor of the Court of Chancery, and judges of the Supreme Court; and it possessed the power "to revise all bills about to be passed into laws by the Legislature" and return them to the house of origin for further revision and consideration. If the council deemed a bill either unconstitutional or inexpedient, the veto could be overridden by a two-thirds vote of the members of the house of origin and by a two-thirds vote of the members *present* in the other house. The council vetoed 169 bills between 1779 and 1820, and 51 vetoes were overridden by the legislature.[6]

MAJOR NINETEENTH-CENTURY DEVELOPMENTS

The constitution of 1777 made no provision for amendment, yet the 1801 legislature enacted a law providing for the election of delegates to a constitutional convention to consider amending the articles dealing with the number of senators and assemblymen, and the right of nomination to office to resolve a dispute between Governor John Jay and senators who were members of the Council of Appointment relative to the authority to nominate candidates for appointment. The governor contended that he possessed the exclusive right of nomination, and Senate members of the council maintained that they possessed the concurrent power of nomination.

The 1801 convention adopted five amendments without providing for their submission to the electorate for ratification.[7] The amendments stipulated that the number of assemblymen would be 100 "and shall never exceed" 150; Assembly seats would be apportioned among the counties in proportion to the number of voters in each county; the number of senators would be 32; the number of assemblymen would be increased by 2 after every census to a maximum of 150; and "the right to nominate all officers, other than those who by the Constitution are directed to be otherwise appointed, is vested concurrently in the person administering the government of this State for the time being and in each of the members of the Council of Appointment."[8]

Politics in the Empire State assumed new forms subsequent to the election of De Witt Clinton as governor in 1817, with a schism developing among the Republicans as the Bucktails, members of the Tammany Society, and the Clintonians sought the support of the remaining fragments of the Federalists. According to several authors, demands increasingly were made to abandon or revise substantially the constitution of 1777.[9] Agitation centered initially on the Council of Appointment, whose appointees received in excess of $1 million per year in compensation. "In 1818, particularly outrageous removals were made and some fifteen thousand offices were dispensed without any public check. The Republicans thus greatly enlarged the spoils system begun by the Federalists."[10] On February 13, 1818, Tammany Assemblyman Ogden Edwards introduced a bill providing for a constitutional convention to devise a new system of making appointments, but Clinton successfully blocked the bill.[11]

Following his election as governor in the spring of 1820, Clinton sent two messages to the legislature recommending appointment process changes and suggesting that the voters should decide whether a constitutional convention should be called.[12] The Bucktails ignored the recommendations and suggestions and enacted a bill authorizing the election of delegates to an unlimited convention. The bill met with an immediate veto by the Council of Revision, and the veto was sustained. Yet on March 13, 1821, a bill providing that voters should decide whether a convention should be called became law, and the electorate by a large margin approved the convening of a third constitutional convention.

The Constitution of 1821

The convention drafted a new constitution, ratified by the electorate in 1822, which removed two checks interposed upon the governor in 1777 by abolishing the Council of Appointment and the Council of Revision. The appointment power was assigned to the governor subject to Senate confirmation, and the veto power also was assigned to the governor subject to an override by a two-thirds vote of the members *present* in each house.[13] The constitution, however, weakened the governorship by reducing the term to two years. The legislature was authorized to elect the attorney general, the comptroller, and the secretary of state.

The new constitution authorized the proposal of constitutional amendments by a majority of the members elected to the Assembly and the Senate in one session and by a two-thirds vote of the members elected to each house in the subsequent session; amendments became effective if ratified by a majority of the electorate.[14] Eight amendments were proposed by the legislature and ratified by the voters between 1825 and 1845, including ones broadening male suffrage, removing the property qualification for holding public office, and providing for the election of justices of the peace.

The Constitution of 1846

The incurring of a substantial state debt as the result of aid for canal and railroad construction resulted in serious state fiscal problems and public disapproval of grants and pledges of state credit. These developments, coupled with Jacksonian democracy, produced growing pressures for a constitutional convention. Fear of a powerful chief executive, reflected in the constitution of 1777, gave way to fear of an irresponsible legislature by 1846.

Meeting from June 1 to October 9, 1846, the convention drafted a new constitution that was ratified by the voters in November. The principal changes were the restrictions placed upon the power of the legislature relative to state finance, corporations, and other matters. Jacksonian democracy resulted in the adoption of a provision for the election of judges formerly appointed by the governor with the consent of the Senate; popular election of the attorney general, canal commissioners, the comptroller, inspectors of prisons, the secretary of state, the state engineer, and the surveyor, as well as for a reduction of the terms of senators from four to two years.[15]

The new constitution contained two additional innovations. First, the compensation of legislators was specified—"a sum not exceeding three dollars a day," with a maximum limit of $300 for the session.[16] Second, the mandatory submission every twenty years to the voters of the question whether a constitutional convention should be called, a provision of the current constitution, made its appearance in the constitution for the first time.[17]

The Convention of 1867–68

The first constitutional convention called by the voters met in 1867–68 and drafted and submitted a new fundamental document in two parts to the voters, who ratified only the judicial article in 1869.[18] Nevertheless, the work of the convention relative to the other parts of the constitution was not in vain.

A Constitutional Commission, appointed by Governor John T. Hoffman with Senate approval in 1872, recommended that the legislature propose many of the amendments contained in the part of the proposed constitution rejected by the voters. Eleven recommended amendments were proposed by the legislature and ratified by the voters, including a three-year term for the governor and repeal of the prohibition of the sale of lease of lateral, nonpaying canals.[19]

The Amendments of 1874

Six proposed constitutional amendments ratified in 1874 restricted the power of the legislature, with the first amendment granting the governor the power to veto items in appropriation bills and to sign bills during a thirty-day postadjournment period.[20] The second amendment forbade the legislature to enact a private or local bill affecting thirteen specified subjects,[21] and the third amendment forbade the legislature to audit or "allow any private claim or account against the State."[22]

The fourth amendment prohibited legislation by "reference" by stipulating that "no act shall be passed which shall provide that any existing law, or any part thereof, shall be made or deemed a part of said act, or which shall enact that any existing law, or any part thereof, shall be applicable, except by inserting it in such act."[23]

Relative to bills imposing, continuing, or reviving a tax or creating a debt, or discharging or commuting a claim of the state, a fifth amendment provided that "the question shall be taken by yeas and nays, which shall be duly entered upon the journals, the three-fifths of all the members elected to either house shall, in all such cases, be necessary to constitute a quorum therein."[24] The final limiting amendment forbade the legislature to "grant any extra compensation to any public officer, servant, agent, or contract."[25] The first five amendments are contained in the current state constitution.

The Constitution of 1894

The new constitution proposed by the constitutional convention on September 29, 1894, was based in large measure upon the 1846 constitution as amended, exceeded 20,000 words in length, and was ratified by the electorate on November 6, 1894.[26]

Rapid population growth produced provisions for a decennial state census and reapportionment of the legislature subsequent to each census.[27] The stalemate on assemblying the convention called by the voters in 1886 led delegates to include in the new constitution a self-executing section for the selection of delegates, date of assembly of the convention, quorum, and submittal of amendments to the voters.[28] These provisions are contained in the current constitution.

To ensure that members of the legislature know what they are voting on, a provision was added that "no bill shall be passed or become law unless it shall be have been printed and upon the desks of the members, in its final form, at least three calendar legislative days prior to its final passage, unless the Governor, or the acting Governor, shall have certified to the necessity of its immediate passage."[29] This provision also is found in the current constitution. Gubernatorial-legislative cooperation, as reflected in the issuance of "messages of necessity" suspending the bill "aging" requirement, is discussed in Chapters VI and VII.

TWENTIETH-CENTURY DEVELOPMENTS

Industrialization and urbanization subsequent to the Civil War led to a need for the provision of additional state services and regulatory activities and resulted in a significant expansion of the executive branch of the state government and an increasing awareness that organizational and budgeting changes were needed.

The electorate in 1914 approved the convening the following year of a constitutional convention. A new constitution was drafted that contained major reforms, including provisions for an executive budget, a short ballot, reorganization of the 152 agencies in the executive branch, serial bonds, and judicial changes.[30]

In November 1915, however, the voters rejected the proposed constitution by a large margin. In common with the convention of 1867–68, many changes contained in the rejected document subsequently became part of the fundamental law of the Empire State, in large measure owing to the efforts of a delegate—Alfred E. Smith—who later became governor.

Governor Smith, although not the first governor to make such proposals, must be given the most credit for securing the adoption of amendments reorganizing the executive branch of the state government and conferring additional formal powers upon the Office of the Governor. In 1919 he appointed the State Reconstruction Commission to study the current organization of the executive branch and make recommendations.[31] Not surprisingly, the commission recommended the consolidation of state departments and agencies and the institution of an executive budget system.[32] These recommendations, however, were not adopted immediately. The

1923 and 1925 legislatures proposed an amended Article V limiting the number of civil departments to nineteen (discussed in Chapter VIII), and the proposed amendment was ratified by the electorate in 1925.

Problems with the judiciary article induced the legislature to call a judiciary constitutional convention in 1921 to investigate the problems and recommend proposed amendments to the legislature.[33] A limited convention is similar to a Constitutional Commission in that neither possesses authority to place proposed amendments directly on the referendum ballot.

The enabling statute specified the convention members—judges, legislators, and attorneys—and as a consequence, no delegate was elected by the voters. In 1925 a judicial amendment incorporating recommendations of the convention was proposed by the legislature and ratified by the voters.

Implementation of the reorganization amendment required enabling legislation, and Governor Alfred E. Smith appointed Charles Evans Hughes to chair a newly appointed State Reorganization Commission whose 1926 report, which subsequently served as the basis for the enabling statutes, recommended the adoption of an executive budget system (discussed in Chapter VII), and an amendment incorporating the recommendation was ratified by the electorate in 1927 and became effective on January 1, 1929.[34]

Voters in November 1936 approved the calling of a constitutional convention whose delegates were elected in November 1937 when the voters approved a constitutional amendment extending to four years the term of office of the governor, the lieutenant governor, the attorney general, and the comptroller.[35]

The convention submitted proposed amendments to the voters as a series of questions rather than as a single package. Approved were the proposed omnibus amendment containing noncontroversial provisions and five other proposed amendments relating to the New York City debt limit; low-rent housing; railroad-grade-crossing elimination; state funds for social welfare; and hours, rights, and wages of employees on public works projects.[36] The electorate refused to sanction proposed amendments increasing the term of senators to four years, prohibiting the use of proportional representation (PR), reapportioning the legislature, and broadening judicial review of administrative action.

The Constitutional Convention of 1967

The legislature placed the question of calling a constitutional convention on the 1965 general election ballot, and the voters approved the convening of a convention. A total of 186 delegates—3 from each of the 57 Senate districts and 15 at-large delegates—were elected on November 8, 1966. Democrats won the 15 at-large delegate seats and 87 of the district delegate seats; 84 Republican district delegates were elected. The convention met between April 4 and September 26, 1967.

The convention drafted a new document and decided to submit the document as one question to the electorate. The proposed constitution was supported by Governor Nelson A. Rockerfeller and the New York American Federation of Labor–Congress of Industrial Organizations (AFL-CIO) but was opposed by the League of Women Voters of New York State, the Citizens Union, the principal New York City newspapers, the Committee for Public Education and Religious Liberty, and numerous protestant leaders. One of the most controversial provisions was the repeal of the provision (Blaine amendment) prohibiting state aid to denominational schools. The proposed constitution was defeated by a vote of 3,478,513 to 1,327,999 on November 7, 1967.

Possibly contributing to the defeat of the proposed document was a report on its cost implications prepared by State Budget Director T. Norman Hurd and released by Governor Rockerfeller on October 4, 1967.[37] The report noted:

an analysis of the proposed new State Constitution contains numerous proposals which will require additional State spending. No provisions are included in the new Constitution for raising the revenues required to pay for such added spending.

A summary of the estimated additional costs shows that in the first year in which all provisions are fully effective, the additional cost to the State could be up to $1.2 billion; in the tenth year it could be up to $3.3 billion.[38]

The major reasons for the estimated higher state governmental costs were constitutional provisions for state assumption of the local share of total welfare costs, financial assistance for public schools based on registration rather than on attendance, state assumption of the total cost of the judicial system, and the cost of acquiring property for state purposes. State financial assistance for private schools would add significantly to state spending because of the repeal of the Blaine amendment.

THE DOCUMENT TODAY

New York State currently operates under an organic law adopted in 1894 and encumbered by 198 amendments, including numerous amendments amending other amendments. As noted earlier, the constitution contains restrictions upon the powers of the legislature adopted in 1846 and 1874, has grown from approximately 18,000 words to more than 60,000 words, and obviously is much too detailed. The constitution basically is a document reflecting distrust of government and public officials.

Looking back over the constitutional history of the Empire State, one can identify the constitution of 1846 as the document initiating the trend toward the minute detailing of the powers of public officials and the placing of limitations upon their powers. This development was the product of the loss of public confidence in public officials in general and legislators in particular. Incorporation of these details into the constitution is a major reason for the length of the fundamental document today. In part, however, the great length of the constitution is a reflection of the Empire State engaging in activities not contemplated when the brief constitution of 1777 was drafted and adopted. Nevertheless, the excessive length of the document is the product of the inclusion of ephemeral and statutorylike provisions and restraints upon the powers of the state and its political subdivisions in the nineteenth century, and the relative ease of amendment. An example of a statutorylike provision is the authorization for the state to construct and maintain "not more than twenty miles of ski trails thirty to eighty feet wide on the north, east, and northwest slope of Whiteface Mountain in Essex County."[39]

Detailed provisions necessitate relatively frequent amendments, and voters are called upon to approve or reject technical amendments that are incomprehensible to the average elector. Simplification of the fundamental document would relieve the citizens of the burden of acting upon proposed amendments at nearly every general election. Furthermore, many of the restrictions have not achieved their purposes because governors and legislatures have employed ingenuity to circumvent the restrictions, (detailed in Chapters VI, VII, and X).

There is widespread agreement among governmental experts and reformers that the Empire State would benefit by the adoption of a short, classic constitution confined to fundamentals as a replacement for the present document, containing improvidently adopted provisions, which largely is a legislative document.[40] Ideally, the constitution should be a brief document guaranteeing civil liberties, establishing the framework of state government, and containing general provisions facilitating flexibility in meeting rapidly changing conditions.

Methods of Amendment

In view of the fact that many provisions were inserted in the constitution as the result of the efforts of interest groups, it is not surprising that interest groups pay close attention to proposals for constitutional amendments. Two methods of proposing amendments may be utilized. One method—the constitutional convention—allows adoption of an entirely new document or major changes within a relatively short period of time, whereas the second method—legislative proposal—results in piecemeal change.

Convention Proposal. The first method involves the convening of a constitutional convention, a temporary body, to draft either a new constitution or amendments for submission to the electorate for ratification. Once every twenty years the question of calling a constitutional convention, a unicameral body, automatically is placed upon the referendum ballot in a year ending in "7"; and the legislature may place the question of calling a convention on the ballot at any time.[41] In 1965 the voters, by a narrow margin, approved the legislature's proposal for the convening of a convention.[42] In 1977, however, the electorate decided not to call a convention by a vote of 1,668,137 to 1,125,906; 7,856,241 persons were registered to vote.

Should voters approve the convening of a convention, no further action by the legislature is required to call the convention. However, the legislature enacts supporting legislation to facilitate the work of the convention by setting forth criminal sanctions and other provisions to protect the integrity of the convention and by providing for the publication of a proposed constitution or amendments in the newspapers of the state.[43] The legislature has required lobbyists for and against proposed constitutional amendments to register and file reports with the secretary of state.[44]

Delegates to the forthcoming convention must be elected at the next general election, and the convention must convene the following April.[45] There is no constitutional limit on the length of a convention, and the last four conventions remained in session until August or September. The constitution stipulates that 3 delegates are to be elected in each Senate district—a total of 180 district delegates—and 15 delegates are to be elected at large. Delegates receive the same compensation as members of the Assembly and are entitled to the same travel expenses as assemblymen.[46] Currently, 195 delegates would receive compensation totaling $4,-582,500 exclusive of expenses. The method of nominating district delegates is the same as the method for nominating candidates for the state legislature, but the candidates for delegates at large are nominated by the state committee of each political party.

A convention possesses the power to determine the form of its organization and rules of procedure and to appoint officers, committees, and employees. The last four conventions based their rules on the rules of the legislature. Committees, similar to committees of each house of the legislature, are appointed by the president of the convention.

Proposals submitted by a convention are placed on the referendum ballot not less than six weeks subsequent to the convention's adjournment. Unless a convention adjourns in September, a special referendum will have to be held on the convention's proposal(s). Ratified amendments become effective on January 1, following their adoption.

Lobbyists flood a constitutional convention because the stakes are high. Warren Moscow reports that lobbyists had a field day at the 1938 constitutional convention and cites the following example:

A distinguished former judge, known for his political and public-utility connections, sat in state on a comfortable bench in the rear of the chamber while delegates were brought back to him one by one. The other delegates were debating the issue on the floor, but a number listened while he explained why they should not vote for state power development at Niagara Falls. He was not a delegate to the Convention, but he exercised more influence than most who were. Actually, he needn't have sat in the rear of the chamber. All lobbyists seemed to have the run of the floor, even while votes were being taken or provisions debated, and the President of the Convention . . . had arranged for his own office to be used for "conferences," a well-meaning gesture that lent prestige to many a malodorous scheme.[47]

Carol S. Greenwald in a study of ninty-one lobbyists at the 1967 constitutional convention found that "the amount of responsibility assigned to the lobbyist tends to increase as the level of specificity increases, . . . 76 percent held upper-echelon decision-making positions within their organizations, . . . and the other 24 percent were members of law firms hired for their expertise."[48] She also reported that some lobbyists were involved at the convention only, whereas other lobbyists were involved at the ratification stage as well as at the convention stage; the former had achieved their goals at the convention and would be unaffected by the referendum result. Interest groups and lobbying are discussed in greater detail in Chapter V.

Controversy has raged over the question of whether a member of the state legislature should be authorized to serve as a delegate to a constitutional convention. Twenty-three percent of the delegates to the 1967 convention were members of the legislature. On the one hand, it is argued that a convention should be composed of "ordinary" citizens rather than "regular" public officials who represent the "establishment"; on the other hand, it is argued that state legislators are more familiar with state problems and issues than any other group of citizens. A constitutional question also is raised relative to whether any identifiable group of citizens can be excluded from service as delegates to a constitutional convention.

If a convention drafts a new document, a decision must be made regarding its submission to the electorate as one document or as several proposals. The 1894 constitutional convention, for example, proposed thirty-one changes but decided to incorporate the changes in a revised constitution to be submitted as two propositions. If a proposed new constitution contains several controversial provisions and is submitted as one proposition, it is possible that opposition to individual sections will cumulate to defeat the document. In 1967 a decision was made to submit a proposed new constitution as one document to the electorate. Assembly Speaker Anthony J. Travia, president of the convention, was convinced that repeal of the Blaine amendment of 1894 prohibiting state financial aid to schools "under the control or direction of any religious denomination" would promote a large turnout of Roman Catholic voters, constituting approximately 40 percent of the electorate, who would benefit from the repeal.[49] Nevertheless, the proposed constitution, less than one half of the length of the current constitution and drafted at a cost of $6.5 million, was defeated by a vote of 3,487,513 to 1,327,999.

A convention often is opposed because of its cost—estimated by opponents to exceed $20 million today. Nevertheless, one should recognize that a convention plays an important civic education role even if the convention's product is not accepted by the electorate. Unfortunately, it is impossible to place a dollar value on this educational function, which cannot be compared with the cost of the convention.

Legislative Proposal. A proposed amendment introduced in either house of the legislature automatically is referred to the attorney general, who has twenty days to issue an opinion relative to the proposed amendment's impact on other constitutional provisions.[50] Subsequent to the receipt of the opinion, the proposal is submitted to a vote of the members of the house of origin and the other chamber.

A proposed amendment approved by one session of the legislature is referred automatically to the next regular session of the legislature held subsequent to the next general election of Assembly members, provided the proposal has been published for a minimum of three months prior to the election. Approval by a majority of the members in each house for a second time results in the proposed amendment being submitted to the voters for their action at a time determined by the legislature. Approval by a majority of the electors voting on the proposal results in the amendments becoming part of the constitution on the following January 1.

All amendments adopted since 1894 were proposed by the legislature, with the exception of six amendments proposed by the 1938 constitutional convention. As pointed out earlier, convention-proposed amendments rejected initially were proposed later by the legislature and ratified by the voters.

The Preparatory Commission. No preparatory research was undertaken prior to the convention of 1846, but a compilation of state constitutions was purchased by the convention, which also prepared a manual.[51] The 1867 legislature charged the attorney general, the comptroller, and the secretary of state with reponsibility for preparing two copies of a manual for each delegate to the forthcoming convention.[52] These same officials were directed by the 1893 legislature to appoint a compiler to prepare a manual for the 1894 convention.[53] The 1914 legislature changed the approach by providing for a five-member commission—the president of the Senate, the speaker of the Assembly, and three others appointed by the governor—to "collect, compile, and print such information and data as it may deem useful for the delegates."[54]

Since the 1937 legislature failed to establish a preparatory commission for the 1938 constitutional convention and the need for a commission was imperative, Governor Herbert H. Lehman appointed Charles Poletti chairman of an "unofficial Commission" to collect data on major issues to be considered by the convention.[55] The commission's membership included the leaders of the legislature. A Temporary State Commission on the Constitutional Convention was created in 1956, but the electorate decided against calling a convention. The 1965 legislature created a Temporary State Commission on the Constitutional Convention that produced fifteen reports dealing with major constitutional issues and a sixteenth report containing a subject index.

Constitutional Restrictions

In addition to forbidding the state government from abridging the civil liberties of citizens, the state constitution contains a number of significant provisions restricting the freedom of action of the state legislature and local governments, which generally have achieved greater success in inhibiting constructive action than in preventing the abuses the restrictions were designed to eliminate.

The inclusion of restrictions in the constitution immediately promoted the use of legislative and gubernatorial ingenuity to discover methods of circumventing the restrictions. Later chapters—dealing with the legislature, the governor, and state finance—provide examples of maneuvers employed to work around the constitutional restrictions. To cite only one illustration, the constitutional limit of twenty civil departments has been circumvented readily by creating the Executive Department, headed by the governor, as a "holding company" for many offices and divisions equal in importance to many of the nineteen civil departments.[56]

Some citizens and groups were convinced that one restriction could be eliminated from the New York State constitution by the application of the United States Supreme Court's one-person, one-vote dictum.[57] The state constitution requires the concurrent approval of city voters as a unit and town voters as a second unit for the adoption of a county charter.[58] Since the populations of the two units of voters are not equal, it was assumed that the provision violated the United States Constitution's guarantee of equal protection of the laws. The District Court for the Western District of New York agreed with this viewpoint, but the United States Supreme Court ruled that the concurrent majority provision did not "violate the Equal Protection Clause of the Fourteenth Amendment."[59]

Increasing Popular Control

The detailed nature of the state constitution is a reflection of widespread popular disillusionment with state government institutions during the nineteenth century. The Citizens Union points out that "the Constitution was to a very large extent envisioned as a device to prevent an inexperienced democracy from 'rocking the boat,' especially by quick or non-deliberate action. This was sought by putting a break on government action generally."[60]

The Recall. If voters were afforded the opportunity to recall officials from the office, the former probably would be inclined to remove many of the restraints from the convention.

A concurrent resolution (S. 7187-A) was filed in the 1978 legislature proposing an amendment authorizing electors to recall public officials from office. The sponsor's memorandum states that "at the present time, if an elected official in New York State neglects the duties of office for which he was elected, there is little the people can do but wait for re-election." The proposed amendment would apply to appointed and elected state and local government officials.

The Initiative. The constitutions of seventeen states authorize the use of the popular initiative to place proposed constitutional amendments on the referendum ballot upon the petition of 5 to 15 percent of the voters. In 1966, S. 3966 and A. 739 proposed adoption of a constitutional amendment authorizing the constitutional initiative, but the proposal failed to secure the required second legislative passage for placement on the referendum ballot.

The Citizens Union of the City of New York has been a major advocate of authorizing the electorate to utilize petitions to place proposed constitutional amendments on the referendum ballot but objects to the system in California, "where petition procedure is too quick and too easy and where ordinary statutes may also be put on the ballot by petition, so that there may be twenty or more questions on the ballot to divide the voters' attention at a single election."[61]

The Citizens Union recommended that supporters of a proposed amendment be required to submit a petition to the attorney general, who would provide advice as to draftmanship; collect 100,000 signatures of registered voters, including at least 200 from each of three fourths of the counties but with no more than one half of the signatures from one city and no more than one third from a single county; obtain certification of the sufficiency of the petitions by the secretary of state, who would submit the proposed amendment to the next regular session of the legislature, which would be allowed two sessions to adopt the proposal as its own; submit a second petition containing 200,000 signatures with the same distribution requirements if the legislature does not approve the amendment at either of the two sessions or fails to approve it the second time; and secure placement of the proposed amendment upon the referendum ballot at the next general election by the secretary of state if a determination is made that sufficient signatures have been filed.[62]

The constitution also could be amended to authorize the statutory initiative permitting voters to propose state laws by petition. Under the direct statutory initiative, a proposed law obtaining the required number of signatures of voters automatically would be placed upon the referendum ballot. Under the indirect statutory initiative, a proposed law obtaining the necessary signatures would be submitted to the legislature, which would be allowed a specified number of days to consider the proposal. If the proposal is enacted by the legislature, the initiative supporters have accomplished their goal. Should the legislature fail to act on the proposal or reject it, the proposal would be placed upon the referendum ballot. To avoid "legislation by referenda," the statutory initiative provision should contain safeguards to ensure that the initiative would be employed only on issues of great importance to the public where the legislature has failed to act.

CONCLUSIONS

Evidence suggests that barring a major crisis the Empire State will continue to tinker with its 1894 constitution to adapt it to changing conditions by adoption of piecemeal amendments. Pressure groups committed to preserving "their sections" of the fundamental document probably will succeed in discouraging voters from calling a convention by using the argument that a convention would be an extravagant method of proposing constitutional change in comparison with legislative proposal of amendments.

If a constitutional convention is held, delegates are urged to give serious consideration to the *Model State Constitution*, drafted by the National Municipal League, and use the model as a starting point to tailor-make a constitution for the Empire State.[63] The model, confined to fundamentals, clearly establishes the framework of government and distributes power among the branches and elected officials. Among other provisions is one for a gubernatorially appointed board to reapportion the legislature following each federal census of population (examined in Chapter VI).[64]

Constitutional changes will occur regardless of whether the constitution of the Empire State is amended formally. Federal and state courts will bring about changes through judicial interpretation, and the governor and the legislature through executive orders and statutes will elaborate constitutional provisions. And one must not overlook the role of partial preemption of functional responsibility by the United States Congress; important changes have been brought about through such action. In the next chapter we examine in detail political parties and interest groups that play major roles in effecting or blocking constitutional change.

NOTES

1. See Charles Z. Lincoln, *The Constitutional History of New York* (Rochester: The Lawyers' Co-operative Publishing Company, 1906), 5 vols.

2. For details, see Bernard Mason, *The Road to Independence: The Revolutionary Movement in New York, 1775–1776* (Lexington: The University of Kentucky Press, 1966), and Allan Nevins, *The American States During and After the Revolution* (New York: The Macmillan Company, 1924), pp. 158–64.

3. The Constitution contained approximately 6,600 words, including the Declaration of Independence.

4. *New York Constitution of 1777*, art. III and XXIII. See also Frank W. Prescott and Joseph F. Zimmerman, *The Council of Revision* (Albany: Graduate School of Public Affairs, State University of New York at Albany, 1973); Alfred B. Street, *The Council of Revision of the State of New York* (Albany, New York: William Gould, Publisher, 1859); J. M. Gitterman, "The Council of Appointment in New York," *The Political Science Quarterly,* May 1892, pp. 80–115; and Hugh M. Flick, "The Council of Appointment in New York State, *New York History,* 1934, pp. 253–80. John Jay, Robert Livingston, and Gouverneur Morris are credited with drafting the constitution.

5. *New York Constitution of 1777*, art. XXIII. The constitution divided the Senate into four "great districts"; each of the four senators selected as members of the council were limited to one-year nonrenewable terms.

6. Prescott and Zimmerman, *The Council of Revision,* p. 42.

7. Francis N. Thorpe, ed., *The Federal and State Constitutions* (Washington, D.C.: United States Government Printing Office, 1909), Vol. V, p. 2638.

8. *New York Constitution of 1777*, amendments I–V.

9. John T. Horton, *James Kent: A Study in Conservatism, 1763–1847* (New York: D. Appleton-Century Company, 1939), p. 243; Dixon Ryan Fox, *The Decline of Aristocracy in the Politics of New York, 1801–1840* (New York: Harper Torch Book Edition, 1965), pp. 229–30; Helen L. Young, "A Study of the Constitutional Convention of New York State in 1821" (New Haven: Ph.D. Dissertation, Yale University, 1910); David M. Ellis, James A. Frost, Harold C. Syrett, and Harry J. Carman, *A Short History of New York State,* (Ithaca: Cornell University Press, 1957), p. 146; and DeAlva S. Alexander, *A Political History of the State of New York* (New York: Henry Holt & Company, 1906), Vol. I, pp. 245–65.

10. David M. Ellis, James A. Frost, Harold C. Syrett, and Harry J. Carman, *A Short History of New York State* (Ithaca: Cornell University Press, 1957), p. 135.

11. Members of the Tammany Society wore "bucktail" hats at various functions, and this faction was labeled the Bucktail party. "The guiding genius of the Bucktails was Van Buren." *Ibid.,* p. 144.

12. Charles Z. Lincoln, ed. State of New York, *Messages from the Governors* (Albany: J. B. Lyon Company, 1909), Vol. II, pp. 1018–21 and 1043–44.

13. *New York Constitution of 1821,* art. I, § 12; art. III, § 1; and art. IV, § 7.

14. *Ibid.,* art. VIII.

15. *New York Constitution of 1846*, art. VI. §§ 2–4, and art. III, § 2. Assemblymen continued to serve a one-year term. *Ibid.,* art. III, § 2.

16. *Ibid.,* art. III, § 6.

17. *Ibid.*, art. XIII, § 2.

18. *Ibid.*, art. VI (1869). Thirty-two delegates were elected at large by limited voting; i.e., no elector could vote for more than sixteen delegates. *New York Laws of 1867,* chap. 286. Limited voting was adopted in an attempt to ensure minority representation at the convention. For further details on limited voting, see Joseph F. Zimmerman, *The Federated City: Community Control in Large Cities* (New York: St. Martin's Press, 1972), pp. 70–72.

19. *New York Constitution of 1846,* art. IV, § 1, and art. VII, § 6 (1874).

20. *Ibid.*, art. IV, § 9 (1874).

21. *Ibid.*, art. III, § 18 (1874).

22. *Ibid.*, art. III, § 19 (1874).

23. *Ibid.*, art. III, § 17.

24. *Ibid.*, art. III, § 21.

25. *Ibid.*, art. III, § 24.

26. *Revised Record of the Constitutional Convention of 1894* (Albany: The Argus Company, 1900).

27. *New York Constitution,* art. III, § 4 (1894).

28. *Ibid.*, art. XIV, § 2.

29. *Ibid.*, art. III, § 15.

30. *Revised Record* (Albany: New York State Constitutional Convention, 1915).

31. *Public Papers of Alfred E. Smith: Governor, 1919* (Albany: J. B. Lyon Company, 1920), pp. 52–53.

32. *Report of Reconstruction Commission on Retrenchment and Reorganization in the State Government, October 10, 1919* (Albany: J. B. Lyon Company, 1919).

33. *New York Laws of 1921,* chap. 348.

34. *Report of the State Reorganization Commission* (Albany: J. B. Lyon Company, 1926), and *New York Constitution,* art. IV (a) (1929).

35. *Ibid.*, art. IV, § 1 (1937).

36. *Ibid.*, art. I–XVII; XIX–XX; VII, §§ 8 and 14; VIII; and I, § 17 (1938).

37. T. Norman Hurd, "Cost Implications of the Proposed New State Constitution," *Ibid.*, pp. 1081–84.

38. *Ibid.*, p. 1081.

39. *New York Constitution,* art. XIV, § 1.

40. Nancy Connell, "State's Constitution Called Worse," *Sunday Times Union,* (Albany, New York), October 29, 1978, p. B-2, and George D. Braden, "How to Rid NYS Constitution of Legalese—Use Reporters," *The Knickerbocker News* (Albany, New York), March 7, 1978, p. 13A.

41. *New York Constitution,* art. XIX, §§ 1–2.

42. Sigmund Diamond, ed., *Modernizing State Government: The New York Constitutional Convention of 1967* (New York: The Academy of Political Science, January 1967).

43. See *New York Laws of 1967,* chap. 7 and 124.

44. *New York Laws of 1967,* chap. 7, and *New York Legislative Law,* § 66-b (McKinney 1978 Supp.).

45. *New York Constitution,* art. XIX, § 2.

46. *Ibid.*

47. Warren Moscow, *Politics in the Empire State* (New York: Alfred A. Knopf, 1948), p. 209.

48. Carol S. Greenwald, "New York State Lobbyists: A Perspective on Styles," *National Civic Review*, October 1972, p. 447.

49. *New York Constitution*, art. XI, § 3. Speaker James G. Blaine of the United States House of Representatives in 1875 proposed a federal constitutional amendment prohibiting state establishment of a religion. Similar state proposals and provisions are referred to as Blaine amendments.

50. *Ibid.*, art. XIX, § 1.

51. *Manual for the Use of the Convention* (New York: Walker and Craighed, 1846).

52. *New York Laws of 1867,* chap. 291. See also Franklin B. Hough, ed., *New York Convention Manual* (Albany, 1867), 2 vols.

53. *New York Laws of 1893,* chap. 14 and 18. See also *New York Laws of 1894,* chap. 400.

54. *New York Laws of 1914,* chap. 261.

55. *Public Papers of Herbert H. Lehman: Forty-Ninth Governor of the State of New York, 1938* (Albany: J. B. Lyon Company, 1942), p. 47.

56. *New York Constitution,* art. V, § 2.

57. *Sanders v. Gray,* 372 U.S. 368 at 381 (1963) and *Reynolds v. Sims,* 377 U.S. 533 (1964).

58. *New York Constitution,* art. IX, § 1 (h).

59. *Town of Lockport v. Citizens for Community Action at the Local Level,* 386 F. Supp. 1 (1974), and *Town of Lockport v. Citizens for Community Action at the Local Level,* 423 U.S. 808 (1977).

60. "A New Simplified Constitution," *New York State Constitutional Convention, 1967: Complete Set of Citizens Union Position Papers* (New York: Citizens Union, 1967), p. 19 (Mimeographed).

61. *Amendments by Popular Initiative* (New York: Citizens Union, 1967), p. 2.

62. *Ibid.*, pp. 2–3. See also Senate 8711 of 1978.

63. *Model State Constitution,* 6th ed. (New York: National Municipal League, 1962).

64. *Ibid.*, art. IV, § 4.04 (b).

CHAPTER V

Political Parties, Elections, and Interest Groups

OUR THEMES OF intergovernmental relations, group politics, and executive integration are pertinent to a discussion of elections, political parties, and pressure groups. State-elected officials—particularly members of the legislature, the governor, and the state comptroller—play important intergovernmental roles, as do political parties, in helping to link federal, state, and local governments. Any discussion of elections and political parties of necessity must emphasize the operation of interest groups. And the struggle to achieve executive integration can be viewed as a battle between interest groups benefiting from executive fragmentation—clientele groups—and other groups—such as taxpayer and good government organizations—seeking greater economy, efficiency, and responsiveness in the executive branch.

Democratic government without political parties and pressure groups is an impossibility, because both play important roles in the governance system. Although parties and groups are not part of the state government, they are recognized by the state constitution and statutes. The constitution stipulates that the political year commences on January 1 and contains two references to political parties. A 1959 amendment to the bill of rights stipulates "that the Legislature may provide that there shall be no primary election held to nominate candidates for public office or to elect persons to party positions for any political party or parties in any unit of representation of the State from which such candidates or persons are nominated or elected whenever there is no contest or contests for such nominations or election."[1] A 1938 amendment authorizes a committee of a party to provide for equal representation by sex on the committee and the state nominating convention to provide for equal representation by sex on any party committee.[2] The Election Law alone is several hundred pages in length and, as one might suspect, was drafted in large measure by the counsels employed by the Democratic and Republican parties.

The functions of a political party and an interest group may appear to be similar, but there is one important difference. The political party recruits and works to elect candidates in order to control the state government and institute the party's policies. The pressure group, although it may help to finance the campaigns of candidates, seeks to influence governmental policy rather than to control the government.

Politics in the Empire State has been typified by an upstate-downstate division and fear upstate of domination by New York City. Trade-offs commonly are made, and the price of a legislative program to aid New York City often is a program designed to benefit upstate areas. International politics also flavors New York State politics because of the large ethnic, racial, and religious groups residing in the state. A Democratic candidate for state or national office must take a strong pro-Israel stand or face the loss of much of the important Jewish vote. Candidates appealing to the Irish vote will often call for British withdrawal from Northern Ireland. Warren Moscow maintains that "any office-seeker of this day who can afford the price of a European vacation automatically plays the three-I Circuit, visiting Ireland, Italy, and Israel impartially."[3]

POLITICAL PARTIES

The history of New York State, commencing in the nineteenth century, has been one of a broadening of the suffrage and the growth of political parties that can be defined as extraconstitutional institutions that serve as compromisers of conflicting interests. However, the Election Law, adopted in 1978, defines a political party as "any political organization which at the last preceding election for Governor polled at least fifty thousand votes for its candidate for Governor."[4] The two parties whose candidates for governor polled the largest number of votes are defined as "major political parties."[5]

Each party may conduct a primary election at state expense, adopt legally binding rules, and select delegates for party conventions. Five parties currently are recognized under state law—Democratic, Republican, Conservative, Liberal, and Right to Life. If a party fails to poll the requisite number of votes for its candidate for governor, its place on the ballot is forfeited. The Election Law also provides that the party receiving the largest number of votes for its candidate for governor receives the first position, or line, on the voting machine in the subsequent elections for all the party's candidates. The second and subsequent lines are allocated to the other parties on the basis of the size of the vote each party's candidate for governor received. The Election Law also authorizes an "independent body" to nominate candidates in a particular election.[6]

The typical political party performs five major functions: (1) recruitment of candidates for election; (2) development of a campaign platform, (3) conduct of election campaigns by informing voters of the issues and urging their participation at the polls; (4) provision of assistance to citizens seeking governmental services; and (5) in the case of the minority party, criticism of the policies of the administration and the efficiency of its service provision.

Party Organization

The Election Law governs the form of party organization, requires each party to have a county committee and a state committee, and specifies the dates of meetings to elect officers.[7]

Whereas the precinct is the lowest level of party organization in other states, the election district with a maximum of 950 registered voters represents the grass-roots level of the party.[8] Currently, there are approximately 13,500 election districts, and each has two voting machines. City councils and town boards draw election district lines with the exceptions of the cities of Buffalo and New York and the counties of Monroe, Nassau, and Suffolk, where the responsibility is exercised by boards of elections.[9] Registered members of a party in each Assembly district elect two committeemen at the primary election; one typically is a man and the other is a woman.[10] Party rules authorize the election of four committeemen in the same districts.

Committeemen within a city, town, or village constitute the local political committee and elect a chairman. The committee is in charge of campaigns and is responsible for recruiting members, raising funds, securing petition signatures, and ensuring that party members and sympathizers vote. The executive committee in a city or town typically selects candidates for local office, and the selections are ratified by the local committee. In a village, candidates for village office may be selected by a party caucus. In New York City and certain other cities, a local political club, which is not an official party organization, may play a major role in nominating and electing candidates.

The Election Law provides that the county committee "shall be constituted by the election in each election district within such county of at least two members and of such additional members not in excess of two, as the rules of the county committee . . . may provide for such district, proportional to the party vote in the district for Governor at the last preceding gubernatorial election."[11] Each county committee has wide latitude under the law in adopting rules. With the exception of the five-county area encompassed by New York City, each county committee has an executive committee composed of the chairman of each local committee and other officers. No party has a single committee within New York City, since each county within the city has an executive committee composed of the leaders of the Assembly districts and other officers elected by the party's voters or members of the county committee residing within each Assembly district.

Members of the state committee are elected "from such units of representation as the state committee shall by rule provide" in the primary election in even-numbered years for a two-year term.[12] Typically, the county chairman determines in practice who the state committeemen from the county will be. A chairman and an executive committee are elected by the state committee, which elects one man and one woman to serve on the national committee, selects delegates at large and chairmen for the quadrennial national convention, raises campaign funds, designates candidates for the statewide officers, and frames and adopts a platform.

The Major Parties

The two major political parties in the Empire State are the Democratic party and the Republican party. Although the names of each party are the names of national political parties, it is a mistake to assume that each major party is identical in each of the fifty states.

To understand politics in the Empire State, one must become aware of the historic upstate-downstate political division. Nevertheless, we agree with Warren Moscow that "there is a tendency to oversimplify the normal voting habits of the state electorate by explaining that 'rural' upstate, the fifty-seven counties outside the big city limits of New York, votes Republican and that New York City votes Democratic."[13] The fallacy of the generalization is apparent when one considers that eight of the state senators from New York City (including one whose district is only partly in the city) are Republicans and that Albany and Utica have been under Democratic control for many years. Rochester, a traditional Republican stronghold, presently is under Democratic control.

The two major parties generally follow the rule of balancing tickets in terms of the ethnic, geographical, and religious backgrounds of their candidates. In 1978, however, the Democratic candidates for governor, lieutenant governor, attorney general, and comptroller resided in New York City. The challenge primary, described in a later section, appears to have hurt the Democratic party's ability to balance its ticket as an insurgent candidate may defeat the leader-endorsed candidate in the primary election, as in 1974 when the leadership-endorsed slate lost the primary election.

Patronage is often described as the lifeblood of a political party, and one party often will seek to deprive the other party of patronage. For example, Senator Roy M. Goodman, who was the Republican candidate for mayor of New York City in 1977, introduced a bill (S. 687A) in the 1975 Senate abolishing the city's eighty-three city marshals, who are unsalaried but receive a fee for each civil judgment collected, by transferring their duties to the city's sheriff's office, thereby allowing the city to increase its annual revenues by more than $1 million. The marshals usually are loyal Democrats appointed by the mayor, whereas the officials in the sheriff's office are salaried civil servants. The bill was approved by the Republican Senate but died in the Democratic Assembly Committee on Cities.

Democrats also can initiate action to reduce patronage available to Republicans. Governor Hugh L. Carey, for example, announced on March 12, 1975, that the state would negotiate directly with carriers of state insurance policies and no longer pay commissions to brokers.[14] The change, according to the governor, was designed to save the state approximately $600,000 in annual commissions. One suspects that many insurance brokers who dealt with the Republican administration during the previous sixteen years had Republican connections.

The two parties cooperate on some matters such as actions to weaken the minor parties (described in a later section), and enter into sweetheart agreements relative to judicial nominations (described in Chapter IX).

The Democratic Party. The party of Jackson, Wilson, and Franklin D. Roosevelt has a significant enrollment edge in New York State over the Republican party, yet failed to achieve dominant status in the state. In 1980, 3,157,199 persons were registered as Democratic party members compared with 2,323,484 registered Republican party members. The role of the independent voter has become more important in recent decades, and independents often exercise the balance of power between the two major parties.

Neal R. Peirce describes the Democratic party in the Empire State "as quarrelsome a group as one can find in American politics, though they had an era of relative unity during the 'Golden Age' of Smith, Roosevelt, and Lehman."[15] Relative to the split between the regular and reform Democrats, Peirce writes that the former includes "a younger set of leftist oriented zealots who take a cataclysmic view of politics—you must say 'yes' to their 10-question set or you don't get a passing grade. Some of the more seasoned reformers tend to be more flexible, and discover the regulars, though more conventional in outlook are not all standpatters, thieves, and rogues, and that there are ways to work with them."[16]

The stronghold of the Democratic party has been New York City where 1,609,612 members resided in 1980. Warren Moscow described the historic political divisions in the state as follows: "It was the city man against the farmer a hundred years ago, the immigrant against the third-generation American, the Irish against the Britishers who populated upstate New York."[17] He adds that the party under Alfred E. Smith did not have a statewide constituency, as "virtually its entire organization and nearly all of its votes were in New York City."[18]

The Democratic party has been the most successful in attracting black voters since the New Deal of the 1930s, and members of many ethnic groups—the Irish in particular—and religious groups—Roman Catholic and Jewish voters. Organized labor also has tended to support the Democrats, although Governor Nelson A. Rockefeller received strong support from construction unions.

In the past, the Democratic party was the party of the workingman and was dominated chiefly by Irish Catholics. By the 1950s the party was attracting a large middle-class vote, especially the vote of New York City Jews, many of whom achieved middle-class status in one generation.[19] Within New York City, two major divisions are apparent within the party—white middle-class members are declining in numbers, and black and Puerto Rican members are growing in numbers. The "organization" in each county has difficulty in getting black and Puerto Rican members to support white candidates against black and Puerto Rican candidates in a primary election.[20] As a greater percentage of the blacks and Puerto Ricans register and vote, the influence of their leaders within the Democratic party in the city will grow. Black and Puerto Rican leaders generally have not worked together, and their political power would be increased significantly if they succeeded in forming an effective coalition.

The Republican Party. According to Moscow, the Republican party in the period 1909 to 1929 was controlled by a group "who believed sincerely that what was good for big business was good for the people of the State."[21] The stock market crash in 1929 and the popularity of the New Deal greatly weakened the party, but it regained strength under Thomas E. Dewey at a time the rural population was declining and the suburban population was growing. Dewey's tight control of the party generated some resentment but no revolt.[22] Peirce credits Dewey with exercising "his patronage powers to change the Republican Party from a group of provincial baronies into a coordinated instrument under his own direction."[23]

Historically, the Republican party found its strength in the rural upstate areas, towns, and the smaller- and medium-sized cities. The decline of the rural population and loss of control of some of the medium-sized cities has been offset to a great extent by the growth in population of the traditional Republican suburban communities. Winning Republican gubernatorial candidates have secured up to 75 percent of their pluralities in Nassau, Suffolk, Westchester, and Queens counties; the latter county is part of New York City. Benjamin attributes much of Rockefeller's electoral success to his appeals to ethnic groups that traditionally support Democratic candidates and refers to thirty-one ethnic political committees that supported Rockefeller.[24]

The Republican party experienced less factionalism than the Democratic party and projected an image of a monolithic party during the Rockefeller years. The party last had more enrolled members than the Democratic party in 1929, yet the party lost control of the legislature since that year only in 1966.

In conformance with the tradition of the two major parties, the Republican party in the Empire State attempts to appeal to all groups and has prepared pamphlets with such titles as *American Labor Belongs in the Republican Party, Ethnic America Belongs in the Republican Pary,* and *Rural America Belongs in the Republican Party.* Nevertheless, the Grand Old Party (GOP) has experienced less success in general than the Democrats in attracting the ethnic and labor vote and has relatively few women and young candidates for office. The party's greatest appeal has been to the middle- and upper-income groups. Benjamin advised Republicans "to seek an attractive Italian-American for the lieutenant governorship in an effort to institutionalize the support given by this group to Republican candidates in 1970 and 1972."[25] The party accepted his advice in 1978 but still lost the gubernatorial election.

Munger and Straetz suggest that the Republican party is influenced by New York City in selecting a candidate for governor:

In the first place, a large bloc of delegates, though less than a majority, are named by the New York City Republican organizations. Since the city Republicans are almost completely dependent on state patronage, these delegates are generally at the command of a sitting Republican governor. . . . Secondly, the party leaders are compelled to give serious consideration to the vote-getting potential of the prospective candidates in the city area. Republicans cannot seriously expect that their candidate will secure a city majority; however, unless he is able to hold down the size of the Democratic margin there, no likely upstate plurality will be sufficient to carry the State.[26]

The leadership of the Republican party commenced to undergo a major change with the resignation of Governor Rockefeller in December 1973, the defeat of Governor Malcolm Wilson in 1974, the resignation of Richard M. Rosenbaum as state party chairman in 1977, and the decision of Attorney General Louis J. Lefkowitz in 1978 not to seek reelection. The resignation of Chairman Rosenbaum severed the last major formal link between former Governor Rockefeller and the Republican party. In June 1977 the Republicans selected Dr. Bernard M. Kilbourne, an Oneida County dentist, as new state chairman. His task was made difficult by the relative lack of patronage, since the national and state administrations, as well as the state assembly, were controlled by the Democrats at the time of his selection.

Republican candidates during the past decade increasingly have been raising their own funds and have been receiving more aid from state legislative campaign committees and less aid from the county committees of the party. Dick Behn in 1977 pointed to the Nassau County GOP committee as an exception that raises approximately $1 million annually and charged that "part of that comes from one percent wage contributions from county workers"; no proof was offered to support the charge other than the statement that "about one-third of Nassau's 2,000 committeemen are on the county's payroll."[27] Macing, the forced contribution from government employees as the price for retaining their jobs, is illegal.

In 1975 the New York Supreme Court denied the motion of four civil service employees of Nassau County seeking a declaratory judgment that various Nassau County officials and the Nassau County Republican chairman had violated the state constitution and the Civil Service Law by macing. The court ruled that "the complaint . . . in no way alleges facts sufficient to connect any of the named defendants with the serious charges alleged against them."[28]

The Smaller Parties

Often referred to as minor or splinter parties, two of the smaller parties occasionally exercised considerable influence in the state's electoral process by their ability to provide the winning votes through cross-endorsements of a major party's candidate in a close election.

According to Lynton K. Caldwell, the leaders of the two major parties have worked together to weaken the smaller parties and the 1947 repeal of proportional representation (PR) for the election of members of the New York City Council "was calculated to deprive the splinter parties of an avenue to influence and publicity."[29] Proposals also have been advanced in the legislature from time to time to prohibit cross-endorsement of candidates. Adoption of such a provision would weaken the leverage exercised by the third parties. The 1947 legislature approved the Wilson-Pakula bill prohibiting a party from endorsing a candidate for party nomination in a primary election unless the candidate was an enrolled party member at the time of the filing of the designating petition, but the bill provided an exception by empowering a party committee to "authorize the designation or nomination of a person as candidate for any office who is not enrolled as a member of such party."[30]

The Liberal Party. Although the founders of the American Labor party (ALP) in 1936 were anti-Communists and pro–New Dealers, members of the Communist party began enrolling in ALP after the Communist party lost its official recognition as a political party when it failed to poll 50,000 votes for its candidate for governor in 1936.[31] The Communists captured control of the ALP in Manhattan in 1938 and by 1943 gained control over the other county organizations. When Sidney Hillman of the Amalgamated Clothing Workers in 1944 proposed that the Communist unions be included in the ALP with the understanding that the party would not nominate a Communist for office, David Dubinsky of the International Ladies' Garment Workers' Union and Alex Rose of the Millinery Workers decided to form the Liberal party.

The founding of the party was made necessary, according to one of its publications, by "the domination of the Republican Party by special interests and the powerful influence of the Dixiecrats and the many corrupt machines of the Democratic Party in big cities."[32] The party was to be a watchdog of the political process and a political balance wheel. The principal planks in the party's current platform are full employment; consumer protection; rent control; protection of voting rights; tax reforms based on the ability to pay; equal rights for women; elimination of discrimination; legislative and judicial reform; and programs for the disadvantaged, the elderly, and the needy.

Frank J. Munger and Ralph A. Straetz described the Liberal party as:

both more than a party and less than a party. It is less than a political party because its role is largely supportive. It attempts to influence the nominating process of the major parties by promises of support or threats to withhold support.

The Liberals are more than a party in the sense that they are to a large extent the political projection of a group of trade unions in the form of a legal political party. They are more issue-oriented on the local level, more conscious of national and international affairs, more of an educative movement than a governing force.[33]

Edward Costikyan, a leader of the Democratic party, presented an interesting view of the Liberal party in 1966:

The Liberal Party now exists in large part as a monument to the past, to the days when there was no way in which the Democratic Party could be revitalized because of the control exercised over it by the Society of Tammany. It exists in large part to satisfy the patronage demands of its small group of activitists.[34]

The following year, Moscow described the party as a "sort of cross between a state of mind and an Elks Convention."[35] With respect to the party's nomination of Franklin D. Roosevelt, Jr., for governor in 1966, Moscow maintained that the leaders of the party "hoped . . . that the Roosevelt name would enable the Party to outpoll the new rival Conservative Party" and "show the Democrats how much they needed the Liberal Party support."[36]

The pragmatic nature of the Liberal party's endorsement policy allows the party to be labeled a swing party. In addition to supporting candidates of one major party in one election and candidates of the other major party in the next election, the Liberal party has withdrawn its candidates to endorse the victors in the Democratic primary election. In 1974 the party withdrew its nominees for governor and lieutenant governor and endorsed Hugh L. Carey and Mary Anne Krupsak, who had won the Democratic primary election for these two offices. In 1976 the party requested Henry Stern, its nominee for the United States Senate, to withdraw his candidacy to enable the party to endorse Daniel P. Moynihan, who had won the Democratic Senate primary election. Interestingly, Governor

Averell Harriman in 1958 vetoed a bill prohibiting a person who had been designated for public office from resigning with the exception of a designee who had been substituted as a candidate by the same party for another office.[37] The bill apparently was directed against the friendly alliances between the Democratic party and the Liberal party.

Over the years, the party has been criticized for close ties to the Democratic party, seeking yet denying that the Liberal party seeks patronage, and endorsing Republican office seekers as well as Democratic office seekers. Many Democratic party leaders in New York City dislike the Liberal party because they believe the party has been siphoning off "their votes."

With New York City Councilman Henry Stern as the only member holding elective office in 1980, it is apparent that the Liberal party lacks the strength to capture control of any government. The party properly may be described as a leverage party in that it uses its relatively reliable bloc of votes to secure concessions from the two major parties.

Many writers, including Peirce, forecasted the demise of the Liberal party, Peirce wrote in 1972 "that without youth, with leadership both aged and tied to the dying garment industry, its future is not bright."[38] The death of longtime Party leader Alex Rose in 1976 raised questions relative to the future of the party, as Rose had dominated and controlled the party for years. Instead of a single dominant leader, the party appears to be entering a period of "collective leadership." The party was unseated as the fourth largest party in the state in the 1978 gubernatorial election by the new Right to Life party, the antiabortion party, which polled 130,193 votes to 123,457 for the Liberal party, which had 67,035 enrolled members in 1980.

The Conservative Party. Dissatisfaction of conservatives within the Republican party with its policies, especially during the Rockefeller administration, led to the formation of the Conservative party. Behn wrote that "the Conservatives originally thought they were the only true Republicans left in New York."[39] In their own words, "the Conservative Party was formed in 1962 to restore a meaningful choice to the voters of New York State."[40] With 100,004 enrolled members in 1980, the party was the third largest one in terms of enrollment.

In its first campaign, the party collected 44,606 signatures on nomination petitions; and its gubernatorial candidate, David H. Jaquith, polled 141,872 votes, an impressive accomplishment. Nevertheless, the party's election strength had little influence on Republican policies, since Governor Rockefeller was reelected by a margin of more than 500,000 votes. Referring to the 1964 election, Moscow wrote in 1967 that "the combination of the Rockefeller win and the Goldwater debacle was hardly an object lesson for the Republican state leaders of any local advantages in the Goldwater approach, and therefore no reason at all for welcoming a Conservative Party alliance based on ideological concessions."[41] Nevertheless, the party in the 1966 election outpolled the Liberal party and became the third largest party in the state. Its vote-getting zenith was reached in 1970 when its candidate for the United States Senate—James L. Buckley—was elected.

The growing conservative mood of many voters in the Empire State during the decade of the 1970s made a conservative alliance more attractive to many Republican candidates. Thirty-nine Republican Senate candidates and ninety Republican Assembly candidates were endorsed by the party in the 1978 election. Only three Democratic Senate candidates and eight Democratic Assembly candidates were endorsed by the party in this election. The relative success of the party is attributed by Peirce to a political vacuum:

Republicans and Democrats were for big government, civil rights, and by their deeds if not their words, high taxes. Practically, there was no difference between the major parties. The Conservatives provided an alternative on spending issues, opposed school busing, took the side of the police in the civilian review board controversy in New York City, and provided the only political voice continuing to call for victory in Vietnam.[42]

The party stands for fiscal responsibility and has proposed "a citizens' commission to investigate all State spending with special emphasis on the areas of welfare and education."[43] In 1978 the party proposed $801 million in state tax cuts and supported a bill (S. 699 and A. 107) proposing a constitutional amendment providing for the popular election of the Board of Regents and commissioner of education to four-year terms. A second bill (A. 2016 and S. 1614) prohibits the imposition of quotas in private employment and the awarding of public contracts; and a third bill (S. 13) exempts home heating fuel from the state sales tax. The party in 1978 also supported the passage of a "court-proof" capital punishment bill.

Whereas the Liberal party vote is concentrated chiefly in New York City, the Conservative party finds its greatest strength in suburban areas where it can siphon away votes from Republican candidates, thereby contributing to their defeat. Local Republican candidates often seek the endorsement of the Conservative party, but the Republican State Committee has steered clear of an alliance with the Conservative party. Nevertheless, the GOP must be careful not to adopt a position considered "too liberal" by the party's conservative members or they may desert the party for the Conservative party. In Behn's view, the departure of Rockefeller for Washington to assume the vice presidency in 1974 made it easier for Republican county chairmen to deal with the Conservative party, since they no longer had to fear Rockefeller's anger.[44]

In contrast with the Liberal party, the Conservative party has not been criticized as a patronage-seeking party. The party has avoided compromising its ideology by refusing to endorse candidates holding a different political philosophy.

The Right to Life Party. Formed as an independent political body in 1969, the Right to Life Party became an official political party when its candidate for governor in 1978 polled more than 50,000 votes. The party originated in Merrick on Long Island in a women's book discussion group and functioned basically as a pressure group until a decision was made to run candidates for governor and lieutenant governor in the 1978 election.[45] The decision was prompted by the Conservative party's endorsement of Republican Perry B. Duryea for governor. Both the Conservative party and the Right to Life party are opposed to abortion, but the Conservative party endorsed Duryea because his position coincided with the party's position on several issues. As a one-issue party, the Right to Life party could not endorse Duryea, as he was responsible for the tie-breaking vote in the 1970 Assembly that led to the approval of a liberalized abortion law.[46]

Polling 130,193 votes for its 1978 candidate for governor, the Right to Life party became the fourth largest party in the Empire State and pushed the Liberal party into fifth place. By becoming officially recognized, the party, with only 8,031 enrolled voters in 1980, became subject to the provisions of the Election Law relative to organization and procedures and must file financial disclosure statements.

NOMINATIONS AND ELECTIONS

The Empire State currently uses the direct primary to nominate candidates except in the case of filling a vacancy where the county committee, city committee, or town committee of each party nominates a candidate. Until 1913 when the direct primary was first employed,[47] the governor, other state officials, and United States senators were nominated by a convention held by each political party. Because of low voter participation and other factors, the direct primary was replaced by the convention system in 1921.[48] In 1967 the state legislature enacted a new primary election law for state-wide candidates.[49]

Utilizing the direct primary system to select members of county and state party committees as well as nominees for public office, the party members should be able to control their party. However, Moscow explains how the system actually works:

Operating under the election law, with ballots paid for out of the public treasury, they [the voters] choose county and state committees of their party . . . and, whether they realize it or not, delegate to these men and women control of the party. These county and state committee members are the "organization," . . . . Right after they are elected they pass their powers on in turn by electing executive committee members, who also pass them on to the leader or chairman. He is the boss, and he is fortified in his position by the fact that the party rules, once adopted at the county or state committee meeting, held every two years, have the force of law unless they conflict with the actual written election law.[50]

Writing in 1935, Alfred E. Smith pointed out that in spite of the direct primary law "the man who is to be a candidate for the State Senate or Assembly is selected by the leader of his district, and upon the leader's judgment in selecting the proper man to represent the district really rests the party's responsibility for picking adequate and suitable legislators."[51] Smith added that when he first ran for the Assembly in 1903 he was nominated by "the local convention system instead of the modern primary election system, but the delegates to the convention invariably followed the suggestion of their leader in selecting candidates."[52]

The Empire State has a closed primary system, and a registered voter may not cast a ballot in the primary election of a political party unless his enrollment in the party appears in the register for his election district.[53] The Election Law defines a primary election as "the mandated election at which enrolled members of a party vote for the purpose of nominating party candidates and electing party officers."[54]

The Runoff Primary

With the exception of New York City, the candidate receiving a plurality (i.e., the largest number of votes) is nominated. To be nominated for a New York City office, a candidate must receive a minimum of 40 percent of the votes cast.[55] Should no candidate receive the required minimum number of votes, a runoff primary election between the two top vote getters is held.

The need for a runoff primary election could be obviated by the adoption of the majority preferential voting system—known as the alternative vote in Great Britain—under which the voter receiving a majority of the number one votes would be nominated. If no candidate received a majority, the one with the fewest votes would be declared defeated and his ballots transferred according to the number two preferences to the other candidates. A candidate receiving a majority of number one and number two votes would be nominated. Should no candidate have a majority of number one and number two votes, the candidate with the fewest votes is declared defeated, and his ballots are transferred to number two and number three choices. The process of counting ballots, declaring defeated the candidate with the fewest votes, and transferring ballots is continued until a candidate receives a majority of the votes.

The Challenge Primary

The Election Law was changed in 1967 to permit a challenge primary for statewide office.[56] The State Central Committee of a political party selects candidates by a majority vote, but any candidate receiving 25 percent of the committee votes may enter the primary election and challenge the committee's designee.[57] Candidates receiving less than 25 percent of the committee's votes may enter the primary election by collecting 25,000 signatures on petitions, with a minimum of 100 signatures collected in each congressional district.

A major impact of the challenge primary system has been the weakening of the party leadership. Democratic voters in the 1974 primary rejected the nominees chosen by the Democratic leaders for the posts of governor, lieutenant governor, and United States senator. With respect to judicial nominations, leaders of the two major parties until 1972 often decided to cross-endorse the nominees of the other party, thereby depriving the voter of a choice in the general election. There have been only a few judicial cross-endorsements subsequent to 1972, since the leaders of the Democratic party often cannot guarantee that their cross-endorsements of Republican candidates will be respected by potential Democratic candidates and voters in the Democratic primary election.

In 1978 the Democratic party state chairman, Dominic Baranello, urged the elimination of the challenge primary provision for a candidate winning 25 percent of the vote at a State Committee meeting automatically qualifying for the primary election ballot. Mr. Baranello described the 25 percent provision as one that "weakens, demeans, makes useless, makes a eunuch out of the State Democratic Committee."[58] He would require a candidate, other than the one designated by the State Committee, to obtain 20,000 signatures of registered party members on nominating petitions.

The Movable Primary Date

The political party controlling the legislature and the governorship has changed the date of a primary election on occasion to facilitate the party's chances of winning the forthcoming election, although the announced reason for the change is different.[59] Governor Thomas E. Dewey in 1953 approved the movement of the date from midsummer to September 15 and reported the change was designed "to encourage greater participation by the voters in the primary elections."[60] In 1958 Governor Averell Harriman disallowed two amendments to the Election Law providing for voting by members of the armed forces and changing the date of the 1958 primary election and nominating conventions from September to

June; he wrote: "it represents a brazen attempt on the part of the majority of the Legislature to play fast and loose with the election process from year to year to suit their own fancies."[61]

In 1974 the Republican-controlled legislature and the Republican governor changed the primary date from June to the first Tuesday after the second Monday in September in the belief that factionalism would split the Democratic party and that a late primary would not allow sufficient time for the factions to reunite before the general election. Republicans described the law as a "good government" one and maintained that a spring primary election made the election campaign unduly long and costly. The Republican strategy failed, as the Democrats captured the governorship and control of the Assembly.

The 1977 legislature approved a bill (A. 2388 and S. 1955) moving the primary election to June, but the bill was vetoed by Governor Hugh L. Carey. In his message to the legislature, the governor advanced four reasons in support of the veto.[62] First, he argued that holding the primary on June 7, 1977, "provides little time for prospective candidates to take the necessary steps to qualify to run. . . . Furthermore, in those parts of the State that continue to suffer from the effects of this year's brutal winter, I am advised that the gathering of petitions . . . will be an extremely difficult and burdensome process." Second, any Election Law change affecting Bronx, Kings, and New York counties must be submitted to the United States attorney general for approval under the Federal Voting Rights Act of 1965, and such approval might require sixty days, thereby adding "uncertainty, doubt, and confusion to an already painfully shortened process." Third, the primary would "be held at the time when the fiscal crisis facing the City is again at a most acute and critical stage." Fourth, approval of the bill would create "the kind of uncertainty and instability that are especially harmful to the conduct of elections."

The governor had been expected to sign the bill, since in 1976 he was a supporter of a spring primary election. The possibility that the Liberal party would endorse Republican Senator Roy M. Goodman for mayor of New York City apparently induced the governor to veto the bill in order to "allow more time for a Democratic-Liberal alliance to develop during the mayoral campaign."[63] The governor feared that Liberal party endorsement of Goodman would put a Republican in the mayor's chair who could injure the governor's reelection campaign by making embarrassing demands. The Liberal party endorsed the governor's initial choice for mayor, Secretary of State Mario Cuomo, who lost in the Democratic party primary election to United States Representative Edward I. Koch. The governor switched his support to Koch, who won the election. Had the Liberal party endorsed Goodman and had he lost the election, the party would have jeopardized its national and state Democratic party patronage.

Suffrage and Elections

The suffrage, or voting privilege, is the subject of Article II of the state constitution. Section 1 of the article establishes the minimum voting age as twenty-one and a residency requirement of three months preceding an election. These requirements, however, have been superseded by the Twenty-sixth Amendment to the United States Constitution, adopted in 1971, lowering the voting age to eighteen and a 1972 United States Supreme Court ruling that "30 days appears to be an ample period of time" for states to prepare lists of registered voters.[64] The estimated number of persons of voting age in the Empire State as of July 1, 1977, was 12,879,000.[65] The number of registered voters totaled 7,215,444 in 1979.

Section 1 of Article II also imposes a literacy test, but the 1970 amendments to the Federal Voting Rights Act suspended all literacy requirements until 1975, and the suspension was made permanent by the 1975 amendments.[66]

Section 2 of Article II authorizes the legislature by general law to provide for absentee voting. Under the Election Law, a voter who will be away from his residence on election day or who is ill or physically disabled may apply to his or her local board of elections for an absentee ballot for general and village elections and primary elections.[67] Applications may be made between thirty and seven days prior to the election, and persons contracting an illness within ten days of an election may apply for an absentee ballot up to 10:00 A.M. on the day prior to the election. Federal courts have held that failure to provide for absentee voting in primary elections does not violate the constitutional rights of voters who will be away from their election districts on the day of a primary election.[68]

Excluded from suffrage by Section 3 of Article II are persons "who shall receive, accept, or offer to receive, or pay, offer or promise to pay, contribute, offer or promise to contribute to another, to be paid or used, any money or other valuable thing as a compensation or reward for the giving or withholding a vote at an election"; persons who wager on the result of an election; and persons convicted of bribery or an infamous crime.[69]

Voter Registration. Section 5 of Article II directs the legislature to provide for the registration of voters at least ten days prior to an election with the exception of town and village elections, unless the legislature otherwise provides, and mandates personal registration for residents of cities and villages exceeding 5,000 population unless the residents are in the armed services or in a "Veterans' Bureau" hospital; ill; physically disabled; or their occupations require them to be outside their counties of residence. A 1975 law allows citizens to register as voters by mail.[70]

When registering as a voter, a person may enroll in a political party, thereby becoming eligible to vote in the party's primary election, participate in party caucuses, sign party petitions, and hold party office.[71] Persons not enrolling in one of the five official parties—Democratic, Republican, Conservative, Right to Life, and Liberal—are listed as "Independents."

The legislature is authorized by Section 6 of Article II to provide for permanent personal registration of a voter "so long as he shall remain qualified to vote from the same address, or for such shorter period as the Legislature may prescribe." In 1967 a system of permanent personal registration was adopted under which a registered voter's name remains on the voting rolls unless he or she moves to a new place of residence or fails to vote in two consecutive elections.[72] A voter who moves within New York City may reregister by mail.

Registration at a local board of elections is closed for thirty days before and registration at polling places commences thirty days after a general election, and for ten days before and five days after other elections.[73] Each local board of elections is required to hold registration for a few days in late September or early October (between the sixth and fourth Saturday prior to a general election).[74]

Election Day. Until 1895, ballots in New York State were printed and distributed by the political parties. Voting machines have been required throughout the state since 1935.[75]

The first Tuesday subsequent to the first Monday in November of an even-numbered year is the date of the general election at which the governor, the lieutenant governor, the attorney general, and the comptroller are elected to four-year terms, and members of the state legislature and the United States House of Representatives are elected to two-year terms. United States senators also are elected at the November general election for a six-year term.

City and town elections are held on the first Tuesday subsequent to the first Monday in November of an odd-numbered year. Elections of village officials occurs on the third Tuesday in March or June unless a village selects a different date.[76]

The Election Law gives ballot position preference to candidates of the party that polled the highest number of votes for governor in the preceding gubernatorial election.[77] In 1970 the Court of Appeals upheld the invalidation by the Supreme Court of a 1970 law providing that the top line on ballots in the New York City primary election would be allocated to incumbents.[78] In supporting the invalidation of the law, Supreme Court Justice Myles J. Lane ruled that is "no rational basis for affording such favoritism to a candidate merely on the basis of his having been successful at a prior election. . . . The odium of the legislation is further enhanced by its restriction to solely the City of New York and only to the primary election to be held this year."[79]

The Election Law stipulates that "names of candidates designated for each public office or party position in a primary . . . shall be placed under the title of the office or position in the alphabetical order of their surnames."[80] In a general election, the names of candidates appear in the row or column containing the names of candidates nominated by a party or independent committee.[81] In 1978 the United States Supreme Court dismissed an appeal from a decision prohibiting Illinois county clerks from placing candidates of their political party at the top of the ballot.[82] If two or more candidates are nominated by the same party or independent committee "for an office to which two or more persons are to be elected," a candidate may demand in writing that the order of names be determined by lot.[83]

Section 8 of Article II mandates that all laws creating boards responsible for registering voters and election administration shall be composed of an equal number of members of each of the two political parties receiving the highest number of votes cast at the preceding general election.

Although state and federal officials usually are elected at the November general elections, Section 2 of Article I of the United States Constitution directs the governor to issue writs of election to fill vacancies in the representation of the state in the United States House of Representatives. The Seventeenth Amendment to the United States Constitution provides that the governor shall issue writs of election to fill a vacancy in the United States Senate unless the state legislature authorizes the governor to make a temporary appointment until the vacancy is filled by an election "as the legislature may direct."

Polls are open from 6:00 A.M. to 9:00 P.M. for general elections and from noon to 9:00 P.M. for primary elections, except in New York City where the hours are the same for the primary and general elections. The Supreme Court and the County Court are required to be in session during an election to hear appeals from citizens who were denied the right to vote by the election inspectors.

The bipartisan board of elections in each county and the New York City Board of Elections are the official boards of canvassers which inspect the returns from the election districts, consolidate the returns, and certify the results to the State Board of Elections and the secretary of state.[84]

Following an election, candidates and any voter may challenge the count of ballots. A recount may be ordered and voting machines may be ordered impounded by the Supreme Court.[85] Election returns are not official until announced by the State Board of Canvassers, located in the State Board of Elections and composed of the Attorney general, one senator, and one assemblyman from the majority party, and one senator and one assemblyman from the minority party.[86] Each winner receives a certificate of election from the board. The Election Law charges the State Board of Elections with responsibility for canvassing primary election returns from county boards of election and the New York City Board of Elections.[87]

The State Board of Elections

Established on June 1, 1974, by the state legislature, the State Board of Elections is responsible for registration of voters, supervision of campaign finance, and conduct of elections.[88] Previously, responsibility for administering elections was placed in the New

York City Board of Elections and fifty-seven county boards of elections, which received advisory opinions from the secretary of state interpreting the Election Law. Local election boards, however, continue to be responsible for the day-to-day administration of elections. Two members of each of the two largest political parties serve as election inspectors in each election district.

The New York State Campaigns, Elections, and Procedures Law of 1974 estblished the State Board of Elections within the Executive Department and provided that the board would have "four Commissioners appointed by the Governor; two commissioners, one each from among not fewer than two persons recommended by the Chairman of the State Committee of each of the major political parties; and two other Commissioners, one upon the joint recommendations of the legislative leaders of one major political party in each house of the Legislature and one upon the joint recommendation of the legislative leaders of the other major political party in each house of the Legislature."[89] Commissioners serve staggered two-year terms.

The board is assigned numerous functions, including issuance of rules and regulations relating to election administration, campaign practices, and campaign finances; examination of records and procedures of local election boards; and conduct of investigations.[90]

A problem with the provision for equal major party representation on the board is the possibility of deadlocks. A major deadlock occurred in 1975 when the two Republican members charged, relative to Governor Carey's campaign committee, "that there was a reckless disregard of the limitations contained in section 455 of the law . . . wherein it is our considered judgment that there is reasonable cause to believe that violation of the law warranting criminal prosecution" had occurred. No action was taken by the equally divided board on the charge.

Corrupt Practices Act

The cost of campaigning for statewide office has skyrocketed during the past two decades, increasing fears that "money" interests will exert undue influence over the successful candidates. Governor Carey spent $5.18 million and amassed a debt of $2,376,000 in his successful 1974 primary and general election campaigns, and he spent $7,018,176 in his successful 1978 campaigns.[91] Attorney General Robert Abrams and Comptroller Edward V. Regan spent $1,151,894 and $776,023, respectively, in their successful 1978 campaigns.[92]

Corrupt Practices Acts regulate campaign finance and attempt to maintain the public's confidence in the integrity of the electoral processes. The early Corrupt Practices Acts primarily were disclosure acts based upon the belief that disclosure would prevent abuses and that the voters would be guided in their electoral decisions by the sources of political contributions. Failure to check the accuracy of reports, inadequate publicity, and the use of "straws"—second, third, and fourth parties—to "launder" campaign funds generally have rendered disclosure provisions of little value. Subsequently, a decision was made to incorporate limitations on contributions in the Corrupt Practices Act and more recently to amend the acts by providing limitations on expenditures.

State Corrupt Practices Acts limiting campaign contributions must operate within the guidelines laid down by the United States Supreme Court in 1976 in *Buckley* v. *Valeo*,[93] a case involving the Federal Election Campaign Act of 1971 and its amendments of 1974.[94] In this case, the Court upheld the individual contribution limits and disclosure and reporting provisions, and the public financing provisions, but ruled "that the limitations on campaign expenditures, on independent expenditures by individuals and groups, and on expenditures by a candidate from his personal funds are constitutionally infirm."[95]

The Court specifically held that "the Act's expenditure ceilings impose direct and substantial restraints on the quantity of political speech."[96] Relative to the limitations on personal expenditures by candidates, the Court ruled the limitation "imposes a substantial restraint on the ability of persons to engage in protected First Amendment expression."[97] The Court added:

The candidate, no less than any other person, has a First Amendment right to engage in the discussion of public issues and vigorously and tirelessly to advocate his own election and the election of other candidates. Indeed, it is of particular importance that candidates have the unfettered opportunity to make their views known so that the electorate may intelligently evaluate the candidates' personal qualities and their positions on vital public issues before choosing among them on election day.[98]

In 1978 the United States Supreme Court struck down a Massachusetts law restricting corporate contributions to issue campaigns "that materially affect its business, property, or assets" by holding that a corporation under the First Amendment to the United States Constitution could spend funds to publicize its views in opposition to a proposed constitutional amendment authorizing the state legislature to levy a graduated income tax.[99]

The restrictions upon the amount of money a candidate or political committee could spend in an election campaign in the Empire State have been repealed, and the Election Law currently limits only campaign contributions. An individual contribution for a statewide office in a primary or general election is limited to a maximum of $0.005 times the number of voters, and the maximum family contribution is limited to $0.025 times the number of voters.[100]

The Campaigns, Elections, and Procedures Law of 1974 allows corporations for the first time to contribute up to $5,000 to any election campaign.[101] Many corporate officials previously contributed funds in their own names or in the names of family members. The 1974 law led to numerous contributions being given in the name of a company, thereby obscuring the identity of the real contributor. Also adding to the difficulty of identifying contributions from business sources is the practice of candidates creating special fundraising committees—such as Concerned Citizens for Carey, Carey for Governor, and Citizens for Carey—each of which files separate campaign receipts reports.

Much to the surprise of many observers and to the anger of some candidates, the State Board of Elections instituted a civil proceeding in the Supreme Court against 62 candidates for failure to file campaign reports or for filing late reports.[102] And on May 1, 1975, the board obtained court orders, including fines, against close to 400 candidates for failure to file one or more reports since the June 1, 1974, effective date of the new campaign finance law.[103] Although the board could have sought prosecution of the involved candidates for a misdemeanor with a maximum sentence of one year in jail, the board decided to institute civil suits because the law was a new one and the old Corrupt Practices Act had not been enforced.

The board of October 30, 1974, found no evidence to support the charge that either Governor Malcolm Wilson or T. David Bullard violated the Election Law relative to the latter's decision to withdraw from the Conservative party's contest for the gubernatorial nomination, since the governor "did not promise Mr. Bullard to appoint any specific person or persons to public office or pledge a specific number of jobs to Conservative Party members."[104]

Republicans charged that Governor Carey violated the state's new campaign finance law in his 1974 election campaign by accepting consolidated loans of $750,000 from his brother in violation of the $66,000 maximum in contributions and loans allowable from one individual, but the board ruled there was no violation, since there was no evidence that "'fresh money' was advanced" subsequent to the June 1, 1974, effective date of the law.[105]

There has been a tendency in recent years for candidates voluntarily to disclose their net worth when campaigning for election. In 1974, for example, Governor Wilson released a net worth statement revealing that his wife and he had combined assets of $632,-580.14—in the form of stocks and bonds, credit in the state retirement system, life insurance, an automobile, savings accounts, and a house—and no liabilities.[106] The governor also reported a total 1973 income of $129,000, including $46,500 from his law firm.

Fair Campaign Code

In compliance with a provision of the Election Law, the State Board of Elections in 1974 issued a 2,200-word "Fair Campaign Code" establishing "ethical standards of conduct for persons, political parties and committees engaged in election campaigns including, but not limited to, specific prohibitions against practices of political espionage and other political practices involving subversion of the political parties and process."[107] The Watergate imbroglio was responsible for the inclusion of the Fair Campaign Code provision in the Election Law, but the provision was declared unconstitutional by a United States district court in 1975, which held that the prohibition of political attacks on the ethnic background, race, religion, or sex of a candidate for public office violated the First Amendment to the United States Constitution.[108] In 1976 the United States Supreme Court unanimously upheld the decision.[109]

The 1977 Election Law revision directs the board to adopt "a 'fair campaign code' setting forth ethical standards of conduct for persons, political parties, and committees engaged in election campaigns"[110] The board, however, has no plans to issue a new code, and sections of the code are still in effect. The board has encouraged local governments to adopt "unofficial" fair campaign codes and to establish boards that would rely upon public opinion for enforcement of the codes.

INTEREST GROUPS

In 1948 Moscow wrote that a public outcry would be heard if a lobbyist participated in the drafting of a bill in Congress, whereas "in Albany it is done all the time and no one gets excited about it. . . . After all, any good lobbyist knows more about the affairs of the industry or pressure group he represents than the members of the Legislature possibly can."[111] In Moscow's view, the most effective lobbyists over the years have been the Roman Catholic church, the teachers' lobby, the Conference of Mayors, the Association of Towns, public utility companies, railroads, newspapers, the New York State Federation of Labor, and the Associated Industries of New York State.[112]

While interest or pressure groups are not a formal part of the institutions of government, the important role played by groups in influencing public policy cannot be overestimated. Groups may be placed in two classes: those with a common economic interest and those with a common attitude or cause such as the Right to Life groups. Groups also may be classified as permanent or ad hoc groups, and as institutional or associational groups. An institutional group, such as a church, may attempt to influence public policy on certain issues, but its activities may not be on a continuing basis. Associational groups, such as the medical societies, typically are engaged in influencing public policy on a permanent basis.

A large, complex state not surprisingly has numerous diverse interests that have formed organizations to bring pressure to bear on political parties, the governor, the legislature, state administrators, and local governments.[113] Relative to the business community, the "Big Three" are the Business Council, the New York Chamber of Commerce and Industry, and the New York State Council of Retail Merchants. Whereas each of the Big Three tended to lobby independently of each other, the groups began joint lobbying in 1978.[114]

While it may have been true in 1948 that "the public-utility and railroad lobbies . . . can pass or kill a bill just as effectively now as they did fifty years ago,"[115] the situation no longer prevails. All major railroads in the state, except the Delaware and Hudson Railway, became bankrupt and were merged by Congress into a nationally controlled system—Conrail—in 1973. The public utilities are still profitable, yet they no longer exercise the influence they did in the past, partly because of the rise of public interest lobbies and the consumer movement.

The growing strength of public interest groups and public employee unions are two of the most important political developments of the past two decades. The League of Women Voters and the Citizens Union of New York City long have been known as good government associations, and they have been joined in recent years by other associations labeled public interest groups, such as the New York State Public Interest Research Group. The latter and the New York Civil Liberties Union frequently file suits in court in an effort to secure their objectives.

The political clout of unions was increased greatly by a 1977 act authorizing a union representing state employees to request the withholding of an agency shop fee from the paychecks of nonunion members in the bargaining unit.[116] The law contains a provision that the union must return upon the demand of an employee a part of the fee representing "the employee's pro-rata share of expenditures by the organization in aid of activities only incidentally related to terms and conditions of employment."

Twenty-two public employee unions, representing 750,000 persons, formed a lobbying coalition to seek changes in the Public Employees Fair Employment Act, popularly known as the Taylor law (discussed in more detail in Chapter VIII). In 1978 the unions were successful in persuading the legislature to amend the Taylor law by deleting the penalty of one year probation for public employees who strike.[117] The unions are seeking to have the law amended to provide that it is an improper labor practice for a public employer to refuse to continue all terms of an expired contract until a new agreement is signed, repeal the section providing double loss of salary for each part of a day an employee was on strike, and provide for compulsory binding arbitration in cases of an impasse.

Moscow wrote in 1948 that the teachers' lobby is "one of the most effective, operating as it does with the cooperation of the parent-teacher associations back home."[118] The alliance is not as strong today because of the Public Employees Fair Employment Act and disputes over the right to strike.

Moscow also ascribed "tremendous influence in Albany with the members of the Legislature" to the Conference of Mayors and the Association of Towns, "since the legislators come from localities and return to them at the end of the session."[119] Peirce calls attention to the New York City lobby and reports its Albany staff "does hundreds of favors for legislators, and in turn hopes to get a favorable ear from them on the multitudinous bills of each session that relate to the City."[120] While not denying the importance of the two associations and the New York City lobby in the legislative process, one should note that the associations and the city were unable to prevent the enactment or secure the repeal of a provision of the Taylor law mandating compulsory binding arbitration of impasses in negotiations with police and fire unions, an indication of the influence exercised by these two organizations in the legislature. To increase their effectiveness in the legislature, four associations— the Association of Counties, the Association of Towns, the Conference of Mayors and Municipal Officials, and the School Boards Association—in 1978 formed the New York State Coalition of Public Employers. Nevertheless, these groups are not in agreement on all issues. For example, the Conference of Mayors and Municipal Officials supports bills providing for the incorporation of new cities, and these bills are opposed by the Association of Towns.

Certain pressure groups seek state recognition of professional status for their members. The State Board of Regents currently licenses and regulates thirty professions. Recommendations relative to professional standards and discipline are made to the Regents by the practice board of each licensed profession. Governor Alfred E. Smith and Governor Franklin D. Roosevelt vetoed bills creating a State Board of Barber Examiners.[121] In 1978 the two teachers' unions launched a major drive to have teaching recognized and licensed as a profession by the Board of Regents.[122] Opposition was organized by the New York State School Boards Association and private schools.

In addition to providing information to legislators and bureaucrats, interest groups attempt to shape public policy by influencing public opinion and contributing financial support to friendly elected officials and other friendly candidates during election campaigns. In 1978 a total of 129 political action committees, organized by various groups, raised funds for contribution to candidates in the general election.[123] To cite two examples, the New York Medical Political Action Committee distributed more than $162,000 to candidates, and Active Industry for the Development of the Economy contributed $88,000.

Former Assemblyman Peter A. A. Berle described the indirect use of money by interest groups to secure their goals in influencing legislators as follows:

Some labor unions, certain professional organizations, and big business interests make it a practice to contribute to legislative campaigns. . . . Another subtle use of money . . . involves allocation of business to financial concerns in a way which profits the legislator. For example, the legislator may be on the banking committee and may also maintain a private law practice. Without any real communication between legislator, lobbyist, or banker, certain routine legal matters are referred by the banks to the legislator's law firm.[124]

The pressure applied by public authorities on the state legislature must not be overlooked. Referring to Robert Moses' Triborough Bridge and Tunnel Authority and other authorities, Robert A. Caro wrote that "having plumbed, in a ten-year series of disputes, the depths of Moses' power in Albany, the Port Authority knew that, deep though theirs ran, his ran deeper."[125] Caro added that:

in the background behind Moses marched a mighty division: the giant automobile manufacturers out of Detroit, the giant aluminum combines, the steel producers, the rubber producers, fifty oil companies, trucking firms in the hundreds, highway contractors in the thousands, consulting engineers, labor union leaders, auto dealers, tire dealers, petroleum dealers, rank upon rank of state highway department officials, Bureau of Public Roads bureaucrats, congressmen, senators—all the selfish interests who author Helen Leavitt was to label "The Highwaymen."[126]

Moses was the originator of the proposal to construct a bridge across Long Island Sound that was authorized by the 1967 legislature and led to a major fight between Governor Rockefeller and bridge supporters against local public officials in Rye and Oyster Bay and environmental interest groups.[127]

Interst groups not only seek to promote or block the enactment of bills but also support or oppose appropriation of funds to implement laws and seek to influence the drafting of implementing rules and regulations by administrative agencies. If unsuccessful in blocking passage of a bill, an interest group might attempt to "starve" the agency responsible for implementing the new law by persuading the legislature to reduce the appropriation for the agency. Similarly, an interest group may be able to persuade an administrative agency to promulgate rules and regulations that will favor the group.

The press and many writers tend to overemphasize the influence exercised by certain interest groups in the governance process. While not denying the important role played by these groups, a statement written in 1948 applies with equal force today:

But it is not only the organized lobbies and pressure groups that influence the votes of legislators and the affairs of government. The great, scantily informed mass of the electorate is also effectively represented by governing officials with knowledge of what is an issue and what is not—what may be used against them and their party effectively if they vote "wrong."[128]

The increased professional staffing of the two houses of the legislature also tends to reduce the amount of influence exercised by interest groups in the legislative process, as members are less dependent upon the groups for expert information.

Interest groups unsuccessful in achieving their objectives on the state level often turn to the federal government and may lobby for federal preemption of responsibility for a governmental function. Interestingly, New York State and many of its local governments lobby heavily in Washington for additional federal financial assistance and enlist the support of private groups.

Lobbyists

The important powers exercised by the state government ensure that lobbyists, the representatives of interest groups, will exert major efforts to promote the enactment, modification, or defeat of proposed legislation and of administrative rules and regulations. Lobbyists also attempt to influence ratemaking decisions by state agencies and commissions. The reference to lobbies as the "third house" of the legislature is an indication of the amount of influence they exert.

Most lobbyists are knowledgeable individuals who provide legislators with expert information. Moscow wrote in 1948 that "many a lobbyist, because of his special knowledge of a problem has saved a legislator from looking foolish. The lobbyist's job is to make friends and influence people. He is co-operative."[129]

While numerous bills are drafted or redrafted for legislators by lobbyists, Berle reports that "some Assemblymen will ask the representatives of the banks, insurance companies, or liquor authority how they feel about a bill. If the lobbyist says his industry wants the bill very badly, the legislator will automatically take the contrary position."[130] The changing nature of legislative lobbying is reflected in a statement by a lobbyist—former State Senator Thomas Laverne: "Years ago a lobbyist could go to the leaders, but you can't do that anymore. You really have to make the rounds. And half the job is knowing who to talk to in an office. You have to know which staff person will bring what you want to the boss' attention."[131] Furthermore, lobbyists today generally attempt to maintain a low profile and no longer provide lavish parties for legislators.

Regulation of Lobbying. The Regulation of Lobbying Act stresses the importance of ensuring that citizens have full opportunity to express their views relative to proposed governmental actions and are made aware of the activities of lobbyists.[132] Prior to 1977 regulation of lobbying was the responsibility of the secretary of state, whose last report on lobbying, issued in 1978, contained an expense list submitted by 463 employers of lobbyists who reported a record high $4,265,000 in fees and payments made in 1977.

The ten employers listed in order of money spent were New York State Common Cause, $86,527; New York State Bankers Association, $77,023; R. H. Macy & Company and Macy's New York, Inc., $76,755; Civil Service Employees Association, $76,227; Association of New York State Life Insurance Companies, $74,319; Associated Industries of New York State, $68,557; National Railroad Passenger Corporation, $61,325; Tobacco Tax Council, $58,290; New York State Broadcasters Association, $51,761; and Medical Society of the State of New York, $43,769. Employers of lobbyists who failed to submit expense statements by March 4, 1978, ranging from Air India to the Upstate S.S.I. Action Coalition of Adult Homes, were turned over to the attorney general.

The constitutionality of lobby disclosure laws has been challenged. In 1974 the United States Supreme Court dismissed an appeal from a Washington State Supreme Court decision holding that the provisions of a state law, requiring the disclosure of contributors of more than $500 a year to a lobbying organization, were constitutional.[133] The Washington State Supreme Court held that:

> Informed as to the identity of the principal of a lobbyist, the members of the Legislature, other public officials, and also the public may more accurately evaluate the pressures to which public officials are subjected. Forewarned of the principals behind proposed legislation, the legislator and others may appropriately evaluate the "sales pitch" of some lobbyists who claim to espouse the public weal, but, in reality, represent purely private or special interests.[134]

The Regulation of Lobbying Act of 1977 transferred responsibility for the exercise of oversight over lobbies from the secretary of state to the six-member Temporary State Commission on Regulation of Lobbying. To lobby legally in the legislature, each lobbyist reasonably anticipating receiving or expending in excess of $1,000 in reportable compensation and expenditures is required to file annually a statement with the commission giving his name, address, and telephone number and the name, address, and telephone number of the person, association, or organization represented.[135] In addition, a lobbyist must file with the commission a copy of the written retainer or employment agreement and quarterly reports on reportable expenditures. Public corporations expending in excess of $1,000 annually for lobbying also must file quarterly reports. In 1980 there were 1,379 lobbyists and designees.

The act exempts from its provisions persons drafting bills, rules, regulations, or rates, provided there "services are not otherwise connected with legislative or executive action on such legislation or administrative action on such rules, regulations, or rates."[136] Also exempted are New York State officials acting in their official capacity; newspapers, other periodicals, radio, and television stations; and "any person who merely appears before an open meeting or public hearing of a standing committee or select committee of the Legislature, or a State agency or agencies."[137] The legislative law forbids any employee of the legislature to "promote or oppose the passage of bills or resolutions by either house" outside "the scope of his legislative employment."[138]

SUMMARY AND CONCLUSIONS

Political parties and interest groups are major participants in the governance processes of the Empire State. The growing independence of voters has reduced the influence of the two major parties, as each has a smaller bloc of dependable adherents on election day and elected officials can act more independently of the desires of party leaders than in the past. The larger third parties have been able to exercise the balance of power in close elections and undoubtedly will continue to do so.

While pressure groups continue to exercise major influence in the governmental decision-making process, interest-group politics has undergone significant changes with the rise of public interest groups, new regulatory laws, greater media coverage of interest-group activities, and increased professional staffing of the legislature. Chapter VI focuses upon the state legislature and the legislative process, revealing points where pressure may be applied to shape legislation.

NOTES

1. *New York Constitution,* art. I, § 1.
2. *Ibid.,* art. XIII, § 1.
3. Warren Moscow, *What Have You Done for Me Lately?* (Englewood CLiffs, N.J.: Prentice-Hall, Inc., 1967), p. 115.
4. *New York Election Law,* § 1-104 (3) (McKinney 1978).
5. *Ibid.,* § 1-104 (24).
6. *Ibid.,* § 1-104 (12).
7. *Ibid.,* §§ 2-100 to 2-128.
8. *Ibid.,* § 4-100 (3).
9. *Ibid.,* § 4-100.
10. *Ibid.,* § 2-100 (2).
11. *Ibid.,* § 2-104.
12. *Ibid.,* § 2-102 (1).
13. Warren Moscow, *Politics in the Empire State* (New York: Alfred A. Knopf, 1948), p. 41.

14. Francis X. Clines, "State Stops Using Insurance Agents," *The New York Times*, March 13, 1975, p. 33.

15. Neal R. Peirce, *The Megastates of America* (New York: W. W. Norton & Company, Inc., 1972), p. 54.

16. *Ibid.*, p. 58.

17. Moscow, *Politics in the Empire State*, pp. 42–43.

18. *Ibid.*, p. 94.

19. Daniel P. Moynihan, "'Bosses' and 'Reformers,'" *Commentary*, June 1961, p. 462.

20. Frank Lynn, "How Many Democratic Parties in the Primary?" *The New York Times*, September 12, 1977, p. 40.

21. Moscow, *Politics in the Empire State*, p. 77.

22. *Ibid.*, p. 82.

23. Peirce, *The Megastates of America,* p. 48.

24. Gerald Benjamin, "Patterns in New York State Politics," in Robert H. Connery and Gerald Benjamin, eds., *Governing New York State: The Rockefeller Years* (New York: The Academy of Political Science, 1974), p. 36.

25. *Ibid.*, p. 44.

26. Frank J. Munger and Ralph A. Straetz, *New York Politics* (New York: New York University Press, 1960), pp. 60–61.

27. Dick Behn, "Rockefeller's Legacy," *Empire State Report*, April 1977, p. 149. Macing and political assessments are illegal. See *New York Civil Service Law*, § 107 (3) (McKinney 1973), and *New York Election Law*, § 17-156 (McKinney 1978).

28. *Cullen et al. v. Margiotta et al.*, 367 N.Y. 2d 638 at 644 (1975).

29. Lynton K. Caldwell, *The Government and Administration of New York* (New York: Thomas Y. Crowell Company, 1954), p. 42.

30. *New York Laws of 1947*, chap. 432, § 1, and *New York Election Law*, § 136-a (1) and (4) (McKinney 1948 Supp.). The Wilson-Pakula law currently is codified as section 6-120 (1) and (3) of the Election Law.

31. Moscow, *Politics in the Empire State*, pp. 103 and 112–13.

32. Ben Davidson, *Liberal Party of New York State* (New York: Liberal Party, n.d.), p. 1.

33. Munger and Straetz, *New York Politics*, pp. 30–31.

34. Edward N. Costikyan, *Behind Closed Doors: Politics in the Public Interest* (New York: Harcourt, Brace and World, Inc., 1966), p. 47.

35. Moscow, *What Have You Done for Me Lately?* p. 64.

36. *Ibid.*, p. 66.

37. *Public Papers of Averell Harriman: Fifty-Second Governor of the State of New York, 1958* (Albany: State of New York, n.d.), p. 314. Hereinafter referred to as *Harriman Public Papers.*

38. Peirce, *The Megastates of America*, p. 61.

39. Dick Behn, "Liberals and Conservatives: The Importance of New York's Two 'Third' Parties," *Empire State Report*, April 1977, p. 164.

40. *Introducing the Conservative Party of New York State* (New York: The Conservative Party, n.d.), p. 1.

41. Moscow, *What Have You Done for Me Lately?* p. 68.

42. Peirce, *The Megastates of America*, p. 63.

43. *Introducing the Conservative Party of New York State*, p. 2.

44. Behn, "Liberals and Conservatives," p. 164.

45. Maurice Carroll, "The Unlikely Beginning of the Right to Life Party," *The New York Times,* November 25, 1978, pp. 25 and 27.

46. Fredric U. Dicker, "Right-to-Life Party Readies Organization," *Sunday Times Union* (Albany, New York), December 17, 1978, pp. 1 and A-18.

47. *New York Laws of 1911,* chap. 649.

48. *New York Laws of 1921,* chap. 479.

49. *New York Laws of 1967,* chap. 716, and *New York Election Law,* § 6-104 (2) (McKinney 1978).

50. Moscow, *Politics in the Empire State,* p. 56.

51. Alfred E. Smith, *The Citizen and His Government* (New York: Harper & Brothers, 1935), p. 48.

52. *Ibid.*

53. *New York Election Law,* § 6-110 (McKinney 1978).

54. *Ibid.,* § 1-104 (9).

55. *Ibid.,* § 6-162.

56. *New York Laws of 1967,* chap. 716, and *New York Election Law,* § 6-104 (2) (McKinney 1978).

57. *New York Election Law,* § 6-104 (2) (McKinney 1978).

58. Frank Lynn, "Democratic Chief Seeks to Curb Number of Statewide Primaries," *The New York Times,* March 27, 1978, p. B-3.

59. For information on primary election dates and registration, consult the "State Political Calendar" in the *Manual for the Use of the Legislature of the State of New York* published by the Department of State.

60. *Public Papers of Thomas E. Dewey: Fifty-First Governor of the State of New York, 1953* (Albany: State of New York, n.d.), pp. 341–42. His special message to the legislature recommended the change in the date of the primary election. See *ibid.,* p. 181.

61. *Harriman Public Papers,* p. 290.

62. *Veto Memorandum #1 of 1977* (Albany: Executive Chamber, March 2, 1977).

63. Frank Lynn, "Carey Seeks to Block Endorsement of Liberals of Goodman for Mayor," *The New York Times,* February 28, 1977, p. 1.

64. *Dunn v. Blumstein,* 405 U.S. 330 (1972). See also *New York Election Law,* § 5-102 (1) (McKinney 1978).

65. *Federal Register,* March 15, 1978, p. 10716.

66. *Voting Rights Act Amendments of 1970,* 84 Stat. 312, 42 U.S.C. 1973 (1970 Supp.). *Voting Rights Act Amendments of 1975,* 89 Stat. 401, 42 U.S.C. 1973b (1975 Supp.).

67. *New York Election Law,* §§ 8-400 to 8-462 (McKinney 1978).

68. *Fidell v. Board of Elections of the City of New York,* 343 F. Supp. 913 (1972), and *Fidell v. Board of Elections of the City of New York,* 409 U.S. 972 (1972).

69. See also *New York Election Law,* § 5-106 (McKinney 1978).

70. *New York Laws of 1975,* chap. 166, and *New York Election Law,* § 5-210 (McKinney 1978).

71. *New York Election Law,* §§ 5-300 to 5-310 (McKinney 1978).

72. *Ibid.,* § 5-210 (4) (a).

73. *Ibid.,* § 5-200 (1).

74. *Ibid.,* § 5-202 (1).

75. *New York Laws of 1935*, chap. 714, and *New York Election Law*, § 7-200 (1) (McKinney 1978). For the manner of voting, including voting machine write-ins, see *New York Election Law*, §§ 8-300 to 8-316 (McKinney 1978).

76. *New York Election Law*, § 15-104 (McKinney 1978). For dates of school board elections, see *New York Education Law*, § 2002 (McKinney 1969 and 1979 Supp.).

77. *New York Election Law*, § 7-116 (a) (McKinney 1964).

78. *Matter of Holtzman v. Power*, 27 N.Y. 2d 628 (1970).

79. *Matter of Holtzman v. Power*, 62 Misc. 2d 1020 at 1024 (1970).

80. *New York Election Law*, § 242-a (7) (McKinney 1978).

81. *Ibid.*, §§ 7-104 and 7-116 (McKinney 1978), and *ibid.*, § 248 (1) (McKinney 1979 Supp.).

82. *Illinois State Board v. Sangmeister*, 435 U.S. 939 (1978).

83. *New York Election Law*, § 7-116 (McKinney 1978).

84. *Ibid.*, §§ 9-204 and 9-206 *et seq.*

85. *Ibid.*, §§ 16-100 to 16-110.

86. *Ibid.*, § 9-216 (1).

87. *Ibid.*, § 9-202.

88. *New York Laws of 1974*, chap. 604, and *New York Election Law*, §§ 3-102, 3-104, 3-106, 3-107, and 14-100 to 14-128 (McKinney, 1978).

89. *New York Election Law*, § 3-100 (McKinney 1978).

90. *Ibid.*, §§ 3-102 and 14-100 to 14-128.

91. Thomas P. Ronan, "Wilson and His Running Mates Spent $2.7-Million," *The New York Times*, November 27, 1974, p. 13; and Lois Uttley, "Carey Spent Record $7 Million in his Re-election Campaign," *The Knickerbocker News* (Albany, New York), January 23, 1979, p. 11A.

92. Lois Uttley, "'78 Elections Cost Abrams a Million," *The Knickerbocker News* (Albany, New York), January 26, 1979, p. 5B.

93. *Buckley v. Valeo*, 424 U.S. 1 (1976).

94. *Federal Election Campaign Act of 1971*, 85 Stat. 3, 2 U.S.C. §§ 431–441 (1971 Supp.), and *Federal Election Campaign Act Amendments of 1974*, 88 Stat. 1263, 2 U.S.C. §§ 431–437 (1976 Supp.).

95. *Buckley v. Valeo*, 424 U.S. 1 at 143 (1976).

96. *Ibid.*, at 39.

97. *Ibid.*, at 52.

98. *Ibid.*, at 52–53.

99. *First National Bank of Boston, et al. v. Bellotti*, 435 U.S. 765 (1978).

100. *New York Election Law*, § 14-114 (1) (a) (McKinney 1978). See also *Guide to the Requirements of the New York State Election Law as Related to Campaign Financing* (Albany: New York State Board of Elections, December 1, 1977), p. 12.

101. *New York Election Law*, § 14-116 (b) (McKinney 1978).

102. "State to Act on 62 Candidates for Lag on Fund Reports," *The New York Times*, October 11, 1974, p. 18.

103. Frank Lynn, "400 of State's Politicians Penalized on Fund Reports," *The New York Times*, May 2, 1975, pp. 1 and 25.

104. "Bullard and Wilson Cleared of Violating Election Law," *The New York Times*, October 31, 1974, p. 35.

105. "Carey Is Cleared on Election Fund," *The New York Times*, February 1, 1975, p. 31.

106. Francis X. Clines, "Wilson Reports His Net Worth as $632,580, No Liabilities," *The New York Times*, September 7, 1974, p. 16.

107. *Official Compilation of Codes, Rules and Regulations of the State of New York*, Subtitle, V, Part 6201 (1974).

108. *Vanasco v. Schwartz*, 401 F. Supp. 87 (1975).

109. *Vanasco v. Schwartz*, 423 U.S. 1041 (1976), and *Schwartz v. Postel*, 423 U.S. 1041 (1976).

110. *New York Election Law*, § 3-106 (a) (1978).

111. Moscow, *Politics in the Empire State*, p. 200.

112. *Ibid.*, pp. 200–204.

113. For a general description of interest groups and lobbies in the Empire State, see Joseph G. Metz, *The Power of People-Power* (Woodbury, N.Y.: Barron's Educational Series, Inc., 1972). For a description and analysis of interest groups in the mid-1930s, see Belle Zeller, *Pressure Politics in New York* (New York: Russell & Russell, 1937).

114. Gerald S. Budgar, "Business Lobby's Voice Booming in Albany," *Sunday Times Union* (Albany, New York), January 7, 1979, pp. 1 and A8.

115. Moscow, *Politics in the Empire State*, p. 202.

116. *New York Laws of 1977*, chap. 677–78.

117. *New York Laws of 1978*, chap. 465.

118. Moscow, *Politics in the Empire State*, p. 201.

119. *Ibid.*, p. 202.

120. Peirce, *The Megastates of America*, p. 47.

121. *Public Papers of Alfred E. Smith, Forty-Seventh Governor of the State of New York, Fourth Term, 1928* (Albany: J. B. Lyon Company, 1937), Vol. VI, pp. 169–70, and *Public Papers of Franklin D. Roosevelt: Forty-Eighth Governor of the State of New York, 1931* (Albany: J. B. Lyon Company, 1937), p. 250.

122. Ari L. Goldman, "Should School Teachers Get Professional State License?" *The New York Times*, February 20, 1978, p. B-2.

123. Lois Uttley, "129 'Political Action' Units Ante Up in State Campaigns," *The Knickerbocker News* (Albany, New York), November 7, 1978, p. 11A.

124. Peter A. A. Berle, *Does the Citizen Stand a Chance? Politics of a State Legislature: New York* (Woodbury, N.Y.: Barron's Educational Series, Inc., 1974), p. 52.

125. Robert A. Caro, *The Power Broker* (New York: Vintage Books, 1975), p. 923.

126. *Ibid.*, pp. 926–27.

127. *New York Laws of 1967*, chap. 717. For further details on this controversy, see Thomas A. Droleskey, "The Politics of the Proposal to Construct a Bridge Crossing from Oyster Bay to Rye, New York" (Albany: Ph.D. Dissertation, Graduate School of Public Affairs, State University of New York at Albany, 1977).

128. Moscow, *Politics in the Empire State*, p. 206.

129. *Ibid.*, p. 200.

130. Berle, *Does the Citizen Stand a Chance?* p. 49.

131. Arlene Bigos, "The Lobbyists' World," *The Knickerbocker News*, March 11, 1976, p. 1C.

132. *New York Laws of 1977,* chap. 937.

133. *Fritz v. Gorton,* 417 U.S. 902 (1974).

134. *Fritz v. Gorton,* 417 P2d 911 at 931 (1974).

135. *Guidelines* (Albany: New York Temporary State Commission on Regulation of Lobbying, 1978).

136. *New York Laws of 1977,* chap. 937, § 12 (a) (1).

137. *Ibid.,* § 12 (a) (2) (3) (4).

138. *New York Legislative Law,* § 66-a (McKinney 1979 Supp.).

CHAPTER VI
The Legislature

THE 60 MEMBERS of the state Senate and the 150 members of the state Assembly are assigned responsibility by the state constitution for the determination of state policy and therefore are responsible for resource allocation, a highly political function, and other important functions. The intergovernmental theme surfaces as the legislature struggles to comply with federal statutes partially preempting responsibility for certain functions and decides how much discretionary authority should be devolved upon local governments. The group politics theme is highlighted because one cannot comprehend the process by which legislation is shaped without an understanding of the role of interest groups. The theme of the most desirable degree of executive integration appears in this chapter because of the historic struggle for political power between the legislature and the governor. The reader, of course, should not overlook the role political parties can play in linking the three levels of government and the legislative and executive branches of government. Parties, however, are not always successful in performing this linking role.

As indicated in Chapter IV, the drafters of the constitution of 1777 provided for legislative dominance of the government, and the governor lacked the appointment power and the veto power, since these powers were vested in the Council of Appointment and the Council of Revision, respectively. Abuses by the legislature in the nineteenth century led to a loss of public trust in the institution and to adoption of constitutional amendments restricting its powers. A number of these shackling provisions remain in the Empire State's constitution today. With respect to the relative power of the legislature and the governor, voter ratification in 1925 of a constitutional amendment limiting the number of civil departments to twenty and a second amendment in 1927 providing for an executive budget system greatly strengthened the formal powers of the governor.

The growing complexity of the issues facing the legislature since World War II and the desire to play an expanded leadership role in the governance of the state induced the legislature to expand greatly its staff and led the Citizens' Conference on State Legislatures in 1971 to rate the New York State legislature as the second most effective state legislature in the nation.[1]

Former Governor Alfred E. Smith, who was elected as assemblyman in 1903, wrote that "after his election the Assemblyman will quickly learn that one of the most important parts of his job is an entirely non-legislative one. He is expected to be an active and helpful assistant to his district leader."[2] Describing a legislator's job as difficult, Smith pointed out that while the legislative session as of 1935 lasted only three or four months a year, the legislator must serve on committees and keep in personal contact with constituents if he desires to be reelected.[3]

FORMAL POWERS

Subject to the restrictions contained in the United States Constitution and the state constitution, the powers reserved to the states by the Tenth Amendment to the United States Constitution are exercisable by the state legislature.[4] The reserved or residual powers may be classified as constituent, legislative, electoral, executive, administrative, and judicial. The first class refers to the power of the legislature to ratify proposed federal constitutional amendments referred to it, propose state constitutional amendments, and convene constitutional conventions.

The power to enact statutes is the legislative power and is the principal focus of this chapter. The legislature's electoral power currently is limited to electing its own officers, and the fifteen members of the Board of Regents to staggered seven-year terms either by a concurrent resolution of the legislature or by a joint session if the two houses fail to agree on a concurrent resolution by the first Tuesday in March.[5] Residence in a particular judicial department is required for eleven members; the other four seats are at-large ones. To be elected, a candidate must receive 106 votes from assemblymen and senators.

An executive power is exercised when the Senate acts upon the governor's nominations for appointments, and an administrative power is exercised through the appropriation process and oversight of the administration of state programs.

Until 1847 the Senate, the chancellor, and judges of the Supreme Court served as a Court for the Correction of Errors, a court of final appellate jurisdiction, when it was replaced by the current Court of Appeals.[6] Each house may exercise a judicial power by trying and disciplining members, and the Assembly—by a majority vote of all members—may impeach members of the executive and judicial branches.[7] A judicial power is exercised when senators and judges of the Court of Appeals serve as a court for the trial of impeachments voted by the Assembly. In the trial of the governor or the lieutenant governor, the temporary president of the Senate does not serve as a member of the Court of Impeachment. If convicted on impeachment charges, an official may be removed from office. In 1913 Governor William Sulzer was impeached, convicted, and removed from office.

The legislature may not annul or correct a judicial determination[8] or grant a new trial or an appeal from the decision of a court.[9]

State Constitutional Restrictions

Many restrictions are the result of agitation by part of the Whig party, antirenters, and Radical ("Barnburner") Democrats leading to the constitutional convention of 1846. The legislature and the governor spend time seeking and finding, in many instances, ways of circumventing constitutional restrictions.

Aging of Bills. To prevent abuses associated with the hasty passage of bills that have not been printed, the constitution has stipulated since 1894 that "no bill shall be passed . . . unless it shall have been printed and upon the desks of the members, in its final form, at least three calendar legislative days prior to its final passage, unless the Governor, or the Acting Governor, shall have certified, . . . the facts which in his opinion necessitate an immediate vote thereon."[10] This requirement results in pageboys each day piling hundreds of bills on each member's desk, and the bills are not read there by the member.

Occasionally, reference is made to a "printer's veto"; that is, failure of copies of printed bills to arrive on members' desks three days prior to adjournment because the bills have been delayed by orders of the leadership. The role of "messages of necessity" in fostering close relationships between the governor and legislative leaders is discussed in Chapter VII. The constitution also stipulates that no bill shall be passed "except by the assent of a majority of the members elected to each branch of the Legislature; and upon the last reading of a bill, no amendment thereof shall be allowed, and the question upon its final message shall be taken immediately thereafter, and the ayes and nays entered on the journal."[11]

One-Subject Bills. Since 1846 the state constitution has stipulated that each private or local bill must be confined to one subject that is expressed in the bill's title in order to alert members and the public as to the interests affected if the bill becomes law.[12] The Court of Appeals has ruled that an act covering all cities is a general (one subject) and not a local act[13] and a deceptive title can invalidate an act.[14]

The origin of this restriction is attributable to the feud between Alexander Hamilton and Aaron Burr. Banking in New York City by 1800 was nearly monopolized by the Bank of New York, chartered in 1791 and headed by Hamilton. Concluding that a competing bank was needed to promote the public weal but blocked from obtaining a bank charter by Federalist control of the legislature, Burr proposed the granting of a charter to a company and authorizing it to raise $2 million to build a waterworks to supply adequate water to eliminate yellow fever and to employ the surplus capital, if any "in any way not inconsistent with the laws and Constitution of the United States or of the State of New York."[15]

Prohibition of Reference. A common practice in many legislative bodies is the incorporation in a new law or provisions of an existing law by reference; that is, by referring to the existing law rather than by reprinting the law. The incorporation of existing laws by reference makes it more difficult for a member or a citizen to understand the full impact of a bill under consideration by the legislature.

The prohibition of reference has been stated clearly in the constitution since 1846.[16] The Court of Appeals in 1938 struck down a section of the Education Law providing that all laws applicable to the New York City Board of Education were applicable to the city's Board of Higher Education.[17] An attempt to incorporate the Fair Trade Law into the Alcoholic Beverage Control Law by reference was invalidated by the court in 1949.[18]

Courts, however, on occasion have not invalidated a challenged law incorporating material by reference. An amendment to the New York City Administrative Code imposing a tax equal to one fourth of the state alcoholic beverage fee was held not to violate the prohibition of reference,[19] and a similar ruling was applied to a 1952 law validating the title of the Town of Huntington Trustees in certain lands by referring to an article in the Civil Practice Act.[20] Similarly, a law stipulating that any violation of the Election Law not specifically covered by the previous section of the Penal Law is a misdemeanor was held to be valid.[21]

Relative to procedural references, courts have held that a law granting power or imposing a duty does not contravene the prohibition of reference by referring to an existing statute detailing the procedures for the execution of the power or the performance of the duty.[22] And the legislature by reference may transfer regulatory authority from one agency to another agency.[23]

Prohibition of Certain Private and Local Bills. The constitution lists fourteen cases where the legislature may not enact a private or local bill, including changing the names of persons, locating or changing county seats, incorporating villages, or regulating the rate of interest on money.[24] Until this prohibition was adopted, the legislature devoted considerable time to consideration of such bills. In 1836, for example, 46 percent of the laws dealt with these topics, an indication that the legislature functioned "as an arena within which local and private interests contended for privileges and influence."[25]

Private Claims. Abuses of the power to allow private claims against the state led to a constitutional amendment forbidding the legislature from auditing or allowing any private claim against the state.[26] This prohibition resulted in the creation of the Court of Claims (described in Chapter VIII). The legislature, however, considers numerous claims bills annually, and the governor typically vetoes many claims bills, granting the claimant an additional period of time to file a claim in the Court of Claims.[27]

Two-Thirds Bills. In addition to requiring a two-thirds vote to override a gubernatorial veto, the constitution requires a two-thirds vote of the total membership of each house to appropriate "public moneys or property for local or private purposes."[28] In 1918 the Court of Appeals held that this provision did not require that Chapter 658 of 1915 be enacted by a two-thirds vote, since the law simply granted an individual additional time to file a claim in the Court of Claims and did not appropriate funds.[29]

Three-Fifths Bills. An 1874 constitutional amendment requires a three-fifths quorum on the vote in each house for final passage of any bill imposing, continuing, or reviving a tax; creating a debt; making, continuing, or reviving "any appropriation of public or trust money or property"; or releasing, discharging, or commuting "any claim or demand of the State."[30] This requirement often forces the legislative leaders to swap votes and arrange trade-offs to secure sufficient votes to pass the budget.

The Blaine Amendment. Perhaps the most controversial restriction upon the powers of the legislature is the so-called Blaine amendment forbidding the state from assisting denominational institutions.[31] The state or a local government, however, may provide for the transportation of pupils to any school and may reimburse denominational schools for the cost of state-mandated duties.

Governor Smith's Views. In 1935 former Governor Smith wrote he would add restrictions upon legislative power because "too much is now done by law that could be done by departmental rules and regulations."[32] As governor, Smith was particularly disturbed by the large number of bills sent to him dealing with the size of fish and conditions under which a person could take fish and game; he vetoed many of these bills, as his predecessors had disallowed similar bills.

STRUCTURE AND SESSIONS

A distinguishing feature of American legislative bodies, other than the Nebraska legislature and local councils, is bicameralism, a two-house legislature.[33] The United States Supreme Court's one-person, one-vote dictum, issued in 1964, rekindled interest in unicameralism, because the Court rejected the federal analogy of one house apportioned on the basis of population and the second house apportioned on the basis of geographical areas.[34] Questions were raised as to whether the decision made bicameralism anachronistic, since there did not appear to be any logical justification for two houses selected on a population basis. In delivering the one-person, one-vote dictum, Chief Justice Earl Warren stressed that the houses could represent different constituencies by having one composed of single-member districts and the other composed partially of multimember districts, and the terms of the two houses could be made to differ.[35]

Commenting upon bicameralism and unicameralism in 1948, Warren Moscow wrote:

While the tendency of one house of the Legislature to pass the buck to the other may be condemned in theory, it works well in practice and is, at least to me, a valid argument against a unicameral legislature of the type in existence in Nebraska. Under the bicameral system, one house may pass a bad bill, and if there is public outcry, the other house can kill the measure without anyone's losing caste.[36]

Apportionment and Reapportionment

The constitution provides for a 50-member Senate and a 150-member Assembly elected by single-member districts.[37] While 150 members is the absolute limit on the number of assemblymen, the constitution contains a provision allowing for the expansion of the size of the Senate, and the current Senate has 60 members.[38] The Assembly had 165 members in 1966 because of a court-ordered reapportionment plan requiring the election of this number in 1965.[39] In 1966, a new reapportionment plan provided for 150 members. The original Assembly and Senate had 70 and 24 members, respectively,[40] and the number of members was increased to 128 and 32, respectively, by the 1821 constitution.[41] The current constitutional provision dates to 1894.[42] Although the constitution does not specify single-member Senate districts, it is possible to imply that this is the intent of the constitution.

Reapportionment must be undertaken by the legislature every decade in the year ending in two.[43] Gerrymandering—the deliberate drawing of district boundary lines to concentrate the minority party in as few districts or distribute it among as many districts as possible—has been a characteristic feature of reapportionment in virtually all states, and the practice has been rendered easier by the United States Supreme Court's one-person, one-vote dictum. Moscow points out that upstate Republicans who controlled the drafting of the 1894 constitution, which is still in effect as amended, took action to ensure that New York City would never be able to elect a majority of members of the legislature by providing that each of the state's sixty-two counties, except Fulton and Hamilton, would be guaranteed at least one seat in the Assembly and "no two counties divided by a river—New York and Kings (Brooklyn) were in mind—could ever have half the Senate seats."[44] Moscow added that a 1917 reapportionment plan "appeared to ensure rural control, but the character of the population changed in several areas, and by 1944, . . . the Democrats had proved that they sometimes could win control of the Senate, if they are carrying the State by landslide or near-landslide proportions for other offices."[45]

Whereas the one-person, one-vote dictum eliminated rural overrepresentation and urban underrepresentation, the dictum made gerrymandering easier because the achievement of near population equality for each district necessitates the ignoring of the section in the state constitution providing that "no country shall be divided in the formation of a Senate district except to make two or more Senate districts wholly in such county. No town, except a town having more than a full ratio of apportionment, and no block in a city inclosed by streets or public ways, shall be divided."[46] A similar provision contains the same prohibition relative to the drawing of Assembly district lines.[47]

To achieve districts with de minimis population variation allowed by the courts,[48] county and town lines have to be ignored and city blocks may have to be broken in order to meet the one-person, one-vote criterion, or at least the majority party can offer this rationale to support blatant gerrymandering. In other words, equally populated districts may have unfair district lines. Gerrymandered districts are not necessarily off-shaped, as symmetrical lines may divide local governments into parts. Writing in 1972, David I. Wells cites a Senate district:

The 34th State Senate District in the Bronx is actually two separate pieces of land connected only by one lane of a drawbridge. When the bridge is open, the district is completely non-contiguous. But whereas the two parts of the district are separated geographically, they have one important thing in common: both are strongly Republican. A district placing most parts of both segments into a single block of territory could, of course, have been drawn—but this would have necessitated inclusion of heavily Democratic Co-op City, a large, union-sponsored housing project, and that would have jeopardized the district's GOP incumbent. Co-op City was therefore cut out of the 34th and attached to the 33rd . . . which was used as a "dumping ground" for Democrats all across the north Bronx.[49]

An Apportionment Commission. To remove partisan motivation from the redrawing of legislative districts lines, numerous proposals have been advanced for taking the responsibility for reapportionment away from the legislature and vesting the responsibility in a nonpartisan apportionment commission. The *Model State Constitution* provides for a gubernatorially appointed board to reapportion the legislature following each decennial federal census.[50] The Citizens Union of New York City made a similar recommendation to the 1967 constitutional convention: "the Governor, after inviting nominations from the presidents of the State's institutions of higher learning, civic, education, professional, and other organizations, should be required to name a ten-member commission to reapportion and redistrict the State legislative districts."[51]

The 1967 constitutional convention ignored the Citizens Union's proposal and advanced to third reading a proposal providing for a commission appointed by the majority and minority leaders of the two houses of the legislature and the Court of Appeals. Reacting to the exclusion of the governor from participation in the reapportionment process, Governor Nelson A. Rockefeller on September 11, 1967, sent a special message to the convention protesting the proposal: "While it purports to remove the matter of reapportionment from the hands of the Legislature the fact is that it merely removes from participation the 207 elected Legislators and concentrates the power in four Legislative Leaders, each of whom is elected by only a small fraction of the total State electorate."[52]

One should bear in mind Wells's statement that a bipartisan apportionment commission may engage in bipartisan gerrymandering with certain districts safely assigned to one party and other districts safely assigned to the other party, or result in a deadlock with the tie-breaking machinery, imposing either a bipartisan gerrymander or "an old-fashioned one-party gerrymander."[53]

The Federal Voting Rights Act and Reapportionment. Reacting to continuing charges of racial discrimination in voting in southern states, Congress in 1965 employed its Fifteenth Amendment powers to enact the Voting Rights Act.[54] Much to the surprise of New Yorkers, the United States attorney general in 1970 made a determination that Bronx, Kings, and New York counties fell under the purview of Section 5 of the act requiring the approval of the United States attorney general before an electoral change can be implemented.[55] Although New York State was successful in obtaining a declaratory judgment from the United States District Court for the District of Columbia exempting the three counties from coverage by the act, the National Association for the Advancement of Colored People (NAACP) intervened in the case.[56] After reopening the declaratory judgment action, the NAACP obtained an order from the United States District Court for the District of Columbia holding that the Voting Rights Act as amended in 1970 applied to congressional and legislative districts in Manhattan, Brooklyn, and the Bronx, thereby necessitating a special session of the state legislature, which on May 29, 1974 redrew congressional and district lines that had been drawn in 1972.[57]

While this redistricting did not change the number of districts with nonwhite majorities, the nonwhite majority percentage was increased in two Senate districts and in two Assembly districts. Objections to some new district lines were advanced by representatives of Brooklyn's Hasidic Jews who argued that the new Assembly districts divided the Hasidic community and made it a victim of a racial gerrymander, thereby diluting the value of their votes in violation of the equal protection of the laws clause and the due process of law clause of the Fourteenth Amendment to the United States Constitution.

On July 1, 1974, the United States attorney general approved the new districts and dismissed the objections of Hasidic Jews and Irish, Italian, and Polish groups on the ground that the act was designed to prevent voting discrimination on the basis of race or color and was not designed to prohibit voting discrimination on the basis of ethnic origin or religious beliefs.[58]

The United States district court dismissed the complaint of the Hasidic Jews on the ground that the petitioners were not disfranchised and that race could be considered in redistricting in order to correct previous racial discrimination.[59] The Circuit Court of Appeals affirmed this decision by reasoning that the redistricting did not underrepresent whites, who constitute 65 percent of the population, since approximately 70 percent of the Assembly and Senate districts in Kings County would have white majorities.[60]

On March 1, 1977, the United States Supreme Court affirmed the lower court ruling by holding that the Voting Rights Act "was itself broadly remedial," that "compliance with the Act in reapportionment cases would often necessitate the use of racial considerations in drawing district lines," and that "a State may revise its reapportionment plan to comply with § 5 by increasing the percentage of black voters in a particular district until it has produced a clear majority."[61]

The Supreme Court's decision in the Hasidic Jews case is disturbing because the Court in effect overturned its 1960 decision in *Gomillion* v. *Lightfoot* invalidating racial gerrymandering.[62] The Court also can be faulted for its uncritical acceptance of a 65 percent nonwhite majority as the magic percentage needed to ensure that the voting rights of nonwhites are not abridged. It is interesting to note that in *Whitcomb* v. *Chavis* the Court refused to accept "the proposition that members of a minority group have a federal right to be represented in legislative bodies in proportion to their number in the general population."[63]

Though decisions of courts are influenced by whether a need exists for remedial action, one cannot support a blatant racial gerrymander when another alternative—use of proportional representation in multimember districts—would provide "fair" representation without encouraging racial segregation.[64]

Sessions

The legislature meets annually in January; may call itself into special session by petition signed by two thirds of the members elected to each house;[65] and may be called into extraordinary session by the governor, who also is authorized to convene the Senate alone in extraordinary session.[66] The constitution also stipulates that "neither house shall, without the consent of the other, adjourn for more than two days."[67] Absenteeism can be a problem, and the leader of each house possesses the power to order the state police to round up members if their presence is necessary.

Between 1919 and 1935, only one session (1923) extended into May. In 1943 the fiscal year was changed from July 1 to April 1, and for the following twenty years the legislature was able to conclude its regular session in March, with the exception of 1955 when the legislature adjourned on April 2.[68] Since 1964 the length of the session has been extended and varied from an adjournment date of April 22 to July 13 until 1976, when the legislature decided to recess instead of adjourn, a practice currently followed.

When called into special session by petition of members, the legislature is limited in its consideration to the subjects listed in the petition. Similarly, the legislature when convened in special session by the governor is limited to passage of the subjects enumerated in his call. In 1975 the extraordinary session convened on September 4 continued into the beginning of the regular session and was not adjourned until January 7, 1976.

Individual legislators on occasion in the past publicly expressed a desire for a veto session of the legislature, but no such session has been held since 1976, the first year the legislature was authorized to call itself into extraordinary session. The 1976 legislature recessed instead of adjourning in June and set July 28 as the date for reconvening to consider the question of overriding the governor's vetoes. On July 26 the legislative leaders announced that the session was unnecessary because the disallowed bills were of insufficient importance to justify a veto session.[69] Arrangements were made to have a member in each house bang the gavel officially opening and closing the session.

The legislature meets in joint session to hear the governor deliver his state of the state and budget messages and to elect members of the Board of Regents if the two houses are unable to agree upon a concurrent resolution to elect Regents by the first Tuesday in March.[70]

Governor Frank S. Black in 1897 and Governor Theodore Roosevelt in 1899 recommended biennial sessions to reduce the volume of legislation.[71] Former Governor Alfred E. Smith favored a brief "budget session" in odd-numbered years with all other matters acted upon in even-numbered years, because such a session "would save a good deal of the large sum of money now expended for the conduct of the yearly legislative sessions and would save legislators themselves a good deal of time and effort."[72]

In his annual message to the legislature in 1957, Governor Averell Harriman suggested the adoption of the "split-session" device with the first part of the session devoted to the introduction of bills followed by a recess to allow committees to hold public hearings and study bills, and members to consult constituents, and the second part of the session reserved for debate and voting.[73] California used the split session between 1911 and 1958.

Although the legislature did not accept Harriman's suggestion, provision has been made for the prefiling of bills commencing on November 15 of each year and for the carryover of bills not enacted or killed in one session to the next session unless an election intervenes.[74] The prefiling of bills and carryover of other bills allows these bills to be printed and studied prior to the convening of the annual session in January.

THE SOLONS

The important role played by members of the state legislature in the governance of the Empire State cannot be overestimated. Governor Smith in 1935 provided advice for a young legislator who desires to play a major role in the legislative process:

If he wants to work hard, study, and get acquainted with legislative procedure, thoroughly familiarize himself with proposals that are put before him, and in other ways really take an interest in his job, the young legislator will be a success. If on the other hand he merely attends the sessions in a perfunctory manner, exhibits interest only in the things that affect his own locality, and fails to be of any material help or assistance to the party as a whole, he will probably never attain any great eminence in public life.[75]

Term of Office

To be eligible for election to the legislature, one must be a United States citizen and a resident of the state for five years and of the Assembly or Senate district for one year prior to the election.[76] No member may be appointed by the governor, the governor and the Senate, the legislature, or a city government to an office created or whose emoluments have been increased during the member's term.[77] If elected to Congress or appointed to a civil or military office in the federal government, the member automatically vacates his seat in the legislature.[78]

Members of the first Senate and the first Assembly served for four years and one year, respectively.[79] The 1846 constitution reduced the term of senators to two years while continuing the term of assemblymen at one year and shifted elections from April following adjournment of the legislature to early November.[80] Members of both houses currently are elected for two-year terms in single-member districts; the Assembly term was increased from one to two years in 1938.[81]

Constitutional amendments are frequently proposed to increase the term of legislators to four years on the ground that members currently spend too much time campaigning for reelection. The necessity for continuous campaigning, according to the New York State Bar Association, also "encourages political cosmetics such as the introduction of multitude of often unnecessary bills to indicate to constituents the great amount of activity which a legislator has undertaken. . . . It also encourages efforts at short-term solutions to difficult long-range fiscal and social problems."[82] Opponents of the four-year term argue that the present term promotes greater responsiveness on the part of members to the electorate.

The state constitution stipulates that "for any speech or debate in either house of the Legislature, the members should not be questioned in any other place."[83] Each house, however, possesses the power to discipline and expel members. After a twenty-four-day trial by the Judiciary Committee, the 1920 Assembly expelled five Socialist assemblymen, an action approved by the *New York Times* and condemned by Governor Alfred E. Smith.[84] A member automatically loses his seat upon conviction for a felony.[85]

Salary and Allowances

The 1777 constitution was silent relative to legislative salaries, and the 1821 constitution allowed the legislature to determine the salaries of members.[86] Reflecting distrust of the legislature, the 1846 constitution restricted the compensation of members to a maximum of $3 a day up to a maximum of $300, except during impeachment proceedings, and authorized "one dollar for every ten miles they travel, in going to and returning from their place of meeting, on the most usual route."[87] The speaker was granted an additional stipend equal to one third of his per diem allowance. The 1894 constitution was the first one to specify an amount—$1,500—as compensation for legislators.[88] Voters in 1911, 1919, and 1921 rejected a proposed constitutional amendment raising the salary of legislators but approved a 1927 amendment increasing the salary to $2,500. A proposed 1947 amendment—appearing on the ballot between an amendment authorizing bonuses for veterans of World War II and an amendment expanding the use of absentee ballots—providing the salary of legislators would "be fixed by law" was ratified by the electorate.[89] The legislature raised the salary to $5,000 in 1948, $7,500 in 1954, $10,000 in 1961, $15,000 in 1963, and $23,500 in 1973. Only members of the California and Michigan legislatures receive a larger annual salary—$25,555 and $24,000, respectively. However, the 1979 legislature voted to raise the salary to $32,960 by 1983. The salary and allowances for additional services may not be increased or decreased during a term for which the legislature is elected.[90] In other words, an election must intervene between the vote to increase the salary or allowance and the receipt of the increased salary or allowance by the legislators.

Members holding leadership positions receive an additional allowance for their added responsibilities, ranging from $3,500 to $30,000 in 1981. In addition, members of the Assembly in 1980 each received $20,000 for the employment of staff and $1,200 for the district office. An assemblyman may not hire more than eight persons with the staff allowance. Senators of the majority party in 1978 each received staff allowances of $35,000, and $2,145,000 was appropriated for staff allowances for minority senators. Each senator also receives an allowance not exceeding $4,500 for the rental of a district office and $1,000 for operating the office. In addition, the Assembly and the Senate each finance three mailings of a newsletter annually for each member.

Until 1974 each member of the legislature received $5,000 annually "in lieu of expenses"—the famous "lulu"—in addition to a regular $15,000 salary. Public criticism of lulus led to the substitution of a $55 daily expense allowance, and a few observers have attributed the increased length of the legislative session to the daily expenses allowance by maintaining that when the lulu was exhausted members went home.

To reduce public criticism of salary increases for members of the legislature, a 1972 law established a nine-member Commission on Legislative and Judicial Salaries appointed by the governor with Senate approval. Although the governor appoints all the members, two members are appointed on the recommendation of the speaker and two on the recommendation of the chief judge of the Court of Appeals.[91] The commission is directed to make an annual review and submit a report to the governor by December 1, and the governor is directed to include in a budget appropriation bill his salary recommendation for the positions reviewed.

Governors, respecting the principle of separation of powers and/ or expecting reciprocity in the legislature's handling of executive office appropriations, usually do not comment on internal legislative matters. In 1975, however, Governor Hugh L. Carey in signing the supplemental budget bill commented on the "individual appropriations for 80 percent of the members of the Legislature as 'allowances for the particular and additional services appertaining to' the special duties of the particular positions" and added: "I would respectfully suggest that the Legislature be prepared next year to offer full explanations for the appropriations for special allowances."[92]

Turnover of Members

Turnover of members in the Assembly was high during the nineteenth century. Whereas 32.4 percent were first-term members during the decade 1777–87, 54.6 percent were first-term members during the decade 1808–17, the percentage rose to 75.5 and 83.3 during the decades 1838–47 and 1848–57, respectively, indicating that legislative inexperience was common.[93] The Senate, on the other hand, generally had fewer than one-quarter new members until 1852–53 and 1856–57, when the percentage of new members was 75.0 and 65.6, respectively.[94]

First-term assemblymen and senators totaled 17.7 percent and 12.1 percent during the period 1925–35, respectively.[95] In 1980 twenty-six assemblymen (17.3 percent) and twelve senators (20.0 percent) were freshmen, a lower percentage than the national average.

Reasons for turnover include defeat in reelection bids and the time demands that interfere with professional and business activities and disrupt family life. In addition, it has been suggested that a number of legislators originally sought election for advertising purposes in their home districts and as their business or professional activities increased they decided to retire from the legislature. In a few instances a legislator is appointed to a state office, necessitating, under the constitution, the resignation of his seat.

The charge occasionally is made that the legislator is "bought out." Alan S. Chartock, for example, wrote in 1976:

> Former Governor Rockefeller was a master at buying Democratic legislators who represented districts that could easily elect Republicans. He merely found a vacancy on an existing commission or managed to establish a new commission and promised the legislator in question a high-level commission job.
>
> A case in point occurred in 1969, when Rockefeller appointed Democratic Assemblyman Charles F. Stockmeister of Rochester to a $35,250 job as a member of the state Civil Service Commission. A Republican won Stockmeister's seat in a special election later that year.[96]

Occupations, Religion, and Race

Farming was the most common occupation of members of the legislature during the decades immediately following 1777. As the Empire State became urbanized and industrialized in the nineteenth century, the number of nonfarmers increased significantly. Only three members listed their occupation as farming in 1980.

Forty-one of the 150 assemblymen and 28 of the 60 senators in 1980 were attorneys; 39 senators and 83 assemblymen identified their occupation as full-time legislators; 15 assemblymen and 7 senators were businessmen; 3 assemblymen and 3 senators were educators; 1 senator was an engineer, 1 a "farmer-businessman"; and 1 assemblyman was a farmer and 1 a "dairyman."

Eight members of the Assembly and four members of the Senate were women. Relative to religion, 81 assemblymen and 27 senators in 1976 were Catholic, 36 assemblymen and 19 senators were Protestant, and 31 assemblymen and 14 senators were Jewish. One hundred and thirty-seven assemblymen and 57 senators were married.[97]

Between 1953 and 1980 the number of black assemblymen increased from 3 to 13, and the number of black senators increased from 1 to 4.[98] Whereas there were no Hispanic members in either house in 1953, there were 3 Hispanic members in the Assembly and 2 Hispanic members in the Senate in 1980.

ORGANIZATION OF THE LEGISLATURE

The state constitution provides that the lieutenant governor "shall be the President of the Senate but shall have only a casting vote therein."[99] The Senate also is directed to "choose a Temporary President and the Assembly shall choose a Speaker."[100] Beyond these constitutional requirements, each house is free to determine its organization and procedural rules, with certain exceptions explained later; elect other officers; and judge "the elections, returns, and qualifications of its own members."[101]

Mr. Speaker

The most powerful member of the Assembly clearly is the speaker, who typically is elected by a majority vote of the members on the first day of the session. The speaker normally is elected under the provision of the "unit rule" that stipulates that once adopted by members of the majority party in caucus or conference, all party members are bound to vote for the candidate selected by the majority. The speaker today is always a member with considerable seniority. This was not true during the first century of the Assembly when the speaker on the average had served only 2.37 years as a member prior to becoming speaker, including a low of nine tenths of a year between 1848 and 1857.[102] The Assembly also elects a speaker pro tempore who presides in the absence of the speaker and earns an extra $14,000 per year for his duties.

Although the speaker always is a member of the majority party, the 1937 Republican Conference—holding a 2-vote majority—was unable to agree on the reelection of Speaker Irving M. Ives. As a compromise, Oswald D. Heck was elected speaker with the aid of Democratic votes, and he appointed Ives the majority floor leader.[103] Similarly, Anthony J. Travia was elected a speaker in 1965 with the help of Republican votes, as a split among the Democrats prevented either of two candidates from receiving a majority of the Democratic votes.[104]

Joseph F. Carlino of Long Beach was elected speaker on July 1, 1959, and became the first Republican leader of either the Assembly or the Senate from the New York City metropolitan area in almost 100 years. Carlino was the first Italian to become speaker, a reflection of the growing importance of this group and of metropolitan New York City suburban areas.[105]

The speaker's authority stems from his powers to appoint the majority leader and committee chairmen, administer rules as presiding officer subject to appeal to the house, recognize members who wish to speak, and refer bills to committee. Assembly Rule I also provides that the speaker is the chairman of the Rules Committee, which is the leadership committee. Rules can be manipulated to reward friends and punish enemies, and favored members can be appointed to the more important committees and bills of friendly assemblymen assigned to a committee that will give the bills a favorable report if the bills are capable of being assigned to more than one committee. The speaker also allocates certain staff to committees. Former Assemblyman Peter A. A. Berle wrote that the speaker "can frequently exert control over what bills are considered and later acted upon favorably by the body he leads."[106]

The speaker can threaten to cut patronage staff members from the payroll to bring recalcitrant legislators into line, allow favored members to sponsor important bills, refuse to allow a member to introduce a bill after the last scheduled day for bill introduction, arrange for a printer's veto (a bill does not arrive from the printer at least three days prior to adjournment), delay action on a bill to ensure that it will be forwarded to the other house late in the session when the bill will not be considered, and create subcommittees jointly with the chairman of a standing committee. In addition, the speaker plays a major role in redrawing Assembly district lines when legislative seats are reapportioned.

One should not conclude that the speaker secures support simply by doing or withholding favors, however. As Moscow pointed out, "the Speaker wins the personal loyalty of the individual members by the tact and care with which he handles their individual problems."[107]

Temporary President of the Senate

Although the state constitution designates the lieutenant governor as the ex officio president of the Senate,[108] the constitution also requires the election of a president pro tempore who always is the majority leader and the dominant figure in the Senate possessing powers similar to those possessed by the speaker.[109]

The majority leader appoints the deputy majority leader, and the chairman, vice chairman, and members of each committee and subcommittee. The majority leader also is chairman of the Rules Committee, appoints all Senate officers and employees, designates the news media representatives entitled to admission to the floor, and administers the rules of the Senate. Along with the deputy majority leader, the minority and deputy minority leader, the majority leader serves as an ex officio member of all committees.

The power of the majority leader is illustrated by a 1938 incident described by Moscow:

> The insurance lobby had the measure bottled up in committee in the Senate. A group of Democratic Senators, for reasons of their own, were listening to the insurance-company arguments rather than to those of their own Governor. By a vote in committee, the bill was killed. It was dead for the session, so far as legislative precedent and procedure were concerned. But John Dunnigan, the Democratic majority leader, proceeded to override the committee with a complete and impertinent disregard for that precedent and procedure. Armed with just another printed copy of the bill—not the original copy—plus a blank committee roll-call, Dunnigan cornered every Democrat on the committee separately and ordered him to sign as approving the measure.
>
> Each protested. They had just voted the other way. The committee couldn't reverse itself, especially without even having a meeting, each one said in turn.

"Who's leader around here, you or me?" Dunnigan stormed. "Sign, I said, sign." They signed.[110]

The ruling of the presiding officer always is challenged when it goes against the wishes of the majority leader or caucus. The *New York Times* reported in 1975:

"The 'Nays' have it," said Lieut. Gov. Mary Anne Krupsak, after the thunder of "ayes" and a thin course of "nays" on a Senate resolution urging Governor Carey to veto a 50 percent increase in tolls by the Port Authority of New York and New Jersey.
The "ayes" demanded a roll call and won it, 41-to-13.[111]

Other Officers

The second in command in the Assembly is the majority leader, who works closely with the speaker. The former, like the latter, is a member of the Rules Committee and ex officio member of each standing committee. If the office of speaker becomes vacant, the majority leader becomes the acting speaker and typically will be elected speaker when the Assembly reconvenes, providing his party retains control.

The Assembly's majority leader is a close confidant of the speaker, shares many of the latter's responsibilities, serves as floor manager since the speaker finds it difficult as presiding officer to get on the floor, and is the party's official spokesman.

The deputy majority leader of the Senate, a position created in 1973, corresponds in some ways to the position of majority leader in the Assembly in that the Senate deputy majority leader is the second in command. He is chairman of the Senate Ethics Committee and an ex officio member of all Senate committees and temporary state commissions. In addition, he coordinates meetings of all Senate committees.

The position of Assembly or Senate minority leader often is a frustrating one, since the minority lacks the votes to pass or reject a bill on its own and possesses real power only when the majority members are divided or a two-thirds vote is required to override the veto of the governor or to appropriate funds or property for local or private use. Should the minority party win control of the legislature in the forthcoming general election, the Assembly minority leader typically becomes speaker and the Senate minority leader typically becomes president pro tempore.

Committees

Standing committees of the legislature were created in the 1780s but were little used in this period, because reliance was placed upon the Committee of the Whole.

The legislature could not function without the assistance of committees because of the large quantities of bills introduced—the number increased from 10,916 in 1965 to 16,034 in 1975, but dropped slightly to 16,009 in 1977 before climbing to 23,426 in 1978.[112]

Each house has standing or permanent committees concerned with rules and substantive topics including agriculture, banks, cities, commerce, corporations, education, elections, insurance, rules, social services, and transportation. Currently, the Assembly and the Senate have thirty and twenty-six standing committees, respectively. The number of members varies from eight on the Ethics Committee to thirty-one on the Rules Committee in the Assembly, with the typical committee having twenty members. The ratio of majority to minority party members tends to be 3 to 2 in order to ensure majority control. The Ethics Committee has four Democrats and four Republicans as members.

In addition to standing committees, each house is free to create subcommittees, task forces, and select committees. In 1980 the Assembly had thirty subcommittees and three task forces, and the Senate had ten subcommittees and a Task Force on Critical State Problems.

In 1980 the Senate had five select committees, which are temporary ones set up to investigate a special subject. Although all select committees today are composed of members of only one house, there were several joint committees in existence from 1973 to 1976 that were called select committees and were replacements for joint legislative committees (JLCs), which had functioned since 1898. Several of the JLCs—such as the ones on aging, interstate cooperation, metropolitan and regional areas study, and transportation—performed important functions; others acquired a bad name for failing to produce useful reports and for serving as a home for "no-shows," sinecurists who reportedly performed no duties other than to collect their paychecks.

Related to the JLC is the Temporary State Commission—composed of an equal number of members appointed by the governor, the Senate president pro tempore, and the speaker—to conduct studies of major state problems. Members often include persons who are not legislators. Many commissions carry the title "temporary," but others—such as the State Study Commission for New York City—adopt a different name, although the joint resolution creating the commission is entitled "The Temporary State Commission to Make a Study of the Governmental Operation of the City of New York."

Joint Assembly-Senate operations in 1980 included the Administrative Regulations Review Committee with a separate Assembly staff and a separate Senate staff, the Legislative Commission on Energy Systems, the Legislative Commission on Expenditure Review, the Legislative Task Force on Education State Aid Information Needs, the Task Force to Study and Evaluate the Parimutuel Racing and Breeding Industry, the Temporary State Commission on Child Welfare, the Temporary State Commission on Management and Productivity in the Public Sector, the Temporary State Commission to Revise the Social Services Law, the Legislative Library, and the Legislative Bill Drafting Commission.

Although the committees are appointed by the speaker and the temporary president of the Senate, they usually follow seniority and preferences of members, to the extent possible, in making appointments and also consult the minority leader regarding appointment of minority members. Party loyalty and competence of members also influence their assignment to committees.

Leadership Committees. The leadership committee in each house is the Rules Committee, chaired by the leader, which administers the rules. This committee acquires additional importance after a specified date in the annual session because all bills are discharged from standing committees and referred to the Rules Committee, which becomes at this point the only committee with authority to introduce bills or to report bills to the floor for action. A large and increasing number of bills are being introduced by the Rules Committee.

The Assembly Ways and Means Committee and the Senate Finance Committee are powerful committees because of their role in formulating and revising appropriation bills. They are "the appropriate committees of the Legislature" referred to by the constitutional amendment establishing the executive budget system, and the head of each state department and agency must furnish simultaneously to these committees copies of their budget requests to the governor.[113] The constitution also provides that upon request of either house "or an appropriate committee thereof," the head of each department must appear before the house or committee during consideration of the budget "to answer inquiries relevant thereto."[114]

The Senate Finance Committee has been assigned the additional function of investigating the nominees of the governor requiring confirmation and reporting findings and recommendations to the Senate.

The oversight role of the fiscal committees is limited by the lack of adequate information on current financial conditions during the course of the year. In a 1978 report, Price Waterhouse & Company stressed that the financial information provided by the executive branch to the legislature is inadequate, as "there is no reporting made to the Legislature apart from that available in the Governor's Budget documents and the mid-year review. The plan presented in the Budget documents is out-of-date before the fiscal year begins, due to changes made by the Legislature to the Governor's recommended appropriations—and a revised version is not provided."[115] The report added that the midyear review is of little value because it contains only a summary of year-end projections. The accuracy of this report is questionable, as an inspection of the midyear summary and the executive budget of the previous January reveal significant differences.

Public Hearings. To gather the views of citizens, organizations, and interested parties, committees hold public hearings in Albany and throughout the state to take testimony. Whereas the hearings on occasion may appear to be a waste of time, they can generate suggestions for the improvement of bills and the introduction of new bills. Furthermore, committee hearings held in different sections of the state perform an educational function by informing the public of state problems and proposed action or actions to remedy the problems. Committees often have stenographic transcripts of important public hearings made, and many transcripts are available in the state library. Other committees tape-record public hearings.

Some public committee hearings may assist a member of the majority party in his reelection bid by providing him with a public forum. In other instances, a public hearing is held by a committee to take local pressure off a member of the majority party experiencing strong constituent pressure by giving the impression that the member is on top of the situation and is instituting remedial action.

Party Organization

Party organization is a prominent feature of the legislature, as party meetings of members in each house elect the leaders and determine whether a party vote will be demanded on certain bills. It is interesting to note that intraparty problems are often greater than interparty problems, since the membership of each party is diverse in terms of both geographical area represented and political philosophy.

Party whips play an important role in the Assembly by assisting the speaker and the minority leader in ensuring that members cast votes when needed on party legislation. By keeping in close contact with members, a whip can keep the speaker or minority leader informed of members' positions in important bills. Whereas the Assembly has had a majority and minority whip for many decades, the positions were not established in the Senate until 1979.

A strong party system in the legislature can strengthen the legislature in its dealings with the governor. In 1960 Frank J. Munger and Ralph A. Straetz wrote that the New York State legislature "possesses a party discipline far superior to that found either in the United States Congress or in all but a few capitals. . . . Consequently, the process of legislation consists of a process of negotiation among the legislative leaders . . . and the Governor."[116]

LEGISLATIVE PROCEDURE

As explained earlier, the state constitution contains procedural requirements relating to the aging of bills, messages of necessity, one-subject bills, two-thirds bills, and three-fifths bills, in addition to stated prohibitions—certain private and local bills, incorporation of existing law by reference, auditing of claims against the state, and the Blaine amendment.[117] The constitution also forbids the amendment of a bill upon its last reading and requires passage of a bill by a majority of the members elected to each house and that "the ayes and nays" on the question of final passage be "entered on the journal."[118]

Each house is free to adopt its own rules of procedure with the exceptions of the constitutional procedural requirements. Rules are adopted at the beginning of a session and usually are the rules of the previous session with minor revisions.

Assembly rules allow the following nonmembers admission to the floor: the governor and lieutenant governor, former members of the Assembly, elected state officers and their deputies, "persons in the exercise of an official duty directly connected with the business of the House," and newsmen designated by the speaker.[119]

Central to the legislative process is the search for compromises acceptable to the major parties and interests when there are sharp differences of opinion on issues. Finding acceptable compromises is exceedingly difficult when issues are emotional and have moral overtones, such as the death penalty for the killing of policemen and medicaid funding of abortions.

Introduction and First Reading

In the contrast to the United States Constitution, the state constitution provides that "any bill may originate in either house of the Legislature, and all bills passed by one house may be amended by the other."[120] The original house, however, must approve the amendment before it becomes effective. Bills may be prefiled after November 15 and introduced by members of either house or multisponsored until the cutoff date for introduction specified in the rules, after which bills may be introduced only by the Rules Committee or, in other words, the leadership.[121] In 1980 the Assembly deadline was March 25 and the Senate deadline was April 21.

Bills may be introduced only by members with the exception of appropriation bills introduced by the governor. In reality, bills have many sources and may be the product of an individual legislator, a committee or subcommittee of either house, the governor, a department of the state government, an interest group, a local government, or an individual citizen. The bulk of the bills introduced by the typical member are of importance chiefly to his constituents.

Former Assemblyman Berle maintained that some legislators will introduce bad bills in response to pressure from constituents, because "this is often easier than telling the constituent or group making demands that the idea for legislation has no merit; that the legislative proposal would embarrass the sponsor if required to defend it in floor debate; or that a legislative solution is totally unconstitutional or beyond the power of the State. The committee then saves the Assemblyman's honor."[122]

Bills of statewide importance tend to be drafted by the Governor's Office, state agencies, legislative leaders, and interest groups. Most bills are drafted by the Legislative Bill Drafting Commission, although the counsel for a department and attorneys employed by interest groups draft proposed legislation in bill form.[123] The leader in each house helps freshmen members of the majority party in their forthcoming bids for reelection by allowing them to sponsor important bills in order to help them establish a record of legislative accomplishments. When the two houses are controlled by different political parties, one-house bills become common, as each house will pass highly partisan bills to place pressure on the other party.

With one exception, all bills are introduced by members and standing committees. The only bill the governor may introduce directly in the legislature is the budget bill or bills.[124] However, bills referred to as the "governor's program bills" are introduced on his behalf by members of the majority party. Bills prepared by departments and not considered important enough to be labeled governor's program bills are introduced by members of the majority party in most instances and are referred to as "department bills."

A "study bill" is one introduced by a sponsor who does not intend to press for its enactment at the current session. The purpose of the study bill is to alert other members, interest groups, and the general public that the sponsor is considering legislation on a given subject and is seeking comments on the study bill. Public committee hearings are held on some study bills for the purpose of gaining input to permit refinement of the bill and its enactment in the following session.

In 1909, 2,893 bills were introduced in the legislature, and the number of bills introduced fluctuated from 3,594 to 4,678 in the period 1930 to 1945. A sharp increase in the number of bills introduced occurred after World War II, rising from 5,200 in 1946 to 6,135 in 1950, to 8,662 in 1960, to 10,916 in 1965, and to 23,426 in

1978. The reader should note that a substantial number of the 1978 bills were carried over from the 1977 session. The output in terms of the number of bills signed into law by the governor has remained relatively constant, varying from 1,002 in 1946 to a high of 1,214 in 1971, but dropping to 895 in 1975 before rising to 982 in 1977 and falling to 819 in 1979. Interestingly, 100 of the 1977 laws dealt with New York City: 65 dealt with the city generally; 25 amended the city's Administrative Code; 2 amended the city charter; 6 amended the City Civil Court Act; and 2 amended the City Criminal Court Act.

The large number of bills introduced is primarily responsible for the $2,546,579 price tag on legislative printing in the biennium 1977–79. In 1980 the cost of 1,500 copies for each single house bill (camera ready copy) was $16.81 per page and $22.26 per page for each "unibill," one introduced simultaneously in each house that carries both an Assembly introductory number and a Senate introductory number. The cost of printing 2,000 copies of appropriation bills is approximately $47 per page. In 1975 the contract cost of printing legislative calendars was $140,000. Calendars have been printed in house since 1976.

Each bill is numbered consecutively as it is introduced in each house. In the Senate the bill is sent to the Introduction and Revision Office where it is examined, corrected if necessary, assigned a number, entered into the Senate computer, deemed to have had its first two readings, printed, and sent to a standing committee. No debate takes place up to this point.

In addition to unibills, other identical bills may be introduced separately in each house, and the *Legislative Record and Index* identifies these bills as being identical even though they were not introduced as unibills. One advantage of unibills is a 50 percent reduction in printing costs, compared with identical bills introduced separately in each house. A second advantage of the unibill is that it eliminates the time-consuming task of comparing two bills to ensure that they are identical in language.

Reference to Committee

After introduction, each bill is referred to an appropriate standing committee that examines and sorts out the bills for approval, amendment, or rejection. Since a bill may fall within the jurisdiction of more than one committee, the power of the speaker and of the Senate temporary president is enhanced, because each can decide the committee of reference. Bills falling within the jurisdiction of a functional committee also are referred to the Ways and Means Committee in the Assembly and the Finance Committee in the Senate if the bills have financial implications. In 1978 an emotionally charged bill requiring parents to be notified prior to a woman under eighteen years of age having an abortion was referred to the Democratic-controlled Ways and Means Committee, which killed the bill by a 13 to 10 vote, reportedly to obviate "the need for another politically damaging veto by Governor Carey."[125] Sponsors and supporters maintained that bill had no fiscal implications.

A committee may, but is not required to, hold a public hearing on each bill. A schedule of forthcoming public hearings by Senate standing committees is available from the Senate Communications Office, a similar schedule is available from the Assembly Information Office. Under rules of each house, a committee may not meet while the house is in session.

The committee's assignment is to examine each bill carefully and report its finding to the house. According to Berle, "a bill is never considered by the Committee unless the sponsor makes a formal written request. Bills which were never intended to be taken seriously by the sponsor can disappear simply if the introducer never requests the Committee to take action upon them. In other situations, sponsors of bills have quietly asked committee members to vote against bills while publicly requesting that the bills be reported."[126]

A committee may take one of several actions: recommend that the bill be: (1) enacted in its present form; (2) enacted with amendments; (3) replaced by a substitute bill (possibly one drafted by the committee); (4) or be pigeonholed—that is, the committee decides to hold the bill for the session, thereby killing it. A majority vote of the house, of course, could force the committee to discharge a bill, but such motions usually fail to win approval. Motions to discharge are used by the minority party to force majority members to vote against a popular bill held in committee for a variety of reasons. To avoid floor debate that might reflect badly upon a bill's sponsor, the Assembly leadership by tradition encourages members to resolve differences in committee.

In an unusual move, the 1975 Assembly Governmental Operations Committee voted to substitute and send to the Ways and Means Committee an identical Republican-sponsored Senate bill creating a separate state agency for mental retardation for a bill sponsored by a Democrat to make it easier for Democrats to vote against the bill, since the governor no longer supported the bill as he had during the 1974 election campaign. The bill was approved by the Assembly but vetoed by the governor.[127] With few exceptions, bills approved by one house are not substituted for bills in the other house until they are ready for floor debate.

The large number of bills referred to the typical committee makes careful analysis of each bill impossible. In consequence, the importance of the chairman is enhanced, and in many instances the appearance is given that the chairman is the committee.

Floor Debate

Once reported out of committee, a bill is placed on the daily calendar, which is the agenda for legislative action. Most Senate bills reported out by committee are placed on the calendar in the "order of first report" section, and advanced to "order of second report" and "order of third report" in the following session days to allow additional time for consideration of the bills. When a bill is on "order of third reading," an identical bill approved by the Assembly may arrive and be substituted for the Senate bill. No debate occurs at these stages in the legislative process. Occasionally, a bill on the order of "special report" with unanimous consent is placed directly on the order of third report and must be acted on that day on third reading or the bill automatically is transferred to the order of first report. When the bill's turn on the order of third report arises, the bill's title and number are read by the clerk in the Senate, and floor debate may take place. If no member objects, the presiding officer will state: "call the roll." On noncontroversial bills, a short roll call is used; that is, the clerk calls the names of the majority and minority leaders, and only the first few and the last few senators on the alphabetical roll call. Should a senator desire to vote no, he may do so by raising a hand. Upon the request of the majority leader or five senators, a slow roll call, involving the calling of the names of all senators, is taken. If a bill is defective or lacks sufficient support for approval, the sponsor may request that the bill be laid aside, returned to committee, or "starred." The majority leader also

can request that a star be placed on a bill, and no action can be
taken until one day after the removal of the star. Starred bills in
the Senate are placed on the Senate starred calendar. The starring
of bills has become a controversial subject, and reform groups generally oppose the practice. However, in many cases starring provides
a type of quality control by providing additional time to perfect
measures.

In the Assembly, bills ordered to a third reading, except una-
mended Senate bills, are sent to the revision and engrossing clerk
to be reprinted incorporating amendments. The Assembly calendar
places most bills in the following groups:

(1) Rules Committee Report—special order of third reading contains
    bills previously reported out by the Rules Committee and advanced
    to third reading.
(2) Rules Committee Report—special order on second and third read-
    ings contains bills that may be considered for second and third
    reading on the first day of the calendar.
(3) Bills on order of second reading may be considered for advancement
    to third reading.
(4) Bills on order of third reading are before the Assembly for final
    passage.
(5) Motions to discharge committee are motions to have bills brought
    to the floor without a favorable committee report. Three days' notice
    is required before the motion to discharge may be made.
(6) Starred bills on order of third reading are bills that sponsors have
    requested that action be deferred on. A starred bill may not be
    considered by the Assembly until one day after the star is removed
    by the sponsor.[128]

Bills reported out of the Assembly Rules Committee are assigned
a rules report number as well as a calendar number. If a bill has
not been on the members' desks for the constitutionally required
three days, the bill will carry an *H*, indicating "high print." When
a Senate bill arrives in the Assembly, the bill is assigned a reception
number (rec. no.) and a calendar number.

The Assembly and the Senate annually consider in excess of
2,000 bills on the floor. Since most bills are of minor importance,
no debate is held, and they are usually approved by voice vote. In
the Assembly each Monday is an "informal" consent calendar day
when only housekeeping and noncontroversial bills are acted upon.

The speaker will say: "Read the last section" and "call the roll." Assembly rules provide that any day can be a consent calendar day. In 1974, 1,462 of the 2,003 bills approved by the Senate were unopposed, and an additional 348 bills were approved with less than 5 negative votes. Even on important bills that are debated, some members sit in the chamber *sub silentio,* and the comments of others are laconic.

To expedite Assembly and Senate action, a fast or short roll call is employed; that is, the clerk calls the names of the majority and minority leaders and the first and last names on the alphabetical roll call list. A member absent from the chamber is voted in the affirmative, as are the present members who have been excused unless they indicate a negative vote by raising a hand to the clerk. In the Assembly, a member's vote is not recorded if he is absent from the chamber on a slow roll call. In the Senate, a member may explain his vote for two minutes on either a fast or a slow roll call. The speaker of the Assembly and the majority leader of the Senate can order the sergeant at arms to lock the doors of the chamber to prevent members from leaving the chamber when an important vote is scheduled and to bring absent members to the chamber.

Warren Moscow reports on the vote on a bill opposed by the speaker:

The clerk, operating on the normally sound theory that a bill that emerges from the Rules Committee is favored by the majority, called the roll and announced the result as ayes 76, nays 49. There were not that many votes in the chamber at the time, but the Democrats did not challenge him. The speaker, however, gave the sign to a majority member, and the legislator duly rose to announce he was changing his vote from aye to nay. Not even that bothered the clerk. Ayes 76, nays 50, he announced as the corrected result. The speaker gave up.[129]

Transcripts of Senate debates since 1960, except the current year, are available from the Senate superintendent of documents at 25 cents per page. A copy of any Senate debate during the current year is available from the Senate Communications Office at 10 cents per page. Transcripts of Assembly debates since 1973 are available through the Assembly Information Office. The status of any bill in the Senate or the Assembly can be obtained by utilizing a toll-free telephone number (1-800-342-9860) to reach the *Senate Journal* clerk's office, where a computer clerk can respond almost instantaneously if the bill number is provided.

Electronic Voting. The use of electronic voting by the Assembly has been a controversial subject. In 1966 the Assembly installed such a voting system, costing $300,000, but the system was abandoned in 1972 because of alleged flaws. Critics of the system of voting in the Assembly pointed out that until 1973 a member could sign in on Monday and leave for the remainder of the week and be voted yes on all noncontroversial bills acted upon during that week. In 1974 the rules were changed to provide that a member must sign in each day, but until 1979 he still could be recorded as voting yes while absent from the chamber.

Reform groups pressured the Assembly to reintroduce electronic voting, and Assembly Speaker Stanley Steingut had an "electronic attendance system" designed, which is referred to as the "member attendance recording system." Under the system introduced in 1979, each member is required to punch his or her member identification card in and out of a card reader at the two entrances to the chamber. On a fast roll call, a member desiring to vote no has to signal the clerk, who pushes a button to record a negative vote rather than the automatic yes vote that otherwise would be recorded. Members absent from the chamber are recorded as absent, but the majority leader and the minority leader each has a mini-computer (Termiflex) used to keep a record of members absent with a valid reason, such as the conduct of negotiations on a bill.

Republican Assemblyman Clark C. Wemple criticized the new system because "a leader could tell someone he can leave and forget about punching out," and he added that a simple rule requiring members to notify the clerk when leaving the chamber would be a better system.[130] Democratic Assemblyman Roland Kidder believes that such an honor system would prove unworkable, and a true electronic attendance and voting system would cost an additional $600,000 and invite abuse: "Speaker Steingut observed such a system in the California Legislature and noticed that one guy was punching the buttons for himself and four other legislators who were absent."[131]

Action by the Other House

The procedural steps involving the approval of a bill in the second house are identical except for minor variations with the steps in the first house. Should the second house approve the bill in the same form as the first house, the bill is transmitted to the governor for his action. One should note, however, that one house may request the other house to return a bill, as in 1979 when the Assembly recalled forty-four bills from the Senate and the latter recalled ninety-four bills from the former.

The 1777 constitution contained a provision for a conference committee in the event a bill passed each house in a different form, but this provision was dropped by the 1821 constitution.[132] Ad hoc conference committees have been used since 1822 both to determine dates for joint meetings and vacations and to develop joint bills and recommendations.

Since conference committees are not used to reconcile differences in bills passed by the two houses, a bill approved by one house and amended by the other house is returned to the first house for concurrence in the amendment. If the first house refuses to adopt the amendment and the second house insists upon the amendment, the bill is dead for that session. Common Cause in 1977 recommended the adoption of the conference committee device, and in 1978 agreement was reached to use the device. Each committee is established on an ad hoc basis by a joint resolution of each house or by the concurrent action of the speaker and the temporary president of the Senate to consider each pair of similar bills. At least five members of each house serve on a conference committee, and the minority party constitutes 25 percent of each house's membership. A sponsor, but not necessarily the prime sponsor, and a chairman of a committee having jurisdiction in each house is included in the membership of each conference committee. No report can be filed with each house except on an affirmative vote of the majority of members of each house, which means that a cross-over majority is not allowed.

Legislation by Fatigue

To the casual observer, the pace of lawmaking appears to be leisurely until the end of the session when an all-night meeting is held at which hundreds of bills, including many that have not been printed, are rushed through each house. In 1959, for example, 508 bills were passed during the last three days of the annual session. Critics maintain that legislation by fatigue means that a trio—the governor, the speaker, and the Senate president pro tempore—determine the bills to be enacted into law.

What the casual observer fails to see is the study of bills by legislators and committees throughout the session, public hearings held by committees, and conferences with interest groups and constituents. The process of seeking public input is time consuming yet essential if hasty and ill-considered legislation is to be avoided and an opportunity for citizen input is to be provided. Unfortunately, long-drawn-out sessions with little public action taken until the approach of adjournment when action becomes hectic does not promote public confidence in the legislature as an institution.

A front-page story in the *Albany Knickerbocker News* described the nineteen-hour finale of the 1976 session in the following terms:

At 12:15 this morning, two Assemblymen literally busted their way out of the chamber. They kicked the glass doors and screamed and finally the guards unlocked the doors.

But that was not the end.

They had been at it more than 12 hours non-stop at that point.

Assemblymen Peter Mirto and Louis DeSalvio, both New York City Democrats, couldn't take it any longer.

"Let me out, let me out," screamed Mirto.

"We're not kids," shouted DeSalvio, who often is in charge of the Assembly from the speaker's chair.

Once they had frightened the guards into unlocking the doors, it was as if a dam had burst. The lawmakers streamed out into the hallways, which smelled now like locker rooms after nine straight days of session, and the session had to stand at ease.[133]

The same article reported that a few members ripped the film from a photographer's camera who later nearly was ejected from the chamber a second time "when somebody did not like the picture he was taking of another dozer."[134] A 1977 headline was entitled "Mass Confusion Reigns in Legislature as Session Nears End."[135] The hectic pace of the end of the session leads to occasional clerical errors. In 1976, for example, the legislature sent the wrong version of a bill to the governor because a "bleary-eyed clerk at the Assembly desk had apparently neglected to put the 'B-print' amendment inside the manila folder containing the 'A-print.'"[136]

The Assembly has a rule limiting a session to a maximum of

eight hours a day, and occasionally an assemblyman will invoke the rule and force a recess until the next day. The eight-hour rule, however, is nullified on the last legislative day of the session because the clock is stopped. Two or three calendar days may pass, yet it is still the same legislative day. Although there is no constitutional limit on the length of the legislative session, leaders of the two houses agree upon a date and time for adjournment, which is established by resolution. By stopping the clock, no bill can be introduced because of the constitutional "aging" requirement unless the governor sends a message of necessity to the legislature, which he does only at the request of the leaders of the two houses. In effect, the governor, the speaker, and the temporary president of the Senate control the agenda relative to new bills during the end of the session.

Former Senate Secretary Albert J. Abrams offers an explanation for late-night sessions in terms of the collective-bargaining function of the legislature: "We are like a school board which can't come to an agreement with a teachers union until 4 a.m., when everybody is exhausted and ready to give in."[137]

Gubernatorial Action

Every bill that passes both the Assembly and the Senate in the same form must be presented to the governor for his action prior to becoming law,[138] with one exception. An appropriation bill submitted by him, "when passed by both houses [shall] be a law immediately without further action by the Governor, except that appropriations for the legislature and judiciary and separate items added to the Governor's bills by the Legislature shall be subject to his approval."[139]

The governor has ten days, excluding Sundays, to act upon a bill. Should he take no action during this period, the bill automatically becomes law unless the legislature by adjournment prevents the governor from returning a bill to the house of origin with his objections, in which instance the bill is pocket-vetoed if the bill is not signed by the governor during the thirty-day postadjournment consideration period. The first memorandum of approval was issued by Governor William L. Marcy in 1837.[140] Whereas only 180 such memoranda had been issued prior to 1900, Governor Herbert H. Lehman issued 178 in 1936 and Governor Nelson A. Rockefeller issued 256 in 1960.[141]

Governor Horatio Seymour in 1863 was the first governor to render a veto during the then ten-day postadjournment period. In 1874 voters amended the constitution by granting the governor a thirty-day bill-signing period following adjournment of the legislature, because governors had not been acting on the bills promptly.[142] A bill becomes effective on the twentieth day after the bill becomes law unless the bill specifies a different date.[143]

Governors usually do not make public announcements of their intention to veto bills being considered by the legislature. Governor Carey, however, on several occasions announced his intention to veto any bill restoring the death penalty or legalizing the use of laetrile by adult cancer patients. Governor Lehman abandoned the practice of holding postsession hearings on bills.[144]

In the typical year, the governor vetoes approximately one fourth of the bills reaching his desk, (explained in Chapter VII). Governor Rockefeller in 1959 started the commendable practice of writing a memorandum on each bill he disallowed giving the reason or reasons for the disallowance, with the result that the pocket veto is no longer exercised.

Senate Majority Leader Warren M. Anderson in 1973 expressed concern relative to vetoes he described as "ill-advised and over-technical," and he introduced a new system in odd-numbered years under which each member can introduce up to five vetoed bills commencing thirty days subsequent to the governor's postadjournment bill consideration period.[145] Previously, a vetoed bill could not be reintroduced until November 15, whereas a bill not acted upon carried over automatically to the next session.

The Item Veto. The item veto, the right of the governor to disallow items in appropriation bills,[146] was a most important power of the governor until the enactment of the constitutional amendment providing for the executive budget[147] and continued to be relatively important until 1943. The item veto has decreased in importance, since the legislature usually is reluctant to add to the items in the governor's budget. Governor Thomas E. Dewey, for example, did not use the item veto until 1947, when he disapproved one item because the symbols indicated a position was not in the exempt class of the civil service when the position was and a second item because the item was not in the proper form.[148]

An Absolute Veto? It appeared that the governor's veto power had become an absolute one, since no veto of a bill had been overridden by the legislature from 1872 until 1976 when the Stavisky-Goodman law (described in Chapter III) was passed over the veto of Governor Carey.[149] There is no evidence, however, that the legislature often will override a gubernatorial veto even though since 1976 the legislature has possessed the authority to call itself into extraordinary session for the purpose of attempting to override vetoes.[150]

Reintroduction of Vetoed Bills. What happens to vetoed bills? Are they reintroduced in identical form in the following session, or are they reintroduced with amendments? Or does the veto end the attempt to enact the bill? All three possibilities occur. Some bills are reintroduced in identical form; others are amended in an attempt to meet the governor's objections; and still others are not reintroduced.

Relative to thirty-four of forty-eight bills vetoed in 1976 as unconstitutional, defective, or unnecessary, twenty-four were not reintroduced. The sponsors of four bills retired from the legislature or were defeated in their reelection bids.[151] With respect to nine bills disallowed on constitutional grounds, only two were reintroduced. The others were not reintroduced because the sponsor could not amend the bills to make them constitutional or did not wish to go against the views of the governor, or an interest group did not want the bill submitted to the governor again. None of the eight bills vetoed on ground of lack of necessity was reintroduced. One sponsor felt that after three tries he should give up.

Nine of the seventeen measures vetoed as technically defective were not refiled in the 1977 session. Interestingly, a bill to create an interdepartmental tourist advisory council—New York State Board of Tourism Commissioners—was vetoed in 1976 but was reintroduced with an amendment by another sponsor, passed the legislature, and was signed into law by Governor Carey.[152]

Three technically deficient bills were approved by the 1977 legislature and vetoed by the governor. A fourth bill vetoed in 1976 was repassed by the 1977 legislature and sent to the governor. However, the bill (A-5405) was recalled from the governor's desk by the Assembly because of objections by Orthodox Jewish organizations to the bill's provisions relative to the disposition, autopsy, and dissection of cadavers. The bill was recalled too late in the session for amendment and resubmission to the governor.

Recall of Bills. The bills forwarded to the governor by the legislature vary in complexity, with a number being extremely complex. Whenever the governor's counsel determines that his staff will be unable to analyze during the forthcoming ten days all bills received, the counsel requests that the Assembly or the Senate recall a number of bills, thereby breaking the ten-day consideration period. When the bills are returned to the governor by the Assembly or the Senate, the ten-day consideration period commences again. The practice of the recall is an old one. In 1913, for example, seventy-four bills were recalled for corrections. The governor, instead of vetoing a bill during the session, on occasion has suggested that the sponsor or sponsors arrange to have the bill recalled to allow the legislature to amend the bill by removing or modifying the provisions found objectionable by the governor. A few sponsors do not agree to suggested amendments because they were opposed to the bills—especially claims bills for constituents—and wanted them vetoed or were opposed philosophically to the suggested changes.

Table I reveals that most bills are recalled only once, although one bill was recalled three times in 1939, 1963, 1966, 1968, and 1976; and three bills were recalled three times in 1977. The largest number of recalled bills sponsored by one legislator—Senator John E. Flynn—involved twenty-eight bills dealing with the age of majority, which were recalled because the governor wanted to sign the bills on the same day, and he did sign the bills on June 15, 1975.[153]

A most interesting recall occurred in 1971 when A. 945—repealing authorization for the Metropolitan Transportation Authority to construct the Rye–Oyster Bay Bridge over Long Island Sound—was approved by the legislature on April 21, presented to the Governor on May 24, recalled by the Assembly on June 3, and returned on June 4 to the governor, who immediately vetoed the bill. Plaintiffs in the court action involving the bill produced evidence that the *Assembly Journal* was "inaccurate since no motion was made to recall the bill either by the sponsor who had introduced the bill and who was the only person authorized under Assembly Rules to make a motion to recall it."[154] The complaint was dismissed by the court, which ruled "there is no cogent authority that in view

TABLE VI.I BILLS RECALLED FROM GOVERNOR'S DESK STATE OF NEW YORK 1932–1980

Year	Total Recalled	Recalled by Senate	Recalled by Assembly	Recalled Once	Recalled Twice	Recalled Returned Law	Recalled Amended Returned Law	Recalled and No Further Action	Recalled Amended and No Further Action	Recalled Amended Returned Vetoed	Recalled Returned Vetoed
1932	18	6	12	17	1	6	6	0	0	1	5
1933	34	17	17	32	2	9	10	6	5	0	4
1934	38	13	25	34	4	9	12	1	3	4	9
1935	78	45	33	77	1	28	10	8	2	2	27
1936	54	25	29	54	0	9	26	9	1	1	8
1937	47	28	19	43	4	2	21	8	8	1	7
1938	35	20	15	34	1	8	8	7	2	2	8
1939*	75	28	47	69	5	24	32	7	0	2	10
1940	39	22	17	38	1	4	10	7	2	3	13
1941	45	22	23	43	2	11	18	7	1	1	7
1942	51	25	26	51	0	13	21	4	3	1	9
1943	26	12	14	26	0	5	9	8	1	1	2
1944	31	17	14	31	0	6	14	7	2	0	2
1945	40	11	29	39	1	8	8	15	0	1	8
1946	52	22	30	50	2	4	12	25	3	1	7
1947	26	17	9	26	0	1	4	14	0	1	6
1948	39	24	15	38	1	3	10	17	1	5	3
1949	111	43	68	110	1	10	26	41	5	3	26
1950	62	33	29	61	1	12	15	19	0	4	12
1951	41	28	13	40	1	6	11	13	1	0	10
1952	46	28	18	46	0	2	10	18	8	3	5
1953	27	16	11	27	0	3	7	12	0	2	3
1954	33	22	11	33	0	5	10	15	2	0	1

Year											
1955	38	18	20	37	1	7	13	9	2	3	4
1956	25	11	14	25	0	6	6	7	2	1	3
1957	30	15	15	30	0	8	12	6	1	0	3
1958	66	31	35	65	1	32	28	20	1	7	7
1959	71	35	36	70	1	10	19	25	1	9	7
1960	82	45	37	80	2	5	36	27	2	7	5
1961	64	26	38	63	1	9	32	16	3	3	1
1962	107	57	50	105	2	17	30	37	5	7	11
1963*	66	25	41	63	2	8	28	18	5	3	4
1964	39	16	23	38	1	2	9	19	3	4	2
1965	144	81	63	141	3	9	42	68	9	11	5
1966*	288	144	144	260	27	85	73	51	25	10	44
1967	90	56	34	90	0	6	29	37	6	4	8
1968*	152	91	61	146	5	24	52	27	26	13	10
1969	77	42	35	77	0	5	30	30	6	4	2
1970	109	49	60	108	1	35	22	24	10	9	9
1971	90	49	41	84	6	20	27	14	1	4	24
1972	37	13	24	37	0	9	19	6	0	0	3
1973	75	34	41	70	5	16	26	13	1	2	17
1974	138	82	56	130	8	74	31	13	0	1	19
1975	78	40	38	71	7	19	15	22	0	0	1
1976*	134	63	71	112	20	54	22	39	0	1	18
1977*	160	69	91	126	26	81	35	22	0	5	17
1978	65	28	37	58	5	11	19	35	5	0	4
1979	67	32	35	64	3	10	12	33	4	1	7
1980	88	51	37	81	7	48	9	12			12
Total	2131	1128	1118	1912	117	464	598	588	112	99	230

SOURCE: *New York Legislative Record and Index* (Albany: The Legislative Index Company, 1932–80).

* One bill was recalled three times in 1939, 1963, 1966, 1968, and 1976. One bill (S. 9353) was recalled four times in 1976. Six bills were recalled three times in 1977, and two bills were recalled three times in 1978.

of the official status accorded such journals, parol [oral] evidence may not be received to impeach the accuracy of the entries therein."[155] The court held that the sponsor should have sought action by the Assembly to correct its *Journal*.

Although the recall of bills provides added flexibility in the legislative process by allowing the correction of errors, thereby preventing the sponsor from being embarrassed and adoption of amendments to meet rapidly changing conditions, a basic political question is raised by the use of the recall of bills that is an extraconstitutional method for resolving differences between the legislature and the governor. If a bill is undesirable for any reason, is it preferable for the governor to veto it, thereby informing the public of the defect(s) of the bill? Does close executive-legislative cooperation in the form of the recall deprive the public of the protection inherent in a system of checks and balances? Among other things, the recall obviously affords interest groups another opportunity to amend or kill certain bills. The recall of bills from the governor's desk and killing them in the Assembly or the Senate excludes the public from knowledge of defects in the bills and the action taken by the governor to prevent their enactment, as the *Journals* of the two houses do not reveal the reason(s) why a bill was recalled.

Public understanding of the legislative process is not facilitated by the recall of bills, since it is difficult for citizens to understand how a bill passed by the Assembly and the Senate and not vetoed by the governor fails to become a law. Furthermore, it is difficult for citizens to determine the location in the legislative process of a bill that may be of great importance to them. And one must not overlook the contribution of the recall to the end-of-the-session logjam.

Legislative-Gubernatorial Cooperation. Another example of the legislature's cooperation with the governor is the agreement between the Senate and the governor's counsel that a specified number of bills, randomly selected, will be forwarded to the governor on each Thursday during the session, thereby allowing the governor an extra day to consider the bills, since the ten-day consideration period will extend over two Sundays, which are not included in the official ten days. A related example of cooperation on the part of the legislature is the purposeful delay in sending particular bills to the governor until the end of the session, thereby making them thirty-day bills.

Emergency Spending in the Interim.   Recognizing the fact that an emergency may necessitate the expenditure of funds when the legislature is not in session, the State Finance Law authorizes the governor to issue a certificate of allocation from the governmental emergency fund upon issuance of a certificate of intent to recommend an appropriation at the next session of the legislature signed by the temporary president of the Senate, the speaker of the Assembly, and the chairmen of the Assembly Ways and Means Committee and the Senate Finance Committee.[156]

Financial Disclosure and Code of Ethics

The first laws enacted to ensure that public officials and employees act in accordance with high moral standards were conflict-of-interest laws dealing with black-and-white situations in which overt unethical conduct—such as embezzlement—is recognized by the overwhelming majority of citizens. To promote integrity in office and ensure that private interests do not benefit unfairly from governmental operations, conflict-of-interest statutes forbid public officials and employees from using confidential information for their private benefit, require competitive public bidding on most government contracts, prohibit public officials and employees from acting as agents or attorneys in the sale of land to the government, forbid the offering of bribes to public officials and the acceptance of bribes, and make it illegal for suppliers to offer and public officials to request or accept commissions or bonuses from suppliers.[157]

Building upon the older conflict-of-interest laws, the legislature enacted a financial disclosure law requiring each member and employee of the legislature annually to file with the secretary of the Senate or clerk of the Assembly a written statement listing:

(1) each financial interest, direct or indirect of himself, his spouse, and his unemancipated children under the age of eighteen years in any activity which is subject to the jurisdiction of a regulatory agency or name of the entity in which the interest is had and whether such interest is over or under five thousand dollars in value.

(2) every office and directorship held by him in any corporation, firm, or enterprise which is subject to the jurisdiction of a regulatory agency, including the name of such corporation, firm, or enterprise.

(3) any other interest or relationship which he determines in his discretion might reasonably be expected to be particularly affected by legislative action or in the public interest should be disclosed.[158]

Outright dishonesty is only one facet of the problem of unethical conduct in a society that is becoming increasingly complex. Recognizing the impossibility anticipating every conceivable ethical question that may arise, the legislature enacted a Code of Ethics containing standards and guidelines for dealing with actions by members of the legislature and public employees in situations falling in the gray area between what clearly is ethical behavior and outright unethical behavior, and providing sanctions for the violations of the standards.[159] In addition, the legislature has enacted "sunshine" laws opening meetings and officials records to the public that seek to promote high ethical standards by making public the actions of members of the legislature and its employees.[160]

Lobbies

No discussion of the enactment of legislation would be complete without reference to lobbies, the so-called third House of the legislature, and their supplications. Although the 1937 Assembly adopted a rule barring lobbyists from the floor of the chamber,[161] lobbyists continued to work closely with committees, as Warren Moscow reported in 1948:

In Washington a stink is occasionally raised over the fact that some lobbyist has sat in with a congressional committee and participated in the drafting of a bill. In Albany it is done all the time and no one gets excited about it. The politically sophisticated members of the state Legislature see no harm in it, and if not done *sub rosa,* it really isn't wrong. After all, any good lobbyist knows more about the affairs of the industry or pressure group he represents than the members of the Legislature possibly could.[162]

Writing twenty-six years later, Assemblyman Berle maintained that "the good legislator can use input from lobbyists to help his decision making process. The danger a legislator faces if he makes decisions solely by hearing arguments from opposing lobbyists is that he will not get a balanced view. Until recently, whole classes of people—consumers, poor people, blind people, and the like had no lobbyists."[163]

In 1973 Speaker Pro Tempore Louis F. DeSalvio, a thirty-eight-year member of the Assembly, stated that "there was a time when lobbyists would try to give you a left-handed deal, try to persuade you to vote for legislation by any means possible. Now I can count on a lobbyist to tell me the truth and in fact I can use them to help background an issue."[164] One should not conclude, however, that certain interest groups lack political power or influence today. In 1976, for example, the harness-racing lobby succeeded in having returned to an Assembly committee a bill requiring harness race-tracks to pay the salaries of starters, judges, and other officials whose salaries currently are paid by the state.[165]

Responsibility for the regulation of lobbying had been vested in the secretary of state when a Temporary State Commission on Lobbying was created in 1977[166] (discussed in more detail in Chapter V). Secretary of State Mario M. Cuomo in 1977 maintained that "lobbying laws are not popular with most office holders: They are regarded by many as a nuisance and an embarrassment. They inevitably irritate some powerful and politically important interest groups. As a result, real reform in the past has been regularly shunned and, when necessary, vigorously resisted by those whose activities it would regulate."[167] Lobbyists reported receiving more than $4 million in fees and payments in 1980, but the real total undoubtedly is considerably higher.

Lobbying can be a legitimate and useful part of the legislative process. However, disclosure of the activities of lobbies is essential if public confidence in the legislature as an institution is to be maintained. Citizens have a right to know how special interests attempt to influence legislation, and lobbying disclosure laws are designed to provide such information.

Carol Greenwald reports that 110 of the 261 organizations registered in 1973 with the New York secretary of state "were represented by professional lobbyists" and that the docket "is heavily weighted towards state regulated industries such as banking, insurance, gambling, nursing homes, drug companies, and highway vehicle business. These businesses and similar interests in the health, welfare, and professional fields created a study core of annual registrants."[168] Lobbyists representing different segments of an industry occasionally clash with each other. In the 1976 session, for example, the savings banks succeeded in obtaining legislative approval for the banks to offer checking accounts, a bill bitterly opposed by the commercial banks.

Perhaps indicative of the strength of volunteer firemen is the fact the first bill approved by the 1977 legislature incorporated a Firemen's Benevolent Association for the members of the Wallkill Hook, Ladder, and Hose Company in the town of Shawangunk in Ulster County. The bill was approved without debate in both houses and signed by the governor.[169] A Firemen's Benevolent Association has been authorized by the State Insurance Law since 1909 to levy and collect a 2 percent tax on fire insurance policies written in its district by insurance companies with headquarters in other states, and the proceeds can be utilized "for the promotion of fraternal intercourse" among members.[170] Assemblyman Maurice D. Hinchey, cosponsor of the bill, was quoted as saying, "it's an easy way for a legislator to do a bit of a favor."[171]

The issues attracting interest groups to the state capitol are many and varied. In recent years an increasing number of nonbusiness and nonprofessional groups have lobbied extensively on such issues as dog licensing and abortion. The issue of medicaid funding of abortions is an extremely emotional one that presents a serious problem for many legislators. Historically, the legislature avoided issues such as abortion and divorce. Right to Life groups appear to be gaining strength and in 1978 succeeded in holding up adoption of the executive budget until an agreement was reached to have a separate bill barring medicaid funding of abortions introduced and voted upon.

Special-interest groups frequently are contributors to legislative elections campaigns. In his 1976 reelection campaign, Chairman Leonard Silverman of the Assembly Insurance Committee received $3,250 in contributions from the insurance industry.[172] Chairman George A. Cincotta of the Assembly Banking Committee in the same year received $10,000 in campaign contributions from savings banks—close to 40 percent of his campaign expenses.[173] The assemblyman was the sponsor of the 1976 bill granting savings banks the right to maintain checking accounts for customers.

A number of lobbyists privately complain that they are taken advantage of by some legislators. One lobbyist was quoted as stating that "being on the list of lobbyists circulated among legislators, I'm hit up for everything—including a baptism in Buffalo at 50 bucks a throw."[174]

Students of the legislative process tend to concentrate on the activities of private-interest groups, completely overlooking the effective lobbying for and against the passage of bills by high-level state administrators. Reference was made earlier to the governor's program bills and department bills that have high executive branch priority. Executive branch lobbyists tend to be highly skilled, and their advice often is prized by legislators. These lobbyists can arrange publicity articles for legislators in agency newsletters and help to solve constituent problems.

PROFESSIONAL STAFF AND MEMBER SERVICES

Historically, the state legislature had few full-time employees. The growing complexity of state problems in the twentieth century and the sharp increase in the number of bills introduced necessitated the enlargement of the number of full-time employees. In 1948 Moscow wrote:

The Legislature has had unnecessary employees, who came to Albany just once a month to draw their pay. This was particularly true when the Republicans were out of power in the state and nation and needed a little legislative payroll padding to eke out their county patronage requirements. The Democrats winked and took a minority share.[175]

Criticisms of no-shows or sinecurists continues, but fewer complaints are heard today.[176]

The budget of the state legislature increased from $32.8 million in 1973–74 to $49.7 million in 1978–79, reflecting in large measure increased professional staffing but also the impact of inflation. The Assembly and the Senate currently employ approximately 2,200 individuals and 1,300 individuals, respectively. The executive budget for fiscal 1981 recommended $24,702,760 for the Senate, $34,091,740 for the Assembly, and $7,172,920 for joint operations— a total of $65,967,420.[177] The actual amount expended will exceed this figure because of reappropriations of funds from the previous fiscal year and additional spending authorized by the deficiency and supplemental budgets.

One of the most important legislative developments, commencing in the 1960s, was the significant expansion of the professional negotiatory, policy developmental, policy audit, and public relations staff paid on a scale equivalent to their counterparts in the executive branch. The New York State legislature was ranked number two in the nation in 1971 by the Citizens' Conference on State Legislatures, in part because of the depth of staff resources of the legislature.[178] While a professionally competent staff will not ensure that the legislature will act responsibly in considering proposed legislation, there probably would be fewer quality bills approved without the professiional input of staff members. Each house determines the staffing for each committee and subcommittee. In practice, the speaker of the Assembly assigns staff to the committees.

Legislative Bill Drafting Commission

The Legislative Bill Drafting Commission—composed of three commissioners, including a chairman, appointed by the president pro tempore of the Senate and speaker of the Assembly and a deputy commissioner appointed by the chairman—must be credited with reducing the percentage of bills introduced that contain technical defects or constitutional infirmities.[179] In addition to drafting and assisting in the drafting of bills, resolutions, and proposed constitutional amendments, the commission advises sponsors of bills on the constitutionality, effect, and consistency of the bills. The commission has a year-round staff of approximately 100 supplemented by an additional 30 to 50 during the session.

Chapter VII contains data on the number of bills disallowed by the governor annually because they contain defective provisions or are unconstitutional. Disallowance of these bills cannot be blamed on the commission, as it does not draft all bills and lacks the staff to check the constitutionality of all bills. Furthermore, the legislature may decide to enact a bill of doubtful constitutionality in order to allow the governor or the courts to settle the issue.

The texts of all New York State laws are stored in computer data banks, and in 1975 a decision was made to computerize the process of bill drafting, thereby eliminating the need to retype and reprint an old law that is being amended. Prior to the placement of the laws in computer data banks, clerks had to check the entire body of laws manually to locate provisions that would be affected by a bill. As a consequence, the cost of bill drafting and printing reportedly was cut by nearly 50 percent.

Fiscal Committees' Staff

The Assembly Ways and Means Committee and the Senate Finance Committee each has a staff of approximately two-score professional budget analysts and economists. The professional staffs of these committees have enabled them to play a more significant role in the appropriation process than had been anticipated by the drafters of the executive budget amendment to the constitution in the 1920s.

Because of the expertise of the staff and its knowledge, members of the committees rely heavily upon the staff for advice. Although the most difficult problems are resolved by negotiations between the governor and speaker and the Senate pro tempore, the fiscal staff still influences the final decisions because they do the analyses and provide the basic information.

Standing Committees' Staff

The Assembly in 1980 had thirty standing committees with thirty subcommittees, and three task forces with funds to employ staff. The Senate in 1980 had twenty-six standing committees, with ten subcommittees, and a Task Force on Critical State Problems. Each standing committee has staff, and not surprisingly the quality of the staff varies from committee to committee.

The New York State Bar Association in a 1975 report was critical of standing committees on the ground that most "have concentrated more on the routine processing of bills than on major decision-making responsibilities in their substantive areas. They are virtually dormant most of the year despite recent steps to increase the activities of committees when the Legislature is not in session."[180] The association rates the legislative leadership highly but adds that "the result has been a by-passing of much of the committee system leading to the failure of many committees to develop adequate expertise, initiate major legislative programs, and exercise effective review over the proposals and operations of the Executive Branch."[181]

Law Revision Commission

Created in 1934, the Law Revision Commission has five members appointed by the governor for five-year terms and four ex officio members—chairmen of the judiciary and codes committees in each house.[182] The commission is charged with the duty of examining the statutes of the state and judicial decisions to discover defective, antiquated, and inequitable provisions and reporting findings annually to the legislature no later than February 1.

The Legislative Library

Composed of a librarian and assistants appointed by the president pro tempore of the Senate and the Speaker of the Assembly, the Legislative Library in the Capitol is open throughout the year to assist members of the legislature and their staffs by providing factual information.

Public Relations Staff

A relatively recent development is the creation of a large public relations staff in each house. Until 1973, the public relations staff of the legislature was small and produced so-called canned press releases containing space for a member to insert his or her name. With a current staff of approximately 100 and supported by cameras, radio, and television equipment, the staff produces millions of copies of newsletters and radio and television tapes for members.[183] No newsletters are produced during the thirty-day period preceding a primary or general election because of the fine line between informing the public and electioneering. In fiscal 1978, $119,000 was appropriated for radio and television services.

Whereas the Senate has only a Communications Office, three separate public relations staffs exist in the Assembly. One is the Communications Office whose function is to publicize the accomplishments of the majority party by preparing newsletters, press releases, and radio tapes. The minority party also has its own Communications Office. In addition, legislative leaders, including many committee chairmen, also have a public information officer.

A 1976 report by a consulting firm quoted a former director of the Assembly's Communications Office as stating that the office was "a communication section to serve the majority member," but the

Assembly's director of administration and operations maintained that assemblymen of both parties were served equally and that he had received no complaints from minority Republicans.[184]

Scientific Staff

According recognition to the role that science and technology can play in helping the legislature solve complex problems, the legislature by concurrent resolution in 1963 created the Science Advisory Council consisting of fifteen members representing the scientific community appointed by the temporary president of the Senate and the speaker of the Assembly.[185] In existence for only two years, the council avoided partisan entanglements even though it reported to the leaders of the legislature, and the council's abolition was the product of the Democratic party gaining control of the legislature in 1965. Professor James E. Underwood of Union College concluded that the council's decision to remain aloof from the regular committees was a major factor in the decision to terminate the council.[186]

Six years later with the Assembly under Republican control, the Assembly scientific staff—composed of three professional scientists, a research and administrative assistant, and two secretaries—was created by the speaker.[187] The assigned duty of the scientific staff was to provide pertinent scientific and technical information for use in the deliberative process of the Assembly. An estimated 5 to 20 percent of the bills considered by the Assembly "have significant technical ramifications depending on definitions,"[188] but there is no evidence that the staff provided information on all of these bills.

In 1979 the staff was merged with the Legislative Commission on Energy Systems to form the Legislative Commission on Science and Technology.

Legislative Commission on Expenditure Review

The twelve members of the bipartisan commission are designated by office: the temporary president of the Senate, the speaker and the majority leader of the Assembly, the chairman of the Senate Majority Conference, the minority leaders of each house, the chairmen of the Assembly Ways and Means Committee and the Senate

Finance Committee, the ranking minority members of both fiscal committees, and two nonlegislative appointees.[189] The chairmanship of the commission rotates annually between the chairman of the Assembly Ways and Means Committee and the chairman of the Senate Finance Committee. The commission's professional staff is hired by the director, who serves at the pleasure of the commission.

As of the beginning of 1980, seventy audits of programs had been published by the commission, including consumer milk protection, criminal justice information systems, fish and wildlife research, marital conciliation, middle-income housing, Department of Transportation real estate program, solid waste management, Boards of Cooperative Educational Services, workmen's compensation for state employees, computers in New York State government, and health planning in New York State. The audits seek to determine the extent to which the administering agencies comply with legislative intent, the efficiency with which resources are being utilized, and the effectiveness of the agencies in achieving programmatic goals. Since the commission only reports its findings and does not make recommendations, the measurement of the effectiveness of its program audits is a difficult task, especially in view of the plethora of other variables influencing executive and legislative decisions relative to programs subsequent to the audits. Nevertheless, there is evidence that the commission's reports are read carefully by the audited agencies and key legislative committees.[190]

LEGISLATIVE REFORM

Critics of state legislatures have advanced numerous reform proposals over the years. Writing in 1935, former Governor Alfred E. Smith maintained that "vast changes" had occurred in legislative procedure since he was a member of the Assembly early in the century and added:

In those early days, . . . the Legislature would spend hours, even days, in debating the state appropriation bill. . . . In recent years, and particularly since the Executive Budget system has been in effect, only a handful of men in the Legislature . . . knows anything about the appropriation bill.

These are the members of the Finance Committee. Once reported from the Committee, the bill seems to pass automatically. This is because the party members have reposed enough confidence in their representatives on the Finance Committees to abide by their decision on the bill.[191]

Today, party caucuses keep members informed on the major issues, and debates take place in the caucuses. Smith also argued that legislators spent too much "time discussing inconsequential matters which could better be handled by the various commissions and departments of the state."[192] Some observers disagree with Smith, pointing out that the relatively late approval of appropriation bills results from time-consuming negotiations with individual legislators to meet their needs in order to gain their support of the bills.

Reform of the Rules

Proposals have been advanced in recent years to amend the rules of each house to reduce the powers of the leaders, provide greater public access to the legislative process, and improve legislative ethics.

The 1975 Assembly made a number of rule changes, including the elimination of the power of the power of the speaker to star bills—terminate action on a bill until the star is removed—and in some instances kill them for the session; publication of committee agendas a week in advance of meetings; and guaranteeing sponsors the right to have recorded votes in committees. It is interesting to note that Humphrey S. Tyler wrote in 1975 that "as the session drew to a close, Steingut retrieved these prerogatives and ran the lower house much as it had been in the past. He controlled the daily calendar, deciding which bills would be called up for consideration. He ordered committee chairmen to kill or report out bills. And, he managed the machinery that produced unread bills at the last minute and forced their passage."[193]

In 1977 the Citizens Union urged a change in Assembly rules to require "the ratification by the Majority Conference of the Speaker's appointments to Committee Chairmanships and other leadership positions. Allowing the Majority Conference to reject appointments (by secret ballot on a position-by-position basis) would help to democratize the decision-making process."[194] Also recommended was "*a speedy implementation of electronic voting* that would end empty chair voting. At present, members may have voted 'FOR' a particular bill on a short roll call even though they are not in the Assembly chamber."[195] The Senate in 1975 ended "empty-chair" voting and in 1974 adopted a rule providing for publication of committee agendas one week in advance of meetings.

The 1975 Assembly authorized sponsors to require that their bills be voted on at a committee meeting, and the Citizens Union in 1977 urged the Senate to adopt a similar rule and a second rule eliminating the power of the majority leader to star bills.[196]

Oversight of Administration

The legislature plays an important role in the administrative process and frequently makes reference to the need for greater legislative oversight of administration, since major policy laws typically are "skeleton" laws outlining a general policy and authorizing an executive agency to issue implementing rules and regulations detailing the general policy, because the agency is in a position to respond faster to changing conditions and to make adjustments for special situations. In drafting, adopting, and implementing rules and regulations, administrative agencies must comply with the State Administrative Procedures Act.[197] Administrative rulemaking is increasing, and the number of rules issued between 1961 and 1977 rose 240 percent.[198] The detailing power, however, can be abused by executive agencies acting as "mini-legislatures" when viewed from the perspective of the legislature. A survey in 1977 revealed that "nearly one-fifth of the rulemakings . . . contained violations"; inadequate notice of a proposed action was the most common violation.[199] Reflecting the changing nature of society, rules have become more complex and have invaded areas previously untouched by rules and regulations. Critics maintain that some administrative agencies, often referred to as "phantom" legislatures, abuse their rulemaking powers and frustrate legislative intent. The spate of environmental rules and regulations issued during the last decade in particular has caused public concern, and the charge is made that some agencies seek to aggrandize political power by means of rules and regulations. Whether it would be constitutional for the legislature to authorize a committee to suspend rules and regulations is unclear. Proponents believe that such requirements would encourage agencies to draft rules and regulations with more care and that the procedures would help the agencies determine legislative intent more precisely and also allow the legislature to amend enabling legislation if necessary. Critics assert that creation of a legislative review committee would afford interest groups another forum for obtaining their self-serving goals and could cause inordinate delays in effectuating needed rules and regulations.

The 1977 legislature enacted a bill (A. 8527-A) requiring agencies to report rules and regulations to a newly created Legislative Commission on Administrative Regulations Review that would possess subpoena powers, but the bill was vetoed by Governor Carey, who ruled that the bill was unnecessary, pointing out that "existing law [§ 101 of the Executive Law] requires that every agency must, at least 21 days prior to the adoption of any rule, notify the Majority Leader of the Senate and the Speaker of the Assembly of the proposed action to be taken."[200]

Although the governor did not refer to it, the Administrative Procedures Act governs the rulemaking process and is designed to ensure that rules are drafted properly and the public is informed fully by requiring publication in the *State Register* of the statutory authority for a proposed rule or rule amendment, date and place of public hearings on the proposal, procedure for presenting views, and text of the proposal. And standing and fiscal committees possess the authority to exercise oversight over administrative agencies but lack the power to veto actions by the agencies. An Administrative Regulations Review Committee, established by resolution prior to the veto in 1977 with each house maintaining a separate staff, was given statutory base in 1978 when the governor signed a bill that did not contain the notification requirements objected to by the governor in his 1977 veto of a similar bill.[201] The committee continues to review rules and regulations for their compliance with legislative intent.

Appropriation of Federal Funds. The increasing number of federal grants-in-aid received by state departments and agencies during the past two decades has been a subject of growing concern to the legislature, since such grants may allow the departments and agencies to engage in activities opposed by the legislature. In order to obtain information on federal grants received, the legislature in 1966 enacted a law forbidding state departments and agencies from applying for federal funds unless the director of the budget and the chairmen of the fiscal committees of the legislature are notified in writing thirty days in advance of an application.[202]

A controversial proposal is the appropriation by the legislature of all federal funds received by departments and agencies. A 1978 bill (S. 7840-B and A. 10244-B) introduced by the leaders of the two houses declares: "it is the finding of the Legislature that comprehensive allocation and planning of state expenditures from all funding sources is necessary to assure a proper priority balance among state functions, and to assure that limited state resources are used to their maximum potential." In particular, the spending of federal funds and private funds by state agencies has significantly lessened the ability of the legislature to establish priorities in state policy. To cite only two examples, the 1976 legislature directed the State Education Department to abolish several administrative positions and associated support personnel but discovered that at least seven of the positions were continued with federal funds.[203] The year previously the legislature reduced the $600,000 request of the Department for the Instructional Support System to $300,000 and discovered that the Department had used $350,000 in federal funds to supplement the state appropriation.

The memorandum in support of the bill providing for appropriation of federal funds states that state agencies received federal and other funds totaling more than $7 billion in fiscal 1977–78 without legislative review, and this amount was equal to 38 percent of all state expenditures. However, one must point out that departments and agencies cannot apply for federal funds without notifying the director of the budget and the chairmen of the fiscal committees of the legislature. The bill stipulates that any money granted to a state agency "shall be paid to the Department of Taxation and Finance to be held by such Department in trust for the uses and purposes specified by the donor." A special revenue fund would be created for this purpose.

The bill amends the State Finance Law to require that proposed expenditures of money in the special revenue fund "shall be set forth in a fifth separate and distinct part of the budget, and shall be further categorized in a manner suitable for comparison with general fund expenditures, or as reimbursements and miscellaneous revenues credited to the general fund." This information currently appears in the budget for each department. In addition, general fund expenditures proposed to be used as state matching funds under federal grants-in-aid must "be distinctly presented in the executive budget." The bill also forbids any state agency to apply for federal funds without approval of the director of the budget, which has been required since 1966.

State agencies, including university research centers, object to the bill because federal and private funds no longer would go directly to the state comptroller for disbursement to the agencies, which might have to wait one year until the funds are appropriated by the legislature in the following session. Fear also has been expressed that federal and private funds would be driven to other states if the bill became law.

Questions have been raised as to the constitutionality of the proposed law, as courts in Colorado and New Mexico ruled that federal funds are not subject to legislative reappropriations, inasmuch as they are "custodial funds" controlled exclusively by the executive branch.[204] In 1973 the United States Supreme Court ruled that a state may reappropriate federal funds provided federal requirements are complied with.[205] In 1979 the Court refused to overturn a ruling of the Pennsylvania Supreme Court upholding the constitutionality of a statute requiring that all federal funds be deposited in the general fund of the commonwealth and be available for appropriation by the legislature.[206]

A literal reading of the New York State constitution appears to authorize the legislature to appropriate federal funds, since "no money shall ever be paid out of the State Treasury or any of its funds under its management except in pursuance of an appropriation by law"; and "subject to the limitations contained in this Constitution, the Legislature may from time to time assign by law new powers and functions to departments, officers, boards, commissions, or executive officers of the Government and increase, modify, or diminish their powers and functions." On April 3, 1981, the New York State Supreme Court, in *Anderson v. Regan*, agreed with this interpretation.[207]

Program Audits. Some observers believe that only a greatly expanded system of program audits will enable the legislature to exercise effectively its oversight responsibilities by reviewing the performance of departments and agencies to determine the need for changes in programs. The view is expressed that the program audits

performed by the Legislative Commission on Expenditure Review
and the state comptroller are inadequate and that what is needed
is a state general accounting office with competence, independence,
and prestige similar to the federal office with a comptroller general
appointed for a long term and not subject to removal.

CONCLUSIONS

The growing complexity of the issues facing the legislature, the
increasing number of bills introduced, and the desire to play a
greater leadership role in the governance of the state induced the
legislature to expand greatly its staff. Evidence suggests that the
legislature will press forward with efforts to achieve a more coordinate status with the governor in the realm of policy development
and leadership. Central to these efforts will be the further buildup
of the legislature's professional staff capacity. Critics fear that continued staff expansion will delay action on important matters and
possibly result in the staff "running the show." There is little evidence that staff expansion will have these undesirable consequences.

Three additional developments will generate pressures for the
enlargement of the legislature's professional staff. First, the continuing fiscal problems of the Empire State will enhance the importance of legislative program auditing as legislators and many
members of the general public will insist that scarce fiscal resources
be expended in a manner designed to ensure the most economical
and efficient provision of services. The Legislative Commission on
Expenditure Review probably will be relied upon more heavily by
the legislature to determine the need for program modification or
termination.

Second, the state's Freedom of Information Law and the Open
Meetings Law, popularly known as sunshine laws, may beget
greater public interest and involvement in the legislative process
and the public affairs of the Empire State, necessitating a larger
professional staff to accommodate the inquiries and needs of the
citizenry.[208] These laws apply to local governments as well as to the
state government. One must point out that as pressures mount for
operating the legislature in a goldfish bowl, a number of competent

members may conclude that a goldfish bowl atmosphere makes them less effective and may decide not to seek reelection.

Related to the sunshine laws is the larger role being played in the legislative process by public interest groups and young people. The former in recent years have been exerting greater pressure and appear to have growing citizen support. The legislative internship programs operated by several colleges and universities, as well as the willingness of individual legislators to employ students as interns with or without pay, are involving a substantial number of young people in the legislative process, and these young people generally are finding the experience stimulating and personally rewarding, leading one to predict that they will retain a continuing interest in the legislative process. Women's groups also probably will be more influential in the future, and additional women legislators probably will be elected.[209] The League of Women Voters has long been an influential group. Also, the changing ethnic and racial composition of the Empire State undoubtedly will lead to the "Black–Puerto Rican caucus" gradually acquiring additional influence in the legislature, particularly if blacks and Puerto Ricans turn out at the polls in larger numbers on election day.[210]

A third development portending a significant professional staff increase is legislative review of rules and regulations issued by agencies of the executive branch. Legislative oversight to administrative rulemaking has been minimal, but evidence suggests that such oversight will increase and that the public will become more involved in rulemaking. Citizens have had little input into the administrative rulemaking process as notices of proposed rules and regulations were published in the unindexed *State Bulletin* that had only 290 paid subscribers in 1978.[211] The Assembly-Senate Administrative Regulations Review Committee in 1978 proposed the replacement of the *State Bulletin* with a *State Register* that would promote public participation and interagency coordination, provide full information expeditiously, and contain an index.[212] The secretary of state in 1979 replaced the *State Bulletin* with the *State Register*.

David Shafer of the *Knickerbocker News* in 1977 offered a theory suggesting that the legislature is an institution that is improving:

In the old days, the Legislature attracted an unambitious crowd of politicians, interested mostly in doing a little time at the Capitol and willing to follow the dictates of their leaders on most major issues. The leaders would get their way, reaching compromises among themselves which they then forced down the throats of the rank-and-file in marathon meetings wrapping up the session in, say, late April or mid-May.

But lately the Legislature, better paid and more frequently an avenue to higher office is attracting a more ambitious and able membership. And these new members, moved by their own spirit of independence and by the general post-Watergate notion that governmental institutions should be "opened up," are demanding a bigger role in its affairs.[213]

The reader should be aware that the legislature performs a symbolic function in providing legitimacy for governmental processes and generation of public support for the state's political system even though the legislature is not a microcosm of the polity. Evidence is lacking that confidence in the legislature as a responsible institution will rise to the point that the electorate will be willing to remove all constitutional restrictions upon legislative powers. The Watergate scandal undoubtedly lowered public confidence in state legislators and made the public more skeptical regarding the integrity of legislators. The voters did remove the constitutional restriction upon the ability of the legislature to call itself into special session effective in 1976, but it is improbable that the legislature will employ this power in the future.

Reflecting upon his twenty years in the legislature, Senator Jack E. Bronston in 1978 wrote:

Under the pressure of purity, the Legislature has imposed higher and higher standards on its own conduct and operations over the last 10 years. Committee meetings and votes are now totally open to public scrutiny and lobbying pressure. Legislative records have become accessible to mountains of computer printouts. Ethical standards, financial disclosure and election expenditures are regulated in a severe and complex way to the point of incomprehensibility. Needless to say, the public's attitude toward the Legislature remains sarcastic at best, insulting at worst.[214]

In concluding our discussion of the state legislature, we must emphasize that the increasing use of preemptory powers by the United States Congress is limiting the traditional broad discretionary role of the legislature in establishing state policy and resulting in the transfer of some power to the governor who is responsible for implementing programs that meet federal partial preemption standards discussed in Chapter II. Since Congress typically uses broad language in partially preempting regulatory responsibility, Congress authorizes federal agencies to draft, adopt, and implement rules and regulations detailing congressional policy. As a consequence, the power of the federal administrative officials is increased, and they work closely with governors. The Assembly and the Senate fully recognize the important role of Congress and federal administrative agencies in establishing domestic policy, and in 1977 each house opened a lobbying office in Washington.

And one must not overlook the limiting rulings of the United States courts. For example, states may not establish residency standards for welfare recipients under a ruling of the United States Supreme Court, and similar rulings of the same Court have limited the discretionary authority of the state legislature and the governor in other traditional state and local functional fields.[215]

We conclude by expressing agreement with Warren Moscow's 1948 statement that "one cannot examine the work of the Legislature over a period of years without concluding that it has been more responsive to public needs and public opinion than most legislative bodies, including Congress,"[216] and cite as evidence pioneering developments such as antidiscrimination, housing, mental health, and old age assistance laws.

NOTES

1. The Citizens Conference on State Legislatures, *State Legislatures: An Evaluation of Their Effectiveness* (New York: Praeger Publishers, 1971), p. 88

2. Alfred E. Smith, *The Citizen and His Government* (New York: Harper & Brothers, 1935), p. 51.

3. *Ibid.*, pp. 64–65.

4. *People v. Bradley,* 207 N.Y. 592, 101 N.E. 766 (1913) and *King v. Incorporated Village of Ocean Beach,* 286 App. Div. 850, 143 N.Y.S. 2d 637 (1954).

5. *New York Laws of 1974,* chap. 5 and 19. *New York Education Law,* § 202 (McKinney 1978 Supp.).

6. *New York Constitution of 1777,* art. XXXII, and *New York Constitution of 1821,* art. V, § 1, and art. VI, § 2.

7. *New York Constitution,* art. VI, § 24.

8. *In re Greene,* 166 N.Y. 485, 60 N.E. 183 (1901).

9. *Ibid.*

10. *New York Constitution,* art. III, § 14. This requirement pertains only to the house of origin. See *People v. Reardon,* 184 N.Y. 431, 77 N.E. 970 (1906).

11. *New York Constitution,* art. III, § 14.

12. *Ibid.,* § 15.

13. *Ferguson v. Ross,* 126 N.Y. 459, 27 N.E. 954 (1891).

14. *Economic Power Company v. Buffalo,* 195 N.Y. 286, 88 N.E. 389 (1909). See also *New York Laws of 1893,* chap. 459.

15. See *Matter of Clinton Ave,* 57 App. Div. 166, 68 N.Y. 196 (1901).

16. *New York Constitution,* art. III, § 16.

17. *Becker v. Eisner,* 277 N.Y. 143, 13 N.E. 2d 747 (1938).

18. *Levine v. O'Connell,* 300 N.Y. 658, 91 N.E. 2d 322 (1949).

19. *O'Gara v. Joseph,* 115 N.Y.S. 2d 469 (1952).

20. *Knapp v. Fasbender,* 1 N.Y. 2d 212, 134 N.E. 2d 482 (1956). See also *New York Laws of 1952,* chap. 816.

21. *People v. McManus,* 187 Misc. 609, 63 N.Y.S. 2d 183 (1946).

22. *People v. Lorillard,* 135 N.Y. 285, 31 N.E. 1011 (1892).

23. *Consolidated Edison Company of New York v. Moore,* 277 App. Div. 954, 99 N.Y.S. 2d 615 (1950).

24. *New York Constitution,* art. III, § 17.

25. L. Ray Gunn, "The New York Legislature, 1777–1846: A Developmental Perspective," a paper presented at the 21st College Conference on New York History, Albany, New York, April 29–30, 1977, p. 7. (Mimeographed).

26. *New York Constitution,* art. III, § 19.

27. *Parmenter v. State,* 135 N.Y. 154, 31 N.E. 1035 (1892). *Munro v. State,* 223 N.Y. 208 (1918).

28. *New York Constitution,* art. III, § 20.

29. *Munro v. State,* 223 N.Y. 208 (1918).

30. *New York Constitution,* art. III, § 23.

31. *Ibid.,* art. XI, § 3.

32. Smith, *The Citizen and His Government,* p. 257.

33. David L. Colvin, *The Bicameral Principle in the New York Legislature* (New York: Columbia University Press, 1913).

34. *Reynolds v. Sims,* 377 U.S. 533 (1964). The New York constitution provides that "no county shall have more than one-third of all the Senators," a provision obviously in conflict with the one-person, one-vote dictum. See *New York Constitution,* art. III, § 4.

35. *Reynolds v. Sims,* 377 U.S. 533 at 576–77 (1964).

36. Warren Moscow, *Politics in the Empire State* (New York: Alfred A. Knopf, 1948), p. 173.

37. *New York Constitution,* art. III, § 2.

38. *Ibid.,* § 4.

39. *Matter of Jerome T. Orans,* 17 N.Y. 107, 509, 550, and 721 (1966).

40. *New York Constitution of 1777,* art. IV and X.

41. *New York Constitution of 1821,* art. I, § 2.

42. *New York Constitution of 1894,* art. III, § 2.

43. *New York Constitution,* art. III, §§ 4–5.

44. Moscow, *Politics in the Empire State,* p. 167.

45. *Ibid.* See also Richard Lehne, *Legislating Reapportionment in New York* (New York: National Municipal League, 1971), pp. 1–7.

46. *New York Constitution,* art. III, § 4.

47. *Ibid.,* § 5.

48. *Chapman v. Meier,* 420 U.S. 1 (1975).

49. David I. Wells, "The Impact of Gerrymandering," *AFL-CIO American Federationist,* March 1972, p. 16.

50. *Model State Constitution,* 6th ed. (New York: National Municipal League, 1962), art. IV., § 4.04 (b). For details on apportionment commissions, see *Legislative Redistricting by Non-Legislative Agencies* (New York: National Municipal League, 1967).

51. "Reapportionment Outside the Legislature," *New York State Constitutional Convention, 1967: Complete set of Citizens Union Position Papers* (New York: Citizens Union, 1967), Position Paper No. 1, p. 1.

52. *Public Papers of Nelson A. Rockefeller: Fifty-Third Governor of the State of New York, 1967* (Albany: State of New York, n.d.), pp. 217–18.

53. "Remarks of David I. Wells, Assistant Director, Political Department, International Ladies' Garment Workers' Union, for Panel Discussion on 'Experience with Reapportionment Commissions,'" a paper presented at the National Conference on Government, Minneapolis, Minnesota, November 27, 1972, pp. 3–4 (Mimeographed).

54. *Voting Rights Act of 1965,* 79 Stat. 437, 42 U.S.C. 1973 (1964 Supp.). For further details on the act and its extension, see Joseph F. Zimmerman, "The Federal Voting Rights Act and Alternative Election Systems," *William & Mary Law Review,* Summer 1978, pp. 621–60.

55. 35 *Federal Register* 12345 (July 31, 1970) and 36 *Federal Register* 5809 (March 21, 1971).

56. *NAACP v. New York,* 413 U.S. 345 (1973).

57. *New York Laws of 1974,* chap. 588–91 and 599.

58. "Memorandum of Decision" (Washington, D.C.: Civil Rights Division, United States Department of Justice, July 1, 1974). (Unpublished.)

59. *United Jewish Organizations of Williamsburg, Incorporated v. Wilson,* 377 F. Supp. 1164 at 1165–66 (1974).

60. *United Jewish Organizations of Williamsburg, Incorporated v. Wilson,* 510 F. 2d 512 at 523 (1975).

61. *United Jewish Organizations of Williamsburg, Incorporated v. Carey,* 430 U.S. 144 at 156 and 159–60 (1977).

62. *Gomillion v. Lightfoot,* 364 U.S. 339 (1960).

63. *Whitcomb v. Chavis,* 403 U.S. 124 at 149 (1971).

64. For details on proportional representation, see Joseph F. Zimmerman, *The Federated City: Community Control in Large Cities* (New York: St. Martin's Press, 1972), pp. 74–79.

65. *New York Constitution,* art. III, § 18, and *New York Legislative Law,* art. 2-A (McKinney 1978 Supp.).

66. *New York Constitution,* art. IV, § 3.

67. *Ibid.,* art. III, § 10.

68. *New York Laws of 1942,* chap. 405 and 815.

69. Lois Uttley, "State Legislators Stuck with Session They Don't Want and Won't Go Away," *The Knickerbocker News* (Albany, New York), July 27, 1976, p. 9A.

70. *New York Laws of 1974,* chap. 5 and 19. *New York Education Law,* § 202 (McKinney 1978 Supp.).

71. Charles Z. Lincoln, ed. *Messages from the Governors* (Albany: J. B. Lyon Company, 1909), Vol. IX, pp. 753–54, and *ibid.,* Vol. X, p. 21.

72. Smith, *The Citizen and His Government,* p. 67.

73. *Public Papers of Averell Harriman: Fifty-Second Governor of the State of New York, 1957* (Albany: State of New York, n.d.), p. 10.

74. *Joint Rules of the New York Senate and Assembly,* Rule 27.

75. Smith, *The Citizen and His Government,* p. 52.

76. *New York Constitution,* art. III, § 7.

77. *Ibid.*

78. *Ibid.*

79. *New York Constitution of 1777,* art. IV and XI.

80. *New York Constitution of 1846,* art. III, §§ 2 'and 9.

81. *New York Constitution,* art. III, § 2. Members are elected on the first Tuesday following the first Monday in November in even-numbered years. *Ibid.,* § 8.

82. *Toward a More Effective Legislature* (Albany: New York State Bar Association, 1975), p. 16.

83. *New York Constitution,* art. III, § 11.

84. *The New York Red Book* (Albany: J. B. Lyon Company, 1920), pp. 20–22; *The New York Times,* April 2, 1920; Alfred E. Smith, *Up to New: An Autobiography* (Garden City, New York: Garden City Publishing Company, 1929), pp. 201–2; and *New York Legislative Law,* § 3 (McKinney 1952).

85. *New York Public Officers Law,* § 30 (1) (e) (McKinney 1978 Supp.).

86. *New York Constitution of 1821,* art. I, § 9.

87. *New York Constitution of 1846,* art. III, § 6.

88. *New York Constitution of 1894,* art. III, § 6.

89. *New York Constitution,* art. III, § 6, and *New York Legislative Law,* § 5 (McKinney 1978 Supp.).

90. *Ibid.* See also *Public Interest Research Group v. Steingut,* 40 N.Y. 2d 250 (1976).

91. *New York Laws of 1972,* chap. 875. *New York Executive Law,* § 815 (McKinney 1978 Supp.).

92. *Memorandum Filed with Senate Bill Number 6940* (Albany: Executive Chamber, August 9, 1975).

93. Gunn, "The New York State Legislature," p. 23.

94. *Ibid.,* p. 24.

95. Charles S. Hyneman, "Tenure and Turnover of Legislative Personnel," *The Annals,* January 1938, p. 23.

96. Alan S. Chartock, "Why Legislators Don't Return to Albany," *Empire State Report,* January–February, 1976, p. 19.

97. "Profile of the Legislature," *Empire State Report,* February 1977, p. 61. Data on sex, religion, and marital status are taken from this source. See also Janice

Prindle, "Women Legislators: A Paradox of Power," *Empire State Report,* January–February 1976, pp. 307 and 26–28.

98. Charles De Christopher, "Ethnic Groups Gaining," *The Legislative Gazette* (Albany, New York), February 21, 1978, p. 4. Data on the number of Hispanic members also are taken from this source.

99. *New York Constitution,* art. IV, § 6. A casting vote is one given to break a tie vote.

100. *Ibid.,* § 9.

101. *Ibid.*

102. Gunn, "The New York State Legislature," p. 15.

103. *The New York Times,* January 3–19, 1937.

104. R. W. Apple, Jr., "Travia Elected Speaker," *The New York Times,* February 5, 1965, pp. 1 and 19.

105. *The New York Times,* July 2, 1959, p. 1, and *The New York Herald Tribune,* July 2, 1959, pp. 1 and 4.

106. Peter A. A. Berle, *Does the Citizen Stand a Chance? Politics of a State Legislature: New York* (Woodbury, N.Y.: Barron's Educational Series, Inc., 1974), p. 14.

107. Moscow, *Politics in the Empire State,* p. 175.

108. *New York Constitution,* art. IV, § 6.

109. *Ibid.,* art. III, § 9.

110. Moscow, *Politics in the Empire State,* p. 171.

111. "Toll Tally," *The New York Times,* April 18, 1975, p. 24.

112. *Manual for the Use of the Legislature of the State of New York: 1975* (Albany: New York State Department of State, 1975), p. 1103 and *New York Legislative Record and Index 1978: From January 4 to June 2, 1978* (Albany: The Legislative Index Company), Vol. I–II.

113. *New York Constitution,* art. VII, § 1.

114. *Ibid.,* § 3.

115. *Information Requirements for Legislative Oversight: A Report to the New York State Ways and Means Committee* (Washington, D.C.: Price Waterhouse and Company, April 1978), p. 4.

116. Frank J. Munger and Ralph A. Straetz, *New York Politics* (New York: New York University Press, 1960).

117. For terminology, see "A Lexicon of Legislative Lingo," *Empire State Report,* January 1975, pp. 42–43.

118. *New York Constitution,* art. III, § 14.

119. *Rules of the Assembly: 1977–1978* (Albany: New York State Assembly, 1978), Rule 1, § 3.

120. *New York Constitution,* art. III, § 12.

121. See Joint Rule 27 in *The Clerk's Manual of the Legislature: 1963–1966* (Albany: New York State Legislature, 1963), p. 134.

122. Berle, *Does the Citizen Stand a Chance?* p. 27.

123. *New York Legislative Law,* §§ 24–25 (McKinney 1978 Supp.).

124. *New York Constitution,* art. VII, § 3.

125. Richard J. Meislin, "Abortion Measure Locked in Albany," *The New York Times,* June 7, 1978, p. 39.

126. Berle, *Does the Citizen Stand a Chance?* p. 27.

127. S. 3876 was substituted for A. 5153. See also *Veto Memorandum 112 of 1975* (Albany: Executive Chamber, August 9, 1975).

128. Stanley Steingut, "Explanation of the Calendar," *In Assembly: Calendar of Bills,* April 17, 1978, pp. 1–2.

129. Moscow, *Politics in the Empire State,* pp. 176–77.

130. Lois Uttley, "Assembly 'Empty-Chair' Voting Reform Questioned," *The Knickerbocker News* (Albany, New York), January 11, 1978, p. 1B.

131. *Ibid.*

132. *New York Constitution of 1777,* art. XV.

133. Peter Slocum, "'Let Me Out, Let Me Out,'" *The Knickerbocker News* (Albany, New York), June 30, 1976, p.1.

134. *Ibid.*

135. Linda Greenhouse, "Mass Confusion Reigns in Legislature as Session Nears End," *The New York Times,* July 9, 1977, p. 30.

136. Linda Greenhouse, "Wrong Version of Bill Is Made Law by Carey," *The New York Times,* July 23, 1976, p. B-2.

137. Vic Ostrowidzki, "Retired after 40 Years, His Work Begins," *The Knickerbocker News,* (Albany, New York), March 21, 1976, p. B-4.

138. *New York Constitution,* art. IV, § 7. The Court of Appeals in 1931 ruled that the legislature alone is not the lawmaking department, as action by the governor is an essential factor in the lawmaking process. See *Matter of Doyle,* 257 N.Y. 244 at 261, 177 N.E. 489 at 506 (1931).

139. *New York Constitution,* art. VII, § 4.

140. Charles Z. Lincoln, *Messages from the Governors* (Albany: J. B. Lyon Printing Company, 1909), Vol. III, pp. 645–46.

141. For details, see Frank W. Prescott and Joseph F. Zimmerman, *The Politics of the Veto Legislation in New York* (Washington, D.C.: University Press of America, Inc., 1980).

142. *New York Constitution of 1846,* art. IV, § 9 (1874).

143. *New York Legislative Law,* § 43 (McKinney 1952).

144. *The New York Herald Tribune,* March 20, 1947, p. 20.

145. *News from Senator Warren M. Anderson* (Albany: New York State Senate, July 11, 1973), p. 1.

146. *New York Constitution,* art. IV, § 7.

147. *Ibid.,* art. VII, §§ 2–7.

148. *Public Papers of Thomas E. Dewey: Fifty-First Governor of the State of New York, 1947* (Albany: State of New York, n.d.), p. 321.

149. For an analysis of the legislative attempt to override Governor Nelson A. Rockefeller's veto of a bill withdrawing authorization for the Metropolitan Transportation Authority to construct a bridge over Long Island Sound, see Thomas A. Droleskey, "The Politics of the Proposal to Construct a Bridge Crossing from Oyster Bay to Rye, New York" (Albany: Ph.D. Dissertation, Graduate School of Public Affairs, State University of New York at Albany, 1977).

150. *New York Constitution,* art. III, § 18, and art. IV, § 3.

151. Mary Jo Braun, "A Study of Legislation Vetoed in the 1976 Legislative Session," unpublished paper submitted in PPOS 522—State Government—Graduate School of Public Affairs, State University of New York at Albany, Autumn 1977.

152. *New York Laws of 1977,* chap. 357.

153. See the following 1974 New York Senate bills: 8285, 8286, 8288, 8289, 8290, 8292, 8293, 8296, 8297, 8298, 8301, 8303, 8305, 8307, 8310, 8311, 8313, 8314, 8316, 8322, 8323, 8326, 8327, 8328, 8329, 8332, and 8333.

154. *City of Rye v. Ronan,* 325 N.Y.S 2d 548 at 551 (1971).

155. *Ibid.* at 553.

156. *New York State Finance Law,* § 94 (1) and (4) (McKinney 1974).

157. For examples of some of these provisions, see *New York Public Officers Law,* §§ 73 and 75–77 (McKinney 1978 Supp.).

158. *Ibid.,* § 73 (6) (McKinney 1978 Supp.).

159. *Ibid.,* § 74 (McKinney 1978 Supp.).

160. *Ibid.,* §§ 84–90 and 95–106 (McKinney 1978 Supp.).

161. *The New York Times,* January 20–21 and February 3, 1937.

162. Moscow, *Politics in the Empire State,* p. 200. For an analysis of lobbying in the mid-1930s, see Belle Zeller, *Pressure Politics in New York* (New York: Russell & Russell, 1937).

163. Berle, *Does the Citizen Stand a Chance?* p. 49. See also Steve Kroft, "The Magic and Myth of the Big Lobbyists," *Empire State Report,* April 1975, pp. 116–27.

164. Patricia Munsell, "Change Has Been Good, DeSalvio Says," *Legislative Gazette* (Albany, New York), April 17, 1978, p. 8.

165. *New York State Assembly,* Bill A-9907 of 1976.

166. *New York Laws of 1977,* chap. 937 and *New York Legislative Law,* art. I (McKinney 1978 Supp.).

167. "Secretary Cuomo's Statement on Lobbying Reform, January 26, 1977," p. 1. Available from the office of the New York Secretary of State, Albany, New York.

168. Carol Greenwald, "Post-Watergate Lobbying Laws: Tokenism v. Real Reform," *National Civic Review,* October, 1974, p. 470.

169. *New York Laws of 1977,* chap. 4. The first three chapter numbers annually are reserved for the appropriation bills passed later in the session.

170. *New York Laws of 1909,* chap. 33. *New York Insurance Law,* § 554 (McKinney 1978 Supp.).

171. Linda Greenhouse, "Carey Gets Volunteer Firemen Bill, First of the Year," *The New York Times,* February 1, 1977, p. 33.

172. "Insurers Gave $3,250 to Silverman," *The Knickerbocker News* (Albany, New York), March 17, 1977, p. 4.

173. "Banking Chairman Given $10,000," *The Knickerbocker News* (Albany, New York), April 5, 1977, p. 6.

174. Sam Roberts, "Home Touch on Legislators' Mortgages," *Sunday News,* April 1, 1973, p. 6C.

175. Moscow, *Politics in the Empire State,* pp. 181–82.

176. See, for example, Humphrey S. Tyler, "Time to Weed Out the Ranks of the No-Shows," *Empire State Report,* October 1975, pp. 404–5.

177. *State of New York Executive Budget for the Fiscal Year April 1, 1980 to March 31, 1981* (Albany: Executive Chamber, January 22, 1980), pp. 670, 673, and 677.

178. The Citizens Conference on State Legislatures, *State Legislatures: An Evaluation of Their Effectiveness,* p. 88.

179. *New York Legislative Law,* §§ 24–25 (McKinney 1978 Supp.).

180. *Toward a More Effective Legislature,* p. 9.

181. *Ibid.*

182. *New York Laws of 1934,* chap. 597. See also *New York Laws of 1961,* chap. 358. *New York Legislative Law,* §§ 70–72 (McKinney 1952).

183. Ronald Smothers, "Legislature Has Refined Public Relations," *The New York Times,* February 16, 1976, p. 24.

184. Gerald S. Budgar, "Assembly Seeks PR 'Facelift,'" *The Times Union* (Albany, New York), October 31, 1976, pp. B-1 and B-14.

185. *New York State Senate Resolution 129 of 1963.*

186. James E. Underwood, *Science/Technology-Related Activities in the Government of New York State: The Organizational Pattern* (Albany: Office of Science and Technology, New York State Department of Education, 1971) pp. 72–77.

187. *The New York State Assembly Scientific Staff* (Albany: The Assembly, January 10, 1975), p. 1.

188. *Ibid.*

189. *New York Laws of 1969,* chap. 176, § 2, and *New York Legislative Law,* art. 5-A (McKinney 1978 Supp.). Interestingly, Governor Herbert H. Lehman in 1939 vetoed a bill creating the position of legislative auditor on the grounds that the bill was a Republican attempt "to destroy the executive budget system" and the constitution did not contemplate the creation of a legislative postauditor. See *Public Papers of Herbert H. Lehman: Forty-Ninth Governor of the State of New York, 1939* (Albany: J. B. Lyon Company, 1942), pp. 21–39.

190. Ray Pethtel and Richard E. Brown, "Conducting Evaluative Studies: A Workshop on Techniques and Problems," in Ray Pethtel and Richard E. Brown, eds., *Legislative Review of State Program Performance* (New Brunswick, N.J.: Eagleton Institute, Rutgers University, 1972), p. 27.

191. Smith, *The Citizen and His Government,* pp. 65–66.

192. *Ibid.,* p. 66.

193. Humphrey S. Tyler, "The Assembly Reforms: Easy Come, Easy Go," *Empire State Report,* August 1975, p. 297.

194. Letter dated January 4, 1977, to Speaker Stanley S. Steingut from Executive Director Stephen Shestakofsky of Citizens Union of New York City, p. 1.

195. *Ibid.,* p. 2. (Emphasis in the original)

196. Letter dated January 4, 1977, to Majority Leader Warren M. Anderson from Executive Director Stephen Shestakofsky of Citizens Union of New York City, p. 1.

197. *New York Laws of 1975,* chap. 167. *State Administrative Procedures Act,* § 201 (McKinney 1977), and *New York Executive Law,* § 160 (McKinney 1978 Supp.).

198. *State Agencies and the State Administrative Procedure Act: A Study of Compliance* (Albany: Administrative Regulations Review Committee, the Assembly, July 1977), pp. 27 and 29.

199. *Ibid.,* p. 1.

200. *Veto Message #142* (Albany: Executive Chamber, August 11, 1977).

201. *New York Assembly Legislative Resolution 75 of 1977* and *New York Senate Legislative Resolution 29 of 1977.* See also *New York Laws of 1978,* chap. 689, and *New York Legislative Law,* §§ 86–88 (McKinney 1979 Supp.).

202. *New York Laws of 1966,* chap. 578, and *New York State Finance Law,* § 53-a (McKinney 1974).

203. "Appropriating Federal Funds in New York State," *The Ways and Means Report,* January 1977, p. 2.

204. *MacManus v. Love,* 499 P2d 609 (1972). *Sego v. Kirkpatrick,* 524 P2d 975 (1974).

205. *Wheeler v. Barrera,* 417 U.S. 402 (1973).

206. *Shapp v. Casey,* 99 S. Ct. 717 (1979). See also *Shapp v. Sloan,* Pa., 391 A2d 595 (1978).

207. *New York Constitution,* art. VII, § 7, and art. V, § 3, respectively.

208. Open Meetings Law," *New York Laws of 1976,* chap. 511, and *New York Public Officers Law,* §§ 95–106 (McKinney 1978 Supp.), and "Freedom of Information Law," *New York Laws of 1977,* chap. 933, and *New York Public Officers Law,* §§ 84–90 (McKinney 1979 Supp.). The latter law was interpreted by the Court of Appeals in 1977 as giving citizens the right to examine the worksheets of a budget examiner. See *Matter of Dunlea v. Goldmark,* 43 N.Y. 2d 754 (1977).

209. Janice Pringle, "Women Legislators: A Paradox of Power," *Empire State Report,* January–February 1976, pp. 3–7 and 26–28.

210. David Shaffer, "How Legislature's Black–Puerto Rican Caucus Won," *The Knickerbocker News* (Albany, New York), April 1, 1977, p. 10-A.

211. *The State Register: An Administrative Journal for New York State* (Albany: Assembly and Senate Administrative Regulations Review Committee, March 1978), p. 9.

212. *Ibid.,* pp. 14–25.

213. David Shaffer, "Are We Finally Getting a Better Legislature?" *The Knickerbocker News* (Albany, New York), July 1, 1977, p. 4-A.

214. Jack E. Bronston, "The Buck Stops There," *The New York Times,* April 29, 1978, p. 23.

215. *Shapiro v. Thompson,* 394 U.S. 618 (1969).

216. Moscow, *Politics in the Empire State,* p. 184.

CHAPTER VII
His Excellency the Governor

THE OFFICE OF governor became so powerful by the 1960s that some obervers referred to "executive dominance" of the state government. Our themes of intergovernmental relations, executive integration, and group politics are helpful in examining the extent to which the governor dominates the state government. The theory of checks and balances also is helpful in assessing the power of the governor, as the Senate acts as a check upon gubernatorial nominations, the legislature may exercise administrative oversight; and the governor may check the legislature through the exercise of the veto, which is subject to being overridden by a two-thirds vote of each house of the legislature.

The office of Governor emerged from a relatively weak one lacking the appointment and veto powers in 1777 to an executive office among the strongest in the nation in terms of formal political powers. The constitution of 1777 assigned the governor relatively few important powers and provided for a dominant legislature. Although the governor was granted by the constitution of 1821 a qualified power to appoint certain members of the executive branch and to veto bills, the legislature was authorized to elect the secretary of state, the treasurer, the attorney general, and the commissary general, thereby preventing the governor from becoming the chief executive.

In the early part of the twentieth century a movement developed to lengthen the term of office of the governor, strengthen his executive powers, increase his salary, and expand his staff. Particularly important in making the governor the strong executive were the constitutional amendments reorganizing the executive branch by limiting the number of major departments to twenty and instituting the executive budget system.

The governor plays several important roles—chief executive, chief legislator, leader of his political party, ceremonial head of state, and intergovernmental representative. While each role is important, his roles as chief executive and chief legislator are the most important. The latter is especially important in terms of time commitments while the legislature is in session and the influence this role has on his prospects for reelection or election to the presidency. If the governor is successful in his role as policy leader, he will be projected into national prominence. However, the legislature often is difficult to deal with even if controlled by the governor's political party. Since the governor's constituency is a statewide one, it is not surprising that his views would differ on important issues from legislators who represent more parochial constituencies.

Warren Moscow contrasts the difficulties of being governor of the Empire State with those faced by the president of the United States and the mayor of New York City by writing that "the Governorship is a soft snap" and adding:

The reason for this is simply that the important part of the job of Governor lies in the field of policymaking rather than in the handling of administrative detail. The Governor is not wakened late at night or early in the morning by recurrent crises in international affairs, nor is his executive domain so vast that the number of minutes in the calendar week is insufficient to permit even abbreviated conversations with each of his lieutenants, a difficulty which plagues a modern President.

The Governor does not have to work overtime every time a snowstorm blocks streets and delays garbage collection, as does a Mayor of New York City; nor does every strike called or threatened land in his lap for settlement. He has his office in the State Capitol and half a dozen blocks away his mansion on Eagle Street, where he can relax or work as he sees fit, without a constant stream of visitors. In addition to his immediate privacy, he has one other priceless advantage over the Mayor of New York City. His own relative isolation in Albany means that the strain of attending four or five public dinners a night can be avoided.[1]

The reader must take into consideration that Moscow was describing the situation existing prior to 1948. The complexities of the governorship of the Empire State have increased significantly during the past three decades—and one governor, Nelson A. Rockefeller—

worked out of his office in New York City and spent relatively little time in Albany. Governor Hugh L. Carey also worked to a large extent out of his New York City office.

THE OFFICE OF GOVERNOR

Article IV of the state constitution stipulates that "no person shall be eligible to the office of Governor or Lieutenant Governor, except a citizen of the United States, of the age of not less than thirty years, and who shall have been five years next preceding his election a resident of this state."[2] These two officials are elected jointly to a four-year term.[3] The term of office was extended to four years by a constitutional amendment ratified by the voters in 1937. George Clinton served as governor for twenty and three-quarters years. Governors Herbert H. Lehman and Nelson A. Rockefeller were elected to four terms, but three of Lehman's terms were two years in length. Lehman resigned as governor during the last month of his fourth term, and Rockefeller resigned nearly thirteen months prior to the expiration of his fourth four-year term.

Prior to 1954 the governor and the lieutenant governor were elected separately, and it was possible for the two officials to be members of different political parties or to be political opponents even though members of the same party. Governor Lehman in 1938, for example, arranged to have the lieutenant governor nomination "given" to Charles Poletti instead of the incumbent, William Bray, who was an anti–New Dealer.

Sponsors of the joint election amendment were influenced by the joint election of the president and the vice president combined with the practice of the former selecting the candidate of his party for the latter position. In 1974, however, insurgents in the Democratic party primary defeated the candidates endorsed by the leaders of the party, and as a result the Democratic candidate for governor did not select the Democratic candidate for lieutenant governor. The relations between the two officials were cool.

For the first time in the state's history a lieutenant governor, Mary Ann Krupsak, stunned the governor, Hugh L. Carey, and the Democratic party on June 12, 1978, the day the governor had scheduled the announcement of his candidacy for reelection, by with-drawing as a candidate for reelection. She charged that "during the past three and one-half years, I have served the Governor with dedication, integrity, and loyalty; I had expected the same dedication from the Governor to the people of this State. This quality I have found lacking."[4]

The decision of Lieutenant Governor Krupsak to challenge Governor Carey for the nomination could have led to an unusual situation, with Mario W. Cuomo running for the election as lieutenant governor on the Democratic party ticket with Mary Anne Krupsak and on the Liberal party ticket with Hugh L. Carey. Matters would have been more complicated in that votes received by Cuomo on the Democratic line probably could not be added to votes received on the Liberal line, since the constitution provides for the election of the governor and the lieutenant governor as a team.

The increasing use of television commercials has significantly increased the cost of running for governor, and a potential candidate has no prospect for success unless he or she can raise several million dollars in campaign funds. In 1966 Governor Rockefeller's campaign committee reported that eight committees spent approximately $5 million. Four years later the governor spent $6,794,627 in his reelection bid, with $4,124,500 contributed by his family, including $287,079 of his own funds. Governor Carey in 1974 spent $4,400,000 in his successful bid for the governorship, including a debt of $1,-200,000 that was not paid until April 1978.

Governors make it a practice to appoint campaign officials to high-level state posts from which they resign prior to the start of the reelection campaign. The governor's press secretary, Thruway Authority chairman, and members of various boards and commissions often resign to assume important positions in the governor's reelection campaign. A 1974 *New York Times* survey revealed that the state spent "more than $2 million a year for 18 boards, authorities, and commissions stacked with 'seldom-shows.'"[5]

The governor or the lieutenant governor may be removed from office through the impeachment process. Should the Assembly approve impeachment charges by a majority vote of all members, a trial will be conducted by the Court for the Trial of Impeachments consisting of the members of the Senate, with the exception of the temporary president and the judges of the Court of Appeals.[6] The only governor ever to be impeached and removed was William

Sulzer. The Assembly on August 12, 1913, voted eight articles of impeachment, and the Court for the Trial of Impeachments found him guilty of three charges—perjury, failure to report $8,500 in campaign expenses, and suppression of evidence—and removed him from office on October 17, 1913.[7] Although a product of Tammany Hall, Governor Sulzer would not follow the orders of Tammany leader Charles Murphy, who controlled the legislature, and many of the 384 bills vetoed by Sulzer in 1913 were Tammany bills.[8]

The governor and the lieutenant governor may resign their offices by notifying the legislature. Governor Lehman resigned as governor on December 3, 1942, as did Governor Rockefeller on December 11, 1973.[9] Whenever the governor is absent from the state or is "unable to discharge the powers and duties of his office, the Lieutenant Governor shall act as Governor"[10] Should the governor-elect fail to take office or the governor dies, resigns, or is removed from office, the lieutenant governor succeeds to the governorship.

The constitution also provides that "in case of vacancy in the offices of both Governor and Lieutenant Governor, a Governor and a Lieutenant Governor shall be elected for the remainder of the term at the next general election happening not less than three months after both offices shall have become vacant."[11] The constitution also stipulates that the temporary president of the Senate shall act as governor whenever there is a vacancy in the offices of governor and lieutenant governor; the speaker of the Assembly becomes acting governor if there is a vacancy in the office of temporary president of the Senate or if he is out of state or unable to perform the duties of the Office of Governor.[12] The legislature is authorized to provide for the further devolution of the office of acting governor.

The annual salary of the governor is determined by the legislature and will be $100,000 in 1983.[13] In addition, the governor is provided with an official residence in Albany—the Executive Mansion with twenty-eight servants—chauffeured limousines, use of a State Department of Environmental Conservation airplane that also is used by other officials, offices in New York City and Washington, and an allowance for official and public functions.[14] His Executive Chamber staff in 1980 totaled 265 permanent employees. The governor's use of the state airplane and state police helicopters to attend "official functions," such as addressing an association or breaking ground for a new facility, increases sharply if the governor is seeking reelection in a given year.

The lieutenant governor in 1981 received an annual salary of $60,000, a $15,000 expense allowance, and $1,000 to attend the annual conference of lieutenant governors. The budget for the lieutenant governor's staff and operations was $611,405 in fiscal 1981. The salary of the lieutenant governor will be increased to $85,000 in 1983.

THE STRONG EXECUTIVE

The adoption of constitutional amendments reorganizing the executive branch, limiting the number of departments to twenty, and establishing an executive budget system in the twentieth century transformed the Office of Governor of the Empire State into an office widely recognized as a strong governmental institution in terms of the formal powers conferred upon it by the constitution.[15]

The governor lacks only two formal powers possessed by several other governors. The governor does not have the power—possessed by the governor in Alaska, California, Hawaii, Massachusetts, New Jersey, Pennsylvania, and Tennessee—to reduce items in appropriation bills. In addition, the New York governor lacks the power—possessed by the governor in Alabama, Massachusetts, New Jersey, and Virginia—to return a bill with suggested amendments to the legislature once as an alternative to vetoing the bill. This "conditional veto" power is not a significant one except in New Jersey and seldom is used in Massachusetts, because the same objective can be achieved by the recall of bills from the governor's desk by the legislature.[16]

The formal powers of the governor may be classified as executive, legislative, and judicial. In addition, the governor, as head of state and political party leader, may play an important leadership role based upon informal powers.

Executive Powers

The appointment, removal, administrative supervision, and military powers, combined with his intergovernmental role, make the governor a strong executive. Whereas one might suggest that certain presidents usurped or expanded powers, the governor of the Empire State was given additional powers by constitutional amendments. Courts lack the constitutional authority to interfere with the governor in the exercise of his executive powers and performance of ministerial duties.[17]

The Appointment Power. Although a 1974 article stated that each of the state's twenty administrative departments is "headed by a Commissioner who holds office at the Governor's pleasure," complete administrative integration has not been achieved as appointments in three of the twenty constitutional departments are not made by the governor, although he has other important controls over these departments.[18] Two departments are headed by popularly elected officials. The Department of Audit and Control is under the direction of the state comptroller, and the Department of Law is under the direction of the attorney general. In addition, the Education Department is under the control of the Regents of the University of the State of New York who appoint and may remove a commissioner of education, the chief administrative officer of the department.[19] The commissioner of social services was appointed by the State Board of Social Welfare until 1971 when the Social Services Law was amended to provide for his appointment by the governor.[20]

The governor, with the advice and consent of the Senate, appoints the members of the Public Service Commission and the Civil Service Commission. He also designates the chairman of the Public Service Commission and the president of the Civil Service Commission who serve as the heads of the Public Service Department and the Civil Service Department, respectively. They serve at the pleasure of the governor, who is the head of the Executive Department and who appoints the commissioners of the other fourteen departments with the advice and consent of the Senate. The governor may make interim appointments when the Senate is not in regular session and is not required to submit interim appointments to the Senate for confirmation during a special session of the legislature.[21] Commencing in 1976, the Senate recessed rather than adjourned, thereby preventing the governor from making interim appointments. The governor appoints without Senate confirmation the director of the Division of the Budget, the counsel, and other key staff members who serve at the pleasure of the governor.[22] In addition, he appoints approximately 1,500 persons outside the civil service merit system.

As explained in Chapter IV, the appointment power was confided in the Council of Appointment by the 1777 constitution, and the governor was not granted the appointment power until a new constitution was adopted in 1821.[23] The only recent governor to experience serious problems in recruiting department heads was Hugh L. Carey. His recruitment problems stemmed in part from the issuance of a 1975 executive order requiring all employees in exempt, noncompetitive, or unclassified positions in the executive branch earning in excess of $30,000 and heads of state departments and agencies appointed by the governor annually to make a public disclosure of their finances by filing with a newly created Board of Public Disclosure in the Department of State a list of assets and liabilities plus a statement of sources of income for amounts exceeding $1,000.[24] In addition, the 2,000 covered officers and employees were forbidden to hold a second position with a government or private firm.

The governor expanded coverage of the financial disclosure requirement in 1976 by issuing an amended executive order covering more than 10,000 employees in "managerial or confidential positions" earning more than $30,000; an amended executive order in 1979 lowered the salary figure to $25,000.[25] Many highly qualified businessmen and professionals, earning more than $30,000 in private employment, felt that the governor was asking them to make too big a public sacrifice by requiring them to make a public disclosure of their personal finances should they accept a lower-paying state position. The governor's failure to fill vacancies led to the filing in the 1978 legislature of fifteen bills (S. 7809 through S. 7825) requiring the governor to fill vacancies in the executive branch within ninety days. Because of recruitment problems, Governor Carey sounded out legislators about accepting appointments, and several agreed to resign from the legislature to become eligible for positions in the executive branch.

One of the unwritten rules of Empire State politics is that the governor is free to pick the top members of his administration provided they are competent and honest. Governor Carey is the first governor within the memory of current observers to have a nominee rejected by the Senate, although there were many cases of delay and several rejections during the administration of Governor Lucius Robinson in 1878 and the administration of Governor David B. Hill in the period 1886 to 1889. On April 13, 1976, the Senate rejected the nomination of Herman Schwartz to be chairman of the Commission of Correction.[26] The rejection was based in part on the strong opposition of sheriffs whose jails the commission was attempting to upgrade, the feeling of many Republicans that the Senate had been too cooperative with the governor in an election year, and a difference in correctional philosophy.

In the 1970s the Senate introduced a new "advise-and-consent" policy involving closer scrutiny of gubernatorial nominations and forcing gubernatorial-legislative negotiations prior to a nomination being forwarded to the Senate for confirmation. On June 28, 1977, the Senate Committee on Corporations, Authorities, and Public Utilities voted not to recommend Peter A. Peyser, a former Republican congressman who joined the Democratic party, for confirmation as a member and probably chairman of the Public Service Commission, and on June 30, 1977, Peyser withdrew as a candidate for the position. In 1978 Governor Carey submitted the name of a Liberal party member to be a replacement for the Republican member of the three-member bipartisan State Mediation Board. The Senate, claiming the appointment would make a mockery of bipartisanship, refused to act on the appointment. The governor withdrew the nomination and submitted the name of a Republican as a member of the board.

The governor appointed all judges with Senate approval between 1821 and 1846, and currently appoints the judges of the Court of Appeals and the Court of Claims.[27] As explained later, the governor appoints judges to the elective bench to fill vacancies. Although the governor does not appoint directly the part-time or seasonal employees of state departments and agencies, these positions are filled under his direction and serve as a source of patronage. There are approximately 4,775 seasonal jobs and 300 provisional appointments in state parks, historic sites, and marine facilities, as well as 500 non-civil-service highway employees and 200 seasonal Barge Canal employees, up to 20 positions at each of the state's 11 racetracks, and 42 lottery sales representatives.[28] The governor also fills vacancies on county legislatures and in the offices of county clerk, district attorney, register, and sheriff.

The Removal Power. The state constitution grants the governor power to remove heads of departments and members of boards and commissions and authorizes the governor to "remove any elective sheriff, county clerk, district attorney, or register," providing the governor gives the concerned official "a copy of the charges against him and an opportunity of being heard in his defense."[29]

The comptroller and the attorney general may be removed from office by the Senate for malversation or misconduct upon the governor's recommendation, and all officers appointed by the governor except heads of departments may be removed by the Senate upon the governor's recommendation.[30] Any officer appointed by the governor whose appointment does not require Senate confirmation may be removed by the governor, "after giving to such officer a copy of the charges against him and an opportunity to be heard in his defense."[31] The governor may remove a department head whenever "the public interest shall require" by filing a statement of the reason for the removal with the secretary of state and informing the legislature at its next session.[32]

The governor seldom removes a state official. In 1917 Governor Charles S. Whitman appointed a commissioner to examine charges against Chairman Frederick A. Wenck of the State Athletic Commission and on March 16, 1917, issued an order removing the chairman.[33] When authorized to do so by a city charter or state law, the governor occasionally removes a local official, as in 1907 when Governor Charles Evans Hughes removed Manhattan Borough President John F. Ahern from office. In 1931 Governor Franklin D. Roosevelt did not "find sufficient justification" to remove Mayor James J. Walker of New York City from office and stressed that "the greatest caution must . . . be used in the exercise of . . . the removal power by the Governor in order not to annul the deliberate decision of the voters of the State or of any municipality thereof."[34] However, the Seabury committee, created by the legislature in March 1931, uncovered evidence of widespread corruption and incompetence in the New York City government, and requested that the governor remove Sheriff Thomas M. Farley of New York County and Mayor Walker.[35] Roosevelt removed Sheriff Farley from office and was holding a hearing on the charges against Mayor Walker when he resigned on September 2, 1932.

The Public Officers Law provides that an office is vacated upon the conviction of the incumbent of a crime constituting a violation of his oath of office. When the Schoharie County sheriff, convicted of eleven counts of official misconduct, attempted to remain in office, Governor Malcolm Wilson in 1974 requested Attorney General Louis J. Lefkowitz to institute an action to confirm the forfeiture of the office.[36]

Administrative Supervision Powers. As the chief executive of the state, the governor may supervise the departments under his control by requiring reports, exercising tight budget control, conducting investigations, and reassigning or removal personnel. The governor is authorized by the Moreland act, a 1907 law, to appoint one or more commissioners with broad powers[37] to investigate any state department or agency and report to the governor. The Insurance Department was the first state agency investigated by a Moreland Act Commission, and in 1908 the Board of Embalming Examiners was investigated. In 1975 Governor Carey appointed a Moreland Act Commission on Nursing and Residential Homes and a second commission to investigate state public authorities.[38]

The 1953 legislature enacted a law creating the Office of Commissioner of Investigation and authorized the governor to appoint the commissioner, who was charged with conducting investigations at the direction of the governor.[39] In 1958 the office was replaced by the four-member Temporary State Commission of Investigations; two members are appointed by the governor, one by the temporary president of the Senate, and one by the speaker of the Assembly.[40] No more than two of the commissioners may belong to the same political party.

Financial Power. Today, the governor is the financial leader of the state government, but this leadership position is a relatively new development, as a legislative budget system was in effect until 1929.

The need for a new state budgetary system was recognized in 1909 by Governor Charles Evans Hughes, who declared that "there should also be provided some permanent method of comparative examination of departmental budgets and proposals for appropriations in advance of the legislative session, so that the Legislature may be aided by preliminary investigation and report in determining, with just proportion, the amounts that can properly be allowed."[41] However, it was not until 1926 that the legislature approved a proposed constitutional amendment establishing an executive budget system. The 1927 legislature approved the proposed amendment for the second time, and voters ratified the amendment on November 8, 1927.[42] The State Finance Law directs the governor to submit with his budget "a bill or bills for all proposed appropriations and reappropriations and for the proposed measures of taxation or other legislation, if any, recommended therein."[43]

On January 28, 1929, Governor Franklin D. Roosevelt transmitted to the legislature "the first constitutional budget of the State of New York." The 411-page document immediately met with a legislative challenge in the form of a requirement that previously appropriated funds could not be spent without the approval of the chairman of the Assembly Ways and Means Committee and the chairman of the Senate Finance Committee. The Court of Appeals in 1929 ruled that making the chairmen coordinate with the governor in the segregation of lump-sum items violated Section 7 of Article III of the constitution that prohibits members of the legislature from holding any other civil office.[44]

Although the 1929 court decision appeared to make it clear that the governor was in complete charge of budget execution, Governor Roosevelt was challenged again in 1930, and a second major legislative attack on the system occurred in 1939 when the legislature enacted a law amending the executive budget bill submitted by the governor by striking out substantially every item contained in the bill and substituting a lump-sum appropriation for each department, division, or bureau, combining in such item appropriations for expenses of maintenance, operations, personal service, travel, and the purchase or exchange of automobiles.[45] The effect of the bill was to substitute a legislative budget for the executive budget. The Court of Appeals held that the bill violated the spirit and purpose of Section 4 of Article VII of the constitution forbidding the legislature to alter an appropriation bill submitted by the governor except to strike out or reduce items of appropriation. The court held that "where, however, a whole appropriation has been stricken out, including the items of which it is made, and compensation for clerks and services as well as maintenance is lumped together, the words of the Constitution have not been followed and such appropriation is illegal."[46] There has been no major legislative challenge of the executive budget system since 1939, although conservative Republican members, without attacking the system, forced Governor Thomas E.

Dewey to compromise on aspects of financing his proposed 1949 expenditures.[47]

The governor's constitutional authority to prepare and execute the state budget allows him to play a preeminent role in policy-making. The constitution allows the governor to amend or supplement the budget for thirty days after its submission without the consent of the legislature.[48] Furthermore, neither house may consider any other appropriation bill "until all the appropriation bills submitted by the Governor shall have been finally acted on by both houses, except on message from the Governor certifying to the necessity of the immediate passage of such a bill."[49] And "the Legislature may not alter an appropriation bill submitted by the Governor except to strike out or reduce items therein, but it may add thereto items of appropriation provided that such additions are stated separately and distinctly from the original items of the bill and refer each to a single object or purpose."[50] These restrictions do not apply to bills appropriating funds for the legislature or the judiciary. A separately approved appropriation bill becomes law "without further action by the Governor," that is, without his signature.[51]

The Empire State's constitution provides for cooperative gubernatorial-legislative relations in the process leading to the appropriation of funds by directing the governor to furnish copies of the budget requests of departments and agencies to the legislature's fiscal committees and entitling the committees to attend the hearings held by the governor on the requests.[52]

Frederick C. Mosher in 1952 wrote that "it is almost impossible for a legislative body which considers a budget for a few weeks each year to appraise a line-item document, or to modify it. . . . In practice detailed itemization seems to prevent the intent of the Legislature from being expressed at all; it operates as an aid to executive dominance."[53] One should recognize, however, that the situation has changed significantly since 1952 because of the development of large, year-round professional staffs in the Assembly Ways and Means Committee and the Senate Finance Committee.

In a rare move, State Comptroller Arthur Levitt in 1972 sought a declaratory judgment in the Supreme Court "to determine whether the budget bills submitted by the Governor for the next fiscal year violate the intent of the Constitution" because of the lack of "sufficient itemization to permit the Legislature to take meaningful action," and whether the broad grant of power to the budget director to make interchanges in the proposed appropriations for capital construction was an excessive delegation of legislative authority.[54] After the court rejected the challenge on the ground that the comptroller lacked standing, the governor agreed to changes the comptroller proposed and announced he would not press his suit.[55]

Governors submit three separate budgets to the legislature. The executive budget, the main budget, is submitted in January and totaled $13.79 billion for fiscal 1980–81. The State Finance Law requires the governor to submit to the legislature a five-year projection of general fund income and expenditures as a supplement to the executive budget.[56] The deficiency budget—totaling approximately $150 million—is usually submitted to the legislature in February and is designed to replenish depleted or rapidly depleting accounts to enable state departments and agencies to operate until the end of the fiscal year on March 31. The governor's 1980 deficiency budget was not acted upon by the legislature, the first time the legislature failed to enact an appropriation bill to implement a governor's deficiency budget. The supplemental budget—totaling approximately $100 million—is enacted as one of the last items of business by the legislature and contains funds for needs not anticipated when the executive budget was submitted and typically restores some funds deleted from the executive budget by the legislature.

In approving budgets, the legislature makes modified lump-sum appropriations that are segregated by the Division of the Budget. Expenditure ceilings lower than the amounts appropriated are often established by the division during periods of fiscal stringency. Actual state spending exceeds the total of the executive, deficiency, and supplemental budgets because a large share of the total expenditures of state public authorities does not appear in these budgets, and certain items are "off budget"; that is, they are placed outside the general fund. Included in off-budget funds are state lottery funds and federal countercyclical assistance funds.

Evaluating the executive budgeting system in 1952, Frederick C. Mosher wrote:

New York budgeting is not particularly effective as a mechanism for public information, education, and debate. The relation between financial plan and working program is obscure if not completely invisible in the published budget. Nor is there adequate provision for holding the administration accountable *post facto* for its financial operations and its program accomplishments.[57]

While some observers believe the situation has not changed significantly since 1952, other observers stress that considerably more factual information is provided on each department than in fiscal 1953: budget summaries are published; a five-year projection of general fund income and expenditures is made annually; and additional summary tables, such as off-budget spending, are included.

The fact that the Empire State uses cash accounting instead of accrual accounting (under which income is recorded when earned and expenditures are recorded when commitments are made) allows the governor to hide "surpluses," since he can order the expediting of income tax refunds prior to the end of the fiscal year, delay crediting income tax payments until the beginning of the next fiscal year, underestimate revenue, use cash instead of bond funds for capital construction, and speed up state aid to local governments and payments to vendors. Reverse actions can be taken to avoid reporting a budget deficit. Accrual accounting also can be subject to management.

The *Empire State Report* in 1975 wrote that "Republicans . . . who a year ago said the budget was perfectly balanced now maintain a surplus exists. Conversely, Democratic legislators who last year had claimed surpluses above $300 million are now singing the 'Empty Pocket Blues.'"[58] The Republican Senate in 1978, for the third time, approved a bill (S. 7006) providing for a system of partial accrual accounting, which had been recommended by Democratic State Comptroller Arthur Levitt, but the bill died in the Democratic Assembly.

Relative to the interchange of items of appropriation, a state department or agency with the approval of the director of the budget may transfer funds with the limitation that "the total amount appropriated for any program or purpose may not be increased or decreased by more than five per cent."[59]

In 1980 the Court of Appeals restricted the governor's budgetary execution powers by ruling "that no authority inheres in the Governor under the State Constitution to impound funds appropriated by law."[60]

Military Powers. The state constitution designates the governor as "Commander-in-Chief of the military and naval forces of the State."[61] In 1943 the Court of Appeals upheld the constitutionality of Section 15 of the Military Law authorizing a justice of the Supreme Court, "in case of any breach of peace, tumult, riot, or resistance to process of this State, or imminent danger thereof," to "call for aid upon the commanding officer of the National Guard or Naval Militia" by ruling that such an action by a justice was not a usurpation of the governor's prerogatives as commander in chief.[62]

As the head of the National Guard, the governor may declare the state or parts of the state to be under martial law should there be an emergency and suspend civil rights. He performs his military functions through the Division of Military and Naval Affairs, which has been part of the Executive Department since January 1, 1927. The organized militia is composed of the New York Army National Guard, New York Air National Guard, and New York Naval Militia. Since October 1, 1973, the State Civil Defense Commission has been part of the division.

The governor has the authority to declare the existence of an emergency because of a natural disaster or civil disorder and may mobilize the National Guard. On January 31, 1977, for example, Governor Carey issued an executive order directing "the organized militia to assist agencies in Lewis and Jefferson Counties . . . in alleviating the effects of the natural disaster resulting from the severe weather conditions existing in the Counties."[63]

Intergovernmental Role. Historically, the governor has played an important state-local relations role, and there is evidence that this role may grow in the future as the governor in his executive budget recommends the amount of local assistance. Should New York City have an ambitious and colorful mayor who is seeking the presidency at the same time a dynamic governor is a candidate for president, clashes are inevitable, as occurred between Mayor John V. Lindsay and Governor Rockefeller. The increasing complexity of the federal system and the necessity of close interstate cooperation and state-federal cooperation has resulted in the governor devoting a considerable amount of time to his intergovernmental role. In particular, the governor has been playing a large intergovernmental role because of laws enacted by Congress delegating substantial rulemaking powers to federal departments and agencies, which in turn delegate important powers to the governor, such as the designation of water quality planning commissions and metropolitan planning organizations for transportation. Because of the growing amount of federal aid and federal incursions into traditional state-local functional areas, the governor maintains an Office of Federal Affairs in Washington.

Legislative Powers

The most significant development in gubernatorial-legislative relations since 1777 has been the rise of the governor to a position of legislative leadership should he choose to exercise such leadership. As a full-time state official, in contrast to the part-time legislature, it is not surprising that the governor has been labeled the chief legislator. He may call upon the entire state bureaucracy as well as special advisory commissions for assistance in preparing a legislative program. Furthermore, the governor's legislative proposals, because of the nature of his constituency, tend to be of state-wide concern and involve major problems, whereas bills introduced by the average legislator tend to reflect the more limited concerns of a narrowly based constituency. The governor's recommendations also tend to reflect the major planks in the party's platform.

The governor's most important legislative powers include the right to submit the executive budget, recommend programs to the legislature, issue messages of necessity, call special sessions of the legislature, veto bills enacted by the legislature, and issue executive orders.

Policy Leadership. The state constitution directs the governor to present a state of the state message and the state budget annually to the legislature.[64] The state of the state message is an important one, as indicated by the constitutional mandate for its submission, and constitutes to a large extent a report on the governor's "stewardship," and state problems and their proposed solutions. Typically, the most important bills introduced in the legislature are sponsored by the governor, and his constitutional authority to prepare and execute the state budget allows him to play a preeminent role in policymaking.

Robert H. Connery reports that Governor Rockefeller made greater use of study groups than the governors of other states and

"named some seventy task forces, appointed five temporary commissions, and convened sixteen governor's conferences."[65] The study
commissions also served as a form of "prestige patronage" for members of the two major parties and enabled some members to continue
as members of the state retirement system. Rockefeller's Executive
Chamber staff of 96 in 1959 grew to 282 by 1966 and was supplemented by a sizable private staff in New York City paid by him.

In 1959 Governor Rockefeller broke precedent by submitting
in advance of the 1960 session memorandums recommending major
programs involving reorganization of the executive branch, local
government, juvenile delinquency, atomic development, highway
safety, and creation of a public works stockpile.[66]

The bills included in the governor's legislative program represent the work of the counsel's office, the Division of the Budget,
program associates in the office of the Governor, and departments
and agencies. The governor's program bills are discussed on a regular basis with legislative leaders during the session; Governor
Dewey held many closed-door presession conferences with legislative leaders. Some observers are convinced that a governor has more
leverage with the legislature if his party controls each house with
only a small majority, as this necessitates that party discipline be
tight and allows the governor to make trades with the opposition
party to gain votes necessary for enactment of a program bill. A
large majority in each house strengthens the bargaining position
of the majority legislative leaders vis-à-vis the governor.

As explained in Chapter VI, the governor may issue messages
of necessity suspending the constitutional requirement that all bills
must be on members' desks in final printed form three days prior
to a final vote being taken on the bills. In practice, the governor
usually does not send a message of necessity to the legislature unless
the legislative leaders request a message. The basic reason for the
issuance of the messages is to expedite action during the closing
days of a legislative session. Only in a few instances is the message
of necessity clearly needed prior to the end of the session. A significant percentage of the bills covered by messages of necessity were
introduced earlier, and flaws requiring corrective action were discovered within three days of the date set for adjournment. Under
such circumstances, only a message of necessity would allow a bill
to be amended and enacted into law during that session of the
legislature.

Whereas a number of legislators complained about Governor Rockefeller's "dominance" of the legislative process, many legislators during the 1974 session complained about the lack of strong gubernatorial leadership. The governor's legislative presence declined in 1974 even though Governor Wilson had served twenty years in the legislature prior to being elected lieutenant governor in 1958. The decline was deliberate, as he had pledged in his state of the state message to cooperate with the legislature:

I am convinced that while the Executive and the Legislature are independent and co-equal branches in government, the interests of the people are best served when these two branches work in cooperation. This Administration will seek to progress in partnership with you—all of you.[67]

Commenting on the 1974 legislative session, Rockefeller stated:

This session was a good session. I think Malcolm accomplished exactly what he set out to do, which was to . . . allow the Legislature, which had been critical of my form of leadership, to have the opportunity to express themselves. And then, of course, as is the case with life, they then said, "Where's the leadership?"[68]

Linda Greenhouse in 1977 wrote, relative to the lack of strong legislative leadership by Governor Carey, that "no Legislature is likely to take the lead in dealing with complicated politically charged issues. It is on these issues—housing and higher education, especially—that no initiative has been forthcoming from Governor Carey."[69]

Call of Special Sessions. The governor may call special sessions of either the entire legislature or only the Senate and is in complete control of the agenda of the extraordinary sessions he calls.[70] Since the legislature is limited to the subjects included in the governor's call, the governor has to call a second special session should a development occur that was not anticipated in the first call. As a result, two special sessions may be held on the same day; in early 1976 considerable confusion existed as to whether the legislature on any given day was meeting in special session called in late 1975 after the legislature had adjourned or was in regular session. The governor occasionally calls a special session during the regular session to demand action on a subject, as occurred in 1978.

Although the legislature since 1976 has possessed the power to call itself into special session by petitions signed by two thirds of the members elected to each house, no special session has been called to date by the legislature, which has preferred to recess, allowing the legislature to reconvene when it wishes without the necessity of utilizing petitions, as required for calling itself into special session, and is thus free to act upon any matter.[71] When the legislature adjourns or recesses without acting upon all of the governor's program bills, he may call a special session, or threaten to, as Governor Carey did in 1978.

Veto Power. As pointed out in Chapter VI, it was not until 1821 that the governor was granted the veto power. The first gubernatorial veto was rendered on April 24, 1823, and was sustained in the Senate.[72]

In 1874 voters ratified a constitutional amendment granting the governor the power to veto items in appropriation bills. The item veto was decreased in importance and has seldom been used since the executive budget system became established firmly in 1939, as the legislature is reluctant to add items to the governor's budget. Governor Carey in 1978, however, vetoed 1 item and deleted 170 items totaling $240 million from the fiscal 1981 appropriation bill. An innovative use of the item veto was made by Governor Carey in 1978 when he approved a deficiency line item in the Commerce Department appropriation but disallowed the item language prohibiting the use of the name and photograph of any state or local government official.[73] Senate Majority Leader Warren M. Anderson requested the attorney general's opinion whether such a veto violated the constitution, and the attorney general responded in the negative.[74] In 1980 the Court of Appeals ruled that the Division of the Budget had exceeded its constitutional authority in 1976 by reducing by $7 million a $26 million local assistance grant for sewer treatment operating expenses. The court ruled that the division was "required to implement policy decisions of the Legislature unless vetoed or judicially invalidated."

During sessions of the legislature, the governor has ten days, excluding Sundays, to act upon a bill after it reaches his office. Failure to take action during this period results in the bill becoming law without the governor's signature unless the legislature has adjourned. Joint resolutions, other than ones expressing opinions such as memorials, must be submitted to the governor for his action. Proposed constitutional amendments are not submitted to the governor and are placed on the ballot by concurrent resolutions, which are similar to joint resolutions. In 1931 the Court of Appeals ruled null and void a joint resolution granting immunity from prosecution to a person testifying before a joint legislative committee.[75] The following year the Court of Appeals and the United States Supreme Court issued decisions nullifying a redistricting of the legislature by a joint resolution that was not submitted to the governor.[76]

Following adjournment of the legislature, the governor has had a thirty-day consideration period since the adoption of a constitutional amendment in 1874. Bills enacted by the legislature that are not signed or vetoed by memorandums during this period are pocket-vetoed, that is, they are killed without explanation. No bill has been pocket-vetoed to date, and Governor Rockefeller initiated the practice of writing a memorandum on each disallowed bill giving the specific reasons for the veto. Governors do not veto all bills containing defects because of the importance of certain bills. When a defective bill is signed, an agreement is usually reached with sponsors and the legislative leaders that corrective amendments will be introduced in the next session of the legislature. Occasionally minor defects are cited as a reason for a veto, and the real reasons are not disclosed.

The governor seldom publicly threatens to veto a bill being considered by the legislature, but in 1978 Governor Carey publicly threatened to veto any bill restoring the death penalty or legalizing the use of laetrile.[77] Because of strong public opposition to his death penalty stand, the governor proposed life imprisonment without parole for convicted murderers.

The record for the largest absolute and relative numbers of vetoes is held by Republic Governor Rockefeller who disapproved 567 (34.6 percent) of the 1,641 bills sent to his desk by the Democratic-controlled 1965 legislature. Table I reveals that a total of 5,783 (21.7 percent) of the bills transmitted to the governors between 1959 and 1979 were disallowed. A decline in the exercise of the veto power has occurred since the resignation of Rockefeller as governor in 1973, and this decline may continue, possibly because of the split in party control of the two houses of the legislature.

The counsel and assistant counsels to the governor play major roles in reviewing bills approved by the legislature and in preparing

TABLE VIII.I VETOES RENDERED BY THE GOVERNOR STATE OF NEW
YORK 1959–1980

Year	Number of Bills Sent to the Governor	Number of Bills Vetoed	Percent of Bills Vetoed	Number of Bills Signed
1959	1,202	322	26.8	881
1960	1,389	300	21.6	1,089
1961	1,293	323	25.0	980
1962	1,278	265	20.7	1,013
1963	1,288	266	20.7	1,022
1964	1,327	352	26.5	974
1965	1,641	567	34.6	1,074
1966	1,328	303	22.8	1,025
1967	1,127	310	27.5	817
1968	1,408	319	22.7	1,096
1969	1,523	368	24.2	1,155
1970	1,340	292	21.8	1,048
1971	1,519	305	20.1	1,214
1972	1,298	282	21.7	1,016
1973	1,331	288	21.6	1,045
1974	1,340	260	19.4	1,082
1975	1,087	192	17.7	895
1976	1,082	121	11.2	966
1977	1,184	201	17.0	983
1978	831	51	6.1	780
1979	819	96	11.7	723
1980	1,018	128	12.5	891
Total	27,653	5,911	21.4	21,769

recommendations for approval or disapproval. There has been a regular counsel to the governor since 1905.

In disallowing bills, the governor does not suggest that each vetoed bill is without merit. Frequently, he renders a mollifying memorandum pointing out that the bill was: (1) premature as a study on the subject had not yet been completed; (2) of such importance that additional study was essential; (3) could be improved significantly by the adoption of the governor's suggestions; (4) did not allow sufficient time for implementation; or (5) contained technical defects. Governor Dewey in 1952 and Governor Rockefeller in 1959 hold the record for issuance of the largest number of mollifying memorandums in a single year—fifty-nine. Several bills each year are disallowed as technically defective because of printing errors or poor draftsmanship.

Based upon interviews with top-level officials in the Rockefeller administration, Professor Andrew J. Di Nitto reports that three types of veto messages were employed:

"The Soft Sell" . . . was used to let friendly legislators "down easy." The message would mention the good efforts made by the individuals and his good intentions, and suggest changes. The purpose of the "Soft Sell" was not to embarrass the sponsor. The second model was the "Straight Message." The language was dry and to the point and it was reserved mostly for members of the opposition party. Finally, there was the "Zinger Message." One executive official explained "we would use these when we wanted to embarrass the sponsors." The intent of the language was "How can you be so stupid to present such a bill." The "Zinger Model" was used most often in vetoing bills of a lobbyist or a private pressure group which made a nuisance of itself.[78]

Di Nitto also reports that the reasons assigned for the vetoes in the governor's memorandums generally are accepted by legislators as the "real reasons" for the disallowances,[79] and legislators deciding to reintroduce vetoed bills often attempt to respond to the governor's objections with new language.[80]

The legislature overrode the governor's veto for the first time in November 24, 1824, by enacting Chapter 298 of the Laws of 1824.[81] In 1860 Governor Edwin D. Morgan vetoed en bloc five bills, but the vetoes were overridden and the bills became Chapters 511–15 of the Laws of 1860.[82]

The governor's veto power in practice has been nearly absolute, as evidenced by only sixteen gubernatorial vetoes overridden by the legislature in the period 1823–72 and only three full vetoes (one in 1976 and two in 1979) overridden by the legislature since 1872.[83] Mosher in 1952 wrote that "the veto power has apparently had the double effect of making the Governor dominant over policy matters, including budget policy, and of encouraging the passing of bills with full anticipation that many of them will be vetoed."[84] Until 1976 the legislature had relatively little opportunity to override vetoes, since the legislature transmitted the bulk of the bills to the governor at the end of the legislative session and he vetoed most bills during the thirty-day postadjournment consideration period.[85] To cite only one example, Governor Malcolm Wilson in 1974 wrote 258 of his 260 veto memorandums subsequent to the adjournment of the legislature.

Senate Majority Leader Warren M. Anderson in 1973 issued a news release characterizing a number of the 1973 vetoes as "ill-advised and over-technical" and instituted a new procedure allowing each senator to introduce a maximum of five bills commencing thirty days subsequent to the end of the governor's postadjournment consideration period to facilitate reintroduction of vetoed bills.[86]

Although individual legislators on occasion publicly express a desire for a veto session of the legislature, no such session has been held since 1976, the first year the legislature was authorized to call itself into special session. Legislative leaders expressed the opinion that the disallowed bills were of insufficient importance or urgency to justify a veto session. It is possible that a veto session would embarrass the sponsors of some disallowed bills.

Gubernatorial-Legislative Cooperation. The veto of a relatively high percentage of the bills reaching the governor's desk does not suggest necessarily a lack of gubernatorial-legislative cooperation or that the governor functions as a "one-man legislature." Most disallowed bills are concerned with matter of interest to individual members and do not deal with major statewide issues. Included among the vetoed bills are ones sponsors do not want to become law that were introduced because of constituent pressure.

Testifying before the United States Senate's Rules Committee, Rockefeller offered the following explanation of the process by which he developed policy proposals:

I worked with Democratic leaders as I had with the Republican leaders. I had them totally in my confidence, took their ideas, tried to accommodate them in the development of legislation. The result of this was by the time I gave a message to the Legislature I was already aware of the general outline of the leaders' positions. They were aware of mine. It appeared that I was dominating but, in actual fact, that was the furthest from the truth.[87]

As pointed out in Chapter VI, indicative of the legislature's willingness to cooperate with the governor are the recall of bills from the governor's desk by the Assembly and the Senate in order to give the governor additional time to consider bills, delays in sending bills approved by both houses to him, and the practice of the Senate transmitting bills on Thursdays in order to give the governor two Sundays to consider bills. In some instances, bills are delayed in transmittal to the governor in order to make them thirty-day bills, thereby giving the governor additional time to study these bills while making it impossible for the legislature to override a veto unless the legislature calls a special session for that purpose, a most unlikely event.

The governor in turn cooperates with the leaders of the legislature by sending messages of necessity at their request and with members by arranging to have the Assembly or Senate recall a bill to remove or modify the provision(s) found objectionable by the governor. Of course there is no opportunity to recall the bills transmitted to the governor at the end of the session. The governor has possessed the power to send messages of necessity since 1894, when the current constitution was adopted. Only four such messages were sent by Governor Levi M. Morton in 1895, but the number increased each year thereafter, and Governor Martin H. Glynn issued ninety-nine in the 1913 special session and the 1914 regular and special sessions of the legislature.

Although free to transmit a message of necessity at his discretion, in practice the governor usually sends messages only at the request of the legislative leaders, and not all requests for messages are granted. Table II reveals that the governor employs this power often during the closing days of the annual legislative session. To cite only one example, Governor Rockefeller transmitted thirty-five of his fifty-two messages on the last day of the 1973 regular session.

The message of necessity is an important tool that helps to link the governor and the legislative leaders in a cooperative relationship. Although the constitution does not limit the length of the legislative session, the bill-aging requirement allows the governor and the legislative leaders to control the bills introduced once the legislature is within three days of the adjournment date set by resolution. If action cannot be completed upon all important bills by the specified adjournment date, the clocks in the chambers are stopped to continue the fictional existence of the same legislative day, thereby preventing any bill introduced within three days of adjournment from aging. As a result, several messages carrying the date of the last legislative day were issued during a period of two to three calendar days.

TABLE VIII.II MESSAGES OF NECESSITY STATE OF NEW YORK 1932–1980

Year	Number of Messages Regular Session	Number Transmitted Last Day of Session	Year	Number of Messages Regular Session	Number Transmitted Last Day of Session
1932	72	6	1957	10	2
1933	104	7	1958	22	8
1934	174	0	1959	80	29
1935	83	0	1960	62	30
1936	64	27	1961	57	5
1937	119	36	1962	45	5
1938	195	147	1963	47	6
1939	1	0	1964	29	10
1940	1	0	1965	20	5
1941	3	1	1966	59	15
1942	3	0	1967	62	7
1943	3	1	1968	95	49
1944	5	4	1969	55	14
1945	5	0	1970	142	67
1946	4	3	1971	115	57
1947	11	2	1972	58	12

Year		
1948	7	2
1949	9	3
1950	9	6
1951	5	4
1952	9	8
1953	17	12
1954	15	13
1955	13	6
1956	3	1
1973[a]		52	35
1974[b]		121	114
1975[c]		66	31
1976[c]		119	44
1977		10	32
1978[d]		70	13
1979[d]		73	3
1980[e]		91	13
Total		2,494	895

SOURCE: Adapted from *Public Papers of the Governors of New York* (Albany: State of New York, 1932–74) and Office of Governor Hugh L. Carey.

[a] Governor Nelson A. Rockefeller transmitted thirteen additional messages of necessity to the extraordinary session of the legislature; two of the thirteen messages were sent on the last day of the extraordinary session.

[b] Governor Malcolm Wilson transmitted ten additional messages of necessity to the extraordinary session of the legislature; three of the ten messages were sent on the last day of the extraordinary session.

[c] Governor Hugh L. Carey sent nine additional messages to the 1975 extraordinary session and two additional messages to the 1976 extraordinary session of the legislature.

[d] Governor Carey sent seven additional messages to the 1978 extraordinary session, and three additional messages to the 1979 extraordinary session of the legislature.

[e] Governor Carey sent twenty-two additional messages to the 1980 extraordinary session of the legislature.

The relatively frequent use of such messages has been criticized over the years as excessive and a subterfuge to evade the aging requirement. Delegate Austin Strong opposed messages of necessity at the 1915 constitutional convention by stating that "the message of emergency has become nothing more than a message of convenience; it has become detrimental to the best interests of the State"[88] Austin favored a constitutional amendment repealing the authorization for the governor to issue messages of necessity and maintained that the amendment would "compel the early consideration of bills of importance which should not be considered in the last two or three days of the sessions when the leaders of both sides are so fatigued that sometimes they could not see a joker if it was there."[89]

Many messages of necessity do not relate to entirely new bills, but rather to amendments to bills introduced early in the session. If the legislature decides that a bill introduced early in the session needs a technical amendment or a compromise has been reached on the bill and adjournment is set for less than three days in the future, only a message of necessity will allow the legislature to adopt the amendment.

Following precedent, Governor David Bennett Hill conferred with the sponsors relative to defects in their bills and indicated a willingness to have the bills recalled.[90] Governor Hill, in vetoing two 1885 bills, wrote that he regretted that the bills had been enacted late in the session, as the bills could not be recalled and amended.[91] Although Hill requested the sponsor of a bill appropriating funds for construction of a drawbridge over the Erie Canal to have the bill recalled, the sponsor "did not deem it advisable to do so," and Hill vetoed the bill.[92]

Executive Orders. As chief executive, the governor may issue executive orders carrying the force of law, provided the orders are not in conflict with the state constitution or statutes. While executive orders may deal with important subjects, such orders are relatively few in number and are outweighed in importance by the rules and regulations issued by various state agencies and commissions under legislative authorization.

Political considerations are involved in the issuance of certain executive orders. In 1978 Governor Carey issued an executive order directing state agencies to consider the labor relations of a company in deciding whether to award a state contract, because "the labor relations practices of a bidder . . . can affect the bidder's reliability . . . to meet the requisite quality or other standards for the articles or services to be supplied."[93] In reality, the order was aimed at J. P. Stevens, a textile company headquartered in New York City, which has been opposing attempts by unions to organize its plants in southern states. By issuing the executive order, the governor strengthened his ties with organized labor, and union success in organizing the southern plants would reduce their competitive advantage over New York State textile companies.

Occasionally, courts strike down an executive order on the ground the governor exceeded his authority in issuing the order. On September 1, 1977, Supreme Court Justice Roger J. Miner ruled that Governor Carey exceeded his authority in issuing an executive order requiring contractors on state projects to institute affirmative action programs to promote the hiring of minorities, because the order "extends and expands requirements of statutes."[94] And on March 29, 1978, the Court of Appeals struck down Governor Carey's extension of the financial disclosure requirement to include civil service employees, although he was free to regulate the activities of public officials "serving at his pleasure."[95]

Judicial Powers

Although justices of all courts except the Court of Claims, the Civil Court of New York City, and the Criminal Court of New York City until 1977 were elected by the voters in accordance with the state constitution, in practice a significant number of justices initially reached the bench by means of an interim appointment by the governor to fill a vacancy. Confirmation of such appointments by the Senate is required only if it is in session. Commencing in 1977, the Senate began the practice of recessing instead of adjourning, with the result the governor has not been free to make interim appointments that do not require Senate confirmation.

A study by Carl L. Swidorski of accession to the New York State Court of Appeals in the period 1950 to 1975 revealed that seven judges reached the bench by means of interim appointments.[96] Furthermore, voters had no choice other than to write in the names of candidates in thirteen of the seventeen elections for Court of Appeals judges in the period 1950 to 1972, because the Republican party and the Democratic party cross-endorsed the same candidate for each of thirteen vacancies.[97] The electorate in 1977 approved a constitutional amendment providing for the appointment of judges of the Court of Appeals by the governor from a list prepared by the twelve-member nonpartisan Commission on Judicial Nominations (discussed in Chapter IX).[98]

Referring to Rockefeller, Kramer and Roberts wrote that "the bench in New York is the ultimate goal of any ambitious lawyer with political connections, and the Governor was willing to accommodate for a favor. As usual, the favors sometimes rewarded friendship, but more often they rewarded an infusion of public spiritedness in a politician who had decided to support a Rockefeller program."[99]

In 1975 Governor Carey issued an executive order establishing in each of the four judicial departments a Judicial Nominating Committee—each with at least four nonlawyers—to examine the qualifications of prospective judicial nominees and announced he would appoint only candidates labeled "well-qualified" by the committees.[100] The governor names four of the eleven members of each screening committee, including the chairman and two nonlawyers; the chief judge of the Court of Appeals appoints four members, including two nonlawyers the presiding justice of the Appellate Division of the Supreme Court in each Judicial Department appoints one member who must be a lawyer; and the four legislative leaders—the speaker, the Assembly minority leader, and the Senate majority and minority leaders—jointly appoint two members, including a lawyer.

Each committee screens appointments to the Supreme Court and its Appellate Division. Relative to prospective nominees for the Court of Claims, a statewide committee is appointed and consists of the chairman of each Judicial Department Committee and a lawyer and a nonlawyer from each Department Committee representing different political parties. With respect to county courts and the Surrogate's Court in New York City, the governor appoints a lawyer and a nonlawyer to the Judicial Department Committee. A judge, elected official, or political party officer may not serve on a screening panel, and no panel member is eligible for a judicial appointment until one year subsequent to the end of service on the panel.

Justices of the Supreme Court are elected by the voters, but the governor designates the presiding justice of each Appellate Division.[101] The other appellate justices are "designed by the Governor, from all the Justices elected to the Supreme Court, for terms of five years or the unexpired portions of their respective terms of office, if less than five years."[102]

The governor also possesses unlimited power to grant pardons exculpating convicts by exempting them from further punishment for a crime, reprieves (stays of execution of sentences), and commutation or shortening of sentences. Referring to a proposed constitutional amendment establishing a Board of Pardons, Smith indicated his opposition because he was convinced "that the full responsibility should rest with the Governor," and creation of such a board would be the equivalent to "the creation of a second Court of Appeals."[103]

If the Court of Appeals certifies to the governor that it is unable to hear and dispose of cases within a reasonable period of time because of a heavy case load, the governor is authorized to designate up to four justices of the Supreme Court to serve as associate judges of the Court of Appeals.[104]

A judicial-type power exercised with relative frequency is the supersession of a district attorney or sheriff by the governor. This power is based upon the constitutional charge to the governor to "take care that the laws are faithfully executed."[105] In some instances, a district attorney requests the governor to supersede the district attorney because of a conflict of interest. For example, in 1974, at the request of the district attorney of New York County, Governor Malcolm Wilson directed Attorney General Louis J. Lefkowitz to supersede the district attorney relative to grand jury investigations and indictments in five specified cases.[106]

Similarly, on February 13, 1976, Governor Carey signed an executive order giving Charles J. Hynes, the state's special prosecutor for nursing homes, superseding powers over the Albany County district attorney at his request in a specified case.[107] In 1978 Hynes's jurisdiction was expanded by the governor to include medicaid frauds, because a separate statewide prosecutor's office was a condition established for the continued receipt of federal funds.[108]

A subject provoking considerable controversy was the superseding of the five district attorneys in New York City and the 1972 appointment by Attorney General Lefkowitz, at the request of Governor Rockefeller, of Maurice H. Nadjari as the deputy attorney general and special prosecutor to handle cases involving corruption of the criminal justice system in New York City.[109] The special prosecutor became controversial, and Governor Carey decided to have Nadjari replaced. The governor, without consulting the attorney general, on December 23, 1975, announced the firing of Nadjari, who charged that the governor lacked the authority to fire a special prosecutor and was aware of an investigation the special prosecutor was conducting of officials of the Carey administration. Attorney General Lefkowitz, the appointing authority, refused to fire Nadjari, but extended his term for only six months. According to Maurice Nessen,

Nadjari's sins were multiple: press leaks of confidential investigations to favored reporters, unfounded accusations of corruption, the destruction of the reputation of a most honorable judge by calling him to a grand jury without confronting him with any accusations, bringing one case (the Goldman case) because of its publicity value and so on.[110]

Nadjari was replaced as special state prosecutor in 1976 by John F. Keenan.

In his 1978 annual report, Special State Prosecutor Keenan noted that twenty-five civilians and criminal justice officials pleaded guilty during the previous twelve months to criminal charges brought by his office, a drop of thirty-seven from the previous year, and answered "absolute" in response to a question whether it was difficult to convict a judge of any crime in New York State.[111]

GUBERNATORIAL LEADERSHIP OR DOMINANCE

As head of state, public attention naturally is centered on the governor, and his every important activity is subject to media comment and analysis. Recognizing the importance of the media in influencing and shaping public opinion, modern governors spend a considerable amount of time projecting an image of leadership and have developed a large public relations staff. Under the governorship of Thomas E. Dewey, press releases were prepared and distributed to newspapers throughout the state with particular attention paid to closing dates for copy of weekly newspapers and the topics that various papers had a special interest in. While conceding there was no favoritism shown by the Dewey administration in making news releases and handouts available, Moscow criticized the system because Dewey attempted "to restrict knowledge of state affairs to what he gives out" and added:

Dewey was spoiled by the time he went to Albany as Governor. He was not used to being covered by men with access to additional information. It was a shock to him when reporters, instead of simply printing his announcement that he planned to save the State $25,000 by having a simple inauguration ceremony, reported also that the entire appropriation for the inaugural, in the budget, was $5,000.[112]

Governor Rockefeller expanded the use of press releases by having all announcements by state departments and agencies channeled through his office, with the result that the governor made nearly all the announcements of actions taken or to be taken by the departments and agencies.

The governor annually issues reams of proclamations designating a given week or day as Puerto Rican Folklore Week, State Fair Week, High School Athletes Week, Freedom of Enterprise Week, National Ladies Auxiliary, Jewish War Veterans Day, Women's Equality Day, and so on. These proclamations are issued in such great number that they are of little or no consequence.

In 1978 Governor Carey's press office initiated an "Audio Information Service" allowing radio stations to use a toll-free Wide Area Telephone Service (WATS) number to record a taped message from the governor, which is changed on an average of three times per day. The taped message is introduced by one of the governor's press assistants, who provides background information, and is followed by a maximum-level tone and a countdown prior to the governor's statement.

The popular image of the legislature during the Rockefeller era was that of an obsequious body. Kramer and Roberts, for example, wrote:

The Legislature, when dominated by the Republicans, as it was for 13 of Rockefeller's 15 years, was rarely more than a rubber stamp. When recalcitrant Republicans fussed over big spending, deals were struck with Democrats. Most of the State's politicians (all of whom, by nature, had vivid imaginations) were reluctant to cross Rockefeller for fear of reprisal.[113]

Governor Rockefeller and members of his staff undoubtedly would question the statement that the legislature was "rarely more than a rubber stamp." The governor's most difficult interpersonal relations involve handling the legislative leaders. Assembly Speaker Joseph F. Carlino (1959–64) and Senate President Pro Tem Walter J. Mahoney (1954–64) were not pro-Rockefeller. Furthermore, Governor Rockefeller went out front on tough issues to spare the legislative leaders and Republican members difficulties.

The governor, as leader of his party, is in a position to draw upon an additional resource in order to persuade members of his party in the legislature to support his bills. In 1952 Mosher wrote that the governor of the Empire State has greater control over his political party than the president has over his party:

This strength is due to a number of factors: the high prestige of the office; the Governor's ability to go directly to the people which he has never been reluctant to utilize; his national prominence, which links the welfare of the whole state party with his career; his control of state patronage which renders virtually every county machine dependent upon him; his power to grant or withhold favors to legislators; his nearly complete control over all the state administrative machinery; and the forcefulness and political leadership of the Governors and the progressiveness and popularity of the programs they have sponsored.[114]

The Mosher statement applies with equal force to the Rockefeller governorship.

A wise governor sees to it that the patronage needs of county chairmen and members of the legislature of his party are accommodated, at least partially. A governor can put pressure upon a legislator of his party by requesting the member's county chairman to speak to the member regarding the governor's wishes or to threaten the withholding of party support.

Some governors believe they must exercise tight control over the party; others are convinced that they need to maintain only loose supervision over the party and that the state chairman should run the party. The latter type of governor, Averell Harriman, for example, usually discovers he is seriously weakened by this laissez-faire policy. Roosevelt kept James Farley on a tight leash, and Lehman projected an image of nonpartisanship as he maintained strict party discipline. Dewey exercised such tight control over the Republican county apparatus that he in effect was the state Republican chairman. By systematizing patronage and helping to finance the party, Rockefeller had the county chairmen in his pocket. Carey entered office with an upstate-downstate split in his party as well as splits within the downstate Democrats. His use of "political novices" as "appointments officers" antagonized many Democratic county chairmen.

To win support for his legislative proposals, Governor Rockefeller was careful to balance upstate and downstate interests, and he worked effectively with the minority party legislative leaders as well as with the majority party legislative leaders. Robert H. Connery in 1974 described Governor Rockefeller's relations with the legislature as follows:

Although his main tactic in dealing with the Legislature was persuasion, an art in which he was particularly effective, he recognized the political realities. He was not above using patronage to influence a member's vote, and he could occasionally act with aggressive effectiveness to compel legislative compliance with his wishes.[115]

Kramer and Roberts wrote that the governor of the Empire State has a large amount of patronage of various forms to dispense:

A governor has lots to give away: millions of dollars of interest-free deposits to deserving banks; fees for professional services to firms owned by party fat cats; unpaid ego-massaging appointments to co-opt image makers and enlist them in the "search for solutions"; promulgation of laws and regulations that would reap ample profits for a favored few; and, of course, the fuel that kept the party machines running smoothly and efficiently—jobs.[116]

Kramer and Roberts also quote Queens County Democratic Chairman Matthew Troy, Jr., as stating that "the state patronage I get is all part of deals, usually for votes he [Rockefeller] needs in the Legislature."[117]

Executive Dominance?

Does the governor dominate the entire government of the Empire State? The answer clearly is in the negative, even though strong governors may create such an impression. The governor appoints judges of the Court of Claims (and judges of the Court of Appeals since 1978) and fills vacancies on other courts, except the New York

City Civil and Criminal Courts, by appointment, yet there is no evidence that any governor has attempted to dominate the judicial branch.

The governor is the constitutional head, or chief executive, of only seventeen of the twenty departments. Relative to these departments, it is apparent that the governor may be the dominant official, but these departments are staffed to a large extent by civil service employees who must follow policies established by the legislature.

A combination of strong formal powers and strong personalities enabled several governors to be the Empire State's principal policy leaders. The myth of "executive dominance" is attributable in large measure to the leadership style of Governor Rockefeller in his relations with the legislature. The leadership displayed by strong governors was not dictatorial and often was subtle and consultative in nature.

While it is apparent that the governor has played a significantly larger role in the policymaking process since the executive budget system went into effect in 1929, the legislature has not been an entirely obsequious institution, and on occasions has handed governors stinging defeats. Furthermore, while there is no denying that many major legislative proposals during the past half century originated in the office of the Governor, one must not overlook major pieces of legislation originating in the legislature, such as the Ives-Quinn law, the first antidiscrimination law in the nation; the law establishing the state university system; the Mitchell-Lama law providing assistance for middle-income housing; and a considerable amount of senior citizen legislation.

CONCLUSIONS

The Watergate scandal of the Nixon administration did not produce a spinoff challenge to the strong executive powers possessed by the governor of the Empire State but did reinforce the public's skeptical attitude toward elected and appointed officials in the state. Evidence is lacking that a serious attempt will be made during the next decade to weaken the formal powers of the governor or add to his formal powers.

Occupation of the office of governor by a forceful personality in the future probably will not result in policy leadership by the governor and what appears to be an acquiescing legislature. The legal and structural restraints upon the governor are far less restricting than environmental factors such as wars, inflation, recessions, shift of industries to the South and the West, and the near financial collapse of certain cities. With respect to the latter, the fiscal problems of New York City, Buffalo, and Yonkers have strained the financial resources of the state in a period when there appears to be a growing popular movement for tax reduction, thereby changing the nature of the governor's leadership role. The lack of revenue to support major innovative programs will undoubtedly lead to more "caretaker" governors, and it is improbable that another dynamic governor of the Rockefeller type will appear on the scene in the foreseeable future. Even Governor Rockefeller became aware of the growing fiscal limitations during his last term and the growing conservatism of the voters as reflected in their rejection of a $3.5 billion transportation capital facilities bond issue in 1973 and their increasing concern with crime and drug addiction.

Trends indicate that executive-legislative cooperation will become more common in the future. Annual sessions probably will become longer because of the growing complexity of problems and may lead to a reduction in the number of gubernatorial vetoes, since additional time will be available for the governor and the legislature to reconcile their differences through extraconstitutional means, as occurred in Massachusetts with a lengthening of the annual session in the 1950s and 1960s. Vetoes, however, will remain difficult for the legislature to override. Furthermore, one should anticipate more legislative initiatives in major policy areas whenever both houses are controlled by the same political party, regardless of who is governor, because of the growth of the professional staff of the legislature and the increase in the number of "marginal" legislative districts.

The former governor whose actions while in office will influence most significantly the future course taken by the Empire State is Nelson A. Rockefeller. His legacy includes a model of strong executive leadership, a model of gubernatorial-legislative cooperation, a great expansion of the state's physical facilities, a large state debt if one includes moral obligation debt, and an expanded number of statewide public authorities. This legacy will significantly influence the policymaking process and the decisional output of the process in the future. In particular, the large full faith and moral obligation debts impose a severe restraint on the ability of the state to launch expensive innovative programs.

In sum, the public will continue to look to the governor for guidance and leadership in solving major public problems. Cooperation between the governor and the legislature will be a hallmark of the governance system as future governors and legislatures tackle difficult problems.

NOTES

1. Warren Moscow, *Politics in the Empire State* (New York: Alfred A. Knopf, 1948), pp. 186–87.

2. *New York Constitution,* art. IV, § 2. In 1972 the South Carolina Supreme Court upheld the state's constitutional five-year residency requirement for the governorship. See "Court Bars Victor in Carolina Race," *The New York Times,* September 24, 1974, p. 21.

3. *New York Constitution,* art. IV, § 1.

4. Frank Lynn, "Miss Krupsak Bars a Re-election Race in Split with Carey," *The New York Times,* June 13, 1978, p. 46.

5. Ralph Blumenthal, "The 'Seldom-Show' Jobs," *The New York Times,* March 25, 1974, p. 14.

6. *New York Constitution,* art. VI, § 24.

7. Jacob A. Friedman, *The Impeachment of Governor William Sulzer* (New York: Columbia University Press, 1939).

8. *Public Papers of Governor William Sulzer* (Albany: J. B. Lyon Company, 1913), pp. 177–204.

9. *Public Papers of Nelson A. Rockefeller: Fifty-Third Governor of the State of New York, 1973* (Albany: State of New York, n.d.), pp. 1371–72. See also *New York Public Officers Law,* § 31 (McKinney 1980 Supp.).

10. *New York Constitution,* art. IV, § 5.

11. *Ibid.,* § 6.

12. *Ibid.*, Speaker Stanley Steingut, who was ill with influenza, was governor on October 22, 1975, without being aware of the fact at the time.

13. *New York State Senate Resolution 108 of 1968*, and *New York Laws of 1980*, chap. 881.

14. *State of New York Executive Budget 1979–80 Submitted by Hugh L. Carey, Governor to the New York State Legislature* (Albany: Executive Chamber, January 31, 1979), p. 6.

15. Joseph A. Schlesinger, "A Comparison of the Relative Positions of Governors," in Thad Beyle and J. Oliver Williams, eds., *The American Governor in Behavioral Perspective* (New York: Harper and Row, Publishers, 1972), pp. 141–50.

16. Joseph F. Zimmerman, The Executive Veto in Massachusetts: 1947–1960," *Social Science,* June 1962, pp. 162–68.

17. *Gaynor V. Rockefeller,* 15 N.Y. 2d 120 (1964). *New York State Employees Council 50 v. Rockefeller,* 55 Misc. 2d 250, 248 N.Y.S. 2d 803 (1967).

18. Robert H. Connery, "Nelson A. Rockefeller as Governor," in Robert H. Connery and Gerald Benjamin, eds., *Governing New York State: The Rockefeller Years* (New York: The Academy of Political Science, 1974) p. 3.

19. In 1976, the Regents removed Ewald B. Nyquist as commissioner. See "Regents Dismiss Nyquist as Education Commissioner," *The New York Times,* November 20, 1976, pp. 1 and 38.

20. *New York Laws of 1971,* chap. 111. *New York Social Service Law,* § 11 (McKinney 1980 Supp.).

21. *Informal Opinions of the Attorney General of the State of New York* (1957), p. 144.

22. *New York Executive Law,* art. 8, § 180 (McKinney 1972).

23. See J. M. Gitterman, "The Council of Appointment," *Political Science Quarterly,* May 1892, pp. 80–115; and Hugh M. Flick, "The Council of Appointment in New York State," *New York History,* 1934, pp. 253–80.

24. *State of New York Executive Order Number 10* (May 22, 1975). In a related development, candidates for governor in recent years have been making voluntary public disclosure of their family income.

25. *State of New York Executive Order Number 10.1* (October 29, 1976). This expansion was invalidated by the Court of Appeals on March 29, 1978. See *State of New York Executive Order Number 10.2* (March 12, 1979).

26. Linda Greenhouse, "Senate in Albany Rejects Schwartz for Prison Post," *The New York Times,* April 14, 1976, p. 52.

27. *New York Constitution,* art. VI, §§ 2 and 9.

28. Frank Lynn, "Party Plum: State Parks Full of Jobs," *The New York Times,* April 28, 1975, p. 28.

29. *New York Constitution,* art. V, § 4, and art. XIII, § 13.

30. *New York Public Officers Law,* § 32 (McKinney 1952).

31. *Ibid.,* § 33 (McKinney 1978 Supp.). For the removal of a local officer, see *People v. Ahearn,* 196 N.Y. 182, 89 N.E. 930 (1909).

32. *New York Public Officers Law,* § 33-a (McKinney 1978 Supp.).

33. *Public Papers of Charles Seymour Whitman: Governor, 1917* (Albany: J. B. Lyon Company, 1919), pp. 441–44.

34. *Public Papers of Charles Evans Hughes: Governor, 1907* (Albany: J. B. Lyon Company, 1908), pp. 275–86; and *Public Papers of Franklin D. Roosevelt: Forty-*

Eighth Governor of the State of New York, 1931 (Albany: J. B. Lyon Company, 1937),
p. 486. The New York City charter currently authorizes the governor to remove the
mayor, comptroller, president of the City Council, and the borough presidents from
office.

    35. David M. Ellis *et al., A History of New York State* (Ithaca: Cornell University
Press, 1967), pp. 414–16.

    36. Letter to Attorney General Lewis J. Lefkowitz from Governor Malcolm
Wilson dated November 1, 1974, *Public Papers of Malcolm Wilson: Fiftieth Governor
of the State of New York, 1973–74* (Albany: State of New York, n.d.), pp. 763–66.
One would expect that Governor Wilson's *Papers* would list him as the fifty-fourth
governor, since Governor Rockefeller's *Papers* list him as the fifty-third governor.
However, some governors served two or more nonconsecutive terms, and Governor
Wilson was the fiftieth person to occupy the office of governor. See also *New York
Public Officers Law,* § 30 (McKinney 1978 Supp.), and *New York Executive Law,*
§ 63-a (McKinney 1972).

    37. *New York Laws of 1907,* chap. 539. *New York Executive Law,* § 6 (McKinney
1972). For further details, see John E. Missall, *The Moreland Act* (New York: King's
Crown Press, 1946).

    38. *State of New York Executive Orders Numbers 2 and 3 of 1975.* See also
Restoring Credit and Confidence (Albany: New York State Moreland Act Commission
on the Urban Development Corporation and Other State Financing Agencies, 1976).

    39. *New York Laws of 1953,* chap. 887.

    40. *New York Laws of 1958,* chap. 989.

    41. *Public Papers of Charles Evans Hughes: Governor, 1909* (Albany: J. B. Lyon
Company, 1910), pp. 78–79.

    42. *New York Constitution,* art. 5, § 2 (1928).

    43. *New York State Finance Law,* § 24 (McKinney 1974).

    44. *People v. Tremaine,* 252 N.Y. 27 (1929).

    45. *New York Laws of 1939,* chap. 460.

    46. *People v. Tremaine,* 281 N.Y. 8 (1939).

    47. Frederick C. Mosher, "The Executive Budget, Empire State Style," *Public
Administration Review,* Spring 1952, p. 80.

    48. *New York Constitution,* art. VII, § 3.

    49. *Ibid.,* § 5.

    50. *Ibid.,* § 4.

    51. *Ibid.*

    52. *Ibid.,* § 1.

    53. Mosher, "The Executive Budget, Empire State Style," p. 82.

    54. William E. Farrell, "Levitt Sues to Test Rockefeller's Budget," *The New
York Times,* February 23, 1972, pp. 1 and 41.

    55. *Levitt v. Rockefeller,* 69 Misc. 2d 337, 329 N.Y.S. 2d 976 (1972). See also
William E. Farrell, "Suit Over Constitutionality of Budget Is Dropped," *The New
York Times,* March 18, 1972, p. 34. In 1971 the Appellate Division upheld a Supreme
Court ruling that "the Comptroller may not be compelled to institute a declaratory
judgment action to test the legality of the budget." *Posner v. Levitt,* 37 A.D. 2d 331,
325 N.Y.S. 2d 519 (1971). See also *Posner v. Levitt,* 67 Misc. 2d 565, 324 N.Y.S. 553
(1971).

    56. *New York State Finance Law,* § 22 (McKinney 1974).

57. Mosher, "The Executive Budget, Empire State Style," p. 84.

58. *Empire State Report,* February/March 1972, p. 89.

59. *New York State Finance Law,* § 51 (McKinney 1974).

60. *County of Oneida v. Berle,* 49 N.Y. 2d 515 (1980).

61. *New York Constitution,* art. IV, § 3.

62. *People v. Bard,* 209 N.Y. 304, 103 N.E. 140 (1943).

63. *State of New York Executive Order Number 48* (January 31, 1977).

64. *New York Constitution,* art. IV, § 3, and art. VII, § 2.

65. Connery, "Nelson A. Rockefeller as Governor," p. 6.

66. *Public Papers of Nelson A. Rockefeller: Fifty-Third Governor of the State of New York, 1960* (Albany: State of New York, n.d.), pp. 157–77.

67. *Malcolm Wilson, Message to the Legislature: January 9, 1974,* State of New York Legislative Document (1974), No. 1, p. 1. The message also is printed in *Public Papers of Malcolm Wilson,* 1973–74, pp. 15–32.

68. Francis X. Clines, "Rockefeller Is Out, but He's in Touch," *The New York Times,* June 8, 1974, p. 33.

68. Linda Greenhouse, "The Slow Season in Albany," *The New York Times,* June 20, 1977, p. 30.

70. *New York Constitution,* art. IV, § 3.

71. *Ibid.,* art. III, § 18. See also *New York Legislative Law,* art. 2-A (McKinney 1978 Supp.).

72. Charles Z. Lincoln, ed., *Messages from the Governors* (Albany: J. B. Lyon Company, 1900), Vol. III, p. 15.

73. *Veto Message #1* (Albany: Executive Chamber, March 13, 1978).

74. Letter from Attorney General Louis J. Lefkowitz to President Pro Tem Warren M. Anderson of the New York State Senate dated April 5, 1978. Available in the Office of the Attorney General.

75. *Doyle v. Hofstader,* 257 N.Y. 244, 177 N.E. 489 (1931).

76. *Koenig v. Flynn,* 258 N.Y. 292, 179 N.E. 705 (1932). *Koenig v. Flynn,* 285 U.S. 375 (1932).

77. *Press Release* (Albany: Executive Chamber, March 11, 1978). For the governor's veto of the 1978 bill restoring the death penalty, see *Veto Memorandum #2 of 1978* (Albany: Executive Chamber, April 10, 1978).

78. For details, see Andrew J. Di Nitto "Governor Rockefeller and the Executive Veto: Uses and Perceptions" (Ph.D. Dissertation, Graduate School of Public Affairs, State University of New York at Albany, 1977). For a historical perspective of the veto, see Frank W. Prescott and Joseph F. Zimmerman, *The Politics of the Veto of Legislation in New York* (Washington, D.C.: University Press of America, Inc., 1980).

79. Di Nitto, *Governor Rockefeller and the Executive Veto,* pp. 171–72.

80. *Ibid.,* p. 208.

81. Lincoln, *Messages from the Governors,* Vol. III, pp. 37–38; *Assembly Journal* (1824), p. 1256; and *Senate Journal* (1824), p. 481.

82. Lincoln, *Messages from the Governors,* Vol. V, pp. 238–42.

83. See Chapter III for a discussion of the 1976 override of the veto. The Senate failed by one vote to override Governor Carey's 1978 veto of a bill restoring the death penalty. On April 16, 1917, the legislature overrode Governor Charles S. Whitman's veto of four items for legislative expenses. See *The New York Times,* April 17, 1917, p. 20.

222   The Government and Politics of New York State

84. Mosher, "The Executive Budget, Empire State Style," p. 80.

85. Legislators on occasion have introduced bills for the stated purpose of curtailing the governor's veto power. A proposed constitutional amendment—A. 8781 of 1972—directed the legislature to reconvene annually fifty days subsequent to the adjournment of the regular session for the sole purpose of considering bills disallowed by the governor during the thirty-day postadjournment consideration period. The proposed amendment died in the Assembly Judiciary Committee.

86. *News from Senate Majority Leader Warren M. Anderson* (Albany: The Capitol, July 11, 1973), p. 1. See also *Joint Rules of the Senate and Assembly Rule 27.*

87. William E. Farrell, "Rockefeller at Hearing: A Partial Picture," *The New York Times,* October 10, 1974, p. 34.

88. *Revised Record of the New York State Constitutional Convention* (Albany: J. B. Lyon Company, 1916), p. 771.

89 *Ibid.*

90. Lincoln, *Messages from the Governors,* Vol. VIII, p. 25.

91. *Ibid.,* pp. 124–25.

92. *Ibid.,* p. 208.

93. *State of New York Executive Order Number 70* (March 1, 1978).

94. Damon Stetson, "Affirmative-Action Order by Carey Exceeded Authority, Court Says," *The New York Times,* September 2, 1977, p. B-3. See also *State of New York Executive Order Number 45* (January 4, 1977).

95. Tom Goldstein, "Court Ruling Made on Financial Status," *The New York Times,* March 30, 1978, p. 39. See also *State of New York Executive Order 10.1* (October 29, 1976).

96. Carl L. Swidorski, "The Politics of Judicial Selection: Accession to the New York Court of Appeals, 1960–1975" (Ph.D. Dissertation, Graduate School of Public Affairs, State University of New York at Albany, 1977), p. 445.

97. *Ibid.,* p. 443.

98. *New York Constitution,* art. VI, § 2.

99. Michael Kramer and Sam Roberts, *"I Never Wanted to Be Vice-President of Anything!": An Investigative Biography of Nelson Rockefeller* (New York: Basic Books, Inc., Publishers, 1976), p. 104.

100. *State of New York Executive Order Number 5* (February 24, 1975). See also Alfonso A. Narvaez, "Governor Sets Up Screening Panel to Select Judges," *The New York Times,* February 24, 1975, pp. 1 and 14.

101. *New York Constitution,* art. VI, § 4 (c).

102. *Ibid.*

103. Alfred E. Smith, *The Citizen and His Government* (New York: Harper and Brothers, Publishers, 1935), p. 94.

104. *New York Constitution,* art. IV, § 2.

105. *Ibid.,* § 3. See also *In re B. Turecamo Contracting Company,* 260 App. Div. 253 (1940) and *New York Executive Law,* § 62 (McKinney 1972).

106. Letter to Attorney General Louis J. Lefkowitz from Governor Malcolm Wilson dated March 18, 1974, *Public Papers of Malcolm Wilson,* pp. 740–41.

107. *State of New York Executive Order Number 31* (February 13, 1976).

108. Richard J. Meislin, "Hynes to Handle Medicaid Fraud; Carey Moves to Expand U.S. Aid," *The New York Times,* April 27, 1978, p. 41.

109. *Public Papers of Nelson A. Rockefeller: Fifty-Third Governor of the State*

of New York, 1972 (Albany: State of New York, n.d.), p. 723. See also David Burnham, "Governor Supersedes D.A.'s Here, Names Special Aide to Corruption and Orders a Staff of 200 Hired," *The New York Times*, September 20, 1972, pp. 1 and 29; and Maurice Nessen, "No More Nadjari, No More Special Prosecuting," *Empire State Report*, February 1977, pp. 51–60 and 85.

110. Nessen, "No More Nadjari, No More Special Prosecuting," p. 57.

111. John F. Keenan, *Annual Progress Report to Governor Hugh L. Carey and Attorney General Louis J. Lefkowitz* (New York: Office of Special State Prosecutor, July 20, 1978), p. 1. See also Charles Kaiser, "Special State Prosecutor Reports Fewer Convictions for Last Year," *The New York Times,* July 24, 1978, p. A-12.

112. Moscow, *Politics in the Empire State*, pp. 195–97.

113. Kramer and Roberts, *"I Never Wanted to Be Vice-President of Anything!"* pp. 7–8. The authors are incorrect in writing that the Republicans controlled the legislature for thirteen of the Rockefeller years, as the Democrats controlled the Assembly in the period 1965–68 and the Senate in 1965.

114. Mosher, "The Executive Budget, Empire State Style," p. 83.

115. Connery, "Nelson A. Rockefeller as Governor," p. 11.

116. Kramer and Roberts, *"I Never Wanted to Be Vice-President of Anything!"* p. 98. The reader should recognize that the governor does not possess unchecked authority to do everything cited by Kramer and Roberts.

117. *Ibid.,* p. 106.

CHAPTER VIII
The Fourth Branch

THE DEPARTMENTS and agencies of the executive branch of the state government commonly are referred to as the "fourth branch" of the government as a sign of their current importance in the system of governance. The themes of executive integration, group politics, and intergovernmental relations appear in this chapter, as much of the history of the Empire State has involved struggles by interest groups over the most desirable degree of executive integration and state control of local government personnel.

In 1777 there was no evidence that administrative agencies would play a prominent role in the future, since the Empire State had a simple administrative structure responsible for relatively few functions, and the principal state administrative officials were elected by the legislature. The office of state comptroller was created in 1797[1] but did not acquire constitutional status until the adoption of a new constitution in 1821. Three canal commissioners and three inspectors of state prisons were accorded constitutional status by a new constitution adopted in 1846.

Industrialization and urbanization subsequent to the Civil War ipso facto produced popular pressures for the state to provide new services, and the response of the Legislature generally was the establishment of a new department or agency for each new function. To cite only two examples, the State Board of Charities was established in 1867 and the State Board of Health was created in 1880.[2] By the end of the nineteenth century, a serious organizational problem had been generated by the proliferation of new departments and agencies, resulting in duplication of responsibility, increased cost, and inability to pinpoint responsibility for administrative fail-ures. Early in the twentieth century, the structural weaknesses of the executive branch led to the emergence of the "administrative reorganization movement."

THE ADMINISTRATIVE REORGANIZATION
MOVEMENT

The municipal reform movement, originating in the 1890s, and the scientific management movement had a spinoff effect by pro-moting interest in the administrative reorganization of state gov-ernment. The first governor to express major concern with the ad-ministrative structure of the Empire State was Charles Evans Hughes, who in 1910 recommended a complete reorganization that would make the governor responsible for the state departments and agencies.

Interest in reorganization was stimulated further by the 1912 report of the Commission on Economy and Efficiency appointed by President William H. Taft. The following year Governor William Sulzer successfully urged the legislature to create a State Board of Estimates and a State Department of Efficiency and Economy.[3]

The 1915 constitutional convention, in addition to proposing an executive budget system, drafted a new constitution providing for the reorganization of the 152 agencies in the executive branch, but the proposed constitution was rejected by the electorate.[4] In January 1919 Governor Alfred E. Smith appointed the State Reconstruction Commission and charged it with examining the administrative or-ganization and procedures of the state government.[5] In its report, the commission recommended consolidation of state departments and agencies into sixteen departments, establishment of an exec-utive budget system, increasing from two to four years the term of the governor, and making changes in the salary schedule and the pension system.[6] Governor Smith proposed that the legislature act to implement the recommendations, including those requiring amendment of the state constitution.[7] The reorganization movement came to a near halt with the election of Governor Nathan L. Miller in 1920, but limited progress was made as various labor and revenue agencies were merged into two new departments.[8]

Assuming the office of governor again in 1923, Smith was successful in persuading the legislature to enact a law consolidating several agencies into the Department of Public Works,[9] and also to approve in two successive years a proposed constitutional amendment reorganizing the executive branch that was ratified by the voters in 1925.[10] As implementation of the amendment required executive and legislative action, Governor Smith and the legislative leaders appointed the State Reorganization Commission, under the chairmanship of Charles Evans Hughes, to examine the administrative structure of the state government. The Hughes Commission report served as the basis for the subsequent administrative reorganization, based upon the organizational principle of span of control, resulting in the merger of 187 agencies into 18 departments.[11] In 1926 the Executive Department was organized as one of the eighteen departments;[12] the Department of Commerce was created by a 1944 law[13] implementing a voter-ratified 1943 constitutional amendment; and the Department of Motor Vehicles was created by a 1960 law[14] implementing a voter-ratified 1959 constitutional amendment.

Although the number of civil departments does not exceed the constitutional maximum of twenty, there are a number of independent or semi-independent agencies within the departments. The Executive Department, for example, has thirty separate units in addition to the Executive Chamber, and the budget of each of several units is larger than the budget of one of the smaller departments— the Civil Service Department, the Commerce Department, and the Department of State.

A 1959 report, prepared by the secretary to the governor, contained a number of major recommendations for the reorganization of the executive branch and a reassignment of responsibility for a number of functions.[15] To implement the secretary's report, popularly known as the Ronan Report, Governor Nelson A. Rockefeller recommended that the legislature initiate a number of actions, including a constitutional amendment providing greater flexibility in establishing civil departments. Ratified by the voters on November 7, 1961, the amendment limited the maximum number of departments to twenty without specifying their names, and it authorized the legislature to create temporary commissions and Executive Offices of the Governor.

Governor Rockefeller proposed and the legislature created several new organizational entities to facilitate solutions to manifold problems. Two major new departments were established during the Rockefeller administration. The 1967 legislature enacted and the governor signed a bill creating a Department of Transportation, the Metropolitan Transportation Authority, and the Niagara Frontier Transportation Authority.[16]

A somewhat similar reorganization occurred in 1970 when the legislature enacted and the governor signed a bill creating a Department of Environmental Conservation.[17] As part of the environmental reorganization, the Pure Waters Authority, created in 1967,[18] was converted into the Environmental Facilities Corporation with enlarged powers, and the commissioner of environmental conservation was designated the chairman of the corporation.[19]

THE MAJOR DEPARTMENTS

Testifying before the Committee on the Executive Branch of the 1967 constitutional convention, Governor Rockefeller suggested that "we eliminate the present artificial restriction on the number of State departments that the Constitution imposes, and that we follow the example of the Federal government which enables the Nation's chief executive to reorganize the executive branch subject to legislative review."[20] Neither suggestion has been adopted, yet the constitutional restriction, in effect, has been circumvented by the establishment of the Executive Department as a holding company.

The Executive Department

The Executive Department, headed by the governor, is composed of the Division of the Budget, other agencies that do not merit departmental status, and developing agencies. In addition to the powerful Division of the Budget, the following agencies officially are part of the Executive Department: Division of Military and

Naval Affairs, Division of State Police, Division of Alcoholic Beverage Control, Division of Housing and Community Renewal, Division of Veterans' Affairs, Division of Human Rights, Division for Youth, State Board of Equalization and Assessment, Office of General Services, Health Planning Commission, St. Lawrence–Eastern Ontario Commission, Council on the Arts, Office for the Aging, Crime Victims Compensation Board, Office of Parks and Recreation, State Consumer Protection Board, Office of Employee Relations, Division of Probation, State Board of Social Welfare, Permanent Commission on Public Employee Pension and Retirement Systems, Commission on Cable Television, Commission on Legislative and Judicial Salaries, Adirondack Park Agency, Division of Criminal Justice Services, Racing and Wagering Board, Commission of Correction, Board of Elections, Interdepartmental Committee on Human Rights, Economic Development Board, and Office of State Ombudsman.

Department of Law

The Department of Law is headed by the attorney general, who serves a four-year term and receives a salary of $60,000 annually, which will be increased to $85,000 in 1983.[21] The attorney general possesses important powers as he prosecutes and defends all proceedings for and against the state.[22] Specifically, the attorney general is in charge of the legal affairs of all state departments and agencies and prosecutes criminal violations of the Conservation Law, provisions of the Education Law relating to the conduct of professions with the exception of the law profession, Insurance Law, Labor Law, Unemployment Insurance Law, and Workmen's Compensation Law.[23] The Executive Law stipulates that "whenever in his judgment the public interest requires it, the Attorney-General may, with the approval of the Governor, and when directed by the Governor, shall, inquire into matters concerning the public peace, public safety, and public justice."[24]

The attorney general also prosecutes persons for the fraudulent sale of securities and violations of the General Business Law provisions prohibiting consumer frauds and restraint of trade. He may investigate the unlawful practice of law[25] and prosecute persons for perjury committed during one of his investigations; and he is chairman of the State Board of Canvassers and a member of the State

Defense Council, the Buffalo and Fort Erie Bridge Authority, and the Crime Control Planning Office. In addition, the attorney general separately or jointly with the governor may appoint special prosecutors and may be directed by the governor to supersede a district attorney (described in Chapter IX).[26]

In terms of the political importance of the office, Arvis Chalmers reports that the attorney general has more patronage jobs to distribute than any other state official except the governor and that Attorney General Robert Abrams, upon assuming office in 1979, had more than $21 million in high-level positions to fill—362 attorneys earning $30,000 to $50,000 annually—and an additional $14 million in lower-level confidential positions.[27]

Department of Audit and Control

The Department of Audit and Control is headed by the state comptroller, who serves a four-year tern and receives an annual salary of $60,000, which will be increased to $85,000 in 1983.[28] The comptroller currently is required by the constitution to (1) audit all vouchers before payment and all official accounts, (2) audit the accrual and collection of all revenues and receipts, and (3) prescribe such methods of accounting as are necessary for the performance of the foregoing duties.[29] The Court of Appeals in 1971, however, ruled that the assigned duties of the comptroller did not require the preauditing of the accounts of public corporations in general or of the Urban Development Corporation in particular.[30]

The legislature may assign the comptroller the following additional powers: "(1) supervision of the accounts of any political subdivision of the State; and (2) powers and duties pertaining to or connected with the assessment and taxation of real estate, including determination of ratios which the assessed valuation of taxable property bears to the full valuation thereof, but not including any of those powers and duties reserved to officers to a county, city, town, or village by virtue of sections seven and eight of article nine of this Constitution."[31] The legislature has assigned the duty of determining the full-value ratio of taxable real property to the State Board of Equalization and Assessment.[32] One important limitation on the legislature is the constitutional provision forbidding the legislature from assigning administrative duties to the comptroller.[33] However, the comptroller may perform other duties or hold other public office, provided the duties entailed are not incompatible with his duties as comptroller.[34] To cite only three examples, the comptroller is the sole trustee of the State Employees' Retirement System, the Policemen's and Firemen's Retirement System, and the Public Employees' Group Life Insurance Plan.

The Citizens Union of the City of New York in 1967 issued a constitutional position paper highly critical of "the present confusion of duties assigned to the State Comptroller, under which the Comptroller audits himself," and added:

He must be an independent, outside auditor, and must not be mixed up in running things, managing funds, drawing pay checks, serving on boards, fixing local boundaries, approving drafts of contracts, selecting deposit banks, issuing bonds, or keeping the books. These are the things we want checked, by a man who has had nothing to do with them, aided by a competent staff which has no interest in proving that the decisions it helped to make are O.K.[35]

The Citizens Union recommended that these functions be shifted to other agencies in the executive branch and that the comptroller's sole function be postauditing.[36]

Welfare Inspector General. Concern with the escalating costs of welfare and evidence of individuals illegally receiving welfare benefits led Governor Rockefeller in 1971 to send a special message on welfare to the legislature proposing the creation of the Office of Welfare Inspector General in the Executive Department to investigate complaints relating to alleged abuses, frauds, and other violations of the system of public welfare.[37] The legislature agreed and enacted the governor's proposal into law.[38] The welfare inspector initially was appointed by the governor with the advice and consent of the Senate and served at the pleasure of the governor. The third annual report of the welfare inspector general revealed that the number of persons on the state's welfare rolls had declined by 145,000 during 1973 and that a large proportion of the decrease was attributable to the office's "deterrent effect, pressure for welfare reforms in work relief, face-to-face recertifications, fraud prosecution, and recoupment and direct prodding of all welfare agencies."[39]

Upon assuming office, Governor Hugh L. Carey decided that the office should be transferred to the Department of Audit and

Control, and the legislature agreed.[40] The new law did not change the powers and functions of the inspector general, but it did provide for his appointment for a five-year term by the state comptroller with the consent of the Senate.

In a 1977 report State Comptroller Arthur Levitt wrote that savings of more than $40 million had been effected by the Office of Welfare Inspector General through a series of studies and investigations during the eighteen months subsequent to the transfer of that office to the Department of Audit and Control.[41]

Testifying before the Senate Social Services Committee and the Governmental Operations Committee on March 22, 1978, Acting Welfare Inspector General Ralph A. Cirpiani reported receiving in excess of 4,000 complaints during 1977 and that "investigations of such individual fraud complaints have resulted in savings and recoupments estimated at $12.5 million from 1971 through the last fiscal year ended March 31, 1977."[42]

Department of Education

The Department of Education is the administrative arm of the Regents of the University of the State of New York. Originally incorporated by the 1784 legislature, the Regents have had constitutional status since 1894.[43]

The first constitutional provision relating to public education was Article IX of the constitution of 1846, which stipulated that the revenue of the "Common School Fund shall be applied to the support of common schools." The 1894 constitution mandated that "the Legislature shall provide for the maintenance and support of a system of free common schools, wherein all the children of this State may be educated."[44]

Currently, there are fifteen Regents, serving overlapping terms of seven years, elected by the legislature.[45] The chancellor and the vice chancellor, elected by the Regents from among their members, are the officers of the board that appoints and may remove a commissioner of education who serves as chief administrative officer of the department.[46]

The University of the State of New York encompasses all education, public and private, from kindergarten through professional and graduate schools. Although local boards of education operate the public schools under Regents' guidelines and policies, the courts have ruled that public education is a state rather than a local function inasmuch as the boards are governmental agencies of the state and are not civil subdivisions.[47] The university also includes libraries, museums, and other educational institutions incorporated by the Regents or admitted to the university, which also is composed of nearly 5,000 elementary and secondary schools and in excess of 200 colleges and universities.

A number of decisions—especially ones designed to promote school integration—made by Commissioner of Education Ewald B. Nyquist infuriated many members of the legislature and led to the enactment of a 1976 law deleting the provisions of the Education Law, making decisions of the commissioner final and not judicially reviewable, thereby making the commission's decisions reviewable in the same manner as administrative determinations of other state officials pursuant to Article 78 of the Civil Practice Law and Rules.[48]

Education Inspector General. With state expenditures for elementary and secondary education amounting to more than one fourth of total state spending, it is not surprising that governors and legislatures have been concerned about the quality of education and the impact of education on the state budget. In his 1973 annual message to the legislature, Governor Rockefeller stated that "educational policy . . . is entirely under [the] jurisdiction of the Regents" and added that "your Honorable Bodies and I must take responsibility for determining and imposing the taxes to provide the States' dollars spent for this purpose—but he can no longer avoid having some direct share of the responsibility for determining how those taxes are spent."[49] His recommendation to solve the problem was the "establishment of the Office of Education Inspector General in the Executive Department to review performance in relation to expenditures under present programs and to recommend means of improving their effectiveness and efficiency."[50]

On April 8, 1973, Governor Rockefeller sent a bill (A. 7308) to the legislature to create a State Office of Education Performance Review, headed by a director, in the Executive Department authorized to review the operations of the Department of Education and "the program performance and organization of the public elementary and secondary educational system."[51]

Not surprisingly, the regents and the commissioner of education strongly opposed the governor's proposal, and they were joined in opposition by State Comptroller Arthur Levitt.[52] As opposition to the bill mounted, the legislature had second thoughts about the bill, and on May 23, 1973, Assembly Speaker Perry B. Duryea had the bill starred.[53] Nevertheless, the supplemental budget, approved on May 27, 1973, contained a $400,000 item "for services and expenses, including travel outside of the State, for a special assistant for educational performance review and staff to investigate and review the cost effectiveness of public expenditures for the operation of the State's system of public elementary and secondary education."[54] On June 23, 1973, Governor Rockefeller issued an executive order establishing an Office of Education Performance Review, which functioned for eighteen months and issued a total of nine reports prior to being abolished when Carey became governor in 1975.[55]

Based upon interviews with close observers, Robert J. Neiderberger wrote:

> About two-thirds of those interviewed expressed the belief that the Office had little or no impact. Two legislative staffers and two former staffers of the Office thought that it did have noticeable impact. . . . When pressed for examples of the Office's impact, individuals who said that there had been impact found it difficult to get specific.[56]

The Other Departments

The other sixteen departments are Agriculture and Markets, Banking, Civil Service (discussed later), Commerce, Environmental Conservation, Correction, Health, Insurance, Labor, Law, Mental Hygiene, Public Service, Social Services, State, Taxation and Finance, and Transportation. The Department of Mental Hygiene was reorganized in 1978 with the establishment of three autonomous offices—Mental Health, Mental Retardation and Developmental Disabilities, and Alcoholism and Substance Abuse—and in effect no longer functions as a department.[57] A three-member Commission on Quality of Care of the Mentally Disabled was created in 1978 and charged with inspecting and investigating alleged abuses at residential facilities for the mentally ill and the retarded.[58]

The departments vary in size from the Department of Commerce with only 443 permanent employees in 1980 to 13,523 permanent employees in the Department of Transportation. Detailed information on each department is contained in the annual executive budget, the *New York Red Book*, and the *Manual for the Use of the Legislature of the State of New York.*

THE PUBLIC AUTHORITIES

A distinction was made in the General Corporation Law until 1973 between municipal, district, and public benefit corporations, with the latter defined as ones "organized to construct or operate a public improvement wholly or partly within the State, the profits from which enure to the benefit of this or other States, or to the people thereof."[59]

A new section on public corporations was added to the constitution in 1938 and provides that each such corporation must be created by a special act of the state legislature; public authorities with the exceptions of interstate ones and ones whose members are appointed by the mayor of a city are subject to supervision by the state comptroller; and the bonds of such corporations are not backed by the "full faith and credit" of the state.[60] Constitutional amendments ratified in 1951, 1961, and 1969 guarantee the full faith and credit of the state as backing for State Thruway Authority bonds, Port Authority of New York and New Jersey bonds for railroad commuter cars, and bonds of a public industrial development corporation.[61]

Since the adoption of a new constitution in 1846, only the voters in a statewide referendum may authorize the issuance of full faith and credit bonds, which have first claim on state revenue and as a result carry a lower rate of interest than moral obligation bonds.[62] Should the legislature fail to appropriate adequate funds for the payment of interest on, and retirement of, the principal of full faith and credit bond issues, the constitution directs the state comptroller to "set apart from the first revenues thereafter received, applicable to the general fund of the State, a sum sufficient to pay such interest, installments of principal, or contributions to such sinking fund, as the case may be, and shall so apply the moneys thus set apart."[63]

The best-known and generally considered the most successful public authority is the Port Authority of New York and New Jersey, established by an interstate compact in 1921, which is governed by a Board of Commissioners, with six members appointed by the governor of each state for overlapping six-year terms.[64] The authority was charged with developing and operating transportation and terminal facilities in an area radiating twenty-five miles out from the Statue of Liberty in New York City Harbor. Currently, the authority has invested $3.8 billion in twenty-six facilities and has a debt exceeding $2.0 billion and 7,700 employees.

The nineteen state public authorities in existence in 1958 were concerned primarily with transportation—bridges, tunnels, marine ports, highways, subways, parks, and marketing.[65] The exceptions were the Industrial Exhibit Authority (1933), the Power Authority (1934), the Dormitory Authority (1944), and the Higher Education Assistance Corporation (1957). These authorities generally financed construction of facilities by issuance of revenue bonds supported by user fees, and the projects were considered to be "self-financing."

The use of public authorities to solve statewide and metropolitan problems increased dramatically during the Rockefeller governorship. Currently, there are forty-two state-controlled public authorities operating on a statewide or regional basis: eighteen for transportation, six for commerce and development, three for port development, thirteen for finance and housing, and two for marketing. Members of the authorities are appointed by the governor with Senate approval.

Prior to the formation of public authorities, the constitutional prohibition against the state borrowing funds without the approval of the voters in a referendum was evaded by lease-purchase agreements, a type of so-called back-door financing, providing that the state would lease a facility under a long-term contract and the developer would issue revenue bonds to be paid off with rent. Upon expiration of the lease, the state acquires title to the facility. A relatively recent example involved the state entering into a lease-purchase arrangement with Albany County for the construction of the Empire State Plaza. Albany County was invited to issue the long-term bonds to provide funds for the project, since counties are not required by the state constitution to submit a proposed full faith and credit bond issue to the electorate.

The Moral Obligation Bond

Whereas the early public authorities relied upon revenue bonds, with principal and interest paid by user fees, to finance construction of facilities, a new type of financing emerged in 1960 when the legislature created the New York Housing Finance Agency (HFA), which is authorized to issue bonds and utilize the proceeds to purchase mortgages from private developers of Mitchell-Lama housing projects.[65] To avoid constitutional problems, the Private Housing Finance Law carefully stipulates that "the State shall not be liable on notes or bonds of the Agency and such notes and bonds shall not be a debt of the State, and such notes and bonds shall contain on the face thereof of statement to such effect."[67]

The enabling statute requires HFA to establish a debt-service reserve fund with bond proceeds equal to one year's debt service. If revenues are insufficient to cover debt service, the reserve fund is drawn upon. Should the fund prove insufficient, the agency certifies this fact to the governor, who notifies the legislature that the fund needs to be restored. Upon receipt of notification by the governor, the statute stipulates that "the Legislature shall apportion" the funds necessary to replenish the reserve. "Apportion" obviously does not command the legislature to "appropriate" the funds. Since one legislature constitutionally cannot bind another legislature, the promise to "apportion" the funds is viewed as a moral obligation of a subsequent legislature. According to the Moreland Act Commission on the Urban Development Corporation and Other State Financing Agencies, "the Legislature approved the moral obligation device on the premise that the projects being constructed would be self-sufficient."[68]

A principal reason for the creation of public authorities during the Rockefeller years was to obtain financing for major programs by the issuance of bonds not subject to voter approval. The long-term nonguaranteed debt of the state increased at a rate approximately two and one-half as great as the increase in the state's full faith and credit debt during the Rockefeller administration. Testifying before the United States Senate in 1974, former Governor Rockefeller offered the following explanation for the reliance he placed upon public authorities when he was governor:

No, I had one other fundamental belief, and that was I believed in self-liquidating financing. The user pays. In other words, I feel that you can sell bonds for important activities, if the beneficiary of the activity pays, in order to pay the interest and amortization on the bond, rather than the general public. That is why I went to the use of authorities.[69]

The state legislature commonly makes "first-instance" appropriations either to provide a new public authority with working capital or to finance the construction of facilities. In theory, first-instance appropriations are loans to be repaid from the proceeds of bonds issued by the authority or from operating revenue generated over a number of years. In practice, the legislature writes off some first-instance appropriations as bad debts, and other such appropriations may not be repaid for decades.[70]

The Metropolitan Transportation Authority

A major problem associated with the use of numerous state-controlled public authorities stems from their creation on an ad hoc basis. To reduce fractionalization problems flowing from the creation of several transportation authorities in the greater New York City area, the 1967 legislature decided to employ the device of the interlocking directorate.[71] Prior to the enactment of the law, three major public transportation authorities—the Metropolitan Commuter Transportation Authority, the New York City Transit Authority, and the Triborough Bridge and Tunnel Authority—operated somewhat autonomously in the area. Another major authority, the Manhattan and Bronx Surface Operating Authority, was controlled by the Transit Authority.

Since the United States Constitution forbids states to impair the obligation of contract and the older public authorities had bonds outstanding, the legislature was unable to replace the existing authorities with a new, consolidated authority.[72] To provide unified direction to public transportation in the area, Governor Rockefeller proposed the use of the interlocking directorate. The Metropolitan Commuter Transportation Authority was converted into the Metropolitan Transportation Authority (MTA), and its board was made the ex officio board for the Long Island Railroad and for each of the other three authorities.[73] The MTA is authorized to establish subsidiary corporations,[74] and it organized the Staten Island Rapid Transit Operating Authority in 1971, the Stewart Airport Land Authority in 1971, and the Metropolitan Suburban Bus Authority in 1973 to operate the bus system in Nassau County. The MTA board serves as the ex officio board of directors of these three subsidiary authorities, which do not possess the power to contact indebtedness, since the state constitution stipulates that a public corporation with power to contract indebtedness can be created only by a special act of the legislature.[75]

The Urban Development Corporation

In 1968 the legislature created three versatile authorities, linked together by an interlocking directorate, to promote urban development by catalytic action.[76] Public attention has centered on the activist roles assigned to the Urban Development Corporation (UDC) and its broad panoply of unique powers to acquire, construct, and improve housing, commercial, educational, recreational, and cultural facilities, and specifically to provide decent housing for low-income families. The UDC's nine-member board of directors consists of the superintendents of banks and insurance and seven others appointed by the governor with the advice and consent of the Senate.

The UDC represents a major state governmental innovation in that the corporation is the first public authority in the United States to become a developer of housing, commercial, and industrial projects in cooperation with private firms and local governments. In fact, the UDC was envisioned as a red-tape cutter, expediting the initial phases—assembling of land, financing, obtaining required governmental approvals—of projects to be completed by others. The UDC would provide "front-end" or "seed money" to initiate developments and, if necessary, carry them through to completion. The UDC's multiple roles include that of actuator, promoter, financier, and developer of a wide range of projects.

Drafters of the UDC statutes anticipated that the corporation would sell its properties as soon as feasible and invest the proceeds in new projects. While designed to circumvent certain constitutional restrictions upon the state government, the corporation was limited by other constitutional provisions effectively prohibiting it from constructing or rehabilitating one- to four-family housing units or expending funds on housing units for persons who can afford to pay unsubsidied rents.[77]

Commenting upon the recruitment of the UDC's staff outside the civil service system, Neal R. Peirce in 1972 wrote, "the result is a much freer, less constrained staff, with those on a professional level—architects, lawyers, planners, and the like—showing much more initiative and energy than in a typical state department."[78] In general, planners and commentators were impressed by the various projects undertaken by the UDC.[79] In a 1969 article, Reilly and Schulman, however, issued the caveat relative to the UDC that "there must be no false congratulations, no premature optimism about a breakthrough on the urban crisis" and added that "the state development corporation device may not be readily exportable, in its present form, to other states."[80]

Major opposition to the UDC came from local governments, particularly in Westchester County, which feared that the corporation would use its powers of preemption and override local building, subdivision, zoning, and other codes in order to construct housing for low-income families. The enabling statute directs the UDC in executing projects to "comply with the requirements of local laws, ordinances, codes, charters, or regulations applicable to such construction, reconstruction rehabilitation, alteration or improvement," but adds the proviso "that when in the discretion of the Corporation, such compliance is not feasible or practicable, the Corporation and any subsidiary thereof shall comply with the requirements of the state building construction code. . . . No municipality shall have power to modify or change the drawings, plans, or specifications for the construction, reconstruction, rehabilitation, alteration, or improvement of any project of the Corporation or of any subsidiary thereof."[81]

Strong opposition to the override provision finally resulted in Governor Rockefeller signing a 1973 bill prohibiting the UDC from proceeding with a plan for a residential project in a town or incorporated village if the governing body of a town or village filed a formal written objection to the project with the UDC within thirty days of the public hearing on the proposed project.[82]

Default. On February 25, 1975, the UDC defaulted on $135 million in short-term notes. At that time, the corporation had partly completed $1 billion in projects, had issued more than $1 billion in bonds, and had daily operating costs of approximately $1 million. A warning had been issued in 1969 by Robert A. Amdurksy, counsel for the Joint Legislative Committee on Housing and Urban Development, that "the continued operation of the program may depend upon periodic appropriations from the State Legislature or Congress and grants from private foundations and corporations."[83]

The precipitating factor leading to the UDC's financial collapse was the announcement by the United States Department of Housing and Urban Development on January 9, 1973, that subsidy payments under Section 236 of the National Housing Act as amended were suspended. The impact of this federal action was potentially catastrophic, since 90.4 percent of the housing units constructed by or with UDC aid were receiving Section 236 subsidies, and "the economic feasibility of some 58 projects then under construction but lacking subsidy contracts was therefore in grave doubt."[84]

The announcement had the immediate impact of raising doubts in the financial community regarding the UDC's ability to finance projects. The corporation's financial problems were compounded by rising interest rates in 1973 and 1974 preventing the corporation from keeping Section 236 projects economically viable unless subsidies were increased. And the UDC's borrowing ability in the spring of 1974 was eroded still further by the state legislature's repeal of the Port Authority of New York and New Jersey bond covenant "pledging that the Authority's revenue would not be used to support deficit producing rail systems other than the Port Authority Trans-Hudson system."[85] This repeal impaired investors' confidence in moral obligation bonds and forced interest rates on a May 1974 UDC note offering to rise to such a high level that the offering was withdrawn. Negotiations between banks, the UDC, and the governor stalemated and resulted in the default.

As one approach to solving the corporation's financial problems, Governor Carey proposed and the legislature enacted a law creating the Project Finance Agency (PFA) with authority to accept state appropriations and raise funds by issuing notes and bonds in order to purchase at a premium UDC mortgages.[86] On March 5, 1975, the legislature appropriated $90 million to the PFA to help finance the UDC's operating expenses and current construction projects, and on March 26 appropriated another $20 million to the PFA. On May 12, 1975, an agreement was reached providing for a $140 million loan by banks and a legislative appropriation of $80 million to the PFA to cover UDC debt service for the fiscal year and $8 million for PFA and UDC operating expenses. In July the state property and liability insurance fund provided $140 million to enable the state to achieve "its goal of arranging for the build-out of all UDC housing under construction."[87]

By 1977 a sharply contracted UDC was able to reenter the financial markets and sold $280 million in long-term bonds.[88] The corporation is continuing to develop new towns near Buffalo and

Syracuse and to complete other residential projects. However, the UDC is no longer a major planning and housing agency and is primarily an implementer of plans developed by other organizations.[89]

The Moreland Act Commission

The UDC fiscal crisis and fear that other state authorities might experience similar financial problems induced Governor Carey on February 5, 1975, to issue an executive order creating a three-member Moreland Act Commission and charging it with the duty of studying and making "recommendations with respect to the management and affairs of the New York State Urban Development Corporation, and any other public benefit corporation, agency, or authority engaged in the financing, construction, or management of housing and related commercial and industrial and public facilities."[90]

The commission criticized UDC's "fast-track" method and the failure of bankers to "concern themselves with the feasibility of the projects because UDC was a development agency which could not be expected to have a cash flow to meet current obligations for years."[91] Growth in the state's debt, both full faith and credit and moral obligation at a faster rate than "the State's ability to support the debt," was identified by the commission as the cause of the fiscal crisis.[92] The commission recommended that authorities be supervised by a Public Authorities Control Commission, that moral obligation financing be discontinued, and that the state establish reserves to support high-risk bonds.[93]

Public Authorities Control Board

Acting upon a message of necessity issued by Governor Carey, the 1976 legislature created the New York State Public Authorities Control Board and charged it with the "duty to receive applications from the New York State Environmental Facilities Corporation, the New York State Housing Finance Agency, the New York State Medical Care Facilities Finance Agency, and the Dormitory Authority for approval of the financing and construction of any project proposed by any of the aforesaid State public benefit corporations."[94]

The three members of the board are appointed by the governor and include one member nominated by the speaker of the Assembly.

The governor designates the chairman, and the board can act only by unanimous vote. None of the above-mentioned authorities may enter into an agreement or incur indebtedness without the approval of the board.

THE CIVIL SERVICE SYSTEM

One of the major developments of the twentieth century has been the growth of the state bureaucracy. While persons holding permanent state positions number approximately 158,000, the number of full-time equivalent employees is approximately 194,000, or 108 per 10,000 of population.[95]

Development of the System

The spoils system was one of the features of the British governmental system that became established in the United States during the colonial period and was continued in the period 1777–1821, with the Council of Appointments distributing patronage. The shift of the appointment power to the governor with the advice and consent of the Senate produced little change in the patronage system.

The patronage system, epitomized by Senator William L. Marcy's 1832 statement that "to the victor belongs the spoils of the enemy," prevented the development of a permanent civil service, because incumbents were discharged if their party lost the election and replaced by loyal supporters of the victorious party. It also should be noted that the appointment of relatives to government positions—nepotism—also was a well-established practice in the colonial period and the post–Revolutionary War period.

Reformers—including the Association for Promotion of Civil Service Reform organized in New York in 1877—made no progress in attempting to replace the spoils system with a merit personnel selection system until the assassination of President James A. Garfield in 1881 by a supporter who was not rewarded with a government position. Public outrage at the assassination pressured Congress to enact the Pendleton Act of 1883 establishing the first civil service system in the nation. Shortly thereafter, the legislature enacted and Governor Grover Cleveland on May 16, 1883, signed into law a bill establishing a civil service system similar to the federal one.[96]

In charge of the original system was a three-member bipartisan Civil Service Commission, appointed by the governor and charged with preparing and administering open competitive examinations to test the qualifications of applicants. The statute also provided that all vacancies in the executive branch were to be filled by applicants scoring the highest on the examinations; new appointees were to serve a probationary period; promotions were to be based upon merit as determined by competition; macing—forced contributions to a political party as a condition for maintaining employment—was prohibited; political activity by civil servants was forbidden; and non-competitive examinations could be used when competitive examinations were not practical. The law also exempted laboring positions and granted the commission power to regulate the civil service system of municipalities exceeding 50,000 population. The following year, all municipalities were required to establish civil service systems.

Opposition to the new system arose, and its constitutionality was challenged by a group of Buffalo residents in 1890. The Court of Appeals ruled that the statute was constitutional and that each municipality must appropriate funds for the establishment of a civil service system.[97] The civil service system acquired a more secure status when a new constitution was adopted in 1894, and New York became the first state with a constitutional civil service requirement.[98]

Whether examination to determine merit for filling a given position is practicable has been a source of some controversy. The Appellate Division of the Supreme Court in 1900 ruled that a competitive examination is not a practicable test for determining the fitness of laborers.[99] In 1912 the Court of Appeals ruled that it would not set aside the action of the legislature or a Civil Service Commission in exempting a position from the requirement of competitive examination where there is reasonable ground for a difference of opinion as to the practicability of examinations in determining fitness.[100] In 1941 the Court of Appeals held that the legislature lacked the power to determine whether examination would be practicable for determining fitness for a particular civil service position unless the legislature considered the duties of each position.[101]

The personnel policies of a state must be in conformance with the decisions of the United States Supreme Court relative to the rights of citizens. In 1976 the United States Supreme Court in *Elrod* v. *Burns* held that patronage dismissals of non-policy-making public employees is violative of the guarantees of the First and Fourteenth Amendments to the United States Constitution because such dismissals severely restrict political beliefs and the right of association.[102] When the newly elected mayor of Cohoes attempted to replace a housing counselor, the incumbent went to court alleging that he was removed without cause, notice, and a hearing, in violation of Sections 62 and 65 of the city charter. The issue involved Section 10 of the charter stipulating that "where the term of an appointive officer is not specifically fixed by statute it shall be deemed to continue only during the pleasure of the officer, officers, board, or body authorized to make the appointment." Citing *Elrod* v. *Burns*, the Appellate Division of the State Supreme Court ruled that "Section 10 of the Cohoes City Charter can be applied constitutionally to all appointive officers in policy making positions, but it cannot be applied constitutionally to the petitioner, since his position was in a non-policy making category."[103]

The United States Supreme Court in 1978 upheld a section of the Executive Law providing that the Empire State may restrict appointment of members of the state police to United States citizens.[104] The Court maintained that "it would be as anomalous to conclude that citizens may be subjected to the broad discretionary powers of non-citizen police officers as it would be to say that judicial officers and jurors with power to judge citizens can be aliens."[105]

The Commission and the Department

The Civil Service Commission is composed of three members, appointed for six-year terms by the governor with the advice and consent of the Senate, who may not hold another state political office. No more than two members may belong to the same political party, and the president is designated by, and serves at, the pleasure of the governor. The president also serves as head of the Department of Civil Service, which is responsible for administering the Civil Service Law.[106]

The principal powers of the commission include jurisdictional classification; determining appeals relating to discipline, disqualifications, examinations, salaries, and job titles; administering the

State Employee Suggestion Program; and exercising the powers of the former Commission on Pensions, including the granting of extensions to members of the State Employees' Retirement System beyond the mandatory retirement age of seventy.

The Taylor Law

Respecting a long-standing tradition, state and local government employees seldom went out on strike. A 1947 strike by Buffalo schoolteachers, however, prompted the legislature to enact a major law—the Condon-Wadlin law—outlawing strikes by public employees and providing that strikers would be dismissed and also would forfeit the guarantees of the Civil Service Law for five years.[107]

The Condon-Wadlin law was considered by unions to be totally punitive in nature, and its draconian penalties were so severe that the legislature enacted laws exempting groups of striking public employees from the penalties. General dissatisfaction with the law induced Governor Rockefeller in 1966 to appoint a panel to make recommendations for protecting the public against disruption of service by illegal strikes under the chairmanship of Professor George W. Taylor of the University of Pennsylvania. [108]

The Taylor Commission in 1966 recommended the replacement of the Condon-Wadlin law with a new law, which the legislature enacted in 1967.[109] Popularly known as the Taylor law, the Public Employees' Fair Employment Act is the first comprehensive labor relations statute for the public service; and it guarantees public employees "the right to form, join and participate in, or to refrain from forming, joining, or participating in, any employee organization of their own choosing" and "the right to be represented by employee organizations to negotiate collectively with their public employers in the determination of their terms and conditions of employment, and the administration of grievances arising thereunder."[110]

The law also established in the Department of Civil Service a three-member Public Employment Relations Board (PERB) to implement the law by assisting in resolving disputes "concerning the representation status of employee organizations"; preventing "improper employer and employee organization practices"; studying problems relating to negotiations and representation; making available mediators and fact-finding boards; and issuing rules and regulations.[111] Members of the board are appointed for six-year terms by the governor with the advice and consent of the Senate; no more than two members may be members of the same political party; and members may hold no other public office in the state. The chairman, a full-time official, is designated by the governor.

The prohibition of strikes by public employees is continued by the Taylor law and has remained a subject of considerable controversy and lobbying described in Chapter V.[112] The prohibition has not been totally effective, as there has been an average of twenty strikes annually, including an occasional major strike by teachers and sanitation workers in New York City. Nevertheless, 99 percent of the contracts are negotiated successfully each year without a strike.

Labor unions have sought the repeal of the two mandatory penalties for striking: (1) being placed on probation for one year without tenure, and (2) having deducted from a striker's compensation "an amount equal to twice his daily rate of pay for each day or part thereof" that the employee was on strike.[113] In 1978 unions were successful in their attempts to have the legislature repeal the provision automatically placing strikers on probation for one year and to restore tenure to public employees on probation because of their participation in a strike.[114]

Unions remain subject to a court-imposed fine for violations of an injunction, and union officers convicted of criminal contempt may be fined up to a maximum of $250 and imprisoned for up to thirty days. President Albert Shanker of the United Federation of Teachers and President John J. De Lury of the Uniformed Sanitationmen's Association have served jail sentences, and a $200,000 fine has been levied against teachers in New York City for striking. Furthermore, if the board determines that an employee organization is guilty of an improper practice, the organization looses its privilege of the agency shop fee checkoff.[115]

Compulsory Binding Arbitration. Local governments have registered strong opposition to the provision of the Taylor law requiring compulsory binding arbitration of impasses between local governments and organizations representing policemen and firemen except in New York City.[116] The Conference of Mayors and Municipal Officials labeled the provision "an irresponsible sell-out of local governments by State government in that it will result in substantial costs being imposed upon the taxpayers of local governments at a time when the State is boasting of cutting State taxes."[117]

A study of compulsory binding arbitration of local governments disputes with organizations of policemen and firemen revealed that the procedure was used in those cases where the local government lacked adequate financial resources; the parties in previous years had reached an impasse and had gone to arbitration, "where one or both of the parties felt it was 'rational' to go to arbitration or to factfinding in order to maximize their ability to achieve a favorable settlement"; and in situations where one or both parties did not engage in bargaining in good faith.[118] "The average arbitration award," according to the study, "closely approximated the average non-arbitrated settlement."[119]

Last Offer Binding Arbitration. In 1979 the Office of Employee Relations and the Civil Service Employees Association, Inc. (CSEA), reached an agreement on a procedure for last offer binding arbitration (LOBA). This procedure provides that in the event of an impasse an arbitration panel must select either the last best offer of the state or CSEA and may not modify either offer, as an arbitration panel may do in making an award settling police and fire impasses. LOBA also differs from police-fire arbitration in that all three members of a LOBA panel must be neutral arbitrators.

LOBA provides that the arbitration panel must accord substantial weight to the financial ability of the state to pay the cost of an award without causing an increase in state taxes over the level of the fiscal year 1978–79 and also must consider the impact of inflation on the employees. The theory behind LOBA is that each side will present more reasonable offers and will be willing to reach a compromise without going to LOBA.

The Retirement System

The Empire State lacked a comprehensive retirement system for public employees until 1921 when the New York State Employees' Retirement System was created and placed within the Department of Audit and Control. Earlier, pension systems had been established for firemen, policemen, sanitation workers in municipalities, and employees of state hospitals and prisons. In 1967 the New York

Policemen's and Firemen's Retirement System was established under the supervision of the state comptroller, and policemen and firemen were transferred to this system. New York City has five separate retirement systems.

The state retirement systems provide for voluntary retirement after age fifty-five and superannuation at age seventy. A constitutional amendment adopted in 1938 stipulates that "membership in any pension or retirement system of the State or of a civil subdivision thereof shall be a contractual relationship, the benefits of which shall not be diminished or impaired."[120] Currently, the state's nine retirement systems have assets of more than $20 billion and in excess of 1,200,000 members employed by the state and local governments, and pay benefits to more than 250,000 pensioners and their beneficiaries.[121] The Empire State's generous pension systems cost approximately $4 billion annually. Referring to skyrocketing pension costs, Neal R. Peirce wrote in 1972:

The problem is centered in New York City, but applies statewide, and it is not new; for years, mayors have been negotiating higher and higher pension benefits with unions, often as a substitute for some immediate wage gains. Such settlements often let a mayor off the hook politically in the short run, but the long-term effect on city budgets—as New York City has been discovering—can be disastrous. All pension agreements have to be approved by the state legislature, and in fact the public employee unions have been exceptionally influential there.[122]

Charles R. Holcomb attributed the pension crisis to several factors, including:

spread of a budget-balancing gimmick New York State launched in 1960, with New York City and other local governments quick to follow. It was called "ITHP," for "Increased Take Home Pay," and few then recognized its staggering cost implications. ITHP was a device by which the employer agreed to assume part, and then all, of the employee's required pension contribution, thereby giving him a substantial take-home pay increase without having to raise salary levels very much.[123]

Two other major contributing factors were the 1966 New York City transit contract allowing retirement on half pay at age fifty following twenty years of service, which encouraged other unions to seek similar benefits, and the enactment in 1967 of the Public

Employees' Fair Employment Act, which promoted the growth of unions.

Not surprisingly, efforts to change the retirement systems generate major political conflicts as unions seek to secure greater benefits for their members and taxpayer organizations and municipal officials seek to keep pension costs from increasing. Holcomb pointed out in 1975 that "the enormous costs of pensions have been all but hidden from the public eye, as governments have agreed to public employee unions' demands but then failed to put up enough cash to pay off the liabilities they have incurred. In effect, government in the State, especially the government of New York City, have mortgaged the future, and future taxpayers will have to pay the price."[124]

Rising public concern about the future cost of the public employee retirement systems in the state and the fiscal crisis that would be generated induced the legislature to create a Temporary Commission on Public Employee Pension and Retirement Systems and in 1971 to make the commission a permanent one.[125] The seven-member commission has five members appointed by the governor with the consent of the Senate, one member appointed by the governor upon the recommendation of the temporary president of the Senate, and one member appointed by the governor upon the recommendation of the speaker of the Assembly. Members serve five-year terms, and the chairman is designated the governor.

Referring to the several dozen pension plans within the public employee retirement systems, the commission in 1973 wrote that "the proliferation of special plans has resulted in a pattern of retirement benefit leap-frogging whereby, as one group of public employees secures liberalized benefits, others seek and attain the same, regardless of the benefits already available to them or the cost to present and future taxpayers."[126] In 1976 the commission proposed a Coordinated Escalator Retirement Plan (CO-ESC) for all public employees who join or rejoin a public retirement system after July 1, 1973. The distinguishing features of the plan are:

1. It takes into account social security benefits paid for by the public employer. It does so by recognizing one half of primary social security—the portion which is taxpayer financed.
2. It makes provisions for an automatic escalation in postretirement, disability, and survivors benefits of up to 3% a year.[127]

The 1976 legislature enacted the proposal into law for all public employees hired after July 1, 1976.[128] The CO-ESC plan requires public employees to contribute 3 percent of their salaries or wages to the system. Furthermore, CO-ESC relates retirement benefits to salary, actuarial factors, and years of service as the other eight systems do, but also reduces the retirement allowance by recognizing public employer contributions to social security. The plan is estimated to save taxpayers approximately $2 billion during its first ten years.

The Heart Law. The aspect of the retirement system most irritating to local government officials is the so-called heart law containing the presumption that heart ailments developed by policemen and firemen are job related, thereby entitling the employees to retire on disability pensions equaling a minimum of 75 percent rather than 50 percent of their salaries.[129] The heart law, as enacted by the legislature in 1969, applied only to New York City,[130] but the law was extended by the legislature in 1973 to all local governments with a paid police department or a paid fire department.

Alleged abuses of the heart law have been highlighted by taxpayer organizations and the media. The Citizens Public Expenditure Survey, Inc., has expressed its opposition to the law in strong terms in the following editorial:

For example, if a New York City policeman and fireman has a heart attack while watching television at home or playing tennis, he is eligible to retire on pension. The same holds true if heart disease is detected at any time while he is working for the municipality. The pension, moreover, is exempt from state income tax and partially exempt from city income tax and partially exempt from federal income tax.[131]

The *New York Times* has labeled the heart law a ripoff and reported that the law has been abused by five physicians, formerly employed by the New York City Police Department on a part-time basis, who retired on annual disability pensions of $21,900 to $25,600 and continue their private practices.[132]

Civil Service Reform

The New York State civil service system has a reputation as one of the best systems in the nation. A survey of state employees, conducted by the National Center for Telephone Research, reported that "overall, Civil Service workers have a high opinion of New York State agencies. Half of all respondents rated New York State's agencies on a par with those of the Federal Government."[133] Much of the criticism of the civil service system focuses upon the fact the system fundamentally is based upon an organizational structure and procedures nearly 100 years old. Yet only a small number of persons have advocated abolition of the system. Among the major proposals for change are replacement of the commission and department with a Department of Personnel Management headed by a director, elimination or modification of the "Rule of Three," and creation of a Senior Management Service.

A Department of Personnel Management. The New York State Personnel Council in 1977 recommended that there should be a Department of Personnel Management headed by a director of state personnel management and a bipartisan Personnel Advisory Board, composed of citizens, as a replacement for the Civil Service Commission.[134] The director would be appointed by, and report directly to, the governor.

The Civil Service Employees Association felt that a change in the name of the department would be of little consequence but strongly opposed replacement of the commission with an advisory board. Samuel Grossfield, chairman of the association's Work Performance, Ratings, and Examination's Committee, commented:

It seems incredible that the Council would turn the safeguarding of employee and management rights over to some sort of political entity that probably would give agencies and management carte blanche to do what they'd like. This is hardly the way any kind of state government should be operated.[135]

The Rule of Three. Considerable dissatisfaction has been expressed relative to the Rule of Three providing that departments and agencies must select one of the top three individuals on an eligibility list in filling a vacancy.[136] A 1977 survey revealed that "68% of all New York State civil servants think that the 'Rule of Three' eliminates qualified people."[137] Supporters of affirmative action programs maintain that the rule limits the recruitment of minorities and women.

The New York State Personnel Council in 1977 recommended block certification, which would allow appointing officials "to consider all candidates within a block of scores on an equal basis," or "Rule of the List" allowing all candidates on an eligible list to be considered for appointment.[138]

Modification or abolition of the rule is opposed strongly by the Civil Service Employees Association. Samuel Grossfield charges that the elimination of the rule "would invite politicians and supervisors of agencies to make decisions on the basis of favoritism, nepotism, and personal bias. It would disregard the lessons of the past and destroy the whole principle of the Merit System that has protected us through these many years."[139]

A Senior Management Service. Civil service reformers generally have been impressed by the results produced by private industry's practice of freely transferring top-level executives to new positions and have sought to apply the practice to government service by means of a Senior Management or Career Executive Service.

The present system, critics charge, stifles incentives for outstanding performance because opportunities for advancement to high-level positions are limited. Furthermore, the present system contains rigid restrictions, making it difficult for administrators to be moved freely from one department or agency to another. Members of the Senior Management Service would serve at a level immediately below that of commissioner.

The Capital District Chapter of the American Society for Public Administration in 1978 endorsed "the establishment of a Career Executive Service within the State Civil Service" in which appointees would serve a probationary period of up to one year prior to being permanently appointed to the service, at which point they would be "subject only to dismissal for demonstrated cause."[140] Members of the Career Executive Service would be outside the existing state salary grade structure and would be required, with one exception, to accept intra- and interagency transfers at the discretion of the appointing official. The consent of the member would be required only if the transfer necessitated a relocation of the member's home. The service would be supervised by a proposed Office of Management Development and Evaluation that would assure "that the high standards and objectives of the Service are maintained through broad consideration of qualified career executives for particular assignments."[141]

Creation of a Senior Management Service has been vigorously opposed by unions, in particular the CSEA with its 300,000 members, as elitism that can result in the return of the spoils system. In 1977, CSEA President Theodore C. Wenzl charged that "the Career Management Service will create an elite corps of civil servants that by cronyism could have an adverse effect on placement, promotion, and assignment of other employees" and that it "could reduce or even eliminate opportunities from within departments as career management service employees were transferred into those positions from elsewhere."[142]

SUMMARY AND CONCLUSIONS

The size and importance of the "fourth branch" have been highlighted in this chapter, with emphasis placed upon the departments of the Executive, Law, Audit and Control, Education, and Civil Service, and certain public authorities. However, the other departments and many of the other public authorities play significant roles in the governance of the Empire State and merit careful study.

To date, there is no evidence suggesting that there will be a comprehensive reorganization of the fourth branch or that public authorities will be abolished as their outstanding bonds are retired. The financial collapse of the Urban Development Corporation taught the state a lesson, and the legislature undoubtedly will adopt a cautious approach in granting public authorities power to borrow funds.

The civil service system continues to be a subject of criticism and study. Although several changes have been made in the Taylor law, it is improbable that the law will undergo major amendments in the foreseeable future. Compulsory binding arbitration of impasses involving fire and police unions, financing the retirement systems, and the heart law will be subjects of annual battles in the legislature between local government officials and public employee unions.

The political strength of public employee unions suggests that the major proposed changes in the civil service system are not apt to be enacted into law by the legislature, and any major change enacted into law probably will be challenged on constitutional grounds in court.

NOTES

1. *New York Laws of 1797*, chap. 21

2. John A. Fairlie, *The Centralization of Administration in New York State* (New York: Columbia University Studies in History, Economics, and Public Law, 1898).

3. *New York Laws of 1913*, chap. 280–81. The board and the department were abolished by Chapter 17 of 1915.

4. *Journal of the New York State Constitutional Convention, 1915* (Albany: J. B. Lyon Company, 1915). See also Gilbert G. Benjamin, "The Attempted Revision of the State Constitution of New York," *The American Political Science Review*, February 1916, pp. 20–43.

5. *Public Papers of Alfred E. Smith, Governor, 1919* (Albany: J. B. Lyon Company, 1920), pp. 31, 48–49, and 52–53.

6. *Report of Reconstruction Commission to Governor Alfred E. Smith on Retrenchment and Reorganization in the State Government, October 10, 1919* (Albany: J. B. Lyon Company, 1919), pp. 13–14. For a detailed discussion of the existing and proposed budget systems, see pp. 303–63.

7. *Ibid.*, pp. iii–iv.

8. *New York Laws of 1921*, chap. 50, 90, and 642. Chapter 90 provided that the three-member State Tax Commission was the head of the Tax Department. The Labor Department was reorganized by Chapter 427 of 1926.

9. *New York Laws of 1923*, chap. 867.

10. *New York Constitution*, art V, §§ 2–4.

11. *Report of the State Reorganization Commission* (Albany: J. B. Lyon Company, 1926). The Appendix to this report contains a proposed constitutional amendment establishing an executive budget system.

12. *New York Laws of 1926*, chap. 546.

13. *New York Laws of 1944*, chap. 4.

14. *New York Laws of 1960*, chap. 464.

15. *Report of the Secretary to the Governor* (Albany: State of New York, December 29, 1959).

16. *New York Laws of 1967*, chap. 717, tit. 5.

17. *New York Laws of 1970*, chap. 140.

18. *New York Laws of 1967*, chap. 722.

19. *New York Laws of 1970*, chap. 744.

20. *Public Papers of Nelson A. Rockefeller: Fifty-Third Governor of the State of New York, 1967* (Albany: State of New York, n.d.), p. 210.

21. *New York Constitution*, art. V, §§ 1 and 4, *New York Executive Law*, § 63 (McKinney 1979 Supp.), and *New York Laws of 1980*, chap. 881.

22. *New York Executive Law*, § 63 (McKinney 1972).

23. For information on the office under former Attorney General Louis F. Lefkowitz, see the four articles by Eric Freedman in *The Knickerbocker News* (Albany, New York), December 26, 1978, pp. 1 and 8A; December 27, 1978, pp. 1 and 2A; December 28, 1978, p. 11A; and December 29, 1978, p. 5B.

24. *New York Executive Law*, § 63 (8) (McKinney 1979 Supp.). See also *People v. Brennan*, 69 Misc. 548, 127 N.Y.S. 958 (1910).

25. *New York Laws of 1958* chap. 261.

26. See *Kent Nursing Home v. Office of Special State Prosecutor for Health and Social Services*, 425 U.S. 974 (1976), and *Berger v. Carey*, 86 Misc. 2d 727, 383 N.Y.S. 2d 171 (1976). See 92 Stat. 460, 31 U.S.C. §§ 521–31.

27. Arvis Chalmers, "Abrams Inherits Patronage Jobs," *The Knickerbocker News*, November 10, 1978, p. 5B.

28. *New York Constitution*, art. V, §§ 1 and 4. See also *Levitt v. Wanamaker*, 12 App. Div. 2d 149, 209 N.Y.S. 2d 75 (1961); *New York Laws of 1926*, chap. 614; *New York Laws of 1928*, chap. 590; and *New York Laws of 1980*, chap. 881.

29. *New York Constitution*, art. V, § 1.

30. *Matter of Smith v. Levitt*, 30 N.Y. 2d 934, 287 N.E. 2d 380 (1971).

31. *New York Constitution*, art. V, § 1.

32. *New York Laws of 1975*, chap. 606.

33. *New York Constitution*, art. 5, § 1.

34. *Petition of Consolidated Edison Company of New York*, 277 App. Div. 245, 98 N.Y.S. 2d 973 (1950). The comptroller supervised state banks between 1843 and 1851. See *New York Laws of 1843*, chap. 218. The comptroller also supervised the insurance industry for eleven years until 1869 when the Insurance Department was created. See *New York Laws of 1859*, chap. 366.

35. *New Job Assignment for the State Comptroller* (New York: Citizens Union of the City of New York, 1967), p. 1.

36. *Ibid.*

37. *Public Papers of Nelson A. Rockefeller: Fifty-Third Governor of the State of New York, 1971* (Albany: State of New York, n.d.), pp.228–35.

38. *New York Laws of 1971*, chap. 601, and *New York Executive Law*, §§ 760–64 (McKinney 1972).

39. *Third Annual Report of the Office of Welfare Inspector General, 1973–74* (New York: Office of Welfare Inspector General, 1974), p. 2.

40. *New York Laws of 1975*, chap. 219, and *New York Executive Law*, §§ 46–50 (McKinney 1979 Supp.).

41. *News Release from the New York State Department of Audit and Control* (Albany: Department of Audit and Control, January 10, 1977).

42. "Testimony of Ralph A. Cipriani, State Acting Welfare Inspector General on Proposed Legislation to Establish a Wage Reporting System Given at Public Hearing of Senate Social Services Committee and Senate Governmental Operations Committee," Albany, New York, March 28, 1978, p. 6. (Mimeographed).

43. *New York Constitution*, art. V, § 4, and art. XI, § 2.

44. *New York Constitution of 1894*, art. IX, § 1.

45. *New York Laws of 1974*, chap. 19, § 1, and *New York Education Law*, § 202 (McKinney 1979 Supp.).

46. *New York Constitution*, art. V, § 4.

47. *Buck v. State*, 198 Misc. 575, 96 N.Y.S. 2d 667 (1950). See also *Union Free School District v. Wilson*, 303 N.Y. 107, 100 N.E. 2d 159 (1951).

48. *New York Laws of 1976*, chap. 857, and *New York Education Law*, § 310 (McKinney 1979 Supp.).

49. *Public Papers of Nelson A. Rockefeller, Fifty-Third Governor of the State of New York, 1973* (Albany: State of New York, n.d.), p. 18.

50. *Ibid.*

51. *Education Performance Review Press Release* (Albany: Executive Chamber, April 8, 1973). The message transmitting the bill is contained in *Public Papers of Nelson A. Rockefeller, 1973*, pp. 825–26.

52. *Regent's Statement on Governor's Proposal for an Inspector General for Education* (Albany: New York State Department of Education, January 24, 1973); Ewald B. Nyquist, "Education and the Legislature, 1973 or the Issue of Governance of Education," a paper presented to the New York Legislative Forum, Albany, New York, April 3, 1973; and Arthur Levitt, "An Inspector General for Education—or Super Regent?" a paper presented to the Municipal Law Section, New York State Bar Association, New York, New York, January 25, 1973.

53. "Education Watchdog Snagged in Assembly," *The Times Union* (Albany, New York), May 24, 1973, p. 5.

54. *New York Laws of 1973*, chap. 600.

55. *State of New York Executive Order Number 77 (June 23, 1973)*. The executive order is printed in *Public Papers of Nelson A. Rockefeller, 1973*, pp. 996–97.

56. Robert J. Neiderberger, "The Creation of the Office of Education Performance Review: Some Perspectives," a paper submitted in PPOS 522, State Government, Graduate School of Public Affairs, State University of New York at Albany, January 25, 1977 pp. 23–24.

57. *New York Laws of 1977*, chap. 978.

58. Maureen M. Dana, "State Mental Health Overseers Rapped on Funding, Organization,"*The Knickerbocker News* (Albany, New York), November 1, 1978, p. 7A.

59. *New York General Corporation Law*, § 3 (McKinney 1943). Parts of Section 3 have been incorporated in the *New York Business Corporation Law*, § 102 (McKinney 1979 Supp.). However, only corporation, domestic corporation, and foreign corporations are defined.

60. *New York Constitution*, art. X, § 5. This section specifically provides that the state shall not "be liable for the payment of any obligations issued by such a public corporation heretofore or hereafter created."

61. *Ibid.*, §§ 6–8.

62. *Ibid.*, art. VII, § 11.

63. *Ibid.*, § 16.

64. *New York Laws of 1921*, chap. 154, and *New Jersey Laws of 1921*, chap. 151.

65. For a description and analysis of New York State public authorities in the 1950s, see *Staff Report on Public Authorities* (Albany: Williams Press, 1956). This report is referred to as the Ronan Report. See also William J. Quirk and Leon E. Wein, "A Short Constitutional History of Entities Commonly Known as Authorities," *Cornell Law Review*, April 1971, pp. 521–97.

66. *New York Laws of 1960*, chap. 671, and *New York Private Housing Finance Law*, §§ 40–61 (McKinney 1976).

67. *New York Private Housing Finance Law*, § 46 (8).

68. *Restoring Credit and Confidence* (New York: New York State Moreland Act Commission on the Urban Development Corporation and Other State Financing Agencies, 1976), p. 111.

69. United States Senate Committee on Rules and Administration, *Nomination of Nelson A. Rockefeller of New York to be Vice President of the United States* (Washington, D.C.: United States Government Printing Office, 1974), p. 26.

70. For details, see *Audit Report on First Instance Advances to Public Authorities* (Albany: Office of the State Comptroller, 1972).

71. *New York Laws of 1967*, chap. 717.

72. *Constitution of the United States*, art. I, § 10.

73. *New York Public Authorities Law*, § 1264 (McKinney 1970).

74. *Ibid.*, § 1266.

75. *New York Constitution*, art. X, § 5.

76. *New York Laws of 1968*, chap. 173–75, and *New York Unconsolidated Laws*, §§ 6251–85, 6301–25, and 6341–60 (McKinney 1978 Supp.).

77. *New York Constitution*, art. VII, VIII, and XVIII.

78. Neal R. Peirce, *The Megastates of America: People, Politics, and Powers in the Ten Great States* (New York: W. W. Norton & Company, Inc., 1972), p. 29.

79. See Richard Schickel, "New York's Mr. Urban Renewal," *The New York Times Magazine*, March 1, 1970, pp. 30–34, 36, 38–39, and 41–42; Vincent J. Moore, "Politics, Planning, and Power in New York State: The Path from Theory to Reality," *Journal of the American Institute of Planners*, March 1971, pp. 72–77; and "A Superagency for Urban Superproblems," *Business Week*, March 7, 1970, pp. 96, 98, and 100.

80. William K. Reilly and S.J. Schulman, "The State Urban Development Corporation: New York's Innovation," *The Urban Lawyer*, Summer 1969, p. 145.

81. *New York Laws of 1968*, chap. 174, § 16 (3).

82. *New York Laws of 1973*, chap. 446, and *New York Unconsolidated Laws*, § 6265 (McKinney 1978 Supp.).

83. Robert S. Amdursky, "A Public-Private Partnership for Urban Progress," *Journal of Urban Law*, Vol. 46, No. 2, 1969, p. 212.

84. *Restoring Credit and Confidence*, p. 141.

85. *New York Laws of 1974*, chap. 993.

86. *New York Laws of 1975*, chap. 7.

87. *Restoring Credit and Confidence*, p. 203.

88. Linda Greenhouse, "Sale of Bonds to Help U.D.C. Repay Its Debt," *The New York Times*, March 9, 1977, pp. 1 and 16.

89. Sharon Reier, "The Urban Development Corporation: Back in Business," *Empire*, December 1978, pp. 5–8.

90. *State of New York Executive Order Number 3*, February 5, 1975.

91. *Restoring Confidence and Credit*, pp. 5 and 224–26.

92. *Ibid.*, p. 9.

93. *Ibid.*, pp. 12–13.

94. *New York Laws of 1976*, chap. 39; *New York Laws of 1976*, chap. 649; and *New York Public Authority Law*, § 50 (McKinney 1979 Supp.).

95. United States Bureau of the Census, *Public Employment in 1977* (Washington, D.C.: United States Government Printing Office, 1978), pp. 30–32.

96. *New York Laws of 1883*, chap. 354.

97. *Kip v. City of Buffalo*, 123 N.Y. 152 (1890).

98. *New York Constitution*, art. V, § 9 (1894).

99. *People v. Dalton*, 49 App. Div. 71, 63 N.Y.S. 258 (1900).

100. *Simmons v. McGuire*, 204 N.Y. 253, 97 N.E. 526 (1912).

101. *Meenagh v. Dewey*, 286 N.Y. 292, 36 N.E. 2d 211 (1941).

102. *Elrod v. Burns*, 427 U.S. 347 (1976).

103. *Corbeil v. Canestrari*, 57 App. Div. 2d 153 (1977).

104. *Foley v. Connelie*, 435 U.S. 291 (1978). See also *New York Executive Law*, § 215 (3) (McKinney 1972).

105. *Foley v. Connelie*, 435 U.S. 291 at 299–300 (1978).

106. For a description of public personnel functions, see Joseph F. Zimmerman, *State and Local Government*, 3d ed. (New York: Barnes and Noble Books, 1978), pp. 218–22.

107. *New York Laws of 1947*, chap. 391.

108. *Public Papers of Nelson A. Rockefeller: Fifty-Third Governor of the State of New York, 1966* (Albany: State of New York, n.d.), p. 710.

109. *New York Laws of 1967*, chap. 392, and *New York Civil Service Law*, §§ 200–214 (McKinney 1973 and 1979 Supp.). The report of the Taylor Commission is printed in *Public Papers of Nelson A. Rockefeller, 1966*, pp. 879–929.

110. "Public Employees' Fair Employment Act," *New York Civil Service Law*, §§ 200–203 (McKinney 1973).

111. *Ibid.*, § 205.

112. The Law's prohibition of strikes by public employees has been held not to violate the equal protection of the laws clauses of the New York State and United States constitutions. See *City of New York v. De Lury*, 23 N.Y. 2d 175, 243 N.E. 2d 128, 396 U.S. 872 (1968).

113. *New York Civil Service Law*, § 210 (f) and (g).

114. *New York Laws of 1978*, chap. 465.

115. The agency shop is a requirement that nonmembers of a union must pay an agency shop fee equal to union dues.

116. *New York Laws of 1974*, chap. 724–25, and *New York Civil Service Law*, § 209 (4) (c) (McKinney 1979 Supp.).

117. *Resolution No. 2* adopted at the Annual Meeting of the New York Conference of Mayors and Municipal Officials, Liberty, New York, June 1974 (Mimeographed).

118. Thomas A. Kochan, Ronald G. Ehrenberg, Jean Baderschneider, Todd Dick, and Mordehai Mironi, *An Evaluation of Impasses Procedures for Police and Firefighters in New York State: A Summary of the Findings, Conclusions, and Recommendations* (Ithaca: New York State School of Industrial and Labor Relations, Cornell University, November 1976), p. 8.

119. *Ibid.*, pp. 3–4.

120. *New York Constitution*, art. V, § 7.

121. The nine systems are the State Employees' Retirement System, State Policemen's and Firemen's Retirement System, State Teachers' Retirement System, Coordinated Escalator Retirement System, and five New York City systems: Employees' Retirement System, Teachers' Retirement System, Police Department Pension Fund, Fire Department Pension Fund, and Board of Education Retirement System.

122. Peirce, *The Megastates of America*, p. 40.

123. Charles R. Holcomb, "The Pension Balloon Is About to Burst," *Empire State Report*, May 1975, pp. 160–61.

124. *Ibid.*, p. 158.

125. *New York Laws of 1971*, chap. 733, and *New York Executive Law*, §§ 800–802 (McKinney 1972).

126. *Report of the Permanent Commission on Public Employee Pension and Retirement Systems* (New York: The Commission, 1973), p. 7.

127. *Recommendation for a New Pension Plan for Public Employees: The 1976 Coordinated Escalator Retirement Plan* (New York: Permanent Commission on Public Employee Pension and Retirement Systems, 1976), pp. 1–2.

128. *New York Laws of 1976*, chap. 890–91, and *New York Retirement and Social Security Law*, §§ 500–520 (McKinney 1978 Supp.).

129. *New York Laws of 1973*, chap. 383, § 9, and chap. 1046, § 62, and *New York General Municipal Law*, § 207–k (McKinney 1976 Supp.).

130. *New York Laws of 1969*, chap. 1106, and *New York City Administrative Code*, § B19–4.0.

131. "Hearts—and Flowers, for Taxpayer's Funeral," *CPES Taxpayer*, February 1977, p. 4.

132. "Another Pension 'Ripoff,'" *The New York Times*, April 21, 1976, p. 34, and "Active Doctors Get Police Pensions," *The New York Times*, February 9, 1977, pp. 1 and B–7.

133. National Center for Telephone Research, *A Study of Attitudes of New York State Civil Service Employees Toward the Civil Service System* (Albany: New York State Temporary Commission on Management and Productivity in the Public Service, April 1977), p. 3.

134. *An Evaluation of Our Merit System: Twenty-One Recommendations for Change* (Albany: New York State Personnel Council, January 1977), p. 1.

135. "Personnel Council Recommendations are 'Ridiculous,'" *Civil Service Leader*, February 25, 1977, p. 16.

136. In 1975 the Court of Appeals upheld the "Rule of Three" by ruling that "the constitutional provision does not mandate the selection of the highest individual on the eligible list." *Cassidy v. Municipal Civil Service Commission*, 37 N.Y. 2d 526, 337 N.E. 2d 752 (1975).

137. National Center for Telephone Research, *A Study of Attitudes of New York State Civil Service Employees*, p. 23.

138. *An Evaluation of Our Merit System*, p. 23. See also *Civil Service Reform* (Albany: Capital District Chapter, American Society for Public Administration, May 1978), p. 1.

139. "Personnel Council Recommendations are 'Ridiculous,'" p. 16.

140. *Career Executive Service* (Albany, New York: Capital District Chapter of the American Society for Public Administration, May 1978), p. 1.

141. *Ibid.*, p. 2.

142. "Wenzl Details Civil Service Reform Stand," *Civil Service Leader*, May 20, 1977, p. 11.

CHAPTER IX
Justice for All

THE THIRD BRANCH of state government, the judiciary, increasingly has played a more important role in the governance of the Empire State, including the resolution of certain state-local and gubernatorial-legislative disputes. Without courts to interpret and apply laws made by legislative bodies, organized society in a post-industrial era would function with difficulty. Among the many functions of the judicial system are the adjudication of civil disputes, determination of the innocence or guilt of individuals charged with commission of crimes, protection of personal rights and property rights, and determination of the constitutionality of laws enacted by legislative bodies.

Citizen perception of the administration of justice is influenced far more by the court systems of the fifty states than by the federal court system, since most civil disputes and criminal cases are handled by state courts, which also have jurisdiction over diversity of citizenship cases—litigants are legal residents of two or more different states—if the amount in dispute is less than $10,000.

The state's legal system is based on common law and equity as modified by constitutional and statutory provisions. Common law originated in England where judges first based their decisions on customs and later relied on the precedents established in the early cases—the principle of *stare decisis*. The common law in time became the basis for civil law—rights and duties of individuals in their relationships with each other—and criminal law—definition and punishment of offenders for breaches of the peace and order.

By the eleventh century the rigidities of the common law became apparent, and a clear need was seen for a system of preventive law. For example, the common law remedies could require a person who damaged property to pay for the damages but could not prevent the person from damaging the property, which might be of incalculable value to the property owner. Courts of equity, or chancery, came into being with powers to provide remedies such as issuing a writ of injunction to prevent a threatened wrong or writ of mandamus to order that a certain nondiscretionary governmental action be taken. The New York State courts are courts of both equity and law.

Bills enacted into law by the state legislature are referred to collectively as statute law and take precedence over common law and equity. In fact, statutory law has superseded most of the common law provisions relating to crimes.

The judicial branch, while performing essential functions, is not coequal with the other two branches of state government in terms of formal powers. The New York State constitution, for example, grants the state legislature considerable authority relative to the establishment and abolition of courts other than constitutional ones and the determination of the jurisdiction of all courts, and it authorizes the governor, with the advice and consent of the Senate, to appoint certain judges.

Article VI of the constitution contains many details relative to the judicial system but also grants the state legislature power to play a major role in determining judicial organization, procedures, and other matters. To cite only one example, the Education Law until 1976 stipulated that decisions of the commissioner of education were "final and conclusive"; that is, the decisions could not be appealed to the courts.[1]

The court system of the Empire State is staffed by approximately 1,000 full-time judges, 2,500 part-time judges, and 11,000 other employees. More than 2 million cases annually are disposed of by the state-funded courts at a cost of approximately $350 million. As explained in later sections, the politics of the judiciary becomes heated over proposals to change the method of selecting judges, merge courts, and decriminalize certain offenses.

ORGANIZATION OF THE JUDICIAL SYSTEM

The state court system historically was a fragmented one but became a unified one supervised by the Administrative Board of the Judicial Conference when voters ratified a proposed constitutional amendment in 1961.[2] Sixteen years later the electorate approved another proposed amendment providing that "the Chief Judge of the Court of Appeals shall be the Chief Judicial Officer of the unified court system."[3] The new amendment provides for an Administrative Board for the Courts consisting of the chief judge of the Court of Appeals, who serves as chairman, and the presiding justice of the Appellate Division of the Supreme Court for each of the four judicial departments. With the consent of the Administrative Board, the Chief Judge appoints a chief administrator of the courts—the chief administrative judge—who serves at the pleasure of the chief judge, possesses powers delegated to him by the chief judge and by law, and received an annual salary of $68,522 in 1981.

The Unified Court Budget Act, effective on April 1, 1977, transferred in excess of 9,000 locally paid court employees to the state payroll and provided for the complete state assumption of the cost of courts by April 1, 1980.[4]

Courts in the Empire State may be placed in four major categories: minor courts, general trial courts, appellate courts, and special courts. In terms of volume of cases, the minor courts, which are courts of first instance, are the most important ones.

The Minor Courts

The state constitution stipulates that town, village, and city courts outside the New York City "shall have the jurisdiction prescribed by the Legislature, but not in any respect greater than the jurisdiction of the district courts as provided in section sixteen of this article."[5] These courts, with the exceptions of specified city courts, are not courts of record; that is, the courts are not empowered to have a court clerk to maintain records of court or use an official seal.

The Justice Court. Justice of the peace courts, dating to 1691, performed important judicial, administrative, and legislative functions in towns. Following independence, justices of the peace were appointed by the Council of Appointment until 1821, when the new constitution provided for the appointment of the justices by the Board of Supervisors of each county and the judges of the County Court.[6] Reflecting Jacksonian democracy, the state constitution was amended in 1826 to provide for the popular election of justices.[7] Until a constitutional amendment was adopted in 1938, justices were paid by fees, and "J.P." frequently was referred to as "justice for the plaintiff," since the justice was paid only if he found for the plaintiff. Today, the governing body of cities, towns, and villages determine the salaries of the justices.

All lower courts of civil jurisdiction are governed today by one of four uniform acts. The New York City Civil Court Act and the Uniform District Court Act became effective in 1963.[8] The Uniform City Court Act governs city courts in sixty-one cities and became effective in 1965.[9] The Uniform Justice Court Act became effective in 1967 and governs all towns and village courts.[10] This act substituted the title of Justice Court for the Justice of the Peace Court in towns and the police justice courts in villages in addition to establishing a uniform jurisdiction, practice, and procedure for the Justice Court in each of the 931 towns and 354 villages in 55 upstate counties.

The jurisdiction of the Criminal Court of New York City— which has authorized strength of ninety-eight judges—is limited to misdemeanors and violations.[11] Members of this court are appointed by the mayor of New York City. The Civil Courts of New York City, whose justices are elected, has civil jurisdiction similar to that of justice courts.[12] Each Criminal Court judge and each Civil Court judge in New York City received an annual salary of $42,451 in 1980.

The jurisdiction of justice courts is limited to civil cases involving disputes not exceeding $3,000 and criminal cases involving misdemeanors or minor crimes, including the less serious traffic violations, and violations of local laws and ordinances. Justice courts may arraign a defendant in a felony case and, unless there is a waiver, conduct a hearing to determine whether the defendant should be referred to a grand jury. Court typically is held two or three nights a week and on Saturday.

Adults twenty-one years of age and older found guilty of a misdemeanor may be sentenced to up to one year in prison, and youths over sixteen and under twenty-one years of age found guilty may be sentenced up to four years in a state reformatory. Decisions of the courts may be appealed to the County Court in the third and fourth departments, and to the appellate term of the Supreme Court in the second department.

Justice courts are the workhorses of the state's judicial system, as they adjudicate approximately 80 percent of the cases. Town and village courts handled 1,756,156 criminal and traffic cases in 1976; the Criminal Court of New York City disposed of 231,500 cases in 1977; and the district courts and courts in cities outside New York City disposed of 1,073,351 criminal cases in 1977.[13] Relative to civil cases, town and village courts disposed of 54,516 cases in 1976; the Civil Court of New York City disposed of 68,566 cases in 1977; and the district courts and courts in cities outside New York City disposed of 111,922 cases in 1977.[14]

With the exceptions of towns in Nassau County and the five western towns in Suffolk County where district courts operate, voters in a town elect one to four justices, based upon the population of the town, for four-year terms; all justices in villages are elected by village voters for the same term.[15] To be eligible for election, a person must be a legal resident of the town or village and over eighteen years of age.[16] Justices are not required to be "learned-in-law," but village boards in appointing acting justices are limited to persons who are "learned-in-law." Newly elected or appointed justices are required to take an advanced course within one year.[17]

Each town with a population greater than 300 must elect two justices, and a village may elect two justices or elect one justice and have an acting village justice appointed by the mayor and confirmed by the Village Board.[18] A village justice may serve as a town justice in the town in which the village is located and also may serve as a village trustee.[19] Justices in second-class towns also serve as members of the Town Board, which is the local governing body.[20]

In towns with a population under 300 and taxable property under $100,000, one justice is elected for a four-year term and one assessor is elected for a term of two years, but no town councilmen are elected.[21] The constitution authorizes the legislature to "abolish the legislative functions on town boards of Justices of the Peace and provide that Town Councilmen be elected in their stead."[22] The legislature in 1976 enacted a law stipulating that a town justice elected after July 1, 1977, could not serve as a member of the Town Board in a second-class town.[23]

A Justice Court in a village may be abolished if the Village

Board makes such a recommendation and village voters approve the recommendation.[24] There is no provision in law for the abolition of a Justice Court in a town because it is a constitutionally established court. However, the constitution provides that "the Legislature may discontinue any town court existing on the effective date of this article only with the approval of a majority of the total votes cast at a general election on the question of a proposed discontinuance of the court in each such town affected thereby."[25]

Justice courts have been subjected to strong criticism over the years, and the suggestion frequently has been made that the courts be abolished. Critics generally attack the part-time feature of the justice courts and the fact that many of the justices are not lawyers. Defenders of the courts emphasize the convenience of having justice courts in every local government and the relatively low cost of providing justice through the courts.

The District Court. The constitution authorizes the legislature to create a district court in an entire county or part of a county at the request of the governing body, provided the voters of the cities as one unit and the voters of the towns as a second unit approve the creation of such a court.[26] Currently, there is a district court in Nassau County and a second district court serving the five western towns of Suffolk County.[27] These courts lack the criminal jurisdiction of the justice courts but do arraign individuals accused of crimes and have civil jurisdiction over actions for the recovery of chattels and funds up to $6,000, interpleader jurisdiction, and the power to enforce an award of an arbitrator. Justices of the district courts in 1980 were paid salaries ranging from $40,990 to $45,330.

The Small Claims Courts. A major charge directed at the traditional court system is the high cost of securing justice, a cost that makes litigation of small claims prohibitive. Recognizing the need for an inexpensive system of adjudicating small claims, the 1934 legislature created a Small Claims Court as part of the New York City Municipal Court.

Currently, small claims courts operate under privisions of the New York City Civil Court Act, the Uniform City Court Act, and the Uniform District Court Act.[28] Small claims courts exist in the sixty-two cities of the state and in the judicial districts in Nassau and Suffolk counties. The Uniform Justice Court Act does not contain a small claims article, since justice courts have jurisdiction over disputes not exceeding $1,000. A small claim is defined as "any cause of action for money only not in excess of fifteen hundred dollars exclusive of interest and costs."[29] The small claims jurisdiction of a city court with a basic monetary jurisdiction under $1,000 is the same as the court's basic monetary jurisdiction.

To provide for speedy and inexpensive justice, the statutes specify that the "practice, procedure, and forms shall differ from the practice, procedure, and forms used in the court for other than small claims. . . . They shall constitute a simple, informal, and inexpensive procedure for the prompt determination of such claims in accordance with the rules and principles of substantive law."[30] Any person may initiate action in a small claims court by payment of a $2 filing fee and the cost of a registered or certified mailing.[31] Notices of the claim are sent to the defendant's residence with a return receipt requested. A Small Claims Court may transfer a small claim to another part of the court, and the person initiating the action is deemed to have waived the right to a jury trial unless the action is transferred to another part of the court.[32]

To prevent the small claims courts from becoming collection agencies for business firms, the enabling statutes stipulate that corporations, partnerships, and assignees of small claims may not initiate an action in a small claims court, and the clerk may compel the initiator of an action "to make application to the Court for leave to prosecute the claim in the small claims part" if the clerk determines that a claimant is utilizing the small claims part "for purposes of oppression or harassment."[33]

The judgment debtor has thirty days following receipt of notice of a judgment to satisfy it; failure to so do empowers the judgment creditor to initiate an action for "treble the amount of such unsatisfied judgment, together with reasonable counsel fees, and the costs and disbursements of such action."[34] A major complaint directed against the Small Claims Court is the difficulty of collecting a judgment; the collection rate is approximately 30 percent.

General Trial Courts

There are two general trial courts—the Supreme Court and the County Court. The jurisdiction of the former court is broader than the jurisdiction of the latter court.

The Supreme Court. The present form of the Supreme Court as a statewide court with unlimited jurisdiction in law and equity dates to the constitution of 1846, which amalgamated the offices of circuit judge and chancery judge with the Supreme Court.[35] The 1894 constitution abolished the Superior Court of the City of New York, the Court of Common Pleas for the City and County of New York, the Superior Court of Buffalo, and the City Court of Brooklyn, "and all actions and proceedings then pending in such Courts shall be transferred to the Supreme Court for hearing and determination."[36] In 1962 the County Court in Bronx, Kings, Queens, and Richmond counties and the Court of General Sessions in New York County were abolished and their functions transferred to the Supreme Court.[37] The court exists as a separate bench in each of the state's eleven judicial districts.

The paramount position of the Supreme Court is stressed in the constitution in each article defining the jurisdiction of other trial courts, with the exception of the Court of Claims, by the statement that the grant of jurisdiction "shall in no way limit or impair the jurisdiction of the Supreme Court as set forth in section seven of this article." In addition, the importance of the court is emphasized by the fact that the intermediate appellate courts are "Appellate Divisions of the Supreme Court," justices serve for a term of fourteen years, and judicial departments and the judicial districts are prescribed by the constitution, and the court's jurisdiction is defined by the Constitution.[38] According to a Temporary State Commission, "for many lawyers who are not judges, and for some now serving in other trial courts, election to the Supreme Court is considered the culmination of a career."[39]

The court in 1980 was staffed by 285 justices, not counting those assigned to the appellate divisions. There also were thirty-two Court of Claims judges sitting as Supreme Court justices for felony cases. Each judge receives an annual salary of $48,998, which will be increased to $65,000 in 1982. Employee and other expenses bring the annual total cost of maintaining each justice to approximately $332,000.

The state constitution grants the Supreme Court "general original jurisdiction in law and equity," which also covers "new classes of actions and proceedings" created by the legislature in the future.[40] The jurisdiction of the court is exclusive relative to "crimes prosecuted by indictment" unless the legislature grants "to the city-wide court of criminal jurisdiction of the City of New York jurisdiction over misdemeanors prosecuted by indictment and to the Family Court in the City of New York jurisdiction over crimes and offenses by or against minors or between parent and child or between members of the same family or household."[41] The legislature has not authorized the Criminal Court of the City of New York to exercise jurisdiction over misdemeanors prosecuted by indictment. The Supreme Court also has exclusive jurisdiction on actions to recover an amount exceeding $10,000, and concurrent jurisdiction with other trial courts in a number of instances.[42]

Although possessing broad jurisdiction, the Supreme Court usually does not handle actions and proceedings that could be originated in the minor trial courts or handled by specialized courts such as the Family Court or the Surrogate's Court. The Supreme Court outside New York City and the County Court each possesses civil and criminal jurisdiction, yet the former court's case load is primarily civil and the latter court's case load is primarily criminal. The Supreme Court generally hears cases involving civil matters exceeding the final limits of the jurisdiction of lower courts; annulment, divorce, and separation proceedings; and felonies.

In view of the backlog of cases, questions have been raised as to the need for additional justices. The constitution provides that the legislature may increase the number of justices provided that the number in a judicial district does not exceed one justice per 50,000 population.[43] The legislature has not created the maximum number of justiceships authorized, and some observers argue the constitution should contain a formula for an automatic increase in the number of justices based upon population increases and the case load of the court. Others question whether an adequate formula could be developed and believe the legislature can best assess the need for additional justices.

The County Court. The highest court in each of the fifty-seven counties outside New York City is the County Court, which has civil and criminal jurisdiction. The Civil Court of New York City has a jurisdiction similar to that of the County Court outside the city.

The County Court is a court of criminal and limited civil jurisdiction. Constitutional amendments, ratified by the electorate in 1962, increased the civil jurisdiction of the County Court from $3,000 to $6,000, authorized the legislature to increase the jurisdiction to $10,000 at the request of a county board of supervisors, and empowered the legislature to determine the number of judges of the County Court in each county provided there is at least one judge.[44] The amendments also increased the term of office of a County Court judge to ten years, required each judge to be a resident of the county that elected him to office, and provided that a County Court judge also may be a Surrogate's or a Family Court judge or both.[45] In 1980 the salary of a County Court judge ranged from $36,000 in seventeen counties to $48,998 in Nassau County.

Proposals to change the state constitutional provisions concerning the County Court relate to whether the court should assume the functions of the Surrogate's Court; whether the County Court's jurisdiction to try felonies and indictable misdemeanors should be transferred to the Supreme Court; and whether the County Court should assume the functions of town, village, and city courts outside New York City. Some observers point out that a constitutional amendment providing for the court to assume the functions of the Surrogate's Court in effect would provide constitutional status for the situation in many counties outside New York City where the same individual serves as County Court and Surrogate's Court judge and provide for more efficient utilization of judges in counties where surrogate and County judges currently are elected.

With respect to the possible transfer of the County Court's jurisdiction to try felonies and indictable misdemeanors, some reformers recommend that County Court judges be made Supreme Court justices and cite as precedent a similar change in New York City. Proponents of the County Court absorbing the functions of the town, village, and city courts outside New York City cite the district courts in Nassau County and the western part of Suffolk County as a model.

The Appellate Courts

The 1777 constitution provided for a Supreme Court, a County Court, a Probate Court, an Admiralty Court, and justices of the peace but made no provision for an intermediate Court of Appeals. Such courts first were provided for by the 1821 constitution, and the highest appellate court, the Court of Appeals, was created by the 1846 constitution. The reader should be alerted to the fact that the state constitution does not guarantee the right of appeal in all cases, as it is a privilege the legislature may grant, withhold, or take away in cases where there is no constitutional right of appeal.[46]

The Appellate Division. The current appellate divisions are traceable to a provision in the 1821 constitution that "the State shall be divided by law into a convenient number of circuits, not less than four nor exceeding eight, subject to alteration by the Legislature . . . ; for each of which a Circuit Judge shall be appointed . . . who shall possess the powers of a Justice of the Supreme Court, and in Courts of Oyer and Terminer and Jail-Delivery."[47] The same provision authorized the state legislature to vest equity powers in the circuit judges.

A major court reorganization was instituted by the 1846 state constitution, which established the Supreme Court as the major court of original jurisdiction and provided for a general term of the court in each of its eight districts to hear appeals.[48] The new court system proved to be unsatisfactory during the following forty-eight years and resulted in the constitutional convention of 1894 proposing a new constitution with a revised judiciary article. The new provisions stipulated that the state be divided into four judicial departments, "the Appellate Divisions of the Supreme Court are continued, and shall consist of seven Justices of the Supreme Court in each of the first and second Departments, and five Justices in each of the other Departments," and the presiding justice of each Appellate Division is to be designated by the governor.[49] Each presiding justice in 1981 received an annual salary of $58,029, and each associate justice received an annual salary of $54,028.

The constitution's judiciary article states that "the Appellate Divisions of the Supreme Court shall have all the jurisdiction possessed by them on the effective date of this article and such additional jurisdiction as may be prescribed by law."[50] In effect, the state legislature possesses the authority to broaden or limit the right of appeal to the appellate divisions from a judgment or order not finally determining an action or special proceeding. All civil appeals are taken to the Appellate Division from trial courts with the exceptions of the New York City Civil Court; district courts; and town, village, and city courts outside New York City. Appeals in criminal matters from the County Court and the Supreme Court are taken to the Appellate Division. Appeals in criminal matters from other trial courts are directed to the appellate term of the

Supreme Court in the first and second judicial departments and to the Supreme Court in the third and fourth judicial departments. The Appellate Division has original jurisdiction in a habeas corpus proceedings; admission of attorneys; actions on submitted facts; and Article 78 proceedings against judges of the Supreme Court and County Court. In addition, each Appellate Division has supervisory powers over courts within its department.

Statistical data reveal that actions of the appellate divisions result in affirmances in approximately 60 percent of the cases, reversals in approximately 20 percent of the cases, granting of a new trial in approximately 5 percent of the cases, and dismissals or appeals or other disposition in the balance of the cases.[51]

Constitutional issues involving the divisions include whether they should be continued as divisions of the Supreme Court and whether the number of judicial departments and the number of justices in each division should be prescribed by the constitution. Some reformers favor a separate intermediate Court of Appeals with justices appointed by the governor; other reformers favor the creation of such a court with justices elected by the voters. A major argument for the proposed change is that it would result in a single intermediate appellate court, but opponents argue "that the current system of election from the Judicial District, combined with designation by the Governor to the Appellate Divisions, assures a proper balance between local and statewide considerations."[52]

The Court of Appeals. Dating from the 1846 state constitution, the Court of Appeals sits at the apex of the state's court system and has achieved a position of preeminence among the highest courts of the fifty states.[53] Under the first two constitutions, the higher appellate court was the Court for the Trial of Impeachments and the Correction of Errors, commonly referred to as the Court of Errors, consisting of the temporary president of the Senate, senators, the chancellor, and justices of the Supreme Court.[54] The Court of Errors, a quasi-judicial and quasi-political body, acted upon appeals from equity decrees and appeals by writ of error upon questions of law from Supreme Court judgments.[55] The Court of Appeals was established to settle the law administered by the appellate courts.

The 1894 constitutional convention proposed and the voters ratified a new constitution containing a judiciary article establishing the four appellate divisions; limiting the jurisdiction of the Court of Appeals, except where a judgment is of death; "to the review of questions of law"; and authorizing the legislature "further to restrict the jurisdiction of the Court of Appeals and the right of appeal thereto, but the right to appeal shall not depend upon the amount involved."[56] The court thus became a court to review law and not fact.

Congestion continued to be a problem, and the 1915 constitutional convention proposed a new constitution increasing the number of judges of the Court of Appeals and limiting further the court's jurisdiction.[57] The electorate rejected the proposed constitution. However, recommendations made by the Judiciary Convention of 1921 were ratified by the voters in 1925, and no other basic changes were made in the structure or jurisdiction of the court until 1977.

The chief judge and the six associate judges of the Court of Appeals were elected by the voters for fourteen-year terms until 1977, when voters approved a constitutional amendment providing for the establishment of a twelve-member Commission on Judicial Nomination and authorizing the governor to "appoint, with the advice and consent of the Senate, from among those recommended by the Judicial Nominating Commission, a person to fill the office of Chief Judge or Associate Judge, as the case may be, whenever a vacancy occurs in the Court of Appeals."[58] In 1982 the chief judge and each associate judge received an annual salary of $85,000 and $77,917, respectively.

Carl L. Swidorski studied the background characteristics of the twenty-three judges who served on the court during the period 1950–76 and reported that twenty-two were born in the state; nineteen received their legal education in the state; eighteen were judges when selected for the Court of Appeals, average years of judicial experience at the time of selection were fifteen, and one-third were Irish and one-third were white Anglo-Saxon Protestants, with the remaining third "split among Italians, Dutch . . . , other western Europeans, and Poles. One Judge was Black."[59] In addition, the judges were between the ages of forty-two and sixty-eight when selected to serve on the bench; twelve were Democrats and eleven were Republicans. By 1979 the court had become an all-white, all-male court with three Catholic, three Jewish, and one Protestant member. Four were Republicans and three were Democrats.

The Court of Appeals lacks original jurisdiction, as the constitution makes the court a court of law, with a few well-defined exceptions, by stipulating that the court's jurisdiction is "limited to the review of questions of law except where the judgment is of death, or where the Appellate Division, on reversing or modifying a final or interlocutory judgment in an action or a final or interlocutory order in a special proceeding, finds new facts and a final judgment or a final order pursuant thereto is entered; but the right to appeal shall not depend upon the amount involved."[60]

Cases appealable to the court fall into two classes: (1) those appealable as a matter of right and (2) those cases considered by permission of the court. The court's jurisdiction is based upon the assumption that the appellate divisions will settle with finality the bulk of the appeals. The legislature lacks the power to change the court's jurisdiction other than to abolish appeal as of right in any class of case based on a dissent, modification, or reversal, and substitute appeal by permission of the court.[61]

Relative to criminal cases, an appeal may be taken directly from a court of original jurisdiction where the judgment is of death, and from an Appellate Division or elsewhere as provided by the legislature in other criminal cases. In other than capital cases, an appeal can be made only by permission of a judge of the Court of Appeals or a justice of the Appellate Division. The constitution also specifies the classes of civil cases and proceedings from which appeals may be taken to the Court of Appeals.

The most common civil case to reach the court comes as a matter of constitutional right from a final determination by an Appellate Division involving a modification, reversal, or dissent. Other cases generally are considered by permission, and the court devotes a considerable amount of time to determining the cases to be decided. By tradition, the court grants permission to appeal if two judges consider the case to be one that should be reviewed. Cases of broad public significance are most apt to receive permission to appeal.

A quorum consists of five members of the court, and the concurrence of four is necessary for a decision. Each case reaching the court comes in the form of a record of appeal and written brief. Mario M. Cuomo pointed out that "at the very heart of the decisional method employed by the Court . . . is the traditional system whereby each appeal becomes the special charge of one of the seven Judges of the Court" who usually prepares a written memorandum that is distributed to the other judges.[62] In deciding a case, a written opinion is not always issued. This practice is followed whenever a decision is affirmed unanimously and no new question of law was involved. Where a decision is written, the first judge to vote for the majority position by tradition writes the opinion unless he declines to do so.

The court's work load is heavy because of the complexity of the cases brought to the court for resolution, including issues of state and municipal finance, welfare, unemployment compensation, and freedom of the press. By random lot, each case is assigned to a judge, who prepares a report. When the court is in session, the judges assemble in the courtroom at 2:00 P.M. to hear oral arguments, and the session may run as late as 9:00 P.M. Each morning the judges meet at 10:00 A.M. in the library of the Court of Appeals Building to discuss cases. The judge handling a case makes a report and is followed by the other judges in reverse seniority order. These conferences continue as late as 1:00 P.M. and are secret. According to Martin Wald, "almost all of the Judges admit that they have felt one way about a case going into a conference, but completely changed their minds before the conference was over."[63]

The two major constitutional issues involving the court concern the restriction of appeals as of right and judicial manpower. Relative to the first issue, two proposals have been advanced as constitutional amendments. Chief Judge Stanley H. Fuld in 1967 wrote that the present constitutional provisions do not limit appeals to "only those cases which merit further appellate review," and "innumerable appeals are brought to the Court as a matter of right, at the option of the litigants, not because they are of any moment or merit but merely because there has been some disagreement, no matter how trivial, either between the Appellate Division and the lower court or within the Appellate Division itself, as to the proper final disposition of the case."[64] Judge Fuld's solution was adoption of a constitutional amendment authorizing the Court of Appeals in its discretion to determine the cases worthy of review.[65]

Opponents of this proposal hold that the present system has "proved wise and workable" and fear that adoption of Judge Fuld's proposal would result in errors made in lower courts not being corrected.[66]

The League of Women Voters in 1966 advanced a second proposal, one that would replace the constitutional definition of the court's jurisdiction by a grant of power to the legislature to determine the court's jurisdiction.[67] Adoption of this proposal would simplify the constitution and make the legislature the forum for determining the court's jurisdiction. Opponents of the proposal maintain that legislative changes in the court's jurisdiction have produced an increase in the number of appeals to the court, thereby causing congestion.

Special Courts

New York State has five special courts of limited jurisdiction—the Family Court, the Surrogate's Court, the Court of Claims, peacemaker courts, and the Court for the Trial of Impeachments. A sixth court of limited jurisdiction—the Court on the Judiciary—was replaced, effective January 1, 1978, by a new procedure for disciplining justices (described in a later section).

Dissatisfaction has been expressed regarding the first three special courts. For example, the Special Committee on the Constitutional Convention of the Association of the Bar of the City of New York in 1967 recommended "the elimination of the Surrogate's Court and the Court of Claims as separate courts" on the basis of the following rationale:

Thus, a judicial settlement of an accounting of *inter vivos* trusts must be carried on in the Supreme Court under present law, but a judicial settlement of an accounting dealing with testamentary trusts is dealt with by the Surrogate's Court. This distinction is not logically supportable—it is a creature of history, not reason. If a citizen of New York has a personal injury claim against a fellow citizen—or indeed against the City of New York—he may seek relief in the Supreme Court (or a lower court), but if that fellow citizen happens to have been an employee of the State acting in an official capacity, suit against the State can only be brought in the Court of Claims. Once again, this distinction is to be explained by the historical antecedents of the doctrine of sovereign immunity rather than by reason.[68]

The Family Court. A court of statewide jurisdiction, the Family Court dates to 1962 when it replaced the Domestic Relations Court of New York City and the Children's Courts in the fifty-seven counties outside New York City, thereby ending the confusion associated with courts in different areas operating under different laws.[69] Judges of the court in New York City are appointed by the mayor for a term of ten years; judges of the court in the remainder of the state are elected for a ten-year term.[70] In 1980 Family Court judges received an annual salary ranging from $36,000 in several counties to $48,998 in Nassau County.

The Family Court is a court of record, supervised by the chief administrator of the courts on behalf of the chief judge of the Court of Appeals, with jurisdiction limited to family problems, including conciliation, adoption and parental rights, annulment and divorce actions, family offenses, neglect, juvenile delinquency, paternity, and support.[71] Although the Family Court Act[72] grants the court "exclusive original jurisdiction," the Constitution stipulates that the Supreme Court has general original jurisdiction in law and equity.[73] The Supreme Court usually declines to hear family cases,[74] and cases originated in the Supreme Court commonly are transferred to the Family Court.[75]

The Family Court is given concurrent jurisdiction with the Surrogate's Court by the Social Services Law to commit a "destitute or dependent" child to an authorized agency.[76] The Family Court is granted by the Education Law jurisdiction over criminal violations of the compulsory school attendance law, and jurisdiction by the Domestic Relations Law over the securing of support for children and dependent wives.[77] The jurisdiction of the court has also been expanded by three interstate compacts—the Uniform Support to Dependents Law, the Interstate Compact on Juveniles, and the Interstate Compact on the Placement of Children.[78]

The reason for creating this specialized court is to allow greater flexibility in adjudicating family problems than would be possible under the common law. In particular, the Family Court can handle the myriad of family problems, and there is no need to refer related problems involving a single family to other courts.

The number of judges in New York City and in each county outside the city is specified in the act creating the court.[79] In counties with a small population the judge of the County Court serves as judge of the Family Court. Terminology differs from that used in civil or criminal proceedings with "petitioners" as the plaintiffs and "respondents" as defendants, and "hearings" instead of trials and "dispositional orders" in place of sentences.

The Family Court is a busy trial court whose calendar has become more crowded in recent years because of amendments to the Social Services Law.[80] As of January 1, 1978, there were 18,696 petitions actively pending in the Family Court in New York City and 27,521 petitions actively pending in the Family Court in the remainder of the state.[81]

Relative to the effectiveness of the court, Attorney Douglas J. Besharov wrote:

> Despite the high hopes accompanying its creation, the Family Court, in the opinion of most observers, has failed to fulfill its early promise. The Court rarely has been accorded the priority it deserves and the resources it needs . . . the most critical problem facing the Family Court is the problem of rapidly ballooning caseloads.[82]

This judgment is supported by a study entitled *Family Court . . . The System That Fails All.*[83]

The Surrogate. Although the surrogate originated in the colonial period, the constitutions of 1777 and 1821 did not refer to the surrogate. A 1778 law, however, provided for the appointment of surrogates by the Council of Appointment, and a 1787 law authorized the governor to appoint a surrogate in each county with the advice and consent of the Council.[84] The surrogate was authorized to probate wills and determine controversies.

The state constitution provides for the popular election of one Surrogate's Court judge in each county and additional judges as determined by the legislature for fourteen-year terms in New York City and ten-year terms outside the city.[85] The salary of the surrogate in 1980 ranged from $36,000 in six counties to $48,998 in Nassau County, Suffolk County, and New York City.

Surrogates' courts have jurisdiction over "the affairs of decedents, probate of wills, administration of estates and actions and proceedings arising thereunder or pertaining thereto, guardianship of the property of minors, and such other actions and proceedings, not within the exclusive jurisdiction of the Supreme Court, as may be provided by law."[86] The constitutional jurisdiction of the court can be expanded by the legislature but cannot be lessened in matters relating to the affairs of a decedent.[87]

Over the years, proposals have been advanced for merging the Surrogate's Court with the County Court in lightly populated counties and with the Supreme Court in heavily populated counties to achieve a more efficient use of personnel and "avoid instances in which different issues arising in one probate proceeding require the determination of different tribunals."[88] Opponents argue that the constitution authorizes the temporary assignment of judges that would assure the efficient use of judges and that issues raised in a probate proceeding seldom require determination by another court.[89] Furthermore, defenders of the Surrogate's Court maintain that specialized knowledge relating to the law of estates and trusts is required for the administration of justice in matters currently under the court's jurisdiction and that the product of the merger of the court might be inordinate delays in the administration of estates and testamentary trusts.

Court of Claims. Under the ancient doctrine of sovereign immunity, the state could not be used for damages without its consent. In 1817 the legislature enacted a law providing for a determination of claims, by disinterested appraisers, resulting from land taken by eminent domain for the construction of the Erie Canal.[90] The waiver of immunity gradually was expanded by the state legislature to include damages caused by canals and in 1870 to claims for injuries resulting from negligence of officers in charge of the canals.[91]

For claims other than those involving canals, the legislature was the only body with power to allow claims against the state. Widespread abuse was associated with the auditing of private claims by the legislature, and the 1867–68 constitutional convention proposed that the legislature be forbidden to audit and allow claims and that a Court of Claims be established.[92] The voters, however, rejected the proposed constitution. Nevertheless, a constitutional amendment was ratified in 1874 providing that "the Legislature shall neither audit nor allow any private claim or account against the State, but may appropriate money to pay such claims as shall have been audited and allowed according to law."[93] This amendment necessitated the creation in 1876 of the State Board of Audit (later the Board of Claims) to hear claims, other than those heard by the Canal Board, against the state.[94] The 1897 legislature replaced the board with the Court of Claims.

The Court of Claims underwent a number of changes as the result of statutory enactments, including its abolishment and replacement in 1911 by a newly created Board of Claims, which in turn was abolished when the Court of Claims was reestablished in 1915.[95] The court in 1949 acquired a constitutional basis with the ratification by the voters of a new amendment designed to free the court of the uncertainty of its powers and existence.[96]

In 1910 the state waived its immunity from suit for damages caused by "defects in State and county highways, maintained by the State by the patrol system."[97] Governor Alfred E. Smith in 1928 vetoed a large number of private bills authorizing the Court of Claims to hear and decide actions based on torts (civil wrongs other than breach of contract) and recommended enactment of a general law granting all tort claimants access to the Court of Claims.[98] In 1929 the legislature accepted Smith's advice and waived the state's sovereign immunity from suits for torts.[99] A major purpose of the waiver was to obviate the need for frequent special acts to compensate individuals who suffered damage caused by the state.

The 1936 legislature waived the immunity from suit of counties, cities, towns, villages, and special districts for the negligent operation of motor vehicles and other transportation facilities.[100] The Court of Appeals in 1945 ruled that the statutory waiver of immunity did not make the state liable for the torts of officials and employees of political subdivisions.[101] However, where an official of a political subdivision acts as an agent of the state, the latter may be held liable.[102]

The Court of Claims, a court of record, is required by the constitution to have a minimum of six judges appointed by the governor, with Senate approval, for terms of nine years. The legislature is free to increase the number of judges. The court has "jurisdiction to hear and determine claims against the State or by the State against the claimant or between conflicting claimants as the Legislature may provide."[103] The court has been granted jurisdiction by statute over claims against the state and certain public authorities for breaches of contract, appropriation of personal and real property, and torts.[104]

Real property appropriation bills authorize the court to hear other claims, yet the court lacks general equity powers other than those incidental to the rendering of a money judgment. And the court lacks the power to adjudicate claims against political subdivisions of the state, as these claims must be adjudicated in the Supreme Court.[105] The work of the court was increased significantly in 1944 when responsibility for the acquisition of land for state highways was transferred from the Board of Supervisors of each county to the State Department of Public Works.[106] Approximately

70 percent of the courts cases in recent years have involved acquisition of land for highway rights-of-way, 10 percent of the cases involved contract disputes, and 10 percent involved torts.

The major constitutional question involving the Court of Claims is whether it should be merged into the Supreme Court. Proponents contend that a merger would provide for more efficient use of judicial manpower, avoid gaps in court jurisdiction relative to claims against the state, and be more convenient for litigants. The first argument is based on the contention that it is easier to assign judges of a merged court to other courts when needed than it would be to assign judges of the Court of Claims to other courts. The second argument would overcome the jurisdictional weakness of the Court of Claims, and the third argument is based upon the greater availability of the Supreme Court in contrast with the Court of Claims, whose rules provide for terms to be held in Albany, Buffalo, New York, Rochester, Syracuse, Binghamton, and Elmira.

Opponents of the proposed merger contend that there have been no serious problems relating to the temporary assignment of judges to other courts, that the jurisdictional gaps can be removed by broadening the court's jurisdiction, and that special terms of the court can be held where the claims arose as determined by the presiding justice. Furthermore, opponents maintain that a heavy burden would be placed upon the attorney general if he had to meet calendars in sixty-two counties rather than the cities where the Court of Claims presently sits.

Peacemaker Courts. The governor is directed by law to appoint a justice of the peace for each Indian reservation, and each justice has the same jurisdiction and receives the same compensation as justices of the peace in towns.[107] In addition to these justices of the peace, the Indian Law establishes a Peacemaker's Court for each of three reservations—the Allegany, the Cattaraugus, and the Tonawanda.[108] In particular, "the Peacemaker's Court of each such reservation shall have authority to hear and determine all matters, disputes, and controversies between any Indians residing upon such reservation, whether arising upon contracts or for wrongs, and particularly for any encroachments or trespass on any land cultivated or occupied by any one of them."[109] The Peacemaker's Court of the Allegany reservation or the Cattaragus reservation "have exclusive jurisdiction to grant divorces between Indians residing on such reservations and to hear and determine all questions and actions between individual Indians residing thereon involving the title to real estate on such reservations."[110]

Court for the Trial of Impeachments. By a majority vote, the Assembly may impeach (bring charges) against a member of the executive or judicial branch.[111] Officials impeached are tried by a court "composed of the President of the Senate, the Senators, or the major part of them, and the Judges of the Court of Appeals, or the major part of them."[112] The lieutenant governor and the temporary president of the Senate are forbidden to act as members of the court when the trial involves the governor or the lieutenant governor.

Conviction on charges of impeachment requires a two-thirds vote of the members present of the Court for the Trial of Impeachments. Punishment for officials found guilty is limited "to removal from office, or removal from office and disqualification to hold and enjoy any public office of honor, trust, or profit under this State; but the party impeached shall be liable to indictment and punishment according to law."[113] The Assembly seldom votes impeachment, and there is no evidence that impeachment charges will be preferred often in the future. The only governor impeached and removed from office was Governor William Sulzer in 1913.[114]

THE JUDGES

The Empire State's court system is among the busiest and largest court systems in the world, with approximately 1,000 full-time and 2,500 part-time judges who are supported by approximately 11,000 other court employees. As of 1981, courts expended approximately $370 million in adjudicating more than 2 million cases.

A major controversy has swirled around the issue of whether judges should be elected by the voters or appointed by the governor. The issue was settled with respect to the Court of Appeals in 1977 when voters approved a constitutional amendment providing for gubernatorial appointment of judges to that court.[115] At the same time, the voters approved an amendment establishing a Commission on Judicial Conduct.[116]

Writing in 1948, Warren Moscow emphasized the amount of job patronage the courts can distribute and added:

> While the New York courts dispense justice in a manner that is remarkably free from justifiable criticism, it is also true that the state judiciary is one of the most valuable assets of the two major political parties. The local party organizations in any county are more intimately concerned with the election of a State Supreme Court Justice than they are with the Presidency of the United States, incredible as that may seem.[117]

Jobs include administrative aides, clerks, law secretaries, and stenographers. Furthermore, Marcia Chambers writes that "the judiciary is also a convenient retiring ground to pay off political debts and to place tired politicians and mediocre campaigners. Often it provides a graceful way for the organization to reward a party stalwart who has failed in the political arena or at a city job."[118]

Selection

All judges under the state constitution of 1777 were appointed by the Council of Appointment (described in Chapter VII). The council was abolished by the adoption of the constitution of 1821, which authorized the governor with the consent of the Senate to appoint judges other than justices of the peace.[119] In 1826, however, the constitution was amended to provide for the popular election of justices of the peace.[120]

The present pattern for the selection of judges, other than judges of the Court of Appeals and the Court of Claims, was established with the adoption of a new constitution in 1846 providing for the election of all judges.[121] Although the judiciary article of the constitution has been amended several times since 1846, no changes were made in the method of selecting judges until voters in 1977 ratified a constitutional amendment, effective on January 1, 1978, providing for a Commission on Judicial Nomination and appointment of judges of the Court of Appeals by the governor.[122] The twelve-member commission consists of four members appointed by the governor; four appointed by the chief judge of the Court of Appeals; and one each appointed by the temporary president of the Senate, the minority leader of the Senate, the speaker of the Assembly, and the minority leader of the Assembly. Relative to the four appointed by the governor and the chief judge, no more than two may be members of the same political party and no more than two shall be members of the bar of the state. Members, with one exception, may hold no other public office for which they receive compensation. However, the governor and the chief judge each may appoint one former judge or justice of the unified court system to the commission. Members are forbidden to hold office in a political party and are ineligible for appointment to any court while serving on the commission and for one year subsequently.

Party voters in each judicial district elect delegates and alternates to a convention that selects nominees for the Supreme Court.[123] Most of the 199 delegates to one 1977 Democratic nominating convention were party workers, according to Glenn Fowler, who stressed that in selecting judicial nominees the Democratic party leaders "put their emphasis on traditional political considerations; ticket-balancing along racial and religious lines, pressure for more women jurists, and obligations to candidates passed over in previous years."[124]

A primary election is used to select party candidates for other elective judgeships.[125] The State Committee of each party is authorized by majority vote to designate candidates "for nomination for any office to be filled by the voters."[126] A candidate receiving 25 percent of the votes of the committee may demand that the State Board of Elections place the candidate's name on the primary ballot, and a "challenge primary" will be held.[127]

Appointment or Election? Currently all judges outside New York City are elected except judges of the Court of Appeals and the Court of Claims, who are appointed by the governor with the consent of the Senate. In New York City the mayor appoints judges of the Criminal Court and the Family Court, and voters elect judges of the Civil Court.[128] The governor also designates the presiding justices and associate justices of the appellate divisions of the Supreme Court and fills vacancies in elective judicial offices except vacancies in the Family Court and the Civil Court in New York City and vacancies in district courts.[129]

Vacancies in the Family Court and the Civil Court in New York City are filled by the mayor, and vacancies in the district courts are filled by "the Board of Supervisors or the Supervisor or Supervisors of the affected district if such district consists of a portion of a county or, in counties with an elected county executive officer, such county executive officer may, subject to confirmation by the Board of Supervisors or the Supervisors of such district, fill such vacancy by an appointment."[130]

Supporters of the elective system advance the following five arguments in support of popular election of judges. First, the system has worked well over the years, and the caliber of judges has been high. Second, popular election is the most democratic system, as it ensures that the judges will be responsible directly to the voters and therefore subject to popular control. Proponents point out that no one has recommended that the governor and legislators be appointed on the ground that the voters cannot be trusted to make rational choices.

Third, popular election of judges makes it possible for all groups in the state—ethnic, racial, religious, and the like—to elect their candidates to judicial office and ensures that the judicial system is a balanced one. Fourth, the judicial system must be reflective of changes in society, and popular election of judges is the best guarantee that judges will be sensitive to societal changes. Finally, the argument is advanced that appointment of judges by the governor would violate the constitutional principle of separation of powers. This principle, however, is not an absolute one, and the governor already possesses the power to appoint certain judges.

Four major arguments are raised in opposition to the popular election of judges. First, it is contended that voters are not sufficiently aware of the qualifications of the candidates for judicial office to make an intelligent decision when casting a ballot, a point made by Governor Smith. The typical voter casts his ballot for the candidate of his political party or for a candidate whose name is familiar or does not vote for a judicial candidate. Polls reveal that many voters do not remember the names of judicial candidates voted for.[131]

A related argument is the unsuitability of a system of popular election for the selection of the most qualified candidates for judicial office. Since the system is a partisan one, leaders of the major political parties advance as candidates individuals who are attractive as vote getters but who may not be the most qualified persons available. An examination of the backgrounds of forty-one Supreme Court justices serving in Brooklyn in 1977 revealed that all justices had progressed up the political ladder from earlier service as district leaders, assemblymen, state senators, assistant district attorneys, assistant federal prosecutors, and tax commissioners.[132]

Opponents of the elective system maintain that many of the most able attorneys are deterred from seeking office as judges by election campaigns and also because they do not wish to feel indebted to leaders of a political party. Consequently, these attorneys do not seek election as judges. On the other hand, the argument is advanced that a Judicial Nominating Commission could encourage these attorneys to allow their names to be forwarded to the governor for appointment.

Should the most highly qualified attorney in a given area be a member of the minority political party, this attorney would stand little chance of election even if nominated by his party in a judicial district dominated by the opposition party. After studying the selection of Court of Appeals judges in the period 1950–76, Carl L. Swidorski reported:

> The trend in New York seems to support some contentions of judicial reform advocates who argue that elective systems of selection produce "locals" as judges. Aspiring judges, it is contended, have to have roots in the community from which they will be elected and have to have good political relations with the local party organizations. But this characteristic also is found in states using other methods, including states such as Missouri which use the merit plan to choose judges.[133]

The third argument against the popular election system is that it generates public doubts relative to the impartiality and independence of the judges. The suggestion is advanced that in order to gain reelection a judge, even though he has been elected to a relatively long term, must not offend the leaders of his political party by his judicial decisions. Of greater concern is the fact that most campaigns for judgeships are financed by contributions from attorneys who often will appear in the courtrooms of the judges the attorneys helped to elect. Swidorski reports that Jacob D. Fuchsberg spent $563,000 and Charles D. Breitel spent $441,000 in seeking election to the Court of Appeals in 1973.[134] Under provisions of the Code of Judicial Conduct, a judge is forbidden to know the names of campaign contributors, and campaign managers are directed not to accept exceptionally large contributions, but no mechanism has been developed to enforce the code.

The fourth argument against the election of judges is the fact that the system often produces a situation in which voters are not afforded a choice of candidates because of cross-endorsements. Swidorski reports that thirteen of twenty-three Court of Appeals elections in the period 1950–75 "featured a single major candidate cross-endorsed by the Republican and Democratic parties."[135] And the Democratic Judicial Nominating Convention and the Republican Judicial Nominating Convention in the third judicial district each endorsed the Democratic candidate and the Republican candidate for the two Supreme Court judgeships voted on in 1978. Interestingly, one of the judgeships had been created by the 1978 legislature, at an estimated annual cost of $332,000, and rumors were rife that the new judgeship was created to facilitate the cross-endorsement of the Republican incumbent by providing an opportunity for the Republican Convention to cross-endorse a Democratic candidate for a judgeship.[136] The 1978 law also increased the number of judges from twenty-two to twenty-four in the eighth judicial district and from twenty-one to twenty-two in the ninth judicial district.

Advocates of gubernatorial appointment of judges with Senate confirmation are convinced that an appointment system results in the selection of the best qualified individuals, since the governor bears the responsibility for the quality of his appointees and will exercise extra care in scrutinizing the qualifications of all potential candidates. Furthermore, the governor possesses the staff to conduct the necessary investigations to ensure that only the most highly qualified individuals are selected. The high-quality judicial appointments made by the governor in Massachusetts since 1780 and by the president of the United States since 1788 also are cited in support of the appointive system of selecting judges.

While this debate cannot be terminated with one side winning with finality, recognition must be given to the fact that a high percentage of the judges reach the bench initially by appointment even though the selection is nominally elective.

Tenure and Removal. The state constitution provides for the superannuation, or compulsory retirement, of judges at age seventy.[137] However, a retired judge of the Court of Appeals or a retired justice of the Supreme Court may perform the duties of a Supreme Court justice for an additional two years if certificated as prescribed by law. The certification may be extended for two-year periods until the age of seventy-six is reached.

Judges of the Court of Appeals, justices of the Supreme Court, and surrogates of the Surrogate's Court in New York City serve fourteen-year terms; surrogates of the Surrogate's Court outside New York City, and judges of the County Court, the Family Court, the Civil Court, and the Criminal Court of New York City serve ten-year terms; judges of the Court of Claims serve nine-year terms; Judges of the district courts serve for six years; and justices of the Justice Court serve for four years. Justices of the Appellate Division of the Supreme Court serve for five-year terms or the portion of their terms as Supreme Court justices remaining, whichever is the lesser.

A life term for each judge, as in the Massachusetts and federal judiciary, is favored by those convinced that such a term helps guarantee the independence of the judiciary. Critics of a limited term for judges express the fear that some judges will temper their decisions in order to please the electorate or the appointing authority rather than reaching decisions in an impartial manner. The critics also argue that a limited term makes it more difficult to attract qualified persons to serve as judges because they fear that their failure to win reelection or reappointment will damage their careers. On the other hand, opponents of life terms for judges maintain that such terms will make it difficult to remove unqualified judges and may result in an unresponsive judiciary.

Judges are governed by the Code of Judicial Conduct developed by the New York State Bar Association.[138] The state constitution authorizes two methods for the removal of judges guilty of misconduct in office. The first method involves removal by the legislature; the second method involves removal by judicial proceedings.

The Assembly, by majority vote of all its members, may impeach a judge by preferring charges; the trial is held by the Court for the Trial of Impeachment, consisting of the president of the Senate, the senators, and judges of the Court of Appeals.[139] Once impeached, a judge may not exercise his office until or unless he is acquitted. Conviction on impeachment charges requires a two-thirds affirmative vote of the members of the court present. A convicted judge may be removed from office, disqualified to hold any public office in the future, and be "liable to indictment and punishment according to law." Only one judge has been convicted and removed from office through the impeachment process, and that removal occurred in 1872.[140]

The constitution authorizes two other types of legislative removal proceedings. First, if two thirds of the members elected to each house so vote, judges of the Court of Appeals and justices of the Supreme Court may be removed from office by concurrent resolution; that is, by legislative address.[141] No judge has been removed by this method. Second, judges of the other constitutional courts and inferior courts as determined by the legislature may be removed by a two-thirds vote of the Senate upon the recommendation of the governor.[142] Prior to action being taken under either of these two types of removal proceedings, the judge in question must be served with a notice of the alleged cause and be granted an opportunity for a hearing. One lower court judge was removed by the latter method in 1872.[143]

Judges of the appellate and major trial courts could be removed only by the legislature until 1948, when a constitutional amendment provided for removal of judges from office by judicial proceedings. Moscow wrote in 1948:

> Probably the principal weakness in the State's judicial system was cleared up by constitutional amendment in 1947. Up to then . . . County or Supreme Court Justices could be kicked off the bench only by the Legislature under a complicated impeachment procedure. The Legislature, full of lawyers, showed consistent reluctance over the years to exercise its impeachment powers.[144]

From its establishment in 1948 until its replacement in 1978, the Court on the Judiciary could be convened by the chief judge of the Court of Appeals "upon his own motion" to consider removing or retiring a judge and had to be convened by the chief judge "upon written request of the Governor or a Presiding Justice of the Appellate Division of the Supreme Court or by a majority of the Executive Committee of the New York State Bar Association thereunto duly authorized."[145] The Court on the Judiciary—composed of the chief judge and senior associate judge of the Court of Appeals and one Appellate Division justice from each of the four judicial departments—was an ad hoc court that could act to remove or retire only judges of the Court of Appeals, the Supreme Court, the Court of Claims, the County Court, the Surrogate's Court, or the Family Court. The Court on the Judiciary was seldom convened, but "reprimanded" two County Court judges in 1960, removed a Supreme Court judge and a Court of Claims judge in 1963, and suspended without pay a Supreme Court judge for six months in 1977.[146] Until 1978, the Appellate Division of the Supreme Court occasionally would investigate charges of judicial misconduct and censure or remove a judge. The division removed a Suffolk County District Court judge in 1976 and a Newburgh City judge in 1977, and it censured a New York City Civil Court judge for abuse of authority in 1977.[147]

In 1974 the legislature created a nine-member Temporary State Commission on Judicial Conduct charged with responsibility of receiving and investigating complaints against a judge, and recommending disciplinary action, including the convening of the Court on the Judiciary.[148] During its first year, the commission recommended five removal proceedings, and two additional removal proceedings were recommended in 1976.[149] This commission was replaced in 1976 by the State Commission on Judicial Conduct authorized to issue private reprimands, public censures, and suspensions for a maximum of six months.[150] A judge had the right to a public hearing to challenge a censure or suspension before the Court on the Judiciary. The commission also could recommend initiation of removal proceedings by the Court on the Judiciary.

One of the first major investigations of the new commission was an investigation of alleged traffic-ticket fixing by one judge. In a 1977 report, the commission stated that its investigation had revealed that "more than 250 Judges—mostly Town and Village Justices—in 38 counties have either made requests of other Judges for special consideration, granted such requests, or done both. Some have granted favors many times—one Judge has acknowledged over 500 favors."[151] In most instances, the requests were granted and the requesting judge often indicated a willingness to return the favor. Frequently, the request was for a reduction of the charge "from driving while intoxicated (a misdemeanor) to speeding (a three-point, moving violation) and even to driving with an unsafe tire (a no-point, non-moving violation)."[152]

Between 1974 and 1978 the temporary and permanent commissions initiated fifty-three removal proceedings that resulted in eight judges resigning prior to the preferment of formal charges, two judges who allowed their term of office to expire, one judge being suspended by the commission, and seven cases that went to trial. The courts removed three judges, suspended one, and publicly censured four judges.[153]

Voters in 1977 approved a constitutional amendment, effective on January 1, 1978, replacing the Court on the Judiciary with a Commission on Judicial Conduct charged with receiving and investigating complaints relative to judges and authorized to determine whether "a Judge or Justice [should] be admonished, censured, or removed from office for cause, including, but not limited to, misconduct in office, persistent failure to perform his duties, habitual intemperance, and conduct, on or off the bench, prejudicial to the administration of justice, or that a Judge or Justice be retired for mental or physical disability preventing the proper performance of his judicial duties."[154] Any such determination is transmitted to the chief judge of the Court of Appeals, who serves written notice of the determination on the judge or justice, who may accept the commission's determination or within thirty days file a written request with the chief judge for a review of the determination by the Court of Appeals, which may censure, remove, or retire the judge.

The commission consists of eleven members appointed as follows: four by the governor, one by the temporary president of the Senate, one by the speaker of the Assembly, one each by the minority leaders of the Senate and the Assembly, and three by the chief judge of the Court of Appeals. After the initial appointments, members serve four-year terms.

Interestingly, on March 16, 1978, the Court of Appeals censured Judge Jacob D. Fuchsberg of the Court of Appeals for trading in New York City and State securities during a period in 1976–77 when the Court of Appeals was hearing appeals on lower court decisions on the city's finances.[155] This was the first time that a member of the Court of Appeals had been the subject of disciplinary proceedings. Although responsibility for investigating complaints relative to judges was transferred to the Commission on Judicial Conduct on January 1, 1978, the Court on the Judiciary that censured Judge Fuchsberg had been convened on September 6, 1977.

THE JURY SYSTEM

Two types of juries—the grand jury and the *petit* or trial jury—
operate in the Empire State. Their origin derives from England,
where the jury initially was a body of witnesses that later became
divided into the two types of juries. Trial by jury in civil and criminal
cases has been guaranteed by the state constitution since 1777.[156]

The Grand Jury

The grand jury's accusatory role is traceable to the Assize of
Clarendon in 1166, and the grand jury's protective role is traceable
to the Stuart period.[157] A constitutional guarantee that a defendant
has the right to indictment by a grand jury· in "capital and other
infamous" crimes did not appear in the original state constitution
but was incorporated in the constitution adopted in 1821.[158]

Composed of twenty-three citizens, the grand jury is an in-
quisitorial body summoned to convene in each of the sixty-two counties to hear evidence alleging that individuals are guilty of criminal
acts.[159] Each grand juror must possess the same qualifications as
a trial juror, and the foreman and acting foreman of a grand jury
are appointed by the judge. It is important to note that grand jury
service is voluntary, and the average term is approximately one
month. If the grand jury determines that there is reasonable doubt
as to the guilt or innocence of the accused, the jury returns a pres-
entment of charges or approves as a "true bill" the indictment
drafted by the district attorney. A quorum is sixteen members and
the concurrence of twelve is required to return an indictment.

The grand jury conducts a "John Doe" investigation to expose
crime and corruption when there is insufficient evidence to support
prima facie charges against an individual. While the grand jury
typically does not subpoena the person against whom charges are
made or notify him of the investigations, a prospective defendant
has the right to testify if he waives immunity.[160] If the grand jury
does not return an indictment, the district attorney can submit the
same case to a second grand jury.[161] If the second grand jury dis-
misses the charge, the case cannot be submitted to a grand jury

again. A district attorney can be superseded by the attorney general, who also is authorized to appoint special state prosecutors.[162]

The grand jury is empowered to conduct investigations to determine the existence of criminal wrongdoing, regardless of whether the matter is called to its attention by the district attorney, and possesses the authority, exercised through the district attorney, to subpoena citizens and public officials to appear before the panel and give sworn testimony.[163] Failure to respond to a subpoena or refusal to testify can lead to punishment for criminal contempt. The legislature has enacted statutes authorizing a grand jury to grant immunity from criminal prosecution in order to obtain information from a witness without violating his constitutional right against self-incrimination.[164]

Until 1959 courts in the Empire State ruled that a grand jury could not initiate an investigation simply because the existence of a crime might be uncovered.[165] In 1959 the Court of Appeals upheld the right of the Tioga County grand jury to investigate possible criminal activity associated with the 1957 "Apalacin" meeting of reputed known criminals.[166] In this case, the court held that the grand jury possessed the authority to confer immunity upon a witness and compel him to answer questions under the pain of prosecution for contempt even though the immunity granted did not protect the individual against prosecution by other states or the federal government.

Historically, grand jury proceedings have been conducted *ex parte* and in secret, and a witness has not been allowed to be accompanied by an attorney to the grand jury room but could consult an attorney outside the room. In 1978 the legislature amended the Criminal Procedure Law to authorize a witness who has signed a waiver of immunity to be advised by a counsel during grand jury proceedings.[167] The court that empanels the grand jury is authorized to remove an attorney from the grand jury room and to assign an attorney to advise a witness financially unable to hire an attorney. Opponents of this provision argue that the previous law allowed witnesses sufficient protection and that the presence of an attorney in the grand jury room will slow down proceedings.

In 1961 the Court of Appeals ruled that a grand jury was not authorized to issue a report criticizing public officials as incompetent or guilty of dereliction of duty.[168] This decision induced the 1964 legislature to authorize a grand jury to issue such a report and granted the officials named the right to answer the charges and appeal the judicial order accepting the report prior to its release to the public.[169]

In practice, the grand jury tends to function at the direction of the district attorney, and this practice has raised questions relative to the value of the grand jury system.[170] Courts have ruled that the district attorney is not required to present evidence to the grand jury if he believes the evidence to be insufficient for an indictment.[171] In addition, the Supreme Court has ruled that "the District Attorney is the legal adviser of the grand jury," but lacks the "power to convene, reconvene, or adjourn it."[172] The charge is made that the grand jury is a rubber stamp for the district attorney because the jury returns a true bill in a high percentage of the cases initiated by the district attorney. Others point out that the high percentage is a product of careful screening of cases by the district attorney.

The grand jury has been controversial, with opponents maintaining it is an expensive, anachronistic, and oppressive mechanism, and proponents contending that the grand jury is necessary to protect citizens and ensure that justice is rendered.[173] A number of critics charge that the socioeconomic characteristics of grand jurors are unrepresentative of the community served, with most jurors being middle class, whereas a high percentage of the persons considered by a grand jury have lower incomes and/or are members of minority groups, thereby resulting in preferential treatment for middle-class persons. An unrepresentative grand jury is not unconstitutional unless there is evidence of deliberate exclusion of members of certain groups from grand jury service.[174]

The Trial Jury

The trial or *petit* jury, composed of either six or twelve citizens, hears evidence presented in court, renders decisions in civil cases, and determines the guilt or innocence of persons accused of crimes.[175] The United States Supreme Court in 1978 invalidated a Georgia law providing for a criminal trial with a five-member jury on the ground that a jury of less than six members creates "a substantial threat to sixth and fourteenth amendment guarantees."[176]

The state constitution guarantees that "trial by jury in all cases in which it has heretofore been guaranteed by constitutional provisions shall remain inviolate forever."[177] Since the present constitution was adopted in 1894, this guarantee means that the legislature may decide whether a jury will be provided only in those cases where the constitution and statutes in 1894 did not require a jury trial. There are two types of civil cases where the constitution requires a jury: (1) civil cases triable by jury under the common law, such as actions for monetary damage and recovery of chattels; and (2) civil cases triable by jury under statutory provisions in effect at the time of the adoption of a new constitution in 1777, 1821, 1846, and 1894, such as divorce actions.[178]

The state constitution authorizes a defendant in open court with the approval of the court to waive in writing a trial by jury except where the punishment for conviction is death.[179] The legislature has prescribed the method of waiving a jury trial and authorized the Appellate Division of the Supreme Court in each judicial department to provide for the effectuation of a waiver.[180] The legislature also has provided that "when it appears in the course of a trial by the court that the relief required, although not originally demanded by a party entitled the adverse party to a trial by jury of certain issues of fact, the court shall give the adverse party an opportunity to demand a jury trial of such issues."[181]

Crimes prosecuted by indictment must be tried by a twelve-member jury unless a jury trial is waived.[182] The constitution also empowers the legislature to authorize a criminal court, except in cases of alleged crimes prosecuted by indictment, to try cases without a jury.[183] Although the Seventh Amendment to the United States Constitution guarantees trial by jury in suits at common law where the amount in controversy exceeds $20, the United States Supreme Court ruled that this guarantee is applicable only to federal court proceedings.[184]

One of the complaints directed against the jury system is that justice is delayed and court congestion is increased by the use of trial juries. Empaneling of a jury can be time consuming, and "a Manhattan Supreme Court Justice estimates that one-third of his time is spent in jury selection, one-third in hearing pre-trial motions, and only one-third in actually trying cases."[185] Furthermore, the actual trial time is greater when a jury is utilized. To help remedy the problem of delays in criminal cases, the 1972 legislature enacted a speedy trial law stipulating that criminal cases must be given preference for trial over civil cases.[186]

REDUCING COURT CONGESTION

A common problem with judicial systems across the nation has been crowded dockets resulting in the delay in the administration of justice. To some, delays in the administration of justice mean the denial of justice. In large measure, the proliferation of automobile cases has been responsible for congestion in many courts.

One approach to the solution of the problem of crowded court dockets has been the creation of additional courts, particularly specialized ones, and additional judgeships. A second and limited approach to relieving criminal court congestion has involved the decriminalization of certain activities. In 1974 the legislature enacted a law deleting the Penal Law section that made public intoxication a criminal offense.[187] The legislature took a similar action in enacting the Marihuana Reform Act of 1977, which stipulates that a person possessing less than twenty-five grams of marihuana is "guilty of unlawful possession of marihuana," a noncriminal violation subject to a maximum fine of $100.[188]

Administrative Adjudication

A third approach is the transfer of certain types of cases from the judicial system to administrative tribunals for adjudication. A 1913 constitutional amendment authorized the legislature to provide for a Workmen's Compensation System and the settlement of injuries to workers "with or without trial by jury."[189] The 1913 legislature assigned workmen's compensation cases to a newly created Workman's Compensation Commission, which was not "bound by common law or statutory rules of evidence or by technical and formal procedures of evidence."[190] In contrast to judicial proceedings that tend to be elaborate and technical, administrative adjudicatory proceedings are simpler, less formal, and speedier because "the primary administrative efforts have been to secure expeditious settlements rather than to umpire the litigation of contenders."[191]

With the number of traffic cases in New York City increasing from 2,896,188 in 1962 to 4,600,191 in 1969, the Criminal Court of New York City became so congested that a defendant pleading innocent to a single parking ticket had to wait ten months for a trial.[192] To solve this problem, the 1969 state legislature decided to decriminalize minor traffic and parking violations in New York City, and established the Administrative Adjudication Bureau in the New York State Department of Motor Vehicles to adjudicate minor traffic infractions and the Parking Violations Bureau in the New York City Transportation Administration to adjudicate parking violations.[193]

Completing a comparative study of judicial and administrative adjudication of parking and minor traffic violations in New York City, Yusuf E. Zarur concluded that administrative adjudication "is more economical, speedier, and more effective in achieving the objectives of traffic law enforcement" and "also has the advantage of reducing court congestion."[194] The success of administrative adjudication in New York City induced the 1972 legislature to extend the system to Buffalo and Rochester.[195]

Several reformers favor taking sumptuary offenses (drug addiction and prostitution), housing and sanitation code violations, and all motor vehicle violations out of the judicial system and transferring the offenses to administrative adjudicatory panels.

Arbitration

Court congestion and new areas of business and environmental controversy led to a lessening of confidence in the ability of judicial adjudication to settle many types of disputes and accelerated the trend upward settling disputes by private arbitration with the number of such disputes so handled increasing to 47,066 in 1978, an increase of more than 50 percent since 1971.[196] Other reformers believe that the judiciary should not expand its involvement in social policy because the "judges are taking tasks beyond the capacity of the judicial system."[197]

Taken completely out of the formal judicial system by arbitration are labor grievances, and arbitration is being used more commonly to settle consumer warranty controversies, family and neighborhood disputes, and small claims. The movement is supported by Chief Justice Warren E. Burger of the United States Supreme Court who stated that "we must in the public interest move toward a large volume of private conflicts out of the courts and into the channels of arbitration."[198]

The 1970 legislature enacted the Compulsory Arbitration Law authorizing the Administrative Board of the Judicial Conference to promulgate rules for the compulsory binding arbitration of claims pending in any court for the recovery of money up to $4,000.[199] An experimental program was launched in Bronx, Broome, Monroe, and Schenectady counties, and a total of 3,064 cases were referred to arbitration panels in 1977.[200] The 1977 total accounted for approximately 20 percent of the civil cases disposed of in those counties by the Supreme Court and the County Court. The Administrative Board evaluated the program and concluded that it "is operating successfully in all four counties."[201] The system is being phased in throughout the state.

Fear is expressed by some observers that with the passage of time lawyers will become more involved and push for courtlike procedures, including stenographic transcripts, which may result in decisions being delayed and being legalistic in nature when rendered.

THE JUDICIARY AND POLICYMAKING

Historically, the judiciary has played a major role in protecting civil liberties of citizens by adjudicating disputes among private individuals. As we have seen, the courts also play an important check-and-balance role in reviewing actions of the legislature and the governor and invalidating actions on occasion if they violate the state constitution or the United States Constitution.

While the Empire State's judiciary has not played the activist role that the Warren Court played on the national level, the state's courts have rendered important decisions necessitating changes in major state policies. As a general rule, the courts are reluctant to challenge decisions made by the legislature, since it is composed of the elected representatives of the voters. In 1812 Justice Smith Thompson of the supreme court commented on the wisdom of the judiciary invalidating acts of the legislature:

But admitting such a power in the judiciary, it ought to be exercised with great caution and circumspection and in extreme cases only. It certainly affords a strong and powerful argument in favor of the constitutionality of a law, that it has passed not only that branch of the legislature which constitutes the greater portion of our Court of Dernier Resort, but also the Council of Revision which is composed of the Governor and the two highest judicial tribunals of the State.[202]

With respect to the law mandating the proportion of the New York City budget that must be spent on education (discussed in Chapter III), Martin Wald quotes Chief Judge Charles D. Breitel of the Court of Appeals as stating that, "it was a terrible law" and adding "it is not up to us to decide that kind of public policy. All we were deciding was whether the Governor's veto had been properly overridden."[203]

The Court of Appeals upheld the constitutionality of the state's "blue laws" until 1976. The court in 1959 held that "we must read the statutes as they are written and, if the consequence seems unwise, unreasonable or undesirable, the argument for change is to be addressed to the Legislature, not to the Courts."[204] In the 1970s the court commenced to block enforcement of the "laws" on the ground that the enforcement had been selective and arbitrary.[205] In effect, the court gave the governor and the legislature opportunities to revise the "laws." When no action was taken, the court struck down the "laws" in 1976 by ruling that "due to the gallimaufry of exceptions which has obliterated any natural nexus between section 9 and the salutory purpose of the Sabbath Laws and the pervasive ambiguity of section 12 we declare both of these sections unconstitutional."[206] The court added: "Should the Legislature continue to deem a Sunday closing law desirable it may readily devise a system of exemptions which could produce an atmosphere appropriate for a common day of rest and one which is consonant with today's needs and mores."[207]

The courts, as explained in Chapter III, arbitrate the boundary lines between state powers and local government powers, and also make the final determination with respect to the respective powers of the governor and the legislature under the constitutional amendment establishing the executive budget system (discussed in Chapter VII).

Consideration will be given in the next chapter to court decisions involving real property assessment for tax purposes and school financing that are having major policy impacts in the Empire State.

NOTES

1. *New York Education Law*, § 310 (McKinney 1969), and *New York Laws of 1976*, chap. 857.

2. *New York Constitution*, art. VI, §§ 1 and 28 (1962).

3. *New York Constitution*, art. VI, §§ 1 and 28 (1978).

4. *New York Laws of 1976*, chap. 966, and *New York Judiciary Law*, § 220 (McKinney 1979 Supp.).

5. *New York Constitution*, art. VI, § 17.

6. *New York Constitution of 1777*, art. XXVIII, and *New York Constitution of 1821*, art. IV, § 7.

7. *New York Constitution*, art. IV, § 7 (1826).

8. *New York City Civil Court Act*, §§ 101–2201 (McKinney 1963). *New York Uniform District Court Act*, §§ 101–2300 (McKinney 1963).

9. *New York Uniform City Court Act*, §§ 101–2300 (McKinney 1979 Supp.).

10. *New York Uniform Justice Court Act*, §§ 101–2300 (McKinney 1979 Supp.).

11. *New York Constitution*, art. VI, § 15 (c).

12. *Ibid.*, § 15 (b).

13. *Twenty-Third Annual Report* (New York: The Administrative Board of the Judicial Conference, 1978), pp. 28–29.

14. *Ibid.*, pp. 35–37.

15. *New York Constitution*, art. VI, § 17.

16. *New York Public Officers Law*, § 3 (McKinney 1977 Supp.).

17. *Twenty-Second Annual Report*, pp. 186–87.

18. *New York Town Law*, § 20 (McKinney 1966), and *New York Village Law*, § 3-301 (McKinney 1973).

19. 19 *Op. State Compt.* 82 (1963).

20. *New York Town Law*, § 31 (2) (McKinney 1968). First-class towns include each town with a population exceeding 10,000 with a few specified exceptions, all towns in Westchester County, and towns that voted to become first-class towns. *New York Town Law*, § 10 (McKinney 1977 Supp.).

21. *New York Town Law*, § 20 (b) (McKinney 1968).

22. *New York Constitution*, art. VI, § 17 (c).

23. *New York Laws of 1976*, chap. 739, and *New York Uniform Justice Court Act*, § 105 (d) (McKinney 1978 Supp.).

24. *New York Village Law*, § 301 (2) (a) (McKinney 1973).

25. *New York Constitution*, art. VI, § 17 (b).

26. *New York Constitution*, art. VI, § 16 (a), (b), (c), and (e).

27. See the *New York Uniform District Court Act*, §§ 101–2300 (McKinney 1963).

28. *New York City Civil Court Act*, §§ 1800–10 (McKinney 1968 and 1978 Supp.). *New York Uniform City Court Act*, §§ 1801–13 (McKinney 1978 Supp.). *New York Uniform District Court Act*, §§ 1801–10 (McKinney 1963).

29. *New York Uniform City Court Act*, § 1801.

30. *Ibid.*, § 1802.

31. *Ibid.*, § 1803.

32. *Ibid.*, §§ 1805–6.

33. *Ibid.*, §§ 1809–10.

34. *Ibid.*, § 1812.

35. *New York Constitution of 1846*, art. VI, § 6.

36. *New York Constitution of 1894*, art. VI, § 5.

37. *New York Constitution*, art. VI, §§ 6 (d) and 7 (a).

38. *Ibid.*, §§ 4 and 6–8.

39. *The Judiciary* (New York: Temporary State Commission on the Constitutional Convention, 1967), p. 142.

40. *New York Constitution*, art. VI, § 7 (a) and (c).

41. *Ibid.*, § 7 (a).

42. *Ibid.*, § 11 (a).

43. *New York Constitution*, art. VI, § 6 (d).

44. *New York Constitution*, art. VI, §§ 10 (a) and 11 (a).

45. *Ibid.*, §§ 10 (a) (b) and 14.

46. *People v. Trezza*, 128 N.Y. 529 (1891). *Croveno v. Atlantic Avenue Railroad Company*, 150 N.Y. 225 (1896).

47. *New York Constitution of 1821*, art. V, § 5.

48. *New York Constitution of 1846*, art. VI, §§ 4 and 6.

49. *New York Constitution*, art. VI, § 4 (a), (b), and (c).

50. *Ibid.*, § 4 (k).

51. *The Judiciary*, p. 129.

52. *Ibid.*, p. 135.

53. *New York Constitution of 1846*, art. VI, § 2.

54. *New York Constitution of 1777*, art. XXXII-XXXIII. *New York Constitution of 1821*, art. V, §§ 1–2.

55. *New York Laws of 1801*, cap. 11.

56. *New York Constitution of 1894*, art. VI, § 9. See also the report of the convention's Judiciary Committee, which was chaired by Elihu Root. *Revised Record of the Constitutional Convention of 1894* (Albany: The Argus Company, 1900), pp. 461–68.

57. *Revised Record.* (Albany: New York State Constitutional Convention, 1915).

58. *New York Constitution*, art. VI, § 2 (c) (d) (1-4), and (e).

59. Carl L. Swidorski, "New York Court of Appeals: Who Are the Judges?" *National Civic Review*, December 1977, p. 560.

60. *New York Constitution*, art. VI, § 3 (a).

61. *Ibid.*, § 3 (b) (8). See also *Charles W. Sommer & Brothers v. Albert Lorsch and Company*, 254 N.Y. 146 (1930) and *People v. Crimins*, 38 N.Y. 2d 407 (1975).

62. Cuomo, "The New York Court of Appeals," p. 206.

63. Martin Wald, "State Court of Appeals: From Lofty Dignity to Lowly Spittoons," *The Times Union* (Albany, New York), February 1, 1978, p. 3.

64. Stanley H. Fuld, "The Role of the Court of Appeals," *New York Law Journal*, January 30, 1967, p. 4.

65. *Ibid.*

66. "Report of Chief Judge Albert Conway, *New York State Bar Bulletin, 1958*, pp. 279–80.

67. *A Model Judiciary Article for the New York Constitution* (Albany: League of Women Voters of New York, May 1966), p. 11.

68. Special Committee on the Constitutional Convention, *Court Structure and Management* (New York: The Association of the Bar of the City of New York, March 1967), p. 2.

69. *New York Laws of 1962*, chap. 686, and *New York Family Court Act*, §§ 111–20 (McKinney 1975). See also Robert H. Twichell, "New York State's Family Court Act," *Syracuse Law Review*, 1962–63, pp. 481–96.

70. *New York Constitution*, art. VI, § 13 (a).

71. For the powers and jurisdiction of the court, see *New York Family Court Act*, § 115, and *Matter of Proceeding for Support Under Article 4 of Family Court Act*, 89 Misc. 2d 1052 (1977). The 1978 Juvenile Offender Law stipulates that juveniles accused of specified crimes are to be tried as adults. See *New York Laws of 1978*, chap. 478.

72. *New York Family Court Act*, § 114.

73. *New York Constitution*, art. VI, § 7. *Kagen v. Kagen*, 21 N.Y. 2d 532 (1968). See also *New York Laws of 1977*, chap. 449, and *New York Laws of 1978*, chap. 628-29.

74. *Healy v. Dollar Savings Bank*, 57 Misc. 834 (1968).

75. *Boscia v. Sellazzo*, 42 App. Div. 2d 781 (1973).

76. *New York Social Services Law*, § 384 (McKinney 1978 Supp.).

77. *New York Education Law*, § 3232 (McKinney 1978 Supp.). *New York Domestic Relations Law*, § 3043 (McKinney 1977).

78. *New York Domestic Relations Law*, § 30-43 (McKinney 1977). *New York Unconsolidated Laws*, § 1801-806 (McKinney 1978 Supp.). *New York Social Services Law*, § 374-a (McKinney 1976).

79. *New York Family Court Act*, §§ 131 and 137 (McKinney 1975).

80. *New York Social Services Law*, §§ 358-a and 392 (McKinney 1978 Supp.).

81. *Twenty-Third Annual Report*, pp. 102–3.

82. Douglas J. Besharov, "Practice Commentaries," *New York Family Court Act*, p. 5 (McKinney 1975).

83. *Family Court . . . The System That Fails All* (Albany: New York Senate Research Service, May 1977).

84. *New York Laws of 1778*, chap. 12 and *New York Laws of 1787*, chap. 38.

85. *New York Constitution*, art. VI, § 12. See also section 14.

86. *Ibid.*, § 12 (d). See also *New York Surrogate's Court Procedure Act* (McKinney 1967).

87. *In re Fornason's Estate*, 88 Misc. 2d 736 (1976).

88. *The Judiciary*, p. 201.

89. *New York Constitution*, art. VI, §§ 26 and 28.

90. *New York Laws of 1817*, chap. 262.

91. *New York Laws of 1870*, chap. 321.

92. *Proceedings and Debates of the Constitutional Convention of the State of New York* (Albany: Weed, Parsons, and Company, 1868), Vol. II, pp. 1319–29.

93. *New York Constitution of 1846*, art. III, § 19 (1874).

94. *New York Laws of 1876*, chap. 444.

95. *New York Laws of 1911*, chap. 856, and *New York Laws of 1915*, chap. 1.

96. *New York Constitution*, art. VI, § 9. The 1949 amendment originally was article VI, § 23, but was renumbered in 1961 as part of a new judiciary article. See also *Easley v. New York Thruway Authority*, 1 N.Y. 2d 374 (1956).

97. *New York Laws of 1910*, chap. 570.

98. *Public Papers of Alfred E. Smith: Forty-Seventh Governor of the State of New York, Fourth Term, 1928* (Albany: J. B. Lyon Company, 1937), pp. 200–202.

99. *New York Laws of 1929*, chap. 467. See also *New York Laws of 1939*, chap. 860, § 8.

100. *New York Laws of 1936*, chap. 323, and *New York General Municipal Law*, § 50-b (McKinney 1978 Supp.).

101. *Bernardine v. City of New York*, 294 N.Y. 361 (1945).

102. *Maltby v. County of Westchester*, 267 N.Y. 375 (1935).

103. *New York Constitution*, art. VI, § 9.

104. *New York Court of Claims Act*, § 9 (McKinney 1963).

105. *Plan of the Temporary Commission on the Courts for a Simplified Statewide Court System* (Albany: The Commission, 1956), p. 67.

106. *New York Laws of 1944*, chap. 554, and *New York Highway Law*, § 30 (McKinney 1945 Supp.).

107. *New York Laws of 1923*, chap. 605, and *New York Indian Law*, § 5-a (McKinney 1968).

108. *New York Indian Law*, § 46.

109. *Ibid.*

110. *Ibid.*

111. *New York Constitution*, art. VI, § 24.

112. *Ibid.*, See also *New York Judiciary Law*, §§ 240–48 (McKinney 1978 Supp.).

113. *Ibid.*

114. For details, see Jacob A. Friedman, *The Impeachment of Governor William Sulzer* (New York: Columbia University Press, 1939).

115. *New York Constitution*, art. VI, § 2.

116. *Ibid.*, § 22.

117. Warren Moscow, *Politics in the Empire State* (New York: Alfred A. Knopf, 1948), p. 149.

118. Marcia Chambers, "How a Judge Is Made in Brooklyn: Case of Borough President Leone," *The New York Times*, January 3, 1977, p. 10.

119. *New York Constitution of 1821*, art. IV, § 7.

120. *New York Constitution of 1821*, amendment one (1826).

121. *New York Constitution of 1846*, art. VI, §§ 12–15 and 17–18.

122. *New York Constitution*, art. VI, § 2 (c) (d) (e).

123. *New York Election Law*, § 6-124 (McKinney 1978 Supp.).

124. Glenn Fowler, "Making of Judges: How Rare Method Works in New York," *The New York Times*, October 10, 1977, p. 48.

125. *New York Election Law*, § 6-104 (McKinney 1978 Supp.).

126. *Ibid.*, § 6-104 (2) (McKinney 1978 Supp.).

127. *Ibid.*

128. *New York Constitution*, art. VI, §§ 13 (a) and 15 (a).

129. *Ibid.*, § 21 (a) (c) (d).

130. *Ibid.*, § 21 (c) (d).

131. "How Much Do Voters Know or Care About Judicial Candidates?" *Journal of the American Judicature Society*, February–April 1955, pp. 141–43, and "Poll Finds Voters Apathetic on Judges," *The New York Times*, January 29, 1967, p. 46.

132. Chambers, "How a Judge Is Made in Brooklyn," p. 10.

133. Swidorski, "New York Court of Appeals," p. 559.

134. Carl Swidorski, "Should New York's Top Judges Be Elected? *Empire State Report*, September 1976, p. 308.

135. Carl L. Swidorski, "The Politics of Judicial Selection: Accession to the New York State Court of Appeals, 1950–1975" (Albany: Ph.D. Dissertation, State University of New York at Albany, 1977), pp. 255–56.

136. *New York Laws of 1978*, chap. 711.

137. *New York Constitution*, art. VI, § 25 (b).

138. *New York Code of Judicial Conduct* (McKinney 1975).

139. *Ibid.*, § 24.

140. Charles Z. Lincoln, *The Constitutional History of New York* (Rochester: The Lawyers Cooperative Publishing Company, 1906), Vol. IV, pp. 605–6.

141. *New York Constitution*, art. VI, § 24.

142. *Ibid.*, § 23.

143. Lincoln, *Constitutional History*, pp. 585–86.

144. Moscow, *Politics in the Empire State*, p. 164.

145. *New York Constitution*, § 22 (d) (1977).

146. *Matter of Sobel*, 8 N.Y. 2d (a) at (i) (Court on the Judiciary, 1960). *Matter of Friedman*, 12 N.Y. 2d (a) at (e) (Court on the Judiciary, 1963). *Matter of Osterman*, 13 N.Y. 2d (a) at (j) (Court on the Judiciary, 1963). *Matter of Vaccaro*, 42 N.Y. 2d (a) at (i) (Court on the Judiciary, 1977). See also Tom Goldstein, "New York Suspends Supreme Court Judge," *The New York Times*, September 27, 1977, pp. 1 and 26.

147. Max H. Siegel, "Judge's Reaction to 'Terrible' Coffee Costs Him $40,990 Position in Suffolk," *The New York Times*, July 10, 1976, p. 24. Tom Goldstein, "Civil Court Judge in Manhattan Censured for 'Abuse of Authority,'" *The New York Times*, March 29, 1977, p. 36. Max H. Siegel, "City Judge in Newburgh Dismissed on Inept-Administration Charges," *The New York Times*, April 26, 1977, p. 41.

148. *New York Laws of 1974*, chap. 739-40 and *New York Judiciary Law*, § 42 (McKinney 1974 Supp.).

149. *First Report* (New York: The Temporary State Commission on Judicial Conduct, October 1975), p. 17, and *Final Report* (New York: The Temporary State Commission on Judicial Conduct, August 31, 1976), p. 8.

150. *New York Laws of 1976*, chap. 691, and *New York Judiciary Law*, §§ 40–44 (McKinney 1978 Supp.).

151. *Ticket-Fixing: The Assertion of Influence in Traffic Cases* (New York: The New York State Commission on Judicial Conduct, June 20, 1977), p. 1.

152. *Ibid.*, p. 6.

153. *Annual Report* (New York: New York State Commission on Judicial Conduct, January 1978), p. iii, and Peter Khiss, "Court Orders Removal of a Judge in Brooklyn for Misusing His Title, *The New York Times*, November 26, 1980, pp. 1 and D-20.

154. *New York Constitution*, § 22 (a). See also *New York Laws of 1976*, chap. 691, and *New York Judiciary Law*, §§ 40–48 (McKinney 1979 Supp.).

155. *Matter of Fuschberg*, 42 N.Y. 2d (a) at (e) (Court of the Judiciary, 1978). See also Tom Goldstein, "Fuschberg Censured for Trading in New York Notes During Appeals," *The New York Times*, March 17, 1978, pp. 1 and A19.

156. *New York Constitution of 1777*, art. XXXV. *New York Constitution*, art. I, § 2.

157. Bruce H. Schneider, "The Grand Jury: Powers, Procedures, and Problems," *Columbia Journal of Law and Social Problems*, Summer 1973, p. 682.

158. *New York Constitution of 1821*, art. VII, § 7.

159. *New York Criminal Procedure Law*, § 190.50 (McKinney 1971).

160. *New York Criminal Procedure Law*, § 190.50. See also *People ex rel. Mleczko v. McCloskey*, 16 App. Div. 2d 878 (4th Dept., 1962).

161. *New York Criminal Procedure Law*, § 190.75 (3) (3) (McKinney 1971).

162. For further details on special state prosecutors, see Chapter VII.

163. *New York Criminal Procedure Law*, § 190.40 (McKinney 1978 Supp.).

164. *Ibid.*, §§ 190.40 and 190.45.

165. *Matter of Morse*, 42 Misc. 644 (1904).

166. *People v. Riela*, N.Y. 2d 571 (1959), and *People v. Riela*, 364 U.S. 915 (1960).

167. *New York Laws of 1978*, chap. 447, and *New York Criminal Procedure Law*, § 190.52 (McKinney 1979 Supp.).

168. *In Matter of Wood v. Hughes*, 9 N.Y. 2d 144 (1961).

169. *New York Criminal Procedure Law*, §§ 190.85 and 190.90 (McKinney 1979 Supp.).

170. For the powers and duties of a district attorney, see *New York County Law*, § 700 (McKinney 1972), and *New York Criminal Procedure Law*, §§ 190.50 and 190.55 (McKinney 1971).

171. *Prentice v. Gulotta*, 13 Misc. 2d 280 (1958). For a contrary decision, see *People v. Rosen*, 74 N.Y. 2d 624 (1947).

172. *People v Radewitz*, 108 N.Y.S. 2d 985 at 989 (1951).

173. For a defense of the grand jury, see Peter M. Brown, "Ten Reasons Why the Grand Jury in New York Should Be Retained and Strengthened," *The Record of the Association of the Bar of the City of New York*, June 1967, pp. 471–78.

174. *Fay v. New York*, 332 U.S. 261 (1947), and *People v. Agron*, 10 N.Y. 2d 130 (1961).

175. For details on the trial jury, see the *New York Judiciary Law*, §§ 500-13 and 515-23 (McKinney 1978 Supp.).

176. *Ballew v. Georgia*, 435 U.S. 223 at 243 (1978).

177. *New York Constitution*, art. I, § 2.

178. *Wynehamer v. People*, 13 N.Y. 378 (1856). *Malone v. Saints Peter and Paul's Church*, 172 N.Y. 269 (1902).

179. *New York Constitution*, art. I, § 2.

180. *New York Civil Practice Law and Rules*, § 4102 (McKinney 1963 and 1978 Supp.), and *New York Surrogate's Court Procedure Act*, § 502 (McKinney 1967).

181. *New York Civil Practice Law and Rules*, § 4103 (McKinney 1978 Supp.).

182. *New York Constitution*, art. VI, § 18 (a).

183. *Ibid.*

184. *Walker v. Sauvinet*, 92 U.S. 90 (1875) and *Malloy v. Hogan*, 378 U.S. 1 at 4 (1964).

185. Alexander B. Smith and Harriet Pollack, "Court Reform," *Empire State Report*, May 1977, p. 205. For a general discussion of the jury system, see Jerome Frank, *Courts on Trial* (Princeton: Princeton University Press, 1950), pp. 108–45.

186. *New York Laws of 1972*, chap. 184, and *New York Criminal Procedure Law*, § 30.20 (McKinney 1979 Supp.).

187. *New York Laws of 1974*, chap. 1068, and *New York Penal Law*, § 240.40 (McKinney 1979 Supp.).

188. *New York Penal Law*, § 221.05 (McKinney 1978 Supp.).

189. *New York Constitution*, art. I, § 18.

190. *New York Laws of 1913*, chap. 816, § 68.

191. Walter Gellhorn, *Federal Administrative Proceedings* (Baltimore: The Johns Hopkins Press, 1941), p. 58.

192. *Seventeenth Annual Report* (New York: The Administrative Board of the Judicial Conference of the State of New York, 1972), p. 343.

193. *New York Vehicle and Traffic Law*, §§ 225 and 235 (McKinney 1970 and 1978 Supp.).

194. Yusuf E. Zarur, "Administrative versus Judicial Adjudication of Minor Traffic and Parking Violations: Program Evaluation" (Albany: D.P.A. Dissertation, State University of New York at Albany, 1974), p. 219.

195. *New York Vehicle and Traffic Law*, § 225.1 (McKinney 1978 Supp.).

196. Jerry Flint, "An Answer to Crowded Courts," *The New York Times*, May 29, 1978, p. D-1.

197. *New Approaches to Conflict Resolution* (New York: The Ford Foundation, 1978), p. 8.

198. Flint, "An Answer to Crowded Courts," p. 276.

199. *New York Laws of 1970*, chap. 1004; *New York Judiciary Law*, § 213 (8) (McKinney 1979 Supp.); and *New York Civil Practice Law and Rules*, §§ 7501–10 (McKinney 1963 and 1979 Supp.).

200. *Twenty-Third Annual Report*, p. 173.

201. *Ibid.*, p. 354.

202. *Livingston v. VanIngen*, 9 Johnson 506 at 564 (1812).

203. Martin Wald, "State's Highest Court a 'Reluctant Dragon,'" *The Times Union* (Albany, New York), February 2, 1978, p. 13.

204. *People v. Kupprat*, 6 N.Y. 2d 88 at 90 (1959).

205. *New York General Business Law*, §§ 9 and 12 (McKinney 1968). *People v. Kupprat*, 6 N.Y. 2d 88 at 90 (1959). *People v. Weston's Shoppers City, Incorporated*, 30 N.Y. 2d 572 (1972). *People v. Acme Markets*, 37 N.Y. 2d 326 at 338 (1975).

206. *People v. Abrahams*, 40 N.Y. 2d 277 at 280 (1976).

207. *Ibid.*, at 286. For additional details on invalidation of legislation by the courts, see Franklin A. Smith, *Judicial Review of Legislation in New York: 1906–1938* (New York: Columbia University Press, 1952).

CHAPTER X

Financing the State

THE MAGNITUDE of intergovernmental fiscal assistance and the struggles by groups over taxation and the allocation of state revenue ensure that intergovernmental relations and group politics are prominent themes in a chapter devoted to state finance. Gubernatorial-legislative relations also are highlighted, since the constitution grants the budget preparation and executive powers to the governor and the appropriation power to the legislature.

With consolidated expenditures of all New York State governmental operating funds totaling nearly $19 billion, it is apparent that the New York State government is a big business. The phenomenal increase in expenditures during the past two decades is attributable to four major developments: (1) population growth; (2) new and expanded services to meet problems associated with unemployment, the increased use of drugs, and the higher percentage of young people; (3) large capital projects including the State University campuses, mental health facilities, the Empire State Plaza in Albany, and transportation facilities; and (4) inflation.

The reader should be alerted to the fact that the control of finance by the state government is limited by the "commerce clause" of the United States Constitution forbidding states to levy taxes that interfere with interstate commerce and the Fourteenth Amendment to the United States Constitution prohibiting the giving of public funds to a private interest for private purposes. The federal government, however, is a major supplier of funds to the Empire State, with federal grants-in-aid totaling $5,473 million in 1979 and general revenue-sharing funds totaling $257 million, or 2.1 percent of state revenue, in 1979.[1] The federal government also provides loan guarantees enabling New York City to borrow funds in the financial markets (described in Chapter II).

Forces external to a state—such as the health of the national economy and interest rates—restrict a state's freedom of action in the area of finance. Should the Federal Reserve System decide to raise market interest rates sharply to curtail inflation, the state may decide that the cost of borrowing funds for a specific project authorized by the voters makes the project's cost prohibitive. And the state constitution, of course, contains a number of restrictions on legislative action in the area of finance, including the requirement that a debt "be paid in equal annual installments," which prevents accelerated repayment of a debt or postponement of payment.[2] Furthermore, the state is forbidden to give or loan money to private organizations for capital construction, including hospitals, except "to a public corporation to be organized for the purpose of making loans to finance the construction of new industrial or manufacturing plants . . . or the acquisition, rehabilitation, or improvement of former industrial or manufacturing plants."[3]

A high-tax state, such as New York, must weigh carefully the impact of a proposed new tax or tax increase, because a significant increase in taxation places the state at a competitive disadvantage with other states in terms of attracting and retaining industry. Because of its relatively high graduated income tax, the state decided to levy a sales tax rather than increase the income tax in 1965 to raise needed revenue.

Not surprisingly, the tax issue frequently is a major electoral campaign issue, as in 1978. Former Governor Alfred E. Smith wrote in 1935:

In every political campaign the cost of government becomes an issue. . . . Everybody knows that claims of tax reduction are made by politicians in the most general terms. For the most part they are simply bait waved before the eyes of the tax-ridden voter to lure him into a favorable vote at the ballot-box with little thought to what will happen after election.[4]

THE STATE BUDGETS

Chapter VII traces the development of the executive budget system and emphasizes the preeminent role of the governor in budget preparation and budget execution. The state constitution, however, provides for a cooperative relationship between the governor and the legislature's fiscal committees by directing the governor to furnish the committees with copies of the budget requests of departments and agencies and authorizing the committees to attend the hearings on the requests held by the governor.[5] In addition, the presiding officer of each house is directed to provide "itemized estimates of the financial needs of the Legislature," and the comptroller is required to provide similar estimates for the judiciary by December 1 "each year for inclusion in the budget without revision."[6]

The Three Budgets

The state lacks a comprehensive financial plan, as three budgets and accompanying appropriation bills are submitted annually by the governor to the legislature, and large expenditures are treated as "off-budget" items, a subject discussed later. The 1,095-page executive budget for fiscal 1979–80, which totaled $12.4 billion and weighed six pounds, was submitted in January. Following a gubernatorial election, the executive budget must be submitted to the legislature no later than February 1; in other years the budget must be submitted by the second Tuesday following the opening of the annual legislative session.

Subsequent to the submission of the executive budget, the governor may amend or supplement the budget for thirty days, and the legislature may not consider another appropriation bill until those submitted by the governor have been finally acted upon, unless the governor sends a message of necessity to the legislature certifying the need for the immediate passage of another appropriation bill.[7] While the legislature is free to delete or reduce items in an appropriation bill submitted by the governor, the legislature may not add items to the bill unless each item refers to a single object and is stated separately from the original items in the bill.[8] An appropriation bill submitted by the governor and approved by the legislature is not subject to a veto or item veto by the governor, with the exceptions of appropriations for the legislature and the judiciary and separate items added to the bill by the legislature.[9] The governor lacks the power to reduce items in appropriation bills, a power possessed by the governor in Alaska, California, Hawaii, Massachusetts, New Jersey, Pennsylvania, and Tennessee.

A five-year projection of general fund income and expenditures must be submitted as a supplement to the executive budget.[10] The five-year projection of general fund income and expenditures, prepared in 1980, shows expenditures rising from $13,790 million in fiscal 1980–81 to $17,138 million in fiscal 1984–85.[11]

The deficiency budget, usually submitted in January and totaling approximately $150 million, is designed to replenish depleted or rapidly depleting accounts to enable departments and agencies to continue operations until March 31, which is the end of the fiscal year. Traditionally, the supplemental budget is one of the last items of business acted upon by the legislature each year and contains funds to meet needs not anticipated in January and typically restores some funds deleted from the executive budget by the legislature. The supplemental budget—totaling approximately $100 million—is the product of intense bargaining between the governor, the speaker of the Assembly, and the temporary president of the Senate. Members of the legislature typically have little opportunity to examine the supplemental budget prior to its adoption. Members, for example, were given the 318-page fiscal 1978 supplemental budget bill at 10:30 A.M. and voted to approve the bill in the evening.

Constitutional Restrictions

The First Amendment to the United States Constitution, applied to the states through the Fourteenth Amendment, restricts the purposes for which public money may be appropriated. In 1977, for example, the United States Supreme Court struck down as violative of the First Amendment a New York law appropriating funds to reimburse sectarian schools for expenses incurred in performing certain recordkeeping and testing services mandated by state law.[12] In 1980 the Court upheld the constitutionality of a similar but not identical law.

To provide a check on the appropriation of funds for local or private purposes, the 1821 state constitution required a two-thirds vote of the members elected to each house before such an appropriation could be made.[13] The first constitutional restriction on the purposes for which state funds could be expended dates to the 1846 constitutional provision forbidding the loan or gift of the credit of the state "to or in aid of any individual, association, or corporation."[14] This restriction, however, did not prevent the legislature from recognizing and allowing claims based upon charity, equity, or gratitude.

The 1894 constitution continued the earlier restrictions, but exceptions were made by amendments proposed by the 1938 constitutional convention and ratified by the voters, and by amendments proposed by the legislature and ratified by the voters in 1965 and 1977. The current exceptions are:

- aid, care, and support of the needy
- hazards of unemployment, sickness, and old age
- education and support of the blind, the deaf, the dumb, and physically handicapped, and mentally ill, the emotionally disturbed, the mentally retarded, and juvenile delinquents
- health and welfare service for all children
- aid, care, and support of neglected and dependent children and of the needy sick
- increase in the amount of pension benefits of any widow or widower of a retired member of the state to whom payable as beneficiary under an optional settlement in connection with the pension of such member
- low-rent housing and nursing home accommodations for persons of low income
- clearance, replanning, reconstruction, and rehabilitation of substandard and insanitary areas[15]

The legislature may recognize the equity of a private claim against the state and provide for the allowance of the claim by the Court of Claims, but the legislative finding of a moral obligation on the part of the state is not binding upon the court.[16]

Although the constitution stipulates that "no money shall ever be paid out of the State Treasury or any of its funds, or any of the funds under its management, except in pursuance of an appropriation by law,"[17] the State Finance Law recognizes that emergencies may require the expenditure of funds when the legislature is not in session. The governor is authorized by the law to issue a certificate of allocation from the governmental emergency fund, created in 1944, upon issuance of a certificate of intent to recommend an appropriation at the next session of the legislature signed by the temporary president of the Senate, the speaker of the Assembly, the chairman of the Assembly Ways and Means Committee, and the chairman of the Senate Finance Committee.[18] Prior to the establishment of the fund, departments and agencies were forced to operate within a "frozen" budget unless the legislature was in session and approved a deficiency or supplemental appropriation.

The constitution is unclear as to whether a "line-item" budget is required. The governor is directed to submit to the legislature the budget and "a bill or bills containing all the proposed appropriations and reappropriations included in the budget and the proposed legislation, if any, recommended there," but the form of the appropriation bills is not specified.[19] The constitution, however, authorizes the legislature "to strike out or reduce items" in the budget, and the courts have ruled that this authorization means that appropriation bills must be in line-item form to the extent possible.[20] In other words, full itemization is not required unless needed to provide information as to the necessity for or purpose of the proposed expenditure. Lump-sum appropriations are lined out in detail by the director of the budget, "for personal services expenditures and for general categories of maintenance and operating expenses."[21]

Federal Funds

An important budgeting principle is comprehensiveness, which means that the budget document should contain data on all proposed expenditures, estimated receipts, and debt. The state's executive budget lacks comprehensiveness, as no information is provided on federal grants-in-aid. Federal revenue-sharing funds, which are only a fraction of the grant funds, are included in the budget. The lack of information on federal grants-in-aid restricts the ability of the legislature to evaluate proposed state spending. A major controversy has swirled around the proposal that all federal funds received by state departments and agencies should be subject to appropriation by the legislature (discussed in greater detail in Chapter VI).

The United States Supreme Court in 1973 ruled that a state

legislature may appropriate federal funds if federal conditions are met on the expenditure of the funds.[22] Nevertheless, strong opposition by the governor and executive branch agencies has blocked the proposed legislative appropriation of federal funds with the arguments that the agencies might have to wait one year until the funds are appropriated by the legislature and federal funds would be driven to other states if the bill became law. In 1981, the New York State Supreme Court in *Anderson v. Regan* ruled legislative approval was required before federal funds can be spent.

Budget Balance and Execution

The constitution requires that the budget be balanced,[23] but the determination of whether the budget actually is balanced is difficult because the state does not use the accrual system of accounting, a subject discussed in more detail in a later section. Governors have been able to present a balanced budget by fiscal legerdemain. Commenting upon the use of different budget surplus figures by the two major gubernatorial candidates in 1978, former Governor Nelson A. Rockefeller stated: "If I'm having problems, I feel for the general public."[24]

Only in the narrowest of instances may the judiciary directly review the state budget. The Court of Appeals in 1976 held that a planned deficit in unconstitutional[25] but ruled in 1977 that two successive deficits do not necessarily mean that there was a planned deficit.[26] The court in the 1977 case stressed that "the proof of improper budget manipulation must be found in the estimates of revenues and expenditures."[27]

Until 1980 it was assumed that once the legislature approved appropriation bills, the governor was in charge of budget execution and was under no requirement to spend all the funds that were appropriated. In other words, the governor could order a freeze on spending for a specific purpose, including a freeze on the hiring of personnel. In 1980, however, the Court of Appeals ruled that the governor could not impound funds appropriated by the legislature.[28]

Taxpayer Challenges

In a most important decision, the Court of Appeals in 1975 reversed its 1963 decision restricting standing to challenge the constitutionality of an appropriation by the legislature to individuals "personally aggrieved thereby" and ruled that a taxpayer has standing to challenge enactments of our State Legislature as contrary to the mandates of State Constitution."[29] In the same year, the legislature enacted a law authorizing any citizen taxpayer to bring an action in court for declaratory and equitable relief "against an officer or employee of the State who in the course of his or her duties has caused, is now causing, or is about to cause a wrongful expenditure, misappropriation, misapplication, or any other illegal or unconstitutional disbursement of State funds or State property."[30]

The following year, the Court of Appeals ruled that there can be no direct judicial review of the state budget, because the courts must exercise "proper restraint . . . in responding to invitations to intervene in the internal affairs of the Legislature as a co-ordinate branch of government."[31] The court in 1977 rejected the argument that the existence of a deficit in two consecutive years is proof that the legislature unconstitutionally adopted an unbalanced budget[32] and added:

Assuming it were feasible to convert a courtroom into a super-auditing office to receive and criticize the budget estimates of a State with an $11 billion budget, the idea is not only a practical monstrosity but would duplicate exactly what the Legislature and the Governor do together, in harmony or in conflict, most often in conflict, for several months of each year.[33]

After losing a challenge to the constitutionality of the executive budget as adopted on the ground they lacked standing,[34] the appellants sought a writ of mandamus to compel the state comptroller to challenge the legality of the budget, but the Appellate Division of the Supreme Court ruled the comptroller cannot be compelled to perform a duty involving the exercise of judgment or discretion.[35]

In 1977 the Court of Appeals affirmed the ruling of the Appellate Division of the Supreme Court that the state's Freedom of Information Law entitled citizens to examine the files and worksheets of budget examiners.[36] The following year, the Court of Appeals unanimously rejected a taxpayer suit alleging that the 1978–79 executive budget failed to contain sufficient details and ruled that the legislature was the proper body to determine whether the degree of budget itemization was inadequate.[37]

The Fund Structure

The state's financial transactions affect the approximately 1,075 funds established by the legislature or by administrative action. The funds, which exist inside and outside the State Treasury, are accounting devices recording financial transactions. The state comptroller and the commissioner of taxation and finance jointly administer the approximately 175 funds within the State Treasury, and each of the so-called sole custody funds outside the State Treasury is administered by a state official.

Funds Within the Treasury. The general fund is composed of the local assistance fund, the state purposes fund, and the capital construction fund, and is the most important inside fund, as nearly all tax revenue and other specified revenue items are recorded in this fund. The executive budget is processed through the general fund, and the budget's implementing appropriation bills account for approximately 63 percent of all state operating expenditures.

The local assistance fund accounts for approximately 60 percent of all general fund expenditures and is utilized for financial assistance to municipalities and school districts for their general purposes, which is referred to as state revenue sharing, and specified education and social services expenditures. Most of these expenditures are mandated by state laws containing a distribution formula and/or providing for partial reimbursement of municipal expenditures for social services. The expenditures, however, are limited to the amounts appropriated.[38]

Approximately one third of general fund expenditures are state purposes fund expenditures covering the cost of operating the three branches of government, including expenditures for general charges such as employee retirement fund contributions. All debt-service expenditures not chargeable to a specific debt-service fund are charged to the state purposes fund.

The capital construction fund is used to finance the construction and reconstruction of capital facilities, such as grade crossings, highways, parkways, and some institutional facilities, and to pay the rent for certain state office buildings. Current revenues and/or funds from the sale of bond anticipation notes are used to finance expenditures.

The legislature also disburses moneys from the three funds contained in the general fund by means of first-instance appropriations made to various state agencies, which are to be repayed in the future. First-instance appropriations are not reflected completely in the executive budget.

By the end of each fiscal year, all assets in the local assistance fund and the state purposes fund must be transferred to their related tax revenue stabilization reserve funds, commonly known as "rainy-day" funds, dating to 1946. Most transferred assets are accounts receivable relating to unreimbursed first-instance appropriations made during the fiscal year. Money in the reserve funds is used to meet operating deficits in the related operating fund. The State Finance Law requires repayment to the reserve funds within the following six years in three equal annual installments of moneys used to finance a deficit unless the reserve fund balance exceeds 45 percent of the total expenditures of the local assistance fund for the fiscal year and 35 percent of the state purposes fund.[39] Loans from the reserve fund may be made on a temporary basis to the state purposes fund or the local assistance fund during the course of a fiscal year.

The state constitution restricts the transfer of moneys from rainy-day funds by stipulating "no moneys shall at anytime be withdrawn from such Fund unless the revenue derived from such tax or taxes during a fiscal year shall fall below the norm for such year; in which event such amount as may be prescribed by law, but in no event an amount exceeding the difference between such revenue and such norm, shall be paid from such fund into the General Fund."[40] Furthermore, the constitution provides that a "law changing the method of determining a norm" is not effective for three years following its enactment.[41] There is no corresponding reserve fund for the capital construction fund. A surplus in this fund at the end of a fiscal year may be used for authorized capital expenditures.

The general fund reflects the largest part of the state's financial transactions each fiscal year, yet numerous other state activities are financed through approximately 175 other funds located within the State Treasury, which may be placed in seven classes: (1) bond funds, (2) debt-service funds, (3) special revenue funds, (4) enterprise funds, (5) intragovernmental service funds, (6) trust and agency funds, and (7) other custodial funds. All funds except the last category are considered to be governmental operating funds.

The largest number of funds are the special revenue funds covering such operations as hunting and fishing license fees, federal grants, State University tuition, and similar sources of revenue based upon user fees or federal funds that are passed through to local governments to help finance state-administered federal programs.

A debt-service fund typically receives revenue dedicated to the payment of principal and interest on state bonds. State park and recreation facilities fees, for example, are deposited in a debt-service fund used to pay the debt service on park and recreation land acquisition bonds.

An enterprise fund receives fees charged for the rendering of services to business organizations, including fees charged hospitals and nursing home companies for inspecting, regulating, and auditing their activities.[42]

A trust and agency fund is used for escrow transactions involving the state, such as the withholding of federal income taxes from the salaries of employees of the state. The moneys in the fund are periodically remitted to the Internal Revenue Service. Escrow-type items not involving state operations are classified as other custodial funds and include the state's common retirement fund.

Funds Outside the Treasury. Approximately 900 funds, established by statute outside the State Treasury, are administered by individual state officials and usually involve a fiduciary relationship, such as the state insurance fund, which insures employers against liability under the Workmen's Compensation Law and funds for the personal needs of inmates and patients at various state institutions. In addition, the mental hygiene program funds of the Facilities Development Corporation and the emergency highway reconditioning and preservation fund of the Thruway Authority are administered outside the State Treasury.

The emergency highway reconditioning and preservation fund was established to avoid the constitutional requirement for voter approval of a bond issue whose proceeds would be used to reconstruct highways. The 1972 law establishing the fund provides for the financing of projects with a first-instance appropriation of $100 million.[43] To finance the improvement program, the New York State Thruway Authority was directed to repay the state first-instance advance by issuing emergency highway reconditioning and preservation bonds and notes. The authority is compensated for all amortization and debt-service expenses from the fund, which has been financed since October 1, 1972, by 25 percent of the 1 percent increase in the motor vehicle and diesel fuel tax imposed on February 1, 1972.

THE ACCOUNTING SYSTEM

The state's fiscal year commenced on October 1 until 1916, when the start of the fiscal year was changed to July 1. Since 1943 the state's fiscal year has started on April 1.

The state employs the cash method of accounting to record its financial transactions for the fiscal year. In 1937 the Joint Legislative Commission on State Fiscal Policies criticized the "checkbook balance" system utilized by the state to keep its accounts because of manipulation of the system.

Tax payments dates have been advanced so that the cash would be collected before such date [beginning of the new fiscal year] and thus reduce the cash deficit. . . . The time of crediting certain tax revenues to the State treasury was advanced to the close of the month in which collected, so that June collections would be credited in June instead of July. In effect thirteen months of revenue was received in the year in which such change was made. . . . To a slight extent the same procedure was followed even in regard to appropriations—notably the appropriation for the employees' retirement system. The appropriation when passed was immediately available and should have been paid into the retirement fund before June 30. Through an exercise of administrative discretion the check was not drawn until July. By thus postponing the payment of a large appropriation, the "check book balance" of the State on June 30 appeared so much the less in the red.[44]

State Comptroller Arthur Levitt was highly critical of the use of what he labeled the "'checkbook' approach to budgeting and therefore reporting" and in 1977 pointed out that this accounting system "has encouraged the Executive to 'manage' the official deficit or surplus at year-end by accelerating or deferring the deposit of revenues or the payment of expenses. Such actions undermine the credibility of both budget estimates and year-end statements."[45] Comptroller Levitt was convinced that cash accounting distorted significantly the public's perception of the fiscal operations of the state and confused the public because of "rollovers," "reverse rollovers," and "accelerations," which he stated represented "manipulations of the financial reporting process and resulted in distortions of $200 to $300 million in fiscal 1973."[46]

Some distortions are the result of legislation such as changes in tax due dates and payments dates for specific local assistance payments. Other distortions are the product of executive action and include, relative to the amount of taxes held as a reserve for tax refunds, acceleration or delays of tax refunds and payments of vendor billings, and acceleration or delays in revenues reporting. Since the date for payment of local assistance for social services aid is not fixed by statute, the payment in some years has included eleven or thirteen months instead of twelve months. Particularly confusing to the public are tax refund reserves adjustments, which make a year-to-year comparison of financial transactions extremely difficult.

A law reduced from twelve to eleven months per capita aid to local governments in the fiscal year 1968–69, thereby reducing state expenditures in the fiscal year by approximately $200 million and imposing a burden on local governments.[47] Similarly, the January and February payment dates for school aid were changed by statute to April and May, thereby reducing fiscal 1972 state expenditures by approximately $380 million.[48]

Although Levitt was a Democrat and recommended the enactment of a bill (S. 7006 of 1978) providing for a system of partial accrual accounting, the bill died in the Democratic-controlled Assembly, although the bill was passed three years in a row by the Republican-controlled Senate. In 1980 Governor Hugh L. Carey vetoed a bill (A. 10493-A) providing for the use of generally accepted accounting principles (GAAP) on the ground that the bill "seriously intrudes upon the constitutional powers of both the Governor and the State Comptroller."[49] The reader should be aware that management also can manipulate an accrual accounting system to some extent, and such a system has difficulty in handling contract obligations and determining tax delinquency reserves.

Public understanding of the state's finances also is clouded by the fact that the executive budget includes only two thirds of all state expenditures and does not reflect expenditures financed by all note and bond proceeds, state-controlled public authorities, most federal funds, and earmarked revenues. "Off-budgeting"—placing certain expenditures such as federal countercyclical aid and lottery funds—outside the general fund also makes it difficult for citizens to understand state finances. Approximately $183 million were off-budgeted in fiscal 1978 and $315 million in fiscal 1979.

THE AUDITING SYSTEM

The state legislature established an auditing system under provisions of the 1777 constitution by electing an auditor general. In 1797 the name of the position was changed to comptroller, and the position continued to be a statutory one until the office was elevated to the constitutional level by the 1821 constitution.[50] The comptroller was elected by the legislature for a three-year term until the constitution of 1846 made the office elective and the term was reduced to two years.[51] The comptroller is responsible for preauditing and postauditing, which are very important financial functions.

The Preaudit

The preaudit involves the inspection of claims and vouchers to ensure that the proposed expenditures have been authorized properly and that sufficient funds are available in the concerned accounts. The state constitution directs the comptroller "to audit all vouchers before payment and all official accounts; to audit the accrual and collection of all revenues and receipts; and to prescribe such methods of accounting as are necessary for the performance of the foregoing duties."[52] The power to prescribe the accounting system to be used is believed to be incidental to the auditing power.

One can argue that preauditing should be the function of an official directly responsible to the governor, as the preaudit should be an administrative function and the postaudit should be conducted by an official independent of the governor. If the preaudit function were a responsibility of the governor, proposed expenditures would be examined for their advisability as well as for their legality. In addition, performance of the preaudit function by the independently elected state comptroller was objected to in the 1930s on the ground that partisan considerations could influence the preaudit should the comptroller be of a different political party than the governor. Furthermore, it was suggested that to promote his own political ambitions a comptroller of the same political party as the governor might arbitrarily disallow proposed expenditures or slow down preauditing. In practice, these criticisms have proved to be unfounded.

The Postaudit

Considerable debate has revolved around the question of the proper office for the conduct of the postaudit. The postaudit initially involved an examination of accounts at the end of the fiscal year to ensure that all expenditures were legally authorized. In some governmental jurisdictions, the postaudit is limited to such an examination. Objections are raised that a limited audit of this nature is the equivalent of locking the barn door after the horse has been stolen.

A more comprehensive view of postauditing has gained general acceptance during recent decades. In addition to checking on the legality of expenditures, the postauditor conducts program audits to determine how economically and efficiently administrative agencies carry out their responsibilities. Writing in 1938, the New York State Constitutional Convention Committee held:

With the control over finances which this type [executive] budget vests in the Executive Department, the Legislature finds that, once it has approved the appropriations and the revenue proposals embodied in the budget, its check over the application of these funds and the administering of the revenue system is negligible. The Finance Committees of the Legislature must therefore remain completely unenlightened on these matters unless provision is made to have some agency responsible to them perform the postaudit functions. Experts agree that only with this provision will the Legislature and its Financial Committees have the opportunity to become fully informed, through a disinterested agency, on how effectively and economically appropriations are expended.[53]

In spite of this 1938 statement, the legislature appeared to be satisfied with the performance of the postauditing function by the comptroller until the creation in 1969 of Legislative Commission on Expenditure Review (discussed in Chapter VI).[54] Currently, postaudits are conducted by the comptroller and the commission. The argument has been advanced that it would be preferable to have the postaudit function performed by an independent agency, responsible to the legislature, that has not been involved in the financial transactions to be audited. The State Budget Bureau in 1937 wrote:

It cannot be said that the Comptroller has auditing functions only because he still retains the financial administrative functions of debt administration, of supervision of funds paid into any court of record and the duties of the former Commissioner of Canals. This means not only the Comptroller is not purely an auditor and does have administrative functions but it also means there is no independent audit of the financial administrative matters controlled by him.[55]

The bureau also argued that "where all centralized accounts and accounting methods are controlled by the Comptroller, there can be no distinction of pre-audit and post-audit because there is generally only one review of expenditures and one set of accounts. The Comptroller issues the warrants, settles the accounts, and allows the expenditure all in one operation."[56] Nevertheless, others are convinced that:

the postaudit function logically belongs in the Comptroller's department, which is one State office having a complete record of all the financial affairs of the State. In discharging his various financial functions the Comptroller acquires knowledge which would be of inestimable value in carrying out the postaudit functions. He, of all people, has that sweeping knowledge of the State's financial administration which is necessary for one whose function is to expose waste and inefficiency and to recommend needed reforms in the application of expenditures. Moreover, it is pointed out that the Comptroller's office carries the prestige and tradition necessary to secure actions on reforms in financial administration.[57]

THE REVENUE SYSTEM

Various writers, commencing with Adam Smith in 1776, developed canons of good taxes.[58] There is general agreement that the tax burden should be equitable and based primarily upon the taxpayer's ability to pay and benefits received. The canon of convenience means that the method, place, and time of tax payment should be fixed; the canon of certainty means that a taxpayer should be able to compute his tax liability in advance of payment and not be subject to arbitrary taxation. The canon of economy holds that the cost of administering a tax should be low, and most writers agree that the administrative cost should not exceed 5 percent. A fifth canon holds that a tax should conserve tax resources and not be so high as to be confiscatory or drive taxpayers from the state. The sixth canon emphasizes stability of yield as this aids financial planning.

An examination of the taxes levied by the Empire State reveals that they measure up differently against the above canons. The graduated state income tax is viewed as measuring up well against the canon of equity, whereas the state sales tax does not measure up well against this canon, as the sales tax imposes a heavier burden on low-income taxpayers.

A study of the New York fiscal system led the United States Advisory Commission on Intergovernmental Relations to classify the state's fiscal role in terms of all state-local tax revenue as a "State Junior Fiscal Partner," since the state collected only 48.4 percent of all tax revenue collected in the state and ranked forty-fourth among the states in terms of percentage of total tax revenue collected by the state.[59] On the other hand, one should not overlook the fact that the Empire State imposes more mandates on local governments necessitating increased local taxation than any other state in the Union (discussed in Chapter III).[60]

Constitutional Restrictions

The United States Constitution and the state constitution restrict the taxing power of the state. Although the former document does not refer specifically to local governments, the restrictions imposed upon the taxation powers of the states also apply to local governments, since they are considered to be creatures of the state.

The United States Constitution forbids states to levy tonnage taxes or duties on imports and exports except for the purpose of "executing its inspection laws"; impede commerce between the states by taxation; or impose taxes that discriminate arbitrarily between persons, thereby denying the persons equal protection of the laws.[61] A provision of a state tax law also is nullified if it conflicts with a treaty on taxation entered into by the United States with a foreign nation.[62] Furthermore, a state may not tax instrumentalities of the federal government, including federal bonds and interest paid on the bonds, without the consent of Congress.

Until 1938, the power to levy taxes was considered to be an inherent power of the state, and only two provisions of the constitution specifically authorized the levying of taxes or restricted the power of the legislature to levy taxes. The 1938 constitutional convention proposed an amendment on taxation, and the voters ratified the proposal on November 8, 1938.[63] The taxation article currently stipulates that "the power of taxation shall never be surrendered, suspended, or contracted away, except as to securities issued for public purposes pursuant to law."[64] The legislature may delegate the taxing power to local governments but must specify the types of taxes to be levied. Tax exemptions may be granted only by general law and "may be altered or repealed except those exempting real or personal property used exclusively for religious, education, or charitable purposes as defined by law and owned by any corporation or association organized or conducted exclusively for one or more of such purposes and not operating for profit."[65] A state public authority, referred to in law as a public benefit corporation (discussed in Chapter VIII), is exempt from the real property tax as a state instrumentality.

The legislature is directed by the constitution to provide for the review and equalization of assessments for purposes of taxation, and assessments are limited to a maximum of full value.[66] The legislature is forbidden to discriminate in terms of taxation between domestic corporations chartered by the state and corporations chartered by the United States engaged in a similar business.[67] The purpose of this provision is to ensure that state-chartered and nationally chartered banks are treated uniformly in terms of taxation. The taxation article also stipulates that the emoluments, except pensions, of state and local government employees are subject to taxation.

The constitutional prohibition of legislation by reference, dating to 1846, prohibited "the automatic alignment of the State income tax base with federal income tax laws" until a constitutional amendment containing such authorization was adopted in 1959.[68]

The present constitution continues a provision of the 1846 constitution requiring a majority vote of each house and a quorum of three fifths of the members elected to each house when a vote is taken on final passage "of any act which imposes, continues, or revives a tax."[69] Also contained in the constitution is a 1901 amendment forbidding the legislature to pass a private or local bill "granting to any person, association, firm, or corporation, an exemption from taxation on real or personal property."[70]

Types of State Taxes

The state currently levies a personal income tax; a sales and use tax; a corporation franchise tax; bank, insurance, and other business taxes; highway user taxes and fees; cigarette and alcohol beverage excise taxes; estate and gift taxes; parimutuel taxes; a real estate mortgage transfer tax; and admissions and boxing taxes. These taxes may be placed in one of four categories: personal income tax, user fees and taxes, general business taxes, and transfer taxes, all of which produce approximately 90 percent of the state's revenue. The state levied a property tax until 1929 when a decision was made to surrender this tax entirely to local governments.

Personal Income Tax. First levied in 1919, the personal income tax is a degressive tax with rates in 1981 starting at 2 percent of taxable income up to $1,000 and increasing by 1 percent per every additional $2,000 of taxable income to a maximum tax of 10 percent on incomes exceeding $23,000. A personal exemption of $650 was allowed, and taxpayers could make itemized deductions for contributions to charitable organizations, specified taxes, interest payments, medical expenses, and life insurance premiums up to a maximum of $150. Employers are required to withhold the tax from employees' wages and salaries and turn the revenue over to the Department of Taxation and Finance. The personal income tax produces approximately 47 percent of current revenue and is projected to produce revenue of $7.7 billion in fiscal 1983.

User Fees and Taxes. User fees and taxes produce nearly one third of state income. First introduced in 1901 for purposes of regulation, motor vehicle registration fees are based upon the class and weight of vehicles. The registration fee for a passenger vehicle is limited to a maximum of $65 per year. Revenue from registration and drivers' license fees rose from $245 million in fiscal 1970 to $273 million in fiscal 1981. Ten percent of the revenue produced by certain fees are returned to the county of origin.

The gasoline tax, first levied in 1929, presently is 8 cents per gallon, and the diesel fuel tax is 10 cents per gallon. Gasoline tax receipts increased from $357 million in fiscal 1970 to $420 million in fiscal 1981, while diesel fuel tax receipts increased from $18 million to $31 million in the same period. One third of the revenue produced by motor fuel taxes is dedicated to a special highway fund created in 1959, and a small percentage of the revenue is earmarked for an outdoor recreation development fund.[71] In addition, 10 percent of the revenue produced by motor fuel taxes, with the exception of the 1-cent increase levied in 1972, is distributed to New York City and the fifty-seven organized county governments to help meet local expenses, including highway construction and maintenance expenses. Furthermore, 25 percent of the revenue produced by the 1 cent per gallon excise tax increase in 1972 is dedicated to the emergency highway reconditioning and preservation fund.[72]

The highway use tax, commonly referred to as the "truck mileage" tax, has been levied since 1951 on heavy trucks for the privilege of using state highways that are not toll facilities, and is based upon the benefit principle. The tax is determined by the number of miles traveled by a truck within the state, and the rates are graduated on the basis of the weight of the truck or its load. Total highway use tax revenue increased from $29.3 million in fiscal 1970 to $36.0 million in fiscal 1981.

An alcoholic beverage tax has been levied by the state since 1895 except during the Prohibition period. The current rate is $3.25 per gallon of distilled spirits containing in excess of 24 percent alcohol and 80 cents per gallon on other liquors. The tax on beer is $4\frac{4}{9}$ cents per gallon and $53\frac{1}{3}$ cents per gallon of naturally sparkling wine. Revenue from alcoholic beverage taxes has increased from $113 million in fiscal 1970 to $149 million in 1981.

Alcoholic beverage license fees—paid by brewers, distillers, wholesalers, retailers, and others—also produce revenue for the state. The fees depend upon the class of coverage and the type and location of the licensed establishment. Approximately 25,000 bars, package stores, and restaurants pay alcoholic beverage license fees. Revenue has ranged from $33.2 million in fiscal 1970 to $35.0 million in fiscal 1981.

The cigarette tax, first levied in 1939 and now imposed at the rate of 15 cents per twenty-cigarette package, produced approximately $333 million in fiscal 1981, an increase of $80 million compared with fiscal 1970.

The state sales and use tax was adopted in 1965 at a rate of 2 percent, and the state assumed responsibility for collecting local sales and use taxes as well as the state sales and use tax.[73] The state tax currently is 4 percent. New York City, certain other cities, and certain counties levy a local sales and use tax. The combined state-city rate in New York City has been 8 percent since July 1, 1974, and the combined state-county-city rate in Yonkers has been 8 percent since January 1, 1976.[74]

All products and services sold or used in the state with specified exceptions—food and medicine, utility service billings, restaurant meals, hotel and motel occupancy rates, and certain admissions and services—are subject to the tax. Sales and use tax revenue increased from $1.0 billion in fiscal 1970 to $2.9 billion in fiscal 1981. The legislature occasionally approves bills broadening the exemptions from the sales and use tax, and the governor typically disallows the bills, as in 1973 when Governor Rockefeller vetoed bills exempting from these taxes catalytic goods and packaging materials used by manufacturers and merchants.[75]

General Business Taxes. The corporation franchise tax, dating to 1880, is levied for the privilege of doing business and is the most important business tax in terms of revenue produced.[76] The rate is 10 percent of federal taxable income less certain deductions and exclusions. The Tax Law also provides three alternative taxes and requires a corporation to pay the highest of the tax figures produced by the alternative taxes: "(1) business and investment capital allocated to New York; or (2) officer's salaries plus 30 per cent of net income, less a proprietary interest of $15,000; or (3) a flat $250."[77] Revenue produced by the corporation franchise tax has risen from $529.3 million in fiscal 1970 to $1.1 billion in fiscal 1981.

Corporation and utilities taxes are levied upon agricultural cooperatives, new corporations, foreign (out-of-state) corporations operating in the state, reorganized corporations, transmission companies, and transportation companies.[78] Until 1974, these taxes were levied on insurance companies. These are formula taxes, and the formulas vary according to the type of business. Foreign corporations, for example, are taxed on the basis of capital stock employed in the state. These taxes produced $271.5 million in fiscal 1974 and $580.0 million in fiscal 1981.

Difficulties with taxation of insurance companies led to the enactment in 1974 of a statute levying a franchise tax on the basis of both net income and the value of premiums written.[79] Revenue produced by this tax has increased from $156.6 million in fiscal 1975 to $224.0 million in fiscal 1981.

The 12 percent bank tax, dating to 1901, is levied on the net income of state and nationally chartered commercial banks, savings banks, savings and loan associations, trust companies, and certain other financial organizations.[80] A mutual savings bank, however, is taxed on a dividend-based formula if this formula produces a higher tax liability than the net income tax. The dividends tax is levied at the rate of 2 percent on the first 3.5 percentage points of dividends or interest paid to depositors. In any event, a mutual savings bank must pay a $250 minimum tax regardless of the amount due under either formula. Revenue produced by the bank tax rose from $86.2 million in fiscal 1970 to $240.0 million in fiscal 1981.

The unincorporated business income tax is levied at the rate of 5.5 percent on the net income of each of the approximately 65,000 unincorporated business firms—sole proprietorships and partnerships—in the state.[81] Income from specified professions—such as architecture, law, and medicine—are exempt from the tax, and a 1977 law provides for a phasing out of the tax on farmers commencing in 1978.[82] Revenue raised by this tax declined from $77.6 million in fiscal 1970 to $35.0 million in fiscal 1981. New York is the only state levying such a tax that is not integrated with the personal income tax.

Transfer Taxes. The estate and gift tax, the parimutuel tax, the real estate transfer tax, and the stock transfer tax are classified as transfer taxes. The first of these taxes is levied on estates of deceased residents and on the portion of a deceased nonresident's estate composed of real and tangible personal property located in the state.[83] Eighty percent of the tax paid may be deducted as a credit against the federal estate and gift tax liability. The number of taxable estates averages approximately 39,500 per year, but a small number accounts for a large proportion of the revenue produced. A 1973 law provides that the tax will not be levied on the personal property, except tangible property located in the state, if the transferrer is a resident of a state that provides reciprocity by means of the Uniform Interstate Compromise of Death Taxes Act.[84]

In 1972 the legislature enacted a law imposing a gift tax, as a complement to the estate tax first levied in 1885, on transfers of property during the lifetime of a grantor.[85] Property located outside the state that is transferred is excluded from the tax as is up to $3,000 annually in gifts. Rates are graduated from 1.5 percent to 15.25 percent. The estate and gift taxes produced revenues of $177 million in fiscal 1972 and $140 million in fiscal 1981.

The parimutuel tax is levied at varying rates on betting at four thoroughbred racing tracks, eight harness racing tracks, and at off-track betting parlors.[86] Each racing association pays 17 percent of the commission, known as the "takeout," to the state for the privilege of conducting parimutuel betting. The state also licenses quarterhorse racetracks in Tioga Park and Parr Meadows.

Off-track betting originated in New York City and became particularly popular at a time that track wagering and attendance declined. The 1973 legislature extended off-track betting to the remainder of the state.[87] In 1974 the law was amended to impose a 5 percent surcharge on off-track betting corporations.[88]

Parimutuel tax revenue increased from $158.5 million in fiscal 1970 to $180.3 million in fiscal 1976, but declined to $109.1 million in fiscal 1981 because of revisions of the taxes to prevent loss of revenue to legalized gambling in adjoining states—jai alai in Connecticut, dog racing in Vermont, and horse racing and casino gambling in New Jersey. A 4 percent tax, lowered from 15 percent in 1973, is levied on the admission charge to racetracks.[89] The tax decrease was designed to make attendance at tracks more competitive with off-track betting parlors.

The federal documentary stamp tax on conveyances of real estate lapsed on January 1, 1968, and the legislature decided to impose a real estate transfer tax, commonly referred to as the mortgage-recording tax, effective August 1, 1968.[90] Each real property deed conveyance of more than $100 is taxed at the rate of 55 cents per $500 or fraction thereof, with the seller usually responsible for paying the tax. Revenue from this tax increased from $5.6 million in fiscal 1970 to $13.2 million in fiscal 1981, reflecting in large measure real estate inflation.

New York State has levied a stock transfer tax since 1905.[91]

The tax rate was increased in 1968 from 2 cents to 2.5 cents on shares with a selling price of more than $5 per share.[92] Fear that the New York Stock Exchange and the American Stock Exchange might move to New Jersey prompted the 1977 legislature to repeal the tax on the transfer of shares by nonresidents of the state.[93]

The Lottery

Voters in 1966 approved a constitutional amendment changing the bill of rights by allowing a state-operated lottery with the net proceeds dedicated to the support of education.[94] The following year, the legislature established a State Lottery Commission and a Division of the Lottery in the Department of Taxation and Finance, but transferred the responsibilities of the division in 1973 to the State Racing and Wagering Board.[95] Although a 1976 law transferred the Lottery Division back to the Department of Taxation and Finance, the division continues to function independently of the department.[96]

The lottery has not proven to be a dependable source of a significant amount of revenue for public education. Annual state aid for public schools, for example, increased by $1.7 billion between fiscal 1968 and fiscal 1977, yet the lottery never produced more than $91.0 million in any year during this period. Lottery revenues have ranged from $26.0 million in fiscal 1970 to $102.0 million in fiscal 1981.

THE DEBT SYSTEM

The net indebtedness of the state on June 30, 1937, was $563,238,908.05 and was a reflection of the borrowing of approximately $800,000,000 during the previous forty years, which was a sharp departure from the pay-as-you-go policy that had been in effect for more than fifty years.[97] The full faith and credit debt of the Empire State, sanctioned by the voters, totaled $3,654 million at the start of the 1980 fiscal year. The outstanding debt will cost $1,727.4 million in interest before the debt is retired. The actual state debt is considerably larger than the full faith and credit debt because of the existence of $11,145.0 million in moral obligation debt instruments, discussed later.

Constitutional Restrictions

Reckless debt financing of public improvement projects and private companies in the 1820s and 1830s necessitated the levying of a direct state property tax and produced a citizen reaction in the form of constitutional provisions in 1846 restricting the ability of the state legislature to incur indebtedness.[98] The constitutional debt incurrence provisions have been amended several times since 1846, but the current provisions are similar to the original ones. The legislature may authorize the incurrence of (1) short-term debt, to be repaid within one year, in anticipation of the receipt of tax and other revenues; (2) short-term debt, to be repaid within two years, in anticipation of proceeds of authorized bond issues; and (3) unlimited debt "to repel invasion, suppress insurrection, or defend the State in war, or to suppress forest fires."[99]

To incur a full faith and credit debt, the legislature by law must authorize a debt "for some single work or purpose, to be distinctly specified therein"; the voters have three months subsequent to its passage to vote on approval or rejection of the proposed issue at a general election when no "other law or bill shall be submitted to be voted for or against."[100] The purpose of this latter provision is to ensure that the voters can concentrate on one issue and not be distracted by others.

Three constitutional amendments allow the state legislature to contract a full faith and credit debt without voter approval in a statewide referendum.[101] A 1941 amendment authorizes the legislature to incur a debt of up to $300 million to eliminate railroad crossings and to construct state highways and parkways; a 1947 amendment authorizes the legislature to incur a debt of up to $400 million to pay a bonus to state residents who served in the armed forces during World War II; and a 1957 amendment authorizes the legislature to contract a debt of up to $250 million for the expansion of State University facilities.

The state constitution prohibits the use of sinking-fund bonds by mandating that all long-term borrowing—except for the purposes of repelling invasions, suppressing insurrections, and fighting forest fires—shall be by means of serial bonds repayable "in equal annual installments, the first of which shall be payable not more than one year, and the last of which shall be payable not more than forty years after" the debt was contracted.[102] In no event may a borrowing exceed "the probable life of the work or purpose for which the debt is to be contracted."[103] The bond indenture may contain a redeemable provision authorizing the recall of bonds by the state prior to maturity. The legislature is directed by the state constitution annually to appropriate funds to pay the interest and installments of principal on all long-term debt when due, and the constitution authorizes the state comptroller to set apart the first general fund revenue to pay the interest and principal installments should the legislature fail to do so.[104]

Wisdom of Constitutional Restrictions. Debt and tax restrictions often are criticized as obsolete and undesirable because they limit the ability of the state legislature to respond to changing conditions. Professor C. Lowell Harriss of Columbia University responds to this criticism as follows:

Constitutional restraint is sometimes assumed to be undesirable by the answers implied to such questions as: "Don't you have faith in the representatives elected by the public? If not, then is not the proper job to get better legislatures and city councils?" Of course, we all wish for high quality in the public service. Unfortunately, success in achieving this aspiration is not a foregone conclusion. The pressures on the most statesmanlike of elected officials, the competition for votes, will operate often and powerfully to lead to compromises which may sacrifice longer-run interests of the public to more immediate concerns. We cannot "wish away" the role of constitutional restrictions by assuming that future lawmakers will act with the wisdom and foresight we desire.[105]

Professor Harriss also stresses that "government borrowing and debt have a 'time horizon' of more nearly constitutional than legislative nature."[106]

The debt limits in practice have been evaded by three methods: issuance of moral obligation bonds, entry into lease-purchase agreements, and establishment of the emergency highway reconditioning fund.

The Moral Obligation Bond

The moral obligation bond in the Empire State is traceable to the 1960 statute, creating the Housing Finance Agency (HFA), which contains a pledge by the legislature that is interpreted as a "moral obligation":

> The State does hereby pledge to and agree with the holders of any notes or bonds issued under this article, that the State will not limit or alter the rights hereby vested in the agency to fulfill the terms of any agreements made with the holders thereof, or in any way impair the rights and remedies of such holders until such notes or bonds, together with the interest thereon, with interest of any unpaid installments of interest, and all costs and expenses in connection with any action or proceedings by or on behalf of such holders, are fully met and discharged. The agency is authorized to include this pledge and agreement of the State in any agreement with the holders of such notes or bonds.[107]

This provision was inserted in the law in an attempt to bring the moral obligation bonds under the protection of the United States Constitution, which forbids states to impair the obligation of contract.[108] One can question whether the United States Constitution protects a contract entered into by the state in violation of a provision of the state constitution requiring a voter referendum on the question of the incurrence of a state debt. Furthermore, while the pledge appears to be unrepealable, the state constitution stipulates that all statutes creating corporations "may be altered from time to time or repealed."[109]

The state's guarantee of the HFA's debt is indirect; that is, any insufficiency in the HFA's reserve fund will be replenished by an appropriation. Although the state does not guarantee directly the repayment of bonds issued by the HFA, the state has provided for the automatic replenishment of the reserve fund used to pay the interest and principal on bonds when due. Interestingly, the Court of Appeals in 1972 ruled that the Urban Development Corporation, a public benefit corporation, "is not a State agency with the intendment of the constitutional and statutory provisions cited."[110]

No public authority failed to meet the debt-service charges on its bonds until February 25, 1975, when the Urban Development Corporation (described in Chapter VIII) experienced serious financial problems and defaulted on $135 million in short-term notes.

homes by authorized agencies, whether under public or private control, or from providing health and welfare services for all children."[116] Furthermore, a county, city, town, or village is authorized to increase the pension benefits payable to retired policemen and firemen or their widows, dependent children, and dependent parents.

A local government may contract debt for a period up to forty years without securing voter approval, provided the unit "pledged its faith and credit for the payment of the principal thereof and the interest thereon."[117] Debt limits, however, are established and vary from 7 percent for a town, village, and city under 125,000 population to 9 percent for cities over 125,000 population except New York City, which has a 10 percent limit, and 10 percent in Nassau County.[118] The complicated local finance article of the constitution contains various exceptions from the debt limits for Buffalo, New York City, Rochester, and Syracuse in recognition of their special problems, which is an indication of their political influence relative to constitutional revision.[119]

A complex section of the local finance article established real estate tax limits, ranging from 1.5 percent to 2 percent of "average full valuation" for local units other than New York City, which has a 2.5 percent limit, but also provides for exceptions.[120] In the famous 1974 *Hurd* decision, the Court of Appeals ordered local governments to stop the practice of excluding from the constitutional tax limit taxes collected to pay for public employee retirement costs, an exclusion authorized by the legislature in 1969.[121] This decision created serious problems for the cities of Buffalo, Rochester, and Yonkers, and sixty-five school districts in cities with a population under 125,000, because the units were deprived of approximately $40 million in taxing authority.

The 1976 legislature, deciding that the *Hurd* decision had created an emergency, enacted the State Real Property Act authorizing municipalities with a population between 125,000 and 1 million and school districts to request state financial aid from a special account; the request triggered the imposition of a state real property tax at a rate equal to the amount of the request.[122] In 1978 the Court of Appeals ruled that the problems caused by the *Hurd* decision were not the equivalent of emergencies by enemy attack, held the 1976 law to be a subterfuge to evade the state constitution, and reaffirmed the decision.[123] Reacting to this decision, the 1978 legislature authorized the affected local governments to adjust upward the recorded full value of real property during the previous five years, a period selected because the constitution sets the tax limit at 2 percent of the average full value of real property during the preceding five years.[124] New York City and Yonkers have been using this technique since 1968 and 1974, respectively.[125]

The local finance article also charges the legislature with the duty "to restrict the power of taxation, assessment, borrowing money, contracting indebtedness, and loaning the credit of counties, cities, towns, and villages, so as to prevent abuses in taxation and assessments and in contracting of indebtedness by them."[126] An example of the exercise of this power is a section of the Real Property Tax Law regulating the assessment of real property and authorizing a court to award an additional allowance to a petitioner if the court finds that "the assessment of the property was increased without adequate cause" or that an assessment "was grossly discriminatory."[127]

Local Government Financial Aid

Most taxes levied in the Empire State, with the exception of federal taxes, raise revenue to support the system of local government. The state commenced to make grants to local governments in 1789, share tax receipts with local governments in 1916 when the proceeds of the state motor vehicle license tax were distributed to local governments, and inaugurated a per capita aid program in 1946 as a replacement for the shared-tax program.[128]

In 1948 Moscow wrote that "the State is not just a money-grubbing miser. It returns to the cities, the towns, and the villages a major portion of its revenues."[129] This statement remains accurate, as the state devotes approximately 61 percent of its budget to aid to local governments, the highest level of support among the fifty states. Of this amount, 75 percent is state aid for education and social services, and 15 percent is for general revenue and tax sharing.

The Temporary State Commission on State and Local Finances in 1975 reported that all studies had identified the following as the major deficiencies of the state aid program:

(1) County units were unfairly excluded; (2) jurisdictional classification is not an accurate indicator of fiscal need, capacity, or effort, and therefore,

it should be replaced as the major determinant of individual aid shares; (3) the formula treats jurisdictions with extensive resources the same as municipalities with little resources; and (4) fixed per capita amounts for the various jurisdictions do little to further the goal of long-term stabilization at the local level. The solution of virtually every group has been the creation of a formula utilizing fiscal need, capacity, and effort as its major components.[130]

Attempts to change in a comprehensive manner the state aid system have been unsuccessful because of the political strength of the units benefiting from the current system. Governor Hugh L. Carey in 1979 proposed a major change in the state aid system that would reduce such aid by $90 million in fiscal 1980 by providing that revenue-sharing funds would be based on 7.25 percent of all state tax collections during the previous year instead of the current 18.0 percent of the personal income tax collections.[131] The 1979 legislature accepted in general the governor's proposal but increased the percentage to 8.0. This new formula will slow the rate of increase in state aid to local governments, since total state tax revenues increase at a slower rate than the increase in the personal income tax revenues.

The great disparity between the flow of state aid to local governments and the flow of revenue to the state creates problems for the state and necessitates that the state borrow on a short-term basis during the second quarter of the calendar year when approximately 75 percent of the state aid is distributed to local governments. The second quarter is the period during which the smallest amount of state revenue is received.

Local Taxation

To cope with the Great Depression, the 1933 legislature allowed New York City to adopt and amend local laws levying any tax that the state legislature possessed the power to levy during the period from September 1, 1933 to February 28, 1934.[132] In 1947 the legislature authorized cities and counties, depending upon their population, to adopt and amend local laws imposing specified nonproperty taxes, that is, retail sales and use tax, restaurant taxes, taxes on retail licensees of the State Liquor Authority for on- or off-premises consumption, admission taxes, license taxes on vending machines, motor vehicle use taxes, a business gross receipts tax, and an occupancy tax on hotel and motel rooms.[133] These taxes produced a substantial amount of revenue for many local governments, yet the real property tax remains as the most important tax levied by local governments and accounts for approximately 69 percent of all local tax revenue.

The Property Tax Problem

While the state has not levied a real property tax since 1929, the legislature determines the classes of real property exempt from local real property taxation.[134] In addition to educational, religious, and charitable properties accorded exemption from the real property tax, the legislature has exempted various types of real property owned by a municipal corporation outside its corporate limits—public parks, public aviation fields, highways, flood control projects, solid waste conservation projects, sewage disposal plants and systems, and New York City aqueducts.[135] Real property acquired by a municipal corporation by means of a tax deed, referee's deed in tax foreclosure, or deed made in lieu of a tax foreclosure is exempt from real property taxes, except for school purposes and special assessments, for three years.[136]

The real property tax increased by 147 percent on a per capita basis between 1966 and 1976, is projected to total $12.6 billion in 1982, and imposes a heavy burden on homeowners of fixed moderate income.[137] To reduce the burden on senior citizens, the legislature enacted a "real property tax circuit breaker credit" authorizing local governments to grant tax exemptions to owners of real property who are sixty-five years of age and older if they fall below the household gross income limits specified in the law.[138]

The Assessment Problem. The Real Property Tax Law contains a provision, adopted in 1788, that "all real property in each assessing unit shall be assessed at the full value thereof," yet assessors generally ignored this provision by deliberately underassessing property.[139] Commonly, residential property was assessed at a lower percentage of true value than commercial and industrial real property, and the failure to reassess residential property periodically meant that owners of new homes had their properties assessed at a higher percentage of full value than purchasers of homes years earlier.

The legislature recognized the disparities in assessing practices throughout the state by creating the five-member State Board of Equalization and Assessment, charged with the duty of establishing an equalization rate—the average percentage of full value in each local assessing unit—to be used for the distribution of state financial aid.[140]

In 1975 the Court of Appeals struck down fractional valuation of real property in the town of Islip and ordered full-value assessment by July 1, 1978.[141] Lawsuits subsequently were filed in courts throughout the state, and the courts, using the *Islip* decision as precedent, ordered local governments to reassess real property at full market value. The 1978 legislature enacted a law stipulating that "whether or not pursuant to a court order" a local assessing unit shall not be required to file a final assessment roll based upon the full value of real property prior to December 31, 1980, and the 1980 legislature extended the deadline to May 15, 1981.[142] The cost of reassessing real property statewide is estimated to be $100 million.

To assist the implementation of full-value assessment, the 1977 legislature established a Temporary State Commission on the Real Property Tax and initiated a special State Financial Aid program to assist local government to reassess all real property at full value.[143] Full-value assessments will hit hard veterans who may receive up to a $5,000 exemption from the assessed value of their real property and senior citizens who receive exemptions based upon their incomes. Burdened the most by the full-value assessment will be senior citizens who purchased homes three or four decades ago that have not been reassessed.

The School Finance Problem

A related problem involving the real property tax is the method of financing public education for more than 3 million pupils. The state constitution requires the legislature to "provide for the maintenance and support of a system of free common schools," and the system currently consists of 743 school districts.[144]

The great disparity in the wealth of the state's school districts has produced a large expenditure-level gap between the wealthiest and the poorest school districts. The New York State Commission on the Quality, Cost, and Financing of Elementary and Secondary

Education, appointed by Governor Nelson A. Rockefeller and the Board of Regents in 1969, issued a three-volume report analyzing the problems of school finance recommending that the "State shall provide all or nearly all the money for the operation of elementary and secondary schools (with the exception of federal aid)" and "shall determine a defensible basis of distributing money to school districts."[145]

The report, popularly known as the Fleischmann Report, received a negative reaction from the state legislature, school boards fearing the loss of local control of educational programs, and the New York State United Teachers concerned about the loss of local control and possible loss of bargaining power. The issue of school finance, however, was not dead, since suits had been filed in courts challenging the constitutionality of the system of financing public elementary and secondary education.

The wealthiest school district in 1978 had real property values totaling $448,451 supporting each public school pupil and allowing an expenditure of $6,093 per student compared with $30,000 in real property supporting each pupil in Levittown and allowing an expenditure of $2,343 for each student. The state aid formula in 1978 provided each wealthy district with a grant of $360 per student and the poorest districts with a maximum grant of $1,450 per pupil for a total of more than $3 billion.[146] In addition, state law contains a "save harmless" provision guaranteeing districts the same amount of aid even if attendance declines.[147] As pointed out in Chapter V, attempts to change the state aid formula mobilize various interest groups determined to maintain the status quo.

In 1978 Supreme Court Justice L. Kingsley Smith issued a decision declaring the state's system of public school finance unconstitutional but did not establish a timetable for implementation of a new system.[148] In December 1978 the Board of Regents released a proposal for reforming state aid to education in response to the *Levittown* decision:

- a two-tier formula for operating aid, with $1,650 per pupil first ceiling and $1,850 for the second to replace the present ceilings of $1,450 and $1,500
- pupil count on the basis of 50 percent attendance and 50 percent active enrollment rather than 100 percent attendance
- pupil count on the basis of the choice of the greater of the 1978–79 count or the average of 1977–78 and 1978–79

- a weighting of .1 for pupils in approved bilingual programs
- flat grant and save harmless eliminated over a four-year period
- operating aid increases limited to the greater of $130 per pupil or 8 percent of approved operating expense
- building and BOCES aid ratios computed on the same pupil count as used for operating aid
- transportation aid equalized on total transportation expense determined on a weighted per pupil basis
- parity in transportation expense provided for by including fringe benefits in both district-owned and contract transportation systems
- expenditure increase caps which if exceeded result in an aid penalty[149]

In his 1979 budget message, Governor Carey responded to the *Levittown* v. *Nyquist* decision by offering the following recommendations to the legislature:

- a state-funded school-year increase of $203 million
- regional equalization of the operating aid formula to shift some $200 million among districts based upon their relative wealth per pupil, guaranteeing all districts in the New York City metropolitan area a per pupil yield of $74 with a local tax effort of $1 per $1,000 of full valuation, and districts in the remainder of the state $63 per pupil
- elimination of save harmless provisions over a two-year period
- a reduction in the minimum guarantee for the state's wealthiest districts to $100 per pupil
- use of an enrollment-based pupil measure to determine operating aid apportionments for the 1979–80 school year[150]

If enacted into law, the governor's recommendations would result in 520 of the state's 705 large school districts receiving increases in state operating assistance of up to $150 per pupil. Districts whose per pupil wealth exceeds 50 percent of the state average would not receive an increase in aid. State legislators, local officials, and the New York State United Teachers blasted the plan, with the latter charging that the plan would result in an "intolerable burden" being placed on nearly one third of the school districts in the state.[151]

A third proposal was advanced by the New York State Educational Conference Board composed of the School Boards Association, the United Teachers, the Congress of Parents and Teachers, the Council of School District Administrators, the School Administrators Association, the Association of School Business Officials, and the Public Education Association. Total state aid, under the board's proposal, would be increased by $323 million in the 1979–80 school year, with the per pupil operating expense ceiling being increased from $1,450 to $1,650, with the state supplying 49 percent; a supplemental ceiling of $1,850 per pupil, with the State providing 20 percent; and districts receiving an increase of 5 to 15 percent in operating expense aid.[152] The board also recommended:

1. The current transportation aid formula should be improved to provide the same allowable expenses for those districts which own their transportation as for those which contract theirs while eliminating expenditure and aid restrictions.
2. The current building aid formula be continued.
3. The salary factor for computing BOCES aid be increased from $9,500 to $11,500.
4. Current high tax rate aid formula be continued.
5. The state funding level for educating handicapped children be increased.[153]

SUMMARY AND CONCLUSIONS

With total spending approaching $20 billion annually, the state of New York is second only to the national government in gross expenditures. Public spending of this magnitude ensures that public resource distribution is an intensely political process. One can predict without fear of contradiction that major political battles will continue to be waged over attempts to change the formulas providing state aid to local governments, including school districts. Whereas the courts will force a relative equalization of school district fiscal resources, the political process will determine the distribution of state aid to general-purpose local governments.

The free-spending era of the 1960s is over, as financial stringencies within the foreseeable future clearly will limit the ability of the state to initiate expensive new services and expensive new capital projects. While inflation will continue to exert upward pressure on state spending, inflation also will help to fill the state's tax coffers.

To understand the behavior of the governor and the legislature in the fiscal area, one must become well acquainted with the constitutional restraints on state-local finance. Legislative and gubernatorial ingenuity will continue to be employed to seek ways around constitutional roadblocks in addition to the use of public authorities, lease-purchase arrangements, and special funds. Available evidence suggests that the strength of the political groups committed to the status quo will prevent the removal of the constitutional restraints.

NOTES

1. *Annual Financial Report of the Comptroller of the State of New York, 1978* (Albany: Office of the State Comptroller, 1980), p. 11.

2. *New York Constitution*, art. VII, § 12.

3. *Ibid.*, § 8 (3). See *Mount Sinai Hospital v. Hyman*, 92 App. Div. 270 (1904).

4. Alfred E. Smith, *The Citizen and His Government* (New York: Harper and Brothers, 1935), p. 198.

5. *New York Constitution*, art. VII, § 1.

6. *Ibid.*

7. *Ibid.*, §§ 3 and 5.

8. *Ibid.*, § 4.

9. *Ibid.*

10. *New York State Finance Law*, § 22 (McKinney 1974).

11. *State of New York Five-Year Projection of Income and Expenditures, General Fund, Fiscal Years 1980–81 through 1984–85* (Albany: Executive Chamber, February 21, 1980), p. 19.

12. *New York v. Cathedral Academy*, 434 U.S. 1205 (1977). See also *New York Laws of 1972*, chap. 996, and *Committee for Public Education v. Regan*, 100 S. Ct. 840 (1980).

13. *New York Constitution*, art. VII, § 9 (1821).

14. *New York Constitution*, art. VII, § 9 (1846).

15. *New York Constitution*, art. VII, § 8 (2), and art. XVIII, § 1.

16. *Frankfater v. State*, 54 Misc. 2d 159 (1967).

17. *New York Constitution*, art. VII, § 7.

18. *New York State Finance Law*, § 94 (4) (McKinney 1974).

19. *New York Constitution*, art. VII, § 3.

20. *Ibid.*, § 4. See also *People v. Tremaine*, 281 N.Y. 1 (1939).

21. John E. Burton, "Budget Administration in New York State," *State Government*, October 1943, p. 206.

22. *Wheeler v. Barrera*, 417 U.S. 402 (1973). In 1978 the Pennsylvania Supreme Court upheld the constitutionality of a statute providing that federal funds be deposited in the general fund and be available for appropriation by the legislature. *Shapp v. Sloan*, 391 A2d 595 (1978). *Shapp v. Casey*, 99 S. Ct. 717 (1979).

23. *New York Constitution*, art. VII, § 2.

24. Vic Ostrowidzki, "Governor's Race Baffles Rocky," *Sunday Times Union* (Albany, New York, October 22, 1978, p. B-1.

25. *Wein v. State of New York*, 39 N.Y. 2d 136 at 148–49 (1976).

26. *Wein v. Carey*, 41 N.Y. 2d 498 at 503 (1977).

27. *Ibid.* at 504–5.

28. *County of Oneida v. Berle*, 49 N.Y. 2d 515 (1980).

29. *St. Clair v. Yonkers Raceway*, 13 N.Y. 2d 72 (1963), and *Boryszewski v. Brydges*, 37 N.Y. 2d 361 at 362 (1975).

30. *New York Laws of 1975*, chap. 827, and *New York State Finance Law*, §§ 123 to 123-j (McKinney 1979 Supp.).

31. *New York Public Interest Research Group v. Steingut*, 40 N.Y. 2d 250 at 257 (1976). See also *New York Laws of 1970*, chap. 460, and *New York Constitution*, art. III, § 6.

32. *Wein v. Carey*, 41 N.Y. 2d 498 at 502–3 (1977).

33. *Ibid.* at 504–5.

34. *Posner v. Rockefeller*, 26 N.Y. 2d 970 (1970).

35. *Posner v. Levitt*, 37 App. Div. 2d 331 (1971).

36. *Dunlea v. Goldmark*, 42 N.Y. 2d 754 (1977); *Dunlea v. Goldmark*, 54 App. Div. 2d 446 (1976); *Dunlea v. Goldmark*, 85 Misc. 2d 198 (1976); and *New York Public Officers Law*, §§ 84–90 (McKinney 1979 Supp.).

37. *Saxton v. Carey*, 44 N.Y. 2d 545 (1978).

38. *New York Constitution*, art. VII, § 6.

39. *New York Laws of 1946*, chap. 303, and *New York State Finance Law*, § 92 (McKinney 1974).

40. *New York Constitution*, art. VII, § 17.

41. *Ibid.*

42. *New York State Finance Law*, § 97-i (McKinney 1974).

43. *New York Laws of 1972*, chap. 648, and *New York State Finance Law*, § 89 (McKinney 1974).

44. *Report of the Joint Legislative Committee on State Fiscal Policies* (Albany: J. B. Lyon Company, 1937), p. 11. The report was printed as Legislative Document Number 41 of 1938.

45. Arthur Levitt, *Annual Report* (Albany: The Comptroller of the State of New York, 1977), Part I, p. 1. See also *Study Project on the Preparation of State Financial Statements in Accordance with GAAP* (Albany: Office of the State Comptroller, December 1978).

46. Levitt, *Discipline in the Fiscal Process*, pp. 1 and 6.

47. *New York Laws of 1968*, chap. 291, and *New York State Finance Law*, § 54 (7) (d) (McKinney 1969 Supp.).

48. *New York Laws of 1972*, chap. 3.

49. *Veto Memorandum 126* (Albany: Executive Chamber, July 1, 1980). See also "Governor Carey's Ledger-de-Main," *The New York Times*, July 8, 1980, p. A-16.

50. *New York Constitution*, art. IV, § 6 (1821).

51. *New York Constitution*, art. V, § 1 (1846).

52. *New York Constitution*, art. V, § 1.

53. New York State Constitutional Convention Committee, *Problems Relating to Taxation and Finance* (Albany: J. B. Lyon Company, 1938), p. 25.

54. *New York Laws of 1969*, chap. 176, § 2, and *New York Legislative Law*, art. 5-A (McKinney 1979 Supp.).

55. "Memorandum Prepared by the New York State Budget Division on the Organization of Pre-Audit and Post-Audit in the Government of the State," in New York State Constitutional Convention Committee, *Problems Relating to Taxation and Finance*, p. 32.

56. *Ibid.*, p. 34.

57. New York State Constitutional Convention Committee, *Problems Relating to Taxation and Finance*, pp. 26–27.

58. See Adam Smith, *An Inquiry into the Nature and Causes of the Wealth of Nations* (Oxford: Clarendon Press, 1976), Vol. II, pp. 825–26.

59. *Local Revenue Diversification: Income, Sales Tax, User Charges* (Washington, D.C.: United States Advisory Commission on Intergovernmental Relations, October 1974), p. 17.

60. See in particular Joseph F. Zimmerman, "Mandating in New York State," *State Mandating of Local Expenditures* (Washington, D.C.: United States Advisory Commission on Intergovernmental Relations, 1978), pp. 69–85.

61. *United States Constitution,* art. I, §§ 8 and 10, and Fourteenth Amendment.

62. *Ibid.*, art. VI. See also *Missouri v. Holland*, 252 U.S. 416 (1920).

63. *New York Constitution*, art. XVI.

64. *Ibid.*, § 1.

65. *Ibid.*

66. *Ibid.*, art. XVI § 2.

67. *Ibid.*, § 4.

68. *Ibid.*, art. III, § 22, and *State Finance*, p. 32.

69. *New York Constitution*, art. III, § 23.

70. *Ibid.*, § 17.

71. *New York Tax Law*, art. 12-A (McKinney 1975).

72. *New York Laws of 1972*, chap. 648, and *New York State Finance Law*, § 89 (McKinney 1974).

73. *New York Laws of 1965*, chap. 93, and *New York Tax Law*, §§ 1105–48 (McKinney 1975).

74. For New York City, see *New York Laws of 1974*, chap. 368. For Yonkers, see *New York Laws of 1975*, chap. 397.

75. See Veto Memoranda 170 and 172 in *Public Papers of Nelson A. Rockefeller: Fifty-Third Governor of the State of New York, 1973* (Albany: State of New York, n.d.), pp. 197 and 200.

76. *New York Laws of 1917*, chap. 726, and *New York Tax Law*, §§ 208–19-a (McKinney 1975).

77. *State of New York Executive Budget for the Fiscal Year April 1, 1978 to*

March 31, 1979 (Albany: Executive Chamber, January 17, 1978), p. A17. See also *New York Tax Law*, art. 9-A (McKinney 1975).

78. *New York Tax Law*, §§ 180–207-b (McKinney 1966).

79. *New York Laws of 1974*, chap. 649, and *New York Tax Law*, §§ 1500–19 (McKinney 1975).

80. *New York Laws of 1975*, chap. 895, and *New York Tax Law*, § 1455 (McKinney 1979 Supp.).

81. *New York Laws of 1960*, chap. 170, and *New York Tax Law*, §§ 701–23 (McKinney 1975).

82. *New York Laws of 1977*, chap. 508.

83. *New York Laws of 1925*, chap. 320, and *New York Tax Law*, §§ 249–249k (McKinney 1966).

84. *New York Laws of 1973*, chap. 640, and *New York Tax Law*, § 249p-A (McKinney 1979 Supp.).

85. *New York Laws of 1972*, chap. 527, and *New York Tax Law*, §§ 1000–1009 (McKinney 1975).

86. *New York Laws of 1926*, chap. 440, and *New York Unconsolidated Laws*, §§ 7901–23 (McKinney 1974). See also *New York Laws of 1978*, chap. 576.

87. *New York Laws of 1973*, chap. 346.

88. *New York Laws of 1974*, chap. 439.

89. *New York Laws of 1973*, chap. 346.

90. *New York Laws of 1968*, chap. 347, and *New York Tax Law*, §§ 1400–10 (McKinney 1975).

91. *New York Laws of 1905*, chap. 241, and *New York Tax Law*, §§ 270–78 (McKinney 1975).

92. *New York Laws of 1968*, chap. 827, and *New York Tax Law*, § 270 (2) (McKinney 1979 Supp.).

93. *New York Laws of 1977*, chap. 878.

94. *New York Constitution*, art. I, § 9 (1). Although there was strong opposition to a state lottery on moral grounds, the proposed amendment was ratified by a vote of 2,464,898 to 1,604,694.

95. *New York Laws of 1967*, chap. 278; *New York Laws of 1973*, chap. 346; and *New York Tax Law*, §§ 1301–15 (McKinney 1975).

96. *New York Laws of 1976*, chap. 92, and *New York Tax Law*, § 1603 (McKinney 1979 Supp.).

97. New York State Constitutional Convention Committee, *Problems Relating to Taxation and Finance*, pp. 95–96.

98. *New York Constitution*, art. VII, §§ 9–12 (1846).

99. *New York Constitution*, art. VII, §§ 9–10. The constitution allows the contraction of short-term debt for housing for a five-year period. *Ibid.*, art. XVIII, § 3.

100. *Ibid.*, art. VII, § 11.

101. *Ibid.*, art. vii, §§ 14 and 18–19.

102. *Ibid.*, art. vii, § 12.

103. *Ibid.*

104. *Ibid.*, § 16.

105. C. Lowell Harriss, *Constitutional Restrictions on Property Taxing and Bor-*

rowing Powers in New York (New York: Citizens Tax Council, Inc., 1967), pp. 1-3 and 1-4.

106. *Ibid.*, p. VII-1.

107. *New York Laws of 1961*, chap. 803, and *New York Private Housing Finance Law*, § 48 (McKinney 1962).

108. *United States Constitution*, art. I, § 10.

109. *New York Constitution*, art. X, § 1.

110. *Matter of Smith v. Levitt*, 30 N.Y. 2d 934 at 935 (1972).

111. *New York Laws of 1975*, chap. 7, and *New York Unconsolidated Laws*, §§ 6361–82 (McKinney 1979 Supp.).

112. For additional details on this lease-purchase arrangement, see *Schuyler v. South Mall Constructors*, 32 App. Div. 2d 454 (1969).

113. *New York Laws of 1972*, chap. 684, and *New York State Finance Law*, § 89 (McKinney 1974).

114. *New York Constitution*, art. VIII, § 1.

115. *Ibid.*

116. *Ibid.*

117. *Ibid.*, § 2.

118. *Ibid.*, § 4.

119. *Ibid.*, §§ 6–7 and 7a.

120. *Ibid.*, §§ 10, 10a, and 11. The tax limits were included in the constitution by an 1884 amendment. See *New York Constitution*, art. VIII, § 11 (1884).

121. *Hurd v. City of Buffalo*, 34 N.Y. 2d 628 (1974). See *New York Laws of 1969*, chap. 1105.

122. *New York Laws of 1976*, chap. 349 and 485.

123. *Bethlehem Steel Corporation v. Board of Education*, 44 N.Y. 2d 831 (1978).

124. *New York Laws of 1978*, chap. 280, and *New York Real Property Tax Law*, § 1252 (McKinney 1979 Supp.).

125. *New York Laws of 1968*, chap. 1069, and *New York Laws of 1973*, chap. 954.

126. *New York Constitution*, art. VIII, § 12.

127. *New York Real Property Tax Law*, § 722 (2) (McKinney 1972).

128. For details, see *State Revenue Sharing* (Albany: Temporary State Commission on State and Local Finances, 1975).

129. Warren Moscow, *Politics in the Empire State* (New York: Alfred A. Knopf, 1948), p. 218.

130. *State Revenue Sharing*, p. 20.

131. *State of New York Executive Budget, Submitted by Hugh L. Carey, Governor, to the New York State Legislature* (Albany: Executive Chamber, 1979), pp. M9, 159–205, 389–95, and 687–703.

132. *New York Laws of 1933*, chap. 815.

133. *New York Laws of 1947*, chap. 278.

134. For a discussion of exempt property and other aspects of real property taxation, see *The Real Property Tax* (Albany: Temporary State Commission on State and Local Finances, 1975).

135. *New York Real Property Tax Law*, § 406 (1-4) (McKinney 1972).

136. *Ibid.*, § 406 (5).

137. "100% Assessments Major SBEA Aim," *Newsvane*, December 1978, p. 134.

138. *New York Tax Law*, § 606 (McKinney 1979 Supp.).

139. *New York Real Property Tax Law*, § 306 (McKinney 1979 Supp.). The state constitution stipulates that "assessments shall in no case exceed full value." *New York Constitution*, art. XVI, § 2.

140. *New York Laws of 1960*, chap. 335, and *New York Real Property Tax Law*, §§ 200–202 (McKinney 1979 Supp.). See also chapter 346 of the *New York Laws of 1949*, which created a Temporary State Board of Equalization and Assessment.

141. *Hellerstein v. Assessors of the Town of Islip*, 37 N.Y. 2d 1 (1975).

142. *New York Laws of 1978*, chap. 163, and *New York Real Property Tax Law*, § 306 (McKinney 1979 Supp.), and *New York Laws of 1980*, chap. 880, and *New York Real Property Tax Law*, § 306 (McKinney 1981 Supp.).

143. *New York Laws of 1977*, chap. 889; *New York Laws of 1977*, chap. 887; and *New York Real Property Tax Law*, § 1572 (McKinney 1979 Supp.).

144. *New York Constitution*, art. XI, § 1.

145. *The Fleischmann Report on the Quality, Cost and Financing of Elementary and Secondary Education in New York State* (New York: The Viking Press, 1973), Vol. I., pp. 62–63.

146. For additional details, see *Apportionment of Operating Aid for the 1977–78 School Year: A Complex Status Quo* (Albany: New York State Division of the Budget, September 1977), and *Current Components of New York State's Educational Finance System: A Review* (Albany: New York State Division of the Budget, October 1977).

147. *New York Education Law*, § 3602 (McKinney 1979 Supp.).

148. *Board of Education v. Nyquist*, 94 Misc. 2d 466 (1978). See also Roy R. Silver, "Use of Realty Taxes to Finance Schools Voided in New York," *The New York Times*, June 24, 1978, pp. 1 and 24.

149. The Regents Proposal for Improving State Aid to Public Education in New York State (Albany: New York State Education Department, December 1978), p. 15.

150. "Message of the Governor," *State of New York Executive Budget, Submitted by Hugh L. Carey, Governor, to the New York State Legislature*, p. m22.

151. Lois Uttley, "Plan to Cut School Aid a 'Paper Threat?'" *The Knickerbocker News* (Albany, New York), February 1, 1979, pp. 1 and 4A. See also Thomas Y. Hobard, Jr., "School Funding Equity Means Balance, Not Robbery of Peter to Pay Paul," *New York Teacher*, December 24, 1978, p. 4.

152. *1979 State Aid Proposal* (Albany: The New York State Educational Conference Board, 1979), pp. 2–3.

153. *Ibid.*, p. 4.

Bibliography

BOOKS AND MONOGRAPHS

Alexander, DeAlva S. *A Political History of the State of New York*. New York: Henry Holt and Company, 1906.

Balhl, Roy W. *The New York State Economy: 1960–1978 and the Outlook*. Syracuse: Metropolitan Studies Program. Syracuse University, 1979.

Bailyn, Bernard. *Origins of American Politics*. New York: Alfred A. Knopf Company, 1968.

Becker, Carl L. *The History of Political Parties in the Province of New York, 1760–1776*. Madison: Bulletin of the University of Wisconsin, No. 386 (April 1909).

Berle, Peter A. A. *Does the Citizen Stand a Chance?* Woodbury, N.Y.: Barron's Educational Series, Inc., 1974.

Brodhead, John R. *History of the State of New York*. 2 vols. New York: Harper and Brothers, 1853–71.

Caldwell, Lynton K. *The Government and Administration of New York*. New York: Thomas Y. Crowell Company, 1954.

Caro, Robert A. *The Power Broker: Robert Moses and the Fall of New York*. New York: Vintage Books, 1975.

The Citizens Conference on State Legislatures. *State Legislatures: An Evaluation of Their Effectiveness*. New York: Praeger Publishers, 1971.

Collier, Peter, and Horowitz, David. *The Rockefellers: An American Dynasty*. New York: Holt, Rinehart, and Winston, Inc., 1976.

Colvin, David L. *The Bicameral Principle in the New York Legislature*. New York: Columbia University Press, 1913.

Connery, Robert H., and Benjamin, Gerald., eds. *Governing New York State: The Rockefeller Years*. New York: The Academy of Political Science, 1974.

————, and Caraley, Demetrios, eds. *Governing the City: Challenges and Options for New York*. New York: The Academy of Political Science, 1969.

Costikyan, Edward N. *Behind Closed Doors: Politics in the Public Interest*. New York: Harcourt, Brace, and World, Inc., 1966.

Debt-Like Commitments of the State of New York. Albany: Office of the State Comptroller, January 1973.

Diamond, Sigmund, ed. *Modernizing State Government: The New York Constitutional Convention of 1967*. New York: The Academy of Political Science, January 1967.

Dickerson, Oliver M. *American Colonial Government: 1696–1765*. New York: Russell and Russell, 1962.

Dorsett, Lyle W. *Franklin D. Roosevelt and the City Bosses*. Port Washington, N.Y.: Kennikat Press, 1977.

Ellis, David M. *New York: State and City* Ithaca: Cornell University Press, 1979.

————; Frost, James A.; Syrett, Harold C.; and Carman, Harry J. A Short History of New York State. Ithaca: Cornell University Press, 1957.

Fairlie, John A. *The Centralization of Administration in New York State*. New York: Columbia University Studies in History, Economics, and Public Law, 1898.

Federal Funds: Budgetary and Appropriation Practices in State Government. Lexington, Ky.: The Council of State Governments, 1978.

Fiske, John. *The Dutch and Quaker Colonies in America*. 2 vols. Boston: Houghton, Mifflin and Company, 1899.

The Fleischmann Report on the Quality, Cost, and Financing of Elementary and Secondary Education in New York State. New York: The Viking Press, 1973.

Flynn, Edward J. *You're the Boss*. New York: The Viking Press, 1947.

Fox, Dixon Ryan. *The Decline of Aristocracy in the Politics of New York, 1801–1840*. New York: Harper Torch Book Edition, 1965.

Frank, Jerome. *Courts on Trial*. Princeton: Princeton University Press, 1950.

Friedman, Jacob A. *The Impeachment of Governor William Sulzer*. New York: Columbia University Press, 1939.

Gellhorn, Walter. *Federal Administrative Proceedings*. Baltimore: The Johns Hopkins Press, 1941.

Goodwin, Maud W. *Dutch and English on the Hudson: A Chronicle of Colonial New York*. New Haven: Yale University Press, 1919.

Greene, Evarts B. *The Foundations of American Nationality*. New York: American Book Company, 1922.

Hevesi, Alan G. *Legislative Politics in New York State: A Comparative Analysis*. New York: Praeger Publishers, 1975.

Horton, John T. *James Kent: A Study in Conservatism, 1763–1847.* New York: D. Appleton-Century Company, 1939.

Ingalls, Robert F. *Herbert H. Lehman and New York's Little New Deal.* New York: New York University Press, 1975.

Jameson, John F. *Narratives of New Netherland, 1604–1664.* New York: C. Scribner's Sons, 1909.

Kallenbach, Joseph E. *The American Chief Executive: The Presidency and the Governorship.* New York: Harper and Row, Publishers, 1966.

Kilpatrick, Wylie. *State Supervision of Local Budgeting.* New York: National Municipal League, 1939.

Kramer, Michael, and Roberts, Sam. *"I Never Wanted to be Vice-President of Anything!" An Investigative Biography of Nelson Rockefeller.* New York: Basic Books, Inc., Publishers, 1976.

Larabee, Leonard W. *Royal Government in America: A Study of the English Colonial System Before 1783.* New Haven: Yale University Press, 1930.

Legislative Redistricting by Non-Legislative Agencies. New York: National Municipal League, 1967.

Lehne, Richard. *Legislating Reapportionment in New York.* New York: National Municipal League, 1971.

Lincoln, Charles Z. *The Constitutional History of New York.* Rochester: The Lawyers Cooperative Publishing Company, 1906.

Mason, Bernard. *The Road to Independence: The Revolutionary Movement in New York, 1775–1776.* Lexington: The University of Kentucky Press, 1966.

McGoldrick, Joseph D. *Law and Practice of Municipal Home Rule: 1916–1930.* New York: Columbia University Press, 1933.

Menzel, Donald; Friedman, Robert; and Feller, Irwin. *Developing a Science and Technology Capability in State Legislatures: Problems and Prospects.* University Park: Center for the Study of Science Policy, Pennsylvania State University, January 1973.

Metz, Joseph G. *The Power of People-Power.* Woodbury, N.Y.: Barron's Educational Series, Inc., 1972.

Model State Constitution. 6th ed. New York: National Municipal League, 1963.

Morgan, David. *The Capitol Press Corps: Newsmen and the Governing of New York State.* Westport, Conn.: Greenwood Press, 1978.

Moscow, Warren. *The Last of the Big-Time Bosses: The Life and Times of Carmine DeSapio and the Rise and Fall of Tammany Hall.* New York: Stein and Day Publishers, 1971.

———. *Politics in the Empire State.* New York: Alfred A. Knopf, 1948.

———. *What Have You Done for Me Lately?* Englewood Cliffs, N.J.: Prentice-Hall, Inc., 1967.

Munger, Frank J., and Straetz, Ralph A. *New York Politics.* New York: New York University Press, 1960.

Nevins, Allan. *The American States During and After the Revolution*. New York: The Macmillan Company, 1925.

The New York Red Book. Albany: Williams Press, 1979.

New York State: A Citizen's Handbook. New York: League of Women Voters of New York State, 1974.

Nissenson, Samuel G. *The Patroon's Domain*. New York: Columbia University Press, 1937.

O'Callaghan, Edmund B. *History of New Netherland: Or New York Under the Dutch*. New York: D. Appleton and Company, 1845.

Peirce, Neal R. *The Megastates of America: People, Politics, and Power in the Ten Great American States*. New York: W. W. Norton and Company, Inc., 1972.

Pethtel, Ray, and Brown, Richard E., eds. *Legislative Review of State Program Performance*. New Brunswick, N.J.: Eagleton Institute, Rutgers University, 1972.

Prendergast, James T., and Costikyan, Edward N. *Judicial Selection—The Prendergast Plan*. New York: The Weber Company, 1967.

Prescott, Frank W., and Zimmerman, Joseph F. *The Council of Revision*. Albany: Graduate School of Public Affairs, State University of New York at Albany, 1973.

———. *The Politics of the Veto of Legislation in New York*. Washington, D.C.: University Press of America, Inc., 1980.

Progressive Democracy: Addresses and State Papers of Alfred E. Smith. New York: Harcourt, Brace and Company, 1928.

Raesly, Ellis L. *Portrait of New Netherland*. New York: Columbia University Press, 1945.

Rienow, Robert. *New York State and Local Government*, 2d rev. ed. Albany: The State Education Department, 1959.

Sayre, Wallace S., and Kaufman, Herbert. *Governing New York City: Politics in the Metropolis*. New York: Russell Sage Foundation, 1960.

Schick, Thomas. *The New York State Constitutional Convention of 1915 and the Modern State Governor*. New York: National Municipal League, 1979.

Shalala, Donna E. *The City and the Constitution: The 1967 New York Convention's Response to the Urban Crisis*. New York: National Municipal League, 1972.

Smith, Adam. *An Inquiry into the Nature and Causes of the Wealth of Nations*. Oxford: Clarendon Press, 1976.

Smith, Alfred E. *The Citizen and His Government*. New York: Harper and Brothers, 1935.

———. *Up to Now: An Autobiography*. Garden City, N.Y.: Garden City Publishing Company, 1929.

Smith, Franklin A. *Judicial Review of Legislation in New York: 1906–1938*. New York: Faculty of Political Science, Columbia University, 1952.

Stelzer, Leigh, and Riedel, James A. *Capitol Goods*. Albany: Graduate
    School of Public Affairs, State University of New York at Albany, 1976.
Wood, Gordon S. *The Creation of the American Republic: 1776–1787*. Chapel
    Hill: University of North Carolina Press, 1969.
Zeller, Belle. *Pressure Politics in New York: A Study of Group Represen-
    tation Before the Legislature*. New York: Russell and Russell, 1937.
Zimmerman, Joseph F. *The Federated City: Community Control in Large
    Cities*. New York: St. Martin's Press, 1972.
––––––. *State and Local Government*. 3d ed. New York: Barnes and Noble
    Books, 1978.

GOVERNMENT REPORTS AND DOCUMENTS

And Justice for All. New York: Temporary State Commission on the State
    Court System, 1973.
Annual Report: 1975–1976. Albany: New York Job Development Authority,
    1976.
Annual Report. New York: New York State Commission on Judicial Con-
    duct, January 1978.
Annual Report: 1977. New York: New York State Project Finance Agency,
    1978.
Annual Report: 1978. Albany: New York Temporary State Commission on
    Regulation of Lobbying, 1979.
Annual Report of the Comptroller of the State of New York, 1978. Part I.
    Albany: Office of the State Comptroller, 1978.
*Apportionment of Operating Aid for the 1977–78 School Year: A Complex
    Status Quo*. Albany: New York State Division of the Budget, September
    1977.
Audit Report on First Instance Advances to Public Authorities. Albany:
    Office of the State Comptroller, 1972.
Bellacosa, Joseph W. *1977 Annual Report of the Clerk of the Court to the
    Judges of the New York Court of Appeals*. Albany: New York Court of
    Appeals, n.d.
*Coordinating Governments Through Regionalism and Reform. Vol. One:
    Land Use Control: Modern Techniques for Modern Problems*. Albany:
    New York State Joint Legislative Committee on Metropolitan and Re-
    gional Areas Study, 1971.
*Current Components of New York State's Educational Finance System: A
    Review*. Albany: New York State Division of the Budget, October 1977.
Family Court . . . The System that Fails All. Albany: New York Senate
    Research Service, 1977.

Final Report. New York: The Temporary State Commission on Judicial Conduct, August 31, 1976.

Final Report of the Casino Gambling Study Panel. New York: The Panel, 1979.

Financial Data for School Districts: Fiscal Year Ended June 30, 1976. Albany: New York State Department of Audit and Control, n.d.

First Annual Report of the Chief Administrator of the Courts. New York: New York State Office of Court Administration, 1979.

First Report. New York: The Temporary State Commission on Judicial Conduct, October 1975.

First Steps Toward a Modern Constitution. New York: The Temporary Commission on the Revision and Simplification of the Constitution, 1959.

Fiscal Effect of State School Mandates. Albany: Legislative Commission on Expenditure Review, 1978.

Foundations of the Fiscal System. Albany: New York Joint Legislative Committee on State-Local Fiscal Relations, 1966. Published as Legislative Document Number 32 of 1966.

The Genesee County Revaluation: Relationship to School Aid and School Tax Levy Apportionment. Albany: New York State Board of Equalization and Assessment, October 1978.

Governing Urban Areas: Realism and Reform. Albany: New York State Joint Legislative Committee on Metropolitan and Regional Areas Study, 1967.

Guide to the Requirements of the New York State Election Law as Related to Campaign Financing. Albany: New York State Board of Elections, December 1, 1977.

Guidelines. Albany: New York Temporary State Commission on Regulation of Lobbying, 1978.

Hough, Franklin B., ed. *New York Convention Manual.* 2 vols. Albany, 1867.

Information Requirements for Legislative Oversight: A Report to the New York State Ways and Means Committee. Washington, D.C.: Price Waterhouse and Company, April 1978.

Journal of the New York State Constitutional Convention, 1915. Albany: J. B. Lyon Company, 1915.

The Judiciary. New York: Temporary State Commission on the Constitutional Convention, 1967.

Levitt, Arthur. *Annual Report.* Albany: The Comptroller of the State of New York, 1977.

———. *Discipline in the Fiscal Process.* Albany: Office of the State Comptroller, September 1973.

Lincoln, Charles Z., ed. *Messages from the Governors Comprising Executive Communications to the Legislature and Other Papers Relating to Legislation from the Organization of the First Colonial Assembly in 1683* to and Including the Year 1906. Albany: J. B. Lyon Printing Company, 1909.

Local Finance. New York: Temporary State Commission on the Constitutional Convention, 1967.

Local Revenue Diversification: Income, Sales Tax, User Charges. Washington, D.C.: United States Advisory Commission on Intergovernmental Relations, October 1974.

Manual for the Use of the Convention. New York: Walker and Craighed, 1846.

Manual for the Use of the Legislature of the State of New York: 1975. Albany: New York State Department of State, 1975.

Municipal Insurance Pools: An Appropriate Alternative for Local Governments? Albany: New York State Assembly Local Governments Committee, 1980.

National Center for Telephone Research. A Study of Attitudes of New York State Civil Service Employees Toward the Civil Service System. Albany: New York State Temporary Commission on Management and Productivity in the Public Service, April 1977.

New York City's Fiscal Problems: A Long Road Still Lies Ahead. Washington, D.C.: United States General Accounting Office, 1979.

New York's Role in the Fiscal Affairs of Its Local Governments: New Directions for a Partnership. Albany: New York State Assembly Local Governments Committee, 1979.

New York State Assembly Scientific Staff. Proceedings of the New York State Assembly/AISLE Conference on Energy and the Environment. Albany: New York State Assembly, 1974.

New York State Budget Summary: 1979–80. Albany: New York State Division of the Budget, November 1979.

New York State Constitutional Convention Committee. Problems Relating to Taxation and Finance. Albany: J. B. Lyon Company, 1938.

Northeastern Energy and Transportation Problems: A Regional Perspective. Washington, D.C.: United States General Accounting Office, 1979.

Operating Practices of the New York City Pension Systems and City Comptroller's Bureau of Investments. Albany: New York State Comptroller, 1979.

Plan of the Temporary Commission on the Courts for a Simplified Statewide Court System. Albany: The Commission, 1956.

Preliminary Report on Governmental Finances in 1976–77. Washington, D.C.: United States Bureau of the Census, September 1978.

Problems Relating to Home Rule and Local Government. Albany: New York State Constitutional Convention, 1938.

Problems Relating to Taxation and Finance. Albany: New York State Constitutional Convention, 1938.

Proceedings of the Constitutional Convention of the State of New York. Albany: Constitutional Convention of the State of New York, 1967.

Proceedings and Debates of the Constitutional Convention of the State of New York. Albany: Weed, Parsons, and Company, 1868.

Property Tax Circuit-Breakers: Current Status and Policy Issues. Washington, D.C.: United States Advisory Commission on Intergovernmental Relations, 1975.

Public Papers of Thomas E. Dewey: Fifty-First Governor of the State of New York, 1953. Albany: State of New York, n.d.

Public Papers of Averell Harriman: Fifty-Second Governor of the State of New York, 1955. Albany: State of New York, n.d.

Public Papers of Charles Evans Hughes. Albany: J. B. Lyon Company, 1908–9.

Public Papers of Herbert H. Lehman: Forty-Ninth Governor of the State of New York, 1937. Albany: J. B. Lyon Company, 1940.

Public Papers of Herbert H. Lehman: Forty-Ninth Governor of the State of New York, 1938. Albany: J. B. Lyon Company, 1942.

Public Papers of Nelson A. Rockefeller: Fifty-Third Governor of the State of New York, 1967. Albany: State of New York, n.d.

Public Papers of Nelson A. Rockefeller: Fifty-Third Governor of the State of New York, 1972. Albany: State of New York, n.d.

Public Papers of Nelson A. Rockefeller: Fifty-Third Governor of the State of New York, 1973. Albany: State of New York, n.d.

Public Papers of Franklin D. Roosevelt: Forty-Eighth Governor of the State of New York, 1931. Albany: J. B. Lyon Company, 1937.

Public Papers of Alfred E. Smith: Governor, 1919. Albany: J. B. Lyon Company, 1925.

Public Papers of Alfred E. Smith: Governor, 1925. Albany: J. B. Lyon Company, 1926.

Public Papers of Governor William Sulzer. Albany: J. B. Lyon Company, 1913.

Public Papers of Charles Seymour Whitman: Governor, 1917. Albany: J. B. Lyon Company, 1919.

Public Papers of Malcolm Wilson, Fiftieth Governor of the State of New York, 1973–74. Albany: State of New York, n.d.

The Real Property Tax. Albany: Temporary State Commission on State and Local Finances, 1975.

Recommendation for a New Pension Plan for Public Employees: The 1976 Coordinated Escalator Retirement Plan. New York: Permanent Commission on Public Employee Pension and Retirement Systems, 1976.

The Regents Proposal for Improving State Aid to Public Education in New York State. Albany: New York State Department of Education, December 1978.

Regents' Statement on Governor's Proposal for an Inspector General for Ed-

ucation. Albany: New York State Department of Education, January 24, 1973.

Report of the Joint Legislative Committee on State Fiscal Policies. Albany: J. B. Lyon Company, 1937.

Report to the Legislature on the Open Meetings Law. Albany: New York State Committee on Public Access to Records, January 31, 1978.

Report of the New York State Reorganization Commission, February 26, 1926. Albany: J. B. Lyon Company, 1926.

Report of the Panel on the Future of Government in New York. Albany: The Commission, December 31, 1979.

Report of the Permanent Commission on Public Employee Pension and Retirement Systems. New York: The Commission, 1973.

Report of the Reconstruction Commission on Retrenchment and Reorganization in the State Government, October 10, 1919. Albany: J. B. Lyon Company, 1919.

Report on the Review of the Proposed New York City Financial Plan for Fiscal Years 1980 through 1983. New York: Office of the Special Deputy State Comptroller for the City of New York, December 10, 1979.

Report of the Secretary to the Governor. Albany: State of New York, December 29, 1959.

Report of the Temporary State Commission on the Real Property Tax. Albany: The Commission, March 27, 1979.

Research Findings and Policy Alternatives: A Second Interim Report. New York: The New York State Special Task Force on Equity and Excellence in Education, 1980.

Restoring Credit and Confidence. New York: New York State Moreland Act Commission on the Urban Development Corporation and Other State Financing Agencies, 1976.

A Review of New York City's Implementation of Its Capital Plan as of September 30, 1979. New York: Office of the Special Deputy State Comptroller for the City of New York, December 10, 1979.

Revised Record of the New York State Constitutional Convention. Albany: J. B. Lyon Company, 1916.

Revised Record of the Constitutional Convention of 1894. Albany: The Argus Company, 1900.

Revision and Simplification. New York: Temporary State Commission on the Constitutional Convention, March 31, 1967.

Rockefeller, Nelson A. *Message to the Legislature*. Albany: Executive Chamber, 1973.

Second Interim Report. New York: The Temporary State Commission on the Constitutional Convention, 1957.

Senate Administrative Regulations Review Commission. *The Laws of 1977: An Analysis of Regulatory Implementation*. Albany: New York State Senate, 1978.

Senate Administrative Regulations Review Commission. *Sales Tax Administration in New York State.* Albany: New York State Senate, 1978.

Senate Legislative Fellows Program. Albany: New York State Senate, 1978.

Seventeenth Annual Report. New York: The Administrative Board of the Judicial Conference of the State of New York, 1972.

Simplifying a Complex Constitution. New York: The Temporary Commission on the Revision and Simplification of the Constitution, 1961.

Staff Report on Public Authorities. Albany: Williams Press, 1956.

State Agencies and the State Administrative Procedure Act: A Study of Compliance. Albany: Administrative Regulations Review Committee, The Assembly, July 1977.

State Finance. New York: Temporary State Commission on the Constitutional Convention, 1967.

State Mandates. Albany: Temporary State Commission on State and Local Finances, 1975.

State of New York Executive Budget for the Fiscal Year April 1, 1978 to March 31, 1979. Albany: Executive Chamber, 1978.

State of New York Executive Budget, Submitted by Hugh L. Carey, Governor, to the New York State Legislature. Albany: Executive Chamber 1979.

State of New York Five-Year Projection of Income and Expenditures, General Fund, Fiscal Years 1978 through 1982–83. Albany: Executive Chamber, February 16, 1978.

State of New York Five-Year Projection of Income and Expenditures, General Fund, Fiscal Years 1979–80 through 1983–84. Albany: New York State Division of the Budget, 1979.

The State Register: An Administrative Journal for New York State. Albany: Assembly and Senate Administrative Regulations Review Committee, March 1978.

State Revenue Sharing. Albany: Temporary State Commission on State and Local Finances, 1975.

Strengthening Local Government in New York. Part I: The Capacity for Change. New York: Temporary State Commission on the Powers of Local Government, March 31, 1973.

Study Project on the Preparation of State Financial Statements in Accordance with GAAP. Albany: Office of the State Comptroller, December 1978.

Third Annual Report to the Governor and the Legislature on the Open Meetings Law. Albany: Committee on Public Access to Records, February 27, 1979.

Thorpe, Francis N., ed. *The Federal and State Constitutions.* Washington, D.C.: United States Government Printing Office, 1909.

Ticket-Fixing: The Assertion of Influence in Traffic Cases. New York: The New York State Commission on Judicial Conduct, June 20, 1977.

Triborough Bridge and Tunnel Authority: Public Authority Financial

Analysis Statement No. 73-10. Albany: Office of the State Comptroller, 1974.

Twenty-Second Annual Report. New York: The Administrative Board of the Judicial Conference, 1977.

Twenty-Third Annual Report. New York: The Administrative Board of the Judicial Conference, 1978.

Underwood, James E. *Science/Technology-Related Activities in the Government of the State of New York: The Organizational Pattern*. Albany: Office of Science and Technology, New York State Department of Education, 1971.

United States Bureau of the Census. *Public Employment in 1977*. Washington, D.C.: United States Government Printing Office, 1978.

United States Senate State Committee on Rules and Administration. *Nomination of Nelson A. Rockefeller of New York to be Vice President fo the United States*. Washington, D.C.: United States Government Printing Office, 1974.

Viability of the New York State Urban Development Corporation Housing Program. Albany: New York State Comptroller, 1979.

Your Day (or Night) in Court: A Study of Small Claims Courts in New York State. Albany: New York State Assembly Standing Committee on Judiciary, 1977.

Zimmerman, Joseph F., ed. *The Crisis in Mass Transportation*. Albany: New York State Joint Legislative Committee on Transportation, 1970.

―――. *Pragmatic Federalism: The Reassignment of Functional Responsibility*. Washington, D.C.: United States Advisory Commission on Intergovernmental Relations, 1976.

OTHER REPORTS

The Attorney-General Should Be Appointive. New York: Citizens Union of the City of New York, 1967.

Career Executive Service. Albany: Capital District Chapter of the American Society for Public Administration, May 1978.

Civil Service Reform. Albany: Capital District Chapter, American Society for Public Administration, May 1978.

Conservatives Support Continued Election of Judges. New York: The Conservative Party of New York State, n.d.

Davidson, Ben. *Liberal Party of New York State*. New York: Liberal Party, n.d.

Democrats Pledge Sweeping Legislative Reforms in Albany: Changes Would Curb Abuses and Open Process to Public. Albany: Assembly Minority

Leader Stanley Steingut and Senator Mary Ann Krupsak, October 27, 1974.

Discontinue Bond Issue Referendums! New York: Citizens Union of the City of New York, 1967.

An Evaluation of Our Merit System: Twenty-One Recommendations for Change. Albany: New York State Personnel Council, January 1977.

Guastello, Richard J., and Zimmerman, Joseph F. *Intergovernmental Service Agreements in New York State.* Albany: New York Conference of Mayors and Municipal Officials, 1973.

Harris, C. Lowell. *Constitutional Restrictions on Property, Taxing and Borrowing Powers in New York.* New York: Citizens Tax Council, Inc., 1967.

Improving Management of the Public Work Force: The Challenge to State and Local Government. New York: Committee for Economic Development, 1978.

Introducting the Conservative Party of New York State. New York: The Conservative Party, n.d.

Justice Courts in New York State: The Courts Closest to the People. Albany: New York State Association of Magistrates and New York Conference of Mayors and Municipal Officials, 1976.

Kochan, Thomas A.; Ehrenberg, Ronald G.; Baderschneider, Jean; Dick, Todd; and Mironi, Mordehai. *An Evaluation of Impasses Procedures for Police and Firefighters in New York State: A Summary of Findings, Conclusions, and Recommendations.* Ithaca: New York State School of Industrial and Labor Relations, Cornell University, November 1976.

Kress, Jack M., with Stanley, Sandra L. *Justice Court in the State of New York.* Albany: New York State Association of Magistrates and New York Conference of Mayors and Municipal Officials, 1976.

Marshlow, Robert W. *Home Rule in New York State: A Brief Survey.* Albany: New York State Office for Local Government, 1965.

Mediating Social Conflict. New York: The Ford Foundation, 1978.

Moynihan, Daniel P. *The Federal Government and the Economy of New York State.* Washington, D.C.: July 15, 1977. Multilithed.

New Approaches to Conflict Resolution. New York: The Ford Foundation, 1978.

New Job Assignment for the State Comptroller. New York: Citizens Union of the City of New York, 1967.

New York City Attrition and Work Force Reduction, Fiscal Years 1975–1978: A Case Study Examination. New York: Citizens Budget Commission, Inc., September 1979.

New York State Constitutional Convention, 1967: Complete Set of Citizens Union Position Papers. New York: Citizens Union, 1967. Mimeographed.

A Plan to Expedite the Rebuilding of New York City's Physical Infrastructure. New York: Citizens Budget Commission, Inc., November 1979.

A Review of New York City's Management Program. New York: Citizens Budget Commission, Inc., October 1979.

Schroeder, Larry. *Property Tax Equalization Rates in New York State: A Review of Their Uses and Fiscal Implications.* Syracuse: Metropolitan Studies Program, Syracuse University, 1979.

Special Committee on the Constitutional Convention. *Court Structure and Management.* New York: The Association of the Bar of the City of New York, March 1967.

Special Committee on the Constitutional Convention. *Removal of Judges.* New York: The Association of the Bar of the City of New York, March 1967.

Special Committee on the Constitutional Convention. *Selection of Judges.* New York: The Association of the Bar of the City of New York, 1967.

1979 State Aid Proposal. Albany: The New York State Educational Conference Board, 1979.

Statement on New York City's Fiscal Situation. New York: Citizens Budget Commission, Inc., January 1980.

Toward a More Effective Legislature. Albany: New York State Bar Association, 1975.

ARTICLES

"Active Doctors Get Police Pensions." *The New York Times* (February 9, 1977), 1 and B-7.

Adler, Madeline, and Bellush, Jewell. "Lawyers and the Legislature: Something New in New York." *National Civic Review,* LXVIII (May 1979), 244–46 and 278.

Amdursky, Robert S. "A Public-Private Partnership for Urban Progress." *Journal of Urban Law,* XLVI (1969), 199–215.

"Another Pension 'Ripoff.'" *The New York Times* (April 21, 1976), 34.

Appleby, Paul. "The Role of the Budget Division." *Public Administration Review,* XVII (Summer 1957), 156–58.

Behn, Dick. "Liberals and Conservatives: The Importance of New York's Two 'Third' Parties." *Empire State Report,* III (April 1977), 164–69.

———. "Rockefeller's Legacy." *Empire State Report,* III (April 1977), 141–63.

Benjamin, A. David. "A Case Against the Appointment of Judges." *The New York Times* (June 2, 1977), 32.

Benjamin, Gerald. "Patterns in New York State Politics." Connery, Robert H. and Benjamin, Gerald, eds. *Governing New York State: The Rockefeller Years.* New York: The Academy of Political Science, 1974. 31–44.

Benjamin, Gilbert G. "The Attempted Revision of the State Constitution of New York." *The American Political Science Review,* X (February 1916), 20–43.

Berle, Adolf A., Jr. "Elected Judges—Or Appointed?" *The New York Times Magazine* (December 11, 1955), 26, 34, 37–38, and 40.

Bigos, Arlene. "The Lobbyists' World." *The Knickerbocker News* (March 11, 1976), 1-C.

———. "State, Local Governments Argue When Mandated Expenses Are Mandatory." *The Knickerbocker News* (February 23, 1976), 2-A.

Blumenthal, Ralph. "The 'Seldom-Show' Jobs." *The New York Times* (March 25, 1974), 14.

Braden, George D. "How to Rid NYS Constitution of Legalese—Use Reporters." *The Knickerbocker News* (March 7, 1978), 13-A.

Breitel, Charles D. "Some Aspects of the Legislative Process." *New York State Bar Association Bulletin,* XXI (July 1949), 271–77.

Bronston, Jack E. "The Buck Stops There." *The New York Times* (April 29, 1978), 23.

———. "The Legislature in Change and Crisis: 1958–78." *Empire,* IV (October–November 1978), 40–41.

Brown, Peter M. "Ten Reasons Why the Grand Jury in New York Should Be Retained and Strengthened." *The Record of the Association of the Bar of the City of New York,* XXII (June 1967), 471–78.

Buck, Rinker. "Redefining Property Assessment." *Empire State Report,* I (June 1975), 220–21.

———. "The State's Indigestion from a Bad Apple." *Empire State Report,* I (October 1975), 371–73 and 401–3.

Budgar, Gerald S. "Assembly Seeks PR 'Facelift.'" *The Times Union* (October 31, 1976), B-1 and B-14.

———. "Business Lobby's Voice Booming in Albany." *Sunday Times Union* (January 7, 1979), 1 and A-8.

———. "2 Albany Pension Funds Rank High." *Sunday Times Union* (January 21, 1979), B-1 and B-2.

"The Budget Process as a Political War Game." *Empire State Report,* IV (February/March, 1978), 89.

"Bullard and Wilson Cleared of Violating Election Law." *The New York Times* (October 31, 1974), 35.

Burks, Edward C. "8 Units Lobby for New York in Washington." *The New York Times* (April 26, 1978), B-1 and B-5.

———. "New York Congressmen Help State Get $500 'Extra' in U.S. Aid." *The New York Times* (December 27, 1977), 30.

Burnham, David. "Governor Supersedes D.A.'s Here, Names Special Aide to Corruption and Orders a Staff of 200 Hired." *The New York Times* (September 20, 1978), 1 and 29.

Burton, John E. "Budget Administration in New York State." *State Government*, XVI (October 1943), 205–7.

———. "New York." *State Government*, XX (May 1947), 138–40 and 153.

———. "Recent Developments in New York State Fiscal Policy." *The Bulletin of the National Tax Association*, XXXII (May 1947), 245–51.

Cagliostro, Anthony, "Let's Junk the Civil Service Merit System." *Empire State Report*, II (January/February 1976), 42.

Cannon, Raymond J. "The New York Court on the Judiciary." *Albany Law Review*, XXVIII (1964), 1–11.

"Carey Is Cleared on Election Fund." *The New York Times* (February 1, 1975), 31.

Carroll, Maurice. "Koch Looks to State to Rescue His Budget." *The New York Times* (February 6, 1978), B-11.

———. "The Unlikely Beginning of the Right to Life Party." *The New York Times* (November 25, 1978), 25 and 27.

Cermak, Mary. "Top County Outlay Rocks Schenectady." *The Knickerbocker News* (September 22, 1976), 1-A.

Chady, Dick. "Court of Appeals Needles the Legislature." *Empire State Report*, II (January/February, 1976), 12–16.

Chalmers, Arvis. "Abrams Inherits Patronage Jobs." *The Knickerbocker News* (November 10, 1978), 5-B.

———. "Attorney General Holds 'Plums' of $13 Million." *The Knickerbocker News* (October 17, 1974), 1.

Chambers, Marcia. "How a Judge Is Made in Brooklyn: Case of Borough President Leone." *The New York Times* (January 3, 1977), 10.

Chartock, Alan S. "Why Legislators Don't Return to Albany." *Empire State Report*, II (January–February 1976), 17–21.

Clines, Francis X. "Rockefeller Is Out, but He's in Touch." *The New York Times* (June 8, 1974), 33.

———. "Wilson Reports His Net Worth as $632,580, No Liabilities." *The New York Times* (September 7, 1974), 16.

Connell, Nancy. "State's Constitution Called Worst." *Sunday Times Union* (October 29, 1978), B-2.

Conway, Albert. "Report of the Chief Judge." *New York State Bar Journal*, XXX (July 1958), 279–87.

Cook, J. Douglas. "New York Troika: Conflicting Roles of the Grand Jury." *Buffalo Law Review*, II (1961–62), 42–53.

"Court KOs Challenge to South Mall Bonds." *The Knickerbocker News (January 16, 1979), 3-A.*

Crane, Frederick E. *"Detail Work of the New York Court of Appeals." New York State Bar Association Bulletin*, X (December 1933), 477–83.

Crawford, Finla G. "The Executive Budget Decision in New York." *The American Political Science Review*, XXIV (May 1930), 403–8.

————. "The New York State Legislative Session of 1921." *The American Political Science Review*, XV (August 1921), 384–86.

————. "New York State Reorganization." *The American Political Science Review*, XX (February 1926), 76–79.

Cuomo, Mario M. "The New York Court of Appeals." *St. John's Law Review*, XXXIV (May 1960), 197–218.

"Cutting Spending in New York City." *The New York Times* (January 8, 1979), A-20.

Dana, Maureen M. "State Mental Health Overseers Rapped on Funding, Organization." *The Knickerbocker News* (November 1, 1978), 7-A.

Dean, William J., and Tyler, Humphrey S. "The Tug of War Over Reforming the Courts." *Empire State Report*, I (May 1975), 155–57 and 174–77.

De Christopher, Charles. "Ethnic Groups Gaining." *The Legislative Gazette* (Albany, New York), February 21, 1978, 4.

Dembert, Lee. "Beame Appoints 13 to Judgeships." *The New York Times* (December 28, 1977), 1.

————. "Rohatyn Urges More City Cuts Now to Avert 'Surgery.'" *The New York Times* (January 6, 1979), 1 and 22.

Desmond, Charles S. "How Many Kings of Courts Do We Need?" *New York State Bar Association Bulletin*, XXI (December 1949), 442–45.

Desmond, Thomas C. "To Help Governors Govern." *The New York Times Magazine* (June 2, 1957), 14–20 and 22.

Dicker, Fredric U. "Right-to-Life Party Readies Organization." *Sunday Times Union* (December 17, 1978), 1 and A-18.

Dionne, E. J., Jr. "'Heart Law' Pension Provision Extended for Police and Firemen." *The New York Times* (June 16, 1978), B-3.

————. "New York City Gives Jobs Upstate." *The New York Times* (January 23, 1977), 1 and A-19.

"Education Watchdog Snagged in Assembly." *The Times Union* (May 24, 1973), 5.

Ellis, David J. "Court Reform in New York State: An Overview for 1975." *Hofstra Law Review*, III (Summer 1975), 663–700.

"An Examination of the Grand Jury in New York." *Columbia Journal of Law and Social Problems*, II (June 1966), 88–108.

Fallon, Beth. "A Very Private Man." *Sunday News Magazine* (March 12, 1978), 4–5, 11, and 20.

Farrell, William E. "Levitt Sues to Test Rockefeller's Budget." *The New York Times* (February 23, 1972), 1 and 41.

————. "Rockefeller at Hearings: A Partial Picture." *The New York Times* (October 10, 1974), 34.

————. "Suit Over Constitutionality of Budget Is Dropped." *The New York Times* (March 18, 1972), 34.

Flacke, Robert F. "The Adirondack Park Agency Comes of Age." *New York State Environment* (February 1977), 5–8.

Flick, Hugh M. "The Council of Appointment in New York State: The First Attempt to Regulate Political Patronage, 1777–1822." New York History, XV (1934), 253–80.

Flint, Jerry. "An Answer to Crowded Courts." *The New York Times* (May 29, 1978), D-1 and D-4.

Fowler, Glenn. "Making of Judges: How Rare Method Works in New York." *The New York Times* (October 10, 1977), 1 and 48.

Freedman, Eric. "Lefkowitz: Kudos and Complaints." *The Knickerbocker News* (December 27, 1978), 1 and 2-A.

———. "Some Consumers Don't Buy the 'People's Lawyer' Image." *The Knickerbocker News* (December 29, 1978), 5-B.

———. "Some State Lances Clang on the Knight's Shining Armor." *The Knickerbocker News* (December 26, 1978), 1 and 6-A.

———. "State Agencies Seeking Freedom from Attorney General." *The Knickerbocker News* (December 28, 1978), 11-A.

Fuld, Stanley H. "The Court of Appeals and the 1967 Constitutional Convention." *New York State Bar Journal,* XXXIX (April 1967), 99–104.

———. "The Role of the Court of Appeals." *New York Law Journal,* CLVII (January 30, 1967), 4.

"David Garth." *E.P.O.* (The Magazine for Elected Public Officials), I (January/February 1979), 52–59.

Gelb, Joyce. "Black Republicans in New York: A Minority Group in a Minority Party." *Urban Affairs Quarterly,* V (June 1970), 454–73.

Ginzberg, Eli. "New York City: Next Turn of the Wheel." *Empire,* V (February 1979), 36–39.

Gitterman, J. M. "The Council of Appointment in New York." *The Political Science Quarterly,* VII (May 1892), 80–115.

Goldstein, Tom. "Civil Court Judge in Manhattan Censured for 'Abuse of Authority.'" *The New York Times* (March 29, 1977), 36.

———. "Fuschberg Censured for Trading in New York Notes During Appeals." *The New York Times* (March 17, 1978), 1 and A-19.

———. "Judicial Penal Will Hear Charges That 38 Justices Fixed Tickets." *The New York Times* (December 15, 1977), B-3.

———. "New York Suspends Supreme Court Judge." *The New York Times* (September 27, 1977), 1 and 26.

Golomb, Barry. "For Elections." *New York County Lawyers Association Bar Bulletin,* XXIV (1966–67), 215–18.

Greenhouse, Linda. "Carey: 'Double Knockout' or a Victory of Sorts?" *The New York Times* (April 15, 1976), 22.

———. "Carey Gets Volunteer Firemen Bill, First of the Year." *The New York Times* (February 1, 1977), 33.

———. "Efforts to Require Deposits on Bottles Opposed by Carey." *The New York Times* (June 1, 1977), 1 and D-13.

————. "Mass Confusion Reigns in Legislature as Session Nears End." *The New York Times* (July 9, 1977), 30.

————. "Sale of Bonds to Help U.D.C. Repay Its Debt." *The New York Times* (March 9, 1977), 1 and 16.

————. "Senate in Albany Rejects Schwartz for Prison Post." *The New York Times* (April 14, 1976), 52.

————. "The Slow Season in Albany." *The New York Times* (June 20, 1977), 30.

————. "Wrong Version of Bill Is Made Law by Carey." *The New York Times* (July 23, 1976), B-2.

Greenwald, Carol S. "New York State Lobbyists: A Perspective on Styles." *National Civic Review*, LXI (October 1972), 447–50 and 487.

————. "Post-Watergate Lobbying Laws: Tokenism v. Real Reform." *National Civic Review*, LXIII (October 1974), 467–71 and 483.

Gutekunst-Roth, Gayle. "New York—A City in Crisis: Fiscal Emergency Legislation and the Constitutional Attacks." *Fordham Urban Law Journal*, VI (Fall 1977), 65–100.

Haider, Donald H. "Sayre and Kaufman Revisited: New York City Government Since 1965." *Urban Affairs Quarterly*, XV (December 1979), 123–45.

Hallett, George. "The Reapportionment Game: Time to Change the Rules?" *Empire*, V (February 1979), 15–16.

"Hearts—And Flowers, for Taxpayer's Funeral." *CPES Taxpayer*, XXXIX (February 1977), 4.

Hiscock, Frank H. "Some Features of the Organization and Work of the Court of Appeals." *Cornell Law Quarterly*, XXVII (April 1942), 307–12.

Hobart, Thomas Y., Jr. "Last Offer Binding Arbitration a Dangerous Device in Talks." *New York Teacher*, XX (February 25, 1979), 4.

————. "School Funding Equity Means Balance, Not Robbery of Peter to Pay Paul." *New York Teacher*, XX (December 24, 1978), 4.

Hoffman, Paul. "Nassau County's GOP." *Empire*, V (February 1979), 32–35.

Hoffman, Richard B. "New York State Court Financing: Developing the Centralized Process." *State Court Journal*, III (Winter 1979), 3–7 and 39–42.

Holcomb, Charles R. "The Pension Balloon Is About to Burst." *Empire State Report*, I (May 1975), 158–65 and 182–84.

"How Much Do Voters Know or Care About Judicial Candidates?" *Journal of the American Judicature Society*, XXXVII (February–April 1958), 141–43.

Hyneman, Charles S. "Tenure and Turnover of Legislative Personnel." *The Annals*, CXCV (January 1938), 21–31.

"Interview: Counsel to the Governor." *Empire State Report*. VI (February 18, 1980), 67–70.

Johnson, Lyndon B. "Air Pollution—Message from the President of the United States." *Congressional Record,* CXIII (January 30, 1967), H737.

Kaiser, Charles. "Special State Prosecutor Reports Fewer Convictions for Last Year." *The New York Times* (July 24, 1978), A-12.

Kaminsky, Martin I. "Judicial Selection: Alternatives to the Status Quo in the Selection of State Court Judges." *St. John's Law Review,* XLVIII (March 1974), 496–524.

Karger, Arthur. "The New York Court of Appeals: Some Aspects of the Limitations on Its Jurisdiction." *Record of the Association of the Bar of the City of New York,* XXVII (June 1972), 370–80.

Keohane, John J., and Vaccari, Michael A. "The Recodified New York Election Law—A Small Step in the Right Direction." *Fordham Urban Law Journal,* VI (Fall 1977), 29–63.

Khiss, Peter. "Court Orders Removal of a Judge in Brooklyn for Misusing His Title." *The New York Times* (November 26, 1980), 1 and D-20.

Kifner, John. "Carey Was Warned on Attica Pardons." *The New York Times* (April 8, 1978), 1.

Korn, Harold L. "Civil Jurisdiction of the New York Court of Appeals and Appellate Divisions." *Buffalo Law Review,* XVI (1966–67), 307–48.

Kremer, Arthur J. "The Resurgent Legislature in New York State." *National Civic Review,* LXVII (April 1978), 179–83.

Kroft, Steve. "The Magic and Myth of the Big Lobbyists." *Empire State Report,* I (April 1975), 116–27.

Lawrence, Al. ". . . With Liberty and Plea Bargaining for All." *Empire State Report,* II (June 1976), 188–93.

"Levitt Asks Change on Pension Control." *The New York Times* (July 11, 1978), B-10.

"A Lexicon of Legislative Lingo." *Empire State Report,* I (January 1975), 42–43.

Lindsay, John V. "The Selection of Judges." *Judicature,* L (March 1967), 223–28.

"Lindsay Seeking More Home Rule." *The New York Times* (October 4, 1966), 1.

Loewenstein, Louis K. "The New York State Urban Development Corporation—A Forgotten Failure or a Precursor of the Future?" *Journal of the American Institute of Planners,* XXXXIV (July 1978), 261–73.

Lynn, Frank. "Carey Seeks to Block Endorsement by Liberals of Goodman for Mayor." *The New York Times* (February 28, 1977), 1.

———. "Conservatives Seek Tie with Right to Life Party." *The New York Times* (March 12, 1979), B-3.

———. "Democratic Chief Seeks to Curb Number of Statewide Primaries." *The New York Times* (March 27, 1978), B-3.

———. "400 of State's Politicians Penalized on Fund Reports." *The New York Times* (May 2, 1975), 1 and 25.

————. "How Many Democratic Parties in the Primary?" *The New York Times* (September 12, 1977), 40.

————. "Miss Krupsak Bars a Reelection Race in Split with Carey." *The New York Times* (June 13, 1978), 46.

————. "Party Plum: State Parks Full of Jobs." *The New York Times* (April 28, 1975), 28.

————. "Right to Life Party Shows Its Strength." *The New York Times* (November 10, 1978), 1 and B-2.

Madden, Richard L. "Moynihan Sees New Way to Get U.S. Aid for City." *The New York Times* (January 18, 1978), 1 and D-15.

Magee, Jane. "SEQR: How the Law Works for You." *New York State Environment* (April 1977), 5–8.

Markwardt, John J. "The Nature and Operation of the New York Small Claims Courts." *Albany Law Review,* XXXVIII (1974), 196–222.

Mayers, Lewis. "The Constitutional Guarantee of Jury Trial in New York." *Brooklyn Law Review,* VII (December 1937), 180–204.

McInnes, Russell. "Legislative Oligarchy Handicaps New York Governors." *National Civic Review,* XXIII (May 1934), 252–54 and 267.

————. "New York Legislature Again Impedes a Progressive Governor." *National Civic Review,* XXIII (July 1934), 383–88.

McNamara, John J., Jr. "The Court of Claims: Its Development and Present Role in the Unified Court System." *St. John's Law Review,* XL (December 1965), 1–49.

Meislin, Richard J. "Abortion Measure Locked in Albany." *The New York Times* (June 7, 1978), 39.

————. "Hynes to Handle Medicaid Fraud: Carey Moves to Expand U.S. Aid." *The New York Times* (April 27, 1978), 41.

————. "Levitt to Change Accounting Plan of State Budget." *The New York Times* (December 6, 1978), B-1 and B-5.

Moley, Raymond. "The Initiation of Criminal Prosecutions by Indictment or Information." *Michigan Law Review,* XXIX (February 1931), 403–31.

Moore, John F. "State School Boards Chief Blames Legislature for High Education Cost." *The Knickerbocker News* (April 27, 1977), 3-A.

Moore, Vincent J. "Politics, Planning, and Power in New York State: The Path from Theory to Reality." *Journal of the American Institute of Planners,* XXXVII (March 1971), 72–77.

Morse, Wayne L. "Survey of the Grand Jury System." *Oregon Law Review,* X (February 1931), 101–60; X (April 1931), 217–57; and X (June 1931), 295–365.

Mosher, Frederick C. "The Executive Budget, Empire State Style." *Public Administration Review,* XII (Spring 1952), 73–84.

Moynihan, Daniel P. " 'Bosses' and 'Reformers.' " *Commentary,* XXXI (June 1961), 461–70.

Munro, William B. "An Ideal State Constitution." *The Annals,* CLXXXI (September 1935), 1–10.

Munsell, Patricia. "Change Has Been Good, DeSalvio Says." *Legislative Gazette* (April 17, 1978), 8.

Narvaez, Alfonso A. "Governor Sets Up Screening Panel to Select Judges." *The New York Times* (February 24, 1975), 1 and 14.

"Nassau Ordered by Court to Complete Assessment at Full Values by 1980." *The New York Times* (May 24, 1977), 37.

Nessen, Maurice. "No More Nadjari, No More Special Prosecuting." *Empire State Report,* III (February 1977), 51–60 and 85.

Netzer, Dick. "Of School Finance and the Constitution." *The New York Times* (July 14, 1978), A-26.

"100% Assessments Major SBEA Air." *Newsvane,* VII (December 1978), 134.

Ordway, Samuel H. "The Civil Service Clause in the Constitution." In *The Revision of the State Constitution.* New York: The New York State Constitutional Convention Commission, 1915. Part I, pp. 251–62.

Ostrowidzki, Vic. "Governor's Race Baffles Rocky." *Sunday Times Union* (October 22, 1978), B-1.

———. "Retired After 40 Years, His Work Begins." *The Knickerbocker News* (March 21, 1976), B-4.

"Panel Says Judges Under Inquiry Should Not Be Allowed to Resign." *The New York Times* (February 21, 1978), 35.

Peck, David W. "Do Juries Delay Justice?" *The New York Times Magazine* (December 25, 1955), 8 and 30–31.

"Personnel Council Recommendations Are 'Ridiculous.'" *Civil Service Leader* (February 25, 1977), 16.

Plumber, Amy. "The Routes to Reform of School Financing." *Empire State Report,* I (June 1975), 214–17 and 226–28.

Prindle, Janice. "Women Legislators: A Paradox of Power." *Empire State Report,* II (January–February 1976), 3–7 and 26–28.

"Profile of the Legislature." *Empire State Report,* III (February 1977), 61.

Pulliam, Russ. "State Senate Hands Carey Twin Slaps." *The Knickerbocker News* (April 14, 1976), 1 and 4.

Quirk, William J., and Wein, Leon E. "Rockefeller's Constitutional Sleight of Hand." *Empire State Report,* I (November 1975), 429–31.

———. "A Short Constitutional History of Entities Commonly Known as Authorities." *Cornell Law Review,* LVI (April 1971), 521–97.

Reier, Sharon. "The Urban Development Corporation: Back in Business." *Empire,* IV (December 1978), 5–8.

Reilly, William K., and Schulman, S. J. "The State Urban Development Corporation: New York's Innovation." *The Urban Lawyer,* I (Summer 1969), 129–46.

"Remedies for Judicial Misconduct and Disabilities: Removal and Discipline of Judges." *New York University Law Review,* XLI (March 1966), 149–97.

Rickles, Robert N. "Mass Transit in New York State: Where Do We Go from Here?" *Empire* V (February 1979), 17–25.

Rinehart, E. G., and Sweinson, R. J. "The New York State Budget Controversy." *New York University Law Quarterly Review,* VI (September 1929), 174–81.

Roberts, Sam. "Home Touch on Legislators' Mortgages." *Sunday News* (April 1, 1973), 6-C.

"The Role of the Small-Claims Court." *Consumer Reports,* XLIV (November 1979), 666–70.

Ronan, Thomas P. "Poll Finds Voters Apathetic on Judges." *The New York Times* (January 29, 1967), 46.

———. "Wilson and His Running Mates Spent $2.7-Million." *The New York Times* (November 27, 1974), 13.

Rule, Sheila. "New York's Senate Modifies U.D.C. Bill." *The New York Times* (July 19, 1978), A-22.

Sandler, Ross; Schoenbrod, David; and Chudd, Richard A. "Report on a New Direction in Transit." *Empire,* V (February 1979), 26–29.

Schickel, Richard. "New York's Mr. Urban Renewal." *The New York Times Magazine* (March 1, 1970), 30–34, 36, 38–39, and 41–42.

Schlesinger, Joseph A. "A Comparison of the Relative Positions of Governors." In Beyle, Thad, and Williams, J. Oliver, eds. *The American Governor in Behavioral Perspective.* New York: Harper and Row, Publishers, 1972. Pp. 141–50.

Schneider, Bruce H. "The Grand Jury: Powers, Procedures, and Problems." *Columbia Journal of Law and Social Problems,* IX (Summer 1973), 681–730.

Shaffer, David. "Are We Finally Getting a Better Legislature?" *The Knickerbocker News* (July 1, 1977), 4-A.

———. "How Legislature's Black–Puerto Rican Caucus Won." *The Knickerbocker News* (April 1, 1977), 10-A.

Shalala, Donna E. "State Aid to Local Governments." In Connery, Robert H., and Benjamin, Gerald, eds. *Governing New York State: The Rockefeller Years.* New York: The Academy of Political Science, 1974. Pp. 96–103.

Siegel, Max H. "City Judge in Newburgh Dismissed on Inept-Administration Charges." *The New York Times* (April 26, 1977), 41.

———. "Judges's Reaction to 'Terrible' Coffee Costs Him $40,990 Position in Suffolk." *The New York Times* (July 10, 1976), 4.

Silver, Roy R. "Senator Dunne Says He Paid 1 Per Cent Kickbacks to G.O.P. in Nassau." *The New York Times* (June 3, 1977), B-3.

———. "Use of Realty Taxes to Finance Schools Voided in New York." *The New York Times* (June 24, 1978), 1 and 24.

Slocum, Peter. "'Let Me Out, Let Me Out.'" *The Knickerbocker News* (June 30, 1976), 1.

Smith, Alexander B., and Pollack, Harriet. "Court Reform." *Empire State Report,* III (May 1977), 203–6.

Smothers, Ronald. "Legislature Has Refined Public Relations." *The New York Times* (February 16, 1976), 24.

———. "Mt. Kisco's Early Example of the Effect of Revaluation." *The New York Times* (February 10, 1979), 21 and 24.

———. "Yonkers, with Spending Curbed, Takes Control from State Today." *The New York Times* (November 27, 1978), 1 and B-2.

Solomon, Samuel R. "The Governor as Legislator." *National Municipal Review,* XL (November 1951), 511–20.

"Sound Rule on Stavisky." *The New York Times* (August 25, 1976), 32.

Special Committee on Revision of the New York State Constitution. "For Appointment." *New York County Lawyers Association Bar Bulletin,* XXIV (1966–67), 214 and 219–20.

"State to Act on 62 Candidates for Lag on Fund Reports." *The New York Times* (October 11, 1974), 18.

"State Bar Poll Opposes Surrogate's Court Shift." *New York Law Journal,* CLXXI (May 23, 1974), 1 and 3.

Stetson, Damon. "Affirmative-Action Order by Carey Exceeded Authority, Court Says." *The New York Times* (September 2, 1977), B-3.

"A Superagency for Urban Superproblems." *Business Week* (March 7, 1970), 96, 98, and 100.

Swidorski, Carl L. "New York Court of Appeals: Who Are the Judges?" *National Civic Review,* LXVI (December 1977), 558–61 and 571.

———. "Should New York's Top Judges Be Elected?" *Empire State Report,* II (September 1976), 308–12.

"Taylor Law Strike Fine Toughened." *The Knickerbocker News* (May 5, 1978), 7-B.

Tully, James H., Jr. "If the U.S. Collected All Cigarette Taxes." *The New York Times* (May 19, 1977), A-34.

Turner, Frederick L. "New York's Executive-Legislative Controversy." *Cornell Law Quarterly,* XXV (February 1943), 278–83.

Twichell, Robert H. "New York State's Family Court Act." *Syracuse Law Review,* XIX (Spring 1963), 481–96.

Tyler, Humphrey S. "The Assembly Reforms: Easy Come, Easy Go." *Empire State Report,* I (August 1975), 296–97 and 311–13.

———. "The Legislature Edges Toward Openness." *Empire State Report,* I (February/March 1975), 56–59 and 84–87.

———. "Time to Weed Out the Ranks of the No-Shows." *Empire State Report* I (October 1975), 404–5.

"U.S. Bars Port Authority's Plan for Bonds to Finance Mass Transit." *The New York Times* (December 17, 1977), 44.

"Upstaters' Tax-Protest Ordinations May Spur New Laws on Exemptions." *The New York Times* (September 24, 1976), B-16.

Usdan, Michael D. "Elementary and Secondary Education." In Connery, Robert H., and Benjamin, Gerald, eds. *Governing New York State: The Rockefeller Years.* New York: The Academy of Political Science, 1974. Pp. 225–38.

Uttley, Lois. "Assembly 'Empty-Chair' Voting Reform Questioned." *The Knickerbocker News* (January 11, 1978), 1-B.

————. "Carey Spent Record $7 Million in His Re-election Campaign." *The Knickerbocker News* (January 23, 1979), 11-A.

————. "Lobby Watchdog's 'Bite' Unknown." *The Knickerbocker News* (December 13, 1978), 1 and 15-A.

————. "Plan to Cut School Aid a 'Paper Threat?'" *The Knickerbocker News* (February 1, 1979), 1 and 4-A.

————. "'78 Elections Cost Abrams a Million." *The Knickerbocker News* (January 26, 1979), 5-B.

————. "State Legislators Stuck with Session They Don't Want and Won't Go Away." *The Knickerbocker News* (July 27, 1976), 9-A.

Vitello, Paul. "Plan Would Hike Local Cost of Mental Health Programs." *The Knickerbocker News* (February 1, 1977), 3-A.

Vosburgh, Royden W. "Surrogates' Courts and Records in the Colony and State of New York, 1664–1847." *Quarterly Journal of the New York State Historical Association,* III (April 1922), 105–16.

Wald, Martin. "State's Highest Court a 'Reluctant Dragon.'" *The Times Union* (February 2, 1978), 13.

Walker, Jack L. "The Diffusion of Innovations Among the American States." *The American Political Science Review,* LXIII (September 1969), 880–99.

Weber, Abraham S. "Executive Budget System in State of New York." *New York State Bar Journal,* VI (April 1934), 168–78.

Wechsler, James A. "John Lindsay and the Republicans." *Progressive,* XXXI (December 1967), 13–16.

Weinstein, Jack B. "Issues for the 1967 Constitutional Convention." *New York State Bar Journal,* XXXVIII (August 1966), 327–38.

Weisman, Steven R. "Carter Aide Says Koch Agreed to More City Budget Cuts Soon." *The New York Times* (January 8, 1979), 1 and B-3.

————. "Rise in Spending for Schools Void: 3,500 Face Ouster." *The New York Times* (August 24, 1976), 1.

Wells, David I. "The Reapportionment Game." *Empire,* V (February 1979), 8–14.

————. "Redistricting in New York State: It's a Question of Slicing the Salami." *Empire,* IV (October–November 1978), 9–13.

"Wenzl Details Civil Service Reform Stand." *Civil Service Leader* (May 20, 1977), 11.

Zimmerman, Joseph F. "The Executive Veto in Massachusetts: 1947–1960." *Social Science,* XXXVII (June 1962), 162–68.

———. "The Federal Voting Rights Act and Alternative Election Systems." *William and Mary Law Review,* XIX (Summer 1978), 621–60.

———. "Mandating in New York State." *State Mandating of Local Expenditures.* Washington, D.C.: United States Advisory Commission on Intergovernmental Relations, 1978. Pp. 69–85.

———. "Neighborhood Control of Schools." In Herrington, J. Bryce. ed. *Revitalizing Cities.* Lexington, Mass.: Lexington Books, 1979. Pp. 243–56.

———. "Public Transportation." In Connery, Robert H., and Benjamin, Gerald, eds. *Governing New York State: The Rockefeller Years.* New York: The Academy of Political Science, 1974. Pp. 214–24.

UNPUBLISHED MATERIALS

Bebout, John E. "The Citizen as Institution Builder in the Making and Remaking of Constitutions and Charters." A paper presented at the National Conference on Government, Williamsburg, Virginia, November 9, 1976. Mimeographed.

Braun, Mary Jo. "A Study of Legislation Vetoed in the 1976 Legislative Session." A paper submitted in PPOS 522—State Government—Graduate School of Public Affairs, State University of New York at Albany, Autumn 1977.

Di Nitto, Andrew J. "Governor Rockefeller and the Executive Veto: Uses and Perceptions." Albany: Ph.D. Dissertation, Graduate School of Public Affairs, State University of New York at Albany, 1977.

Gunn, L. Ray. "The New York State Legislature, 1777–1846: A Developmental Perspective." A paper presented at the Twenty-first College Conference on New York History, Albany, New York, April 29–30, 1977.

Logue, Edward J. "The UDC and What We Are Trying to Do with It." Remarks presented at the Bard Awards Luncheon, the City Club of New York, May 23, 1969. Mimeographed.

Neiderberger, Robert J. "The Creation of the Office of Education Performance Review: Some Perspectives." A paper submitted in PPOS 522—State Government—Graduate School of Public Affairs, State University of New York at Albany, January 25, 1977.

Solomon, Samuel R. "The Executive Veto in New York." Ph.D. Dissertation, Syracuse University, 1949.

Swidorski, Carl L. "The Politics of Judicial Selection: Accession to the New York Court of Appeals, 1950–1975." Ph.D. Dissertation, Graduate School of Public Affairs, State University of New York At Albany, 1977.

"Testimony of Ralph A. Ciprinani, State Acting Welfare Inspector General on Proposed Legislation to Establish a Wage Reporting System Given at Public Hearing of Senate Social Services Committee and Senate Governmental Operations Committee," Albany, New York, March 28, 1978. Mimeographed.

Young, Helen L. "A Study of the Constitutional Convention of New York State in 1821." New Haven: Ph.D. Dissertation, Yale University, 1910.

Zarur, Yusef E. "Administrative versus Judicial Adjudication of Minor Traffic and Parking Violations: Program Evaluation." Albany: D.P.A. Dissertation, Graduate School of Public Affairs, State University of New York at Albany, 1974.

Zimmerman, Joseph F. "The Federal Voting Rights Act and Alternative Electoral Systems." A paper presented at the Annual Meeting of the Association of American Law Schools, Atlanta, Georgia, December 29, 1977.

———. "The Impact of Federal Preemption on the American Governance System." A paper presented at the Annual Conference of the American Politics Group of the United Kingdom Political Studies Association, Manchester, England, January 4, 1980.

———. "New York State Government: Retrospect and Prospect." A paper presented at the Twenty-first College Conference on New York History, Albany, New York, April 30, 1977.

———. "Partial Federal Preemption and Changing Intergovernmental Relations. A paper delivered at the 1979 Annual Meeting of the American Political Science Association, Washington, D,C., September 3, 1979.

———. "Preemption, Federal Mandates, and Goal Achievement." A paper presented at the Annual Conference of the Council of University Institutes of Urban Affairs, Washington, D.C., March 20, 1980.

———. "Professional Management in Local Government." A paper delivered at the Annual Meeting of the New York State Conference of Mayors and Other Municipal Officials, Grossinger, New York, June 11, 1980.

———. "State-Local Relations: State Dominance of Local Autonomy?" A paper delivered at the 1980 Annual Meeting of the American Political Science Association, Washington, D.C., August 30, 1980.

———. "State Mandates on Counties: A Major Fiscal Problem." A paper presented at the Spring Seminar of the New York State Association of Counties, Grossinger, New York, April 23, 1979.

———. "The State Mandate Issue in New York." A paper presented at the Nineteenth Conference of the Municipal Management Association of New York State, Kiamesha Lake, New York, May 17, 1978.

Index